THE JESUIT *RELATIONS*

McGILL-QUEEN'S STUDIES IN EARLY CANADA / AVANT LE CANADA

Series Editors / Directeurs de la collection:
Allan Greer and Carolyn Podruchny

This series features studies of the history of the northern half of North America – a vast expanse that would eventually be known as Canada – in the era before extensive European settlement and extending into the nineteenth century. Long neglected, Canada-before-Canada is a fascinating area of study experiencing an intellectual renaissance as researchers in a range of disciplines, including history, geography, archeology, anthropology, literary studies, and law, contribute to a new and enriched understanding of the distant past. The editors welcome manuscripts in English or French on all aspects of the period, including work on Indigenous history, the Atlantic fisheries, the fur trade, exploration, French or British imperial expansion, colonial life, culture, language, law, science, religion, and the environment.

Cette série de monographies est consacrée à l'histoire de la partie septentrionale du continent de l'Amérique du Nord, autrement dit le grand espace qui deviendra le Canada, dans les siècles qui s'étendent jusqu'au début du 19ᵉ. Longtemps négligé par les chercheurs, ce Canada-avant-le-Canada suscite beaucoup d'intérêt de la part de spécialistes dans plusieurs disciplines, entre autres, l'histoire, la géographie, l'archéologie, l'anthropologie, les études littéraires et le droit. Nous assistons à une renaissance intellectuelle dans ce champ d'étude axé sur l'interaction de Premières Nations, d'empires européens et de colonies. Les directeurs de cette série sollicitent des manuscrits, en français ou en anglais, qui portent sur tout aspect de cette période, y compris l'histoire des Autochtones, celle des pêcheries de l'Atlantique, de la traite des fourrures, de l'exploration, de l'expansion de l'empire français ou britannique, de la vie coloniale (la Nouvelle-France, l'Acadie, Terre-Neuve, les provinces maritimes, etc.), de la culture, de la langue, du droit, des sciences, de la religion ou de l'environnement.

Recent titles in the series

6 Enthusiasms and Loyalties
The Public History of Private Feelings in the Enlightenment Atlantic
Keith Shepherd Grant

7 Fashioning Acadians
Clothing in the Atlantic World, 1650–1750
Hilary Doda

8 Before Canada
Northern North America in a Connected World
Edited by Allan Greer

9 Regards sur l'âme en Nouvelle-France
Histoire des spiritualités individuelles et collectives en espace colonial
Sous la direction de Joy Palacios et Anne Régent-Susini

10 Workers of War and Empire from New France to British America, 1688–1783
Richard H. Tomczak

11 The Jesuit *Relations*
A Biography
Micah True

The Jesuit *Relations*

A Biography

MICAH TRUE

McGill-Queen's University Press
Montreal & Kingston • London • Chicago

ISBN 978-0-2280-2463-7 (cloth)
ISBN 978-0-2280-2464-4 (paper)
ISBN 978-0-2280-2542-9 (ePDF)
ISBN 978-0-2280-2543-6 (ePUB)

Legal deposit second quarter 2025
Bibliothèque et Archives nationales du Québec

Printed in Canada on acid-free paper that is 100% ancient-forest-free, containing 100% sustainable, recycled fibre, and processed chlorine-free.

This book has been published with the help of a grant from the Federation for the Humanities and Social Sciences, through the Awards to Scholarly Publications Program, using funds provided by the Social Sciences and Humanities Research Council of Canada.

Funded by the Government of Canada | Financé par le gouvernement du Canada | Canada | Canada Council for the Arts | Conseil des arts du Canada

We acknowledge the support of the Canada Council for the Arts.

Nous remercions le Conseil des arts du Canada de son soutien.

McGill-Queen's University Press in Montreal is on land which long served as a site of meeting and exchange amongst Indigenous Peoples, including the Haudenosaunee and Anishinabeg nations. In Kingston it is situated on the territory of the Haudenosaunee and Anishinaabek. We acknowledge and thank the diverse Indigenous Peoples whose footsteps have marked these territories on which peoples of the world now gather.

Library and Archives Canada Cataloguing in Publication

Title: The Jesuit relations: a biography / Micah True.

Names: True, Micah, 1981- author

Series: McGill-Queen's studies in early Canada / Avant le Canada ; 11.

Description: Series statement: McGill-Queen's studies in early Canada / Avant le Canada ; 11 | Includes bibliographical references and index.

Identifiers: Canadiana (print) 20250115557 | Canadiana (ebook) 20250115565 | ISBN 9780228024637 (cloth) | ISBN 9780228024644 (paper) | ISBN 9780228025436 (ePUB) | ISBN 9780228025429 (ePDF)

Subjects: LCSH: Jesuits—Missions—Canada, Eastern. | LCSH: Canada—History—To 1763 (New France)

Classification: LCC FC315 .T78 2025 | DDC 271/.530971309032—dc23

This book was typeset by Marquis Interscript in 10.5/13 Sabon.
Copyediting by Kate Merriman.

McGill-Queen's University Press
Suite 1720, 1010 Sherbrooke St West, Montreal, QC, H3A 2R7

Authorized safety representative in the EU: Mare Nostrum Group BV, Mauritskade 21D, 1091 GC Amsterdam, the Netherlands, gpsr@mare-nostrum.co.uk

For Zoe

Contents

Figures

Acknowledgments

The seed of this book was planted in May 2017, when Dr Christopher Parsons of Northeastern University's history department drew my attention to a news report about Canadian prime minister Justin Trudeau's audience with Pope Francis, and especially his gift to the pontiff of a set of the seventeenth-century Jesuit *Relations* from New France. Trudeau's gift – given just after he had requested an apology for the Church's role in Canada's residential school system – captured my attention at a time when I thought I had already said everything I wanted to say about these annual mission reports in my 2015 book *Masters and Students: Jesuit Mission Ethnography in Seventeenth-Century New France*. Trudeau's comments about the *Relations* in this particular setting, which are discussed in this book's conclusion, caused me to begin reflecting on the texts again. As a settler who moved to Canada in midlife, I found myself particularly interested in how the common descriptions of the *Relations* that Trudeau echoed often seem at odds with contemporary and emerging understandings of Canada's colonial past. As I began to seriously consider whether I might have a new and different story to tell about these texts, I read Alice Kaplan's 2016 *Looking for the Stranger*, a fascinating study of Albert Camus' famous novel. It introduced me to the idea that it is possible to tell the life story of a book, an approach that seemed well suited to the study of the *Relations* that was taking shape in my mind.

As I moved on from these earliest beginnings and began in earnest to research and write this book, I benefited from various forms of help from many people. At the University of Alberta, these included three PhD students – Peter Morley, Dominika Tabor, and Malou Brouwer – whom I was fortunate to be able to hire to help with tasks including bibliographical research, compiling and checking the works-cited list, formatting and verifying references, proofreading, and tracking down relevant secondary sources. The insightful questions and thoughtful feedback of audience members in a variety of forums were also of great value. I presented a preliminary version of some of the material in chapters 3 and 4 at the University of Manitoba's Jesuit Centre for Catholic Studies lunch-hour lecture series in early 2020. An early version of chapter 1 benefited from the sharp eyes and critical minds of North Carolina's multi-institutional Triangle French History and Culture Seminar in 2021. And in 2023 I presented a nearly final version of chapter 4 at Brown University's French Embassy Centre of Excellence, in the Zoom lecture series "New Approaches to New France." Early versions of some of the material in this book were also shared at the annual conferences of the Modern Languages Association, the Society for Interdisciplinary Seventeenth-Century Studies, KFLC: The Languages, Literatures, and Cultures Conference, and at an international symposium in Midland, Ontario, organized by the Ricci Institute for Chinese-Western Cultural History (then at the University of San Francisco, now at Boston College) and the Martyr's Shrine on the theme "Life and Death in the Missions of New France and East Asia: Narratives of Faith and Martyrdom." I presented a very short overview of the entire project to members of my home department at the University of Alberta – Modern Languages and Cultural Studies – in a Zoom event in the early days of the pandemic. I am grateful to the organizers of these events for their kind invitations to present my work, and to those who attended for their generous engagement with it. The penultimate version of this book benefited from the thoughtful, detailed, and generous advice of the two anonymous readers commissioned by the press. Other valued interlocutors over the years – both in general and on some of the specific points discussed in this book – have included Luca Codignola, Christopher Parsons, Robert Morrissey, Michael Harrigan, Michèle Longino, Seth Meehan, and Fr Casey Beaumier. I also wish to acknowledge the professionalism and expertise of the excellent team at McGill-Queen's University Press, especially Kyla Madden. All of this generous attention and assistance has made this book better than it otherwise would have been, and I am grateful to everyone who engaged with it along the way.

I have received generous institutional support while researching and writing this book. Funding from the Social Sciences and Humanities Research Council of Canada in the form of an Insight Grant enabled me to hire the graduate student research assistants named above. I was able to write this book while simultaneously performing an at-times very demanding administrative job thanks to the teaching release and annual research stipend from the University of Alberta that accompanied my appointment as associate dean of the Faculty of Graduate and Postdoctoral Studies. Some of the material in chapter 3, much revised and expanded here, appeared in "From Manuscript to Jesuit *Relation* in New France: The Case of the Torture and Death of Jean de Brébeuf and Gabriel Lalemant," *Papers on French Seventeenth-Century Literature* 66, no. 90 (2019): 53–66. And much of the first third of chapter 7 was previously published as "'En écrivant à une personne, je parle à plusieurs': Responding to Readers in the Jesuit Relations from New France," *Cahiers du dix-septième* 20 (2023): 151–67. I am grateful to both journals for permission to reuse this material.

As always, I am deeply grateful to my family – Kim, Alex, and Zoe – for allowing me the time and space for the periods of intense and all-consuming work that come with writing a book.

THE JESUIT *RELATIONS*

INTRODUCTION

The story scholars usually tell about how the seventeenth-century Jesuit *Relations* from New France came to exist goes something like this: the superior of the Society of Jesus's mission in what is now eastern Canada received news in the form of letters and oral reports from individual missionaries in the field. Drawing on this material as well as his own knowledge, experiences, and best judgment, he crafted a gripping and coherent account of the year's most noteworthy events, fulfilling a longstanding expectation that Jesuits would report regularly on their activities. The resulting text was superficially addressed to the leader of the Society's province of France, in Paris, but was also prepared with the knowledge that it would be published. One of the merchant ships that departed the colony each autumn carried this manuscript to Paris, where it was edited by Jesuit authorities in light of political and social conditions to remove anything that might cause offence. Upon delivery to the bookseller Sébastien Cramoisy, the revised text was printed in inexpensive volumes that were eagerly awaited by devout and politically connected readers every year from 1632 to 1673.

In these books, interested parties could follow the progress of missionaries who endured the hazards and harsh conditions of life in a distant and unfamiliar land in order to induce religious change in the Indigenous Peoples they found there. Readers could also find in them the missionaries' detailed portraits of these potential converts, including their particular ways of life, the sweeping transformations they experienced as the trans-Atlantic fur trade reoriented their economies, and the ways in which they received – or endured – many previously unknown phenomena that were introduced by European settlers: metal tools, Christianity, and various deadly diseases, among others. Enthusiasm for these texts in France was such that they sometimes had to be reprinted to keep up with demand.

This story tends to be told in just a few sentences, usually in a more fragmentary form than above and often only as background information in scholarship that focuses not on the *Relations*, but rather on the French settlement of New France, the characteristics of the Indigenous Peoples with which the Jesuits were in contact, and uneasy encounters between those peoples and French settlers.[1] Scholarship that draws on the Jesuits' annual reports as a source of information about the past is abundant, but studies of the texts themselves are comparatively rare, limited mostly to brief overviews and introductory articles.[2] Only one book, Léon Pouliot's 1940 *Étude sur les Relations des Jésuites de la Nouvelle-France (1632–1672)*, attempts to tell the story of these texts from conception to reception, and only from the celebratory standpoint of a fellow member of the Society of Jesus.[3] Even scholarship that examines the *Relations* as texts instead of as a source of facts about the past usually does not say much more than what is said in the preceding two paragraphs about how they were prepared and received, focusing instead on their relationship to particular genres like ethnography, travel narrative, utopia, and epic, or studying the rhetorical features of specific texts in the series or the writerly choices of individual Jesuit authors as they attempted to describe an unfamiliar place and its inhabitants.[4] The way scholars usually describe the Jesuits' annual reports from New France is not necessarily wrong, within its limits, but it leaves unexplored many aspects of this large and varied set of texts.

This book tells a detailed story about the Jesuit *Relations*, one that probes beyond the usual understanding of the texts to highlight aspects that have either gone unnoticed or that tend to be discussed so briefly that their significance has remained unclear. It considers how they were shaped by contextual factors like the standards and practices of the Society of Jesus, the annual rhythm of the merchant ships moving between France and New France, and the book trade in Paris, factors that have sometimes been mentioned in passing but never fully explored. It also brings into the foreground the individuals who shaped the mission reports in various ways, including not only the Jesuit superiors who prepared them and who have received varying amounts of scholarly attention, but also the many others who have gone mostly unnoticed, including lay settlers, female religious, Indigenous people, and various figures in Paris. And finally, it examines who was on the receiving end of these reports in seventeenth-century France, as well as their reception at other moments in history up to the present. In short, this book tells a new and unfamiliar story about this well-known set of texts, one that begins with the writing traditions of the Society of Jesus that long predated the New France mission and continues to the present, when the missionaries' annual reports continue to be read and interpreted from a variety of perspectives. As its title indicates, this is a biography of the Jesuit *Relations* from New France.

The idea that one can tell the life story of a book – or, in this case, a whole set of them – is not new. It was the subject of a detailed exploration as early as 1924, when the French journalist and literary critic Pierre Audiat offered a method for such an approach.[5] More recently, fine studies have considered Albert Camus' *The Stranger*, James Joyce's *Ulysses*, Henry James's *Portrait of a Lady*, Samuel Johnson's dictionary, and other famous books from this point of view.[6] Princeton University Press has produced an entire series of books, titled "The Lives of Great Religious Books," that "examine the historical origins of texts from the great religious traditions, and trace how their reception, interpretation, and influence have changed – often radically – over time," including volumes dedicated to individual books of the Bible, the Koran, the Dead Sea Scrolls, the Bhagavad Gita, the I Ching, and many others.[7] Such works examine how the books they take as their subjects came to be and continue to resonate, with attention to the people who shaped them and to contextual factors. This approach shares with *critique génétique* a concern for how a given book came to exist in its published form, but also pays attention to its relationship to the intentions, preoccupations, and desires of its author. It does not, however, consider the book solely as the result of the writing life of a particular person, and therefore is distinct from the biography of the book's author. In sum, the biography of a book traces the forces at work in its creation and legacy, including social and political context, the author's life and particular choices, and its resonance at various moments in history. As one listener summarized this approach upon hearing Alice Kaplan present her then-in-progress study of Albert Camus' *The Stranger*, "Like an historian looking for the causes of a war, the biographer of a book looks for the causes of that book."[8] The present study aims not to extol yet again the well-established historical importance, documentary value, or rhetorical richness of the Jesuit *Relations*, but rather to tell the story of this series of annual reports from their earliest beginnings to the present, with particular emphasis on episodes that have not been part of scholarly accounts.

Telling the story of the *Relations* is a more complicated task than telling that of a novel like *Ulysses* or *The Stranger*, for several reasons. This is not the story of a single book written by one author, but rather of an entire series of books that appeared one at a time over the course of forty years, adding up to thousands of pages. Eight different Jesuits oversaw the composition of the texts over the course of the series, their names usually recorded on the title page of each instalment: Paul Le Jeune, Jean de Brébeuf, Barthélemy Vimont, Jérôme Lalemant, Paul Ragueneau, François-Joseph Le Mercier, Jean de Quen, and Claude Dablon. Although these men were all members of the same religious order, trained in the same ways in its colleges, and steeped in similar experiences in the New France mission, the texts they produced did not always look much alike. Paul Le Jeune's inaugural 1632 *Relation*, the first in the series, was a sixty-eight-page letter. The next year's text, also written by Le Jeune in the form of a letter, was nearly three times as long, stretching to 216 pages. Barthélemy Vimont's *Relation* for 1642–43 filled more than three hundred pages and was, like most after 1634, divided into thematic chapters, and François-Joseph Le Mercier could muster just forty-seven pages for his similarly organized report on events in 1665 and 1666.[9] Some of the texts also included long chronological journals or letters that were interspersed among the chapters or appended to the end of the book. They also could vary widely in content. Unlike most of the texts, the first instalment in the annual series, published in 1632, resembles the travel narratives that were beginning to come into fashion in France, and that would eventually rival novels in popularity.[10] It recounts Le Jeune's preparations to depart France, the discomforts he endured during the Atlantic crossing, and his initial impressions of a new and unfamiliar place and its inhabitants. Many of the *Relations* account for the highlights of a full year's worth of events, focusing especially on the missionaries' efforts to induce Indigenous people to convert to Christianity. And others focus mostly on a single set of events in just one location, instead of attempting to account for what happened everywhere the Jesuits were working. Such was the case, for example, of Paul Ragueneau's report for 1649, which reports on the mortal peril posed by Haudenosaunee attacks on the Wendat that forced their dispersal and the dissolution of the mission, and contains no news at all of events in Quebec. Telling the story of the Jesuit *Relations* from New

France is complicated, then, by the sheer size of the series, the number of authors involved, and the texts' diversity in form and content.

This book's account of the *Relations* is therefore unavoidably selective. Any study that proceeded by considering each of the individual texts and authors in turn would quickly become tedious and repetitive, not to mention extremely long. Each of the following chapters examines instead an aspect of the New France Jesuits' annual reports that has not received the detailed exploration it deserves or, in some cases, has gone entirely unremarked. Care has been taken to select topics and examples that shed light on all of the major moments in the texts' creation: the preparation of the draft report by the mission superior on the basis of a variety of raw materials, its transport to France and the editorial work performed there, and the reactions of readers from the seventeenth century to the present. Although each chapter of this book focuses on a different aspect of the process by which the Jesuits' annual reports were created and received, they are united by three over-arching preoccupations: a care to balance attention to individual writers with an understanding of the series as a whole, a commitment to bringing out of obscurity at least some of the many individuals other than Jesuit missionaries in New France who could sometimes play significant roles in the texts' creation, and a desire to place the *Relations* as much as possible in the broader context of writing in seventeenth-century New France. It is worth briefly explaining in turn each of these aspects of the approach taken here.

First, instead of following most scholarship and choosing either to treat the *Relations* as a coherent corpus or to focus instead on particular authors or volumes in the series, this book attempts to balance these two approaches. In scholarship that uses the series as a source of facts about events that occurred long ago, information is frequently drawn from an assortment of texts written by various authors and woven together into new narratives about the past. This approach is perhaps fair enough, because the documentary value of the annual reports is not attached to any single text or author. All instalments in the series offer detailed if obviously far from disinterested accounts of Indigenous cultures, the French missions and settlements, or both. Scholars who take a more literary approach, on the other hand, have devoted entire books and articles to the writings of individual Jesuits and how they were marked by these authors' experiences, circumstances, preoccupations, and personal characteristics. Paul Le Jeune in particular has been singled out, and the same is true to a lesser extent of Jean de Brébeuf and Paul Ragueneau.[11] Both of these scholarly tendencies have resulted in excellent work that has advanced knowledge about the settlement of New France, Indigenous Peoples and their interactions with the French, and the rhetorical qualities of the texts themselves. But neither is by itself adequate for a full understanding of the Jesuits' annual reports. Approaches that foreground the series as a whole, and its importance as a rich source of information, tend to obscure from view the various individuals who wrote the texts. Examinations of particular texts or of the work of specific authors, on the other hand, do not usually pay much attention to their relationship to the rest of the series. And so, this book highlights individual writers and how the way they approached the task of preparing the *Relations* differed from their peers, but it also strives to offer insights about the series as a whole.

Three Jesuit missionaries to New France in particular receive sustained attention in this book. Paul Le Jeune is by far the most prolific and oft-studied author of the *Relations*. He inaugurated the series and had at least a hand in the preparation of more than one-third of its instalments, including some that were not attributed to him at the time. His abnormally large role, explored in various chapters of this book, simply cannot go unaccounted for in any close examination of the New France Jesuits' annual reports. The other two missionaries whose work is examined closely here, Jérôme Lalemant and Paul Ragueneau, are much less frequently studied. Lalemant was responsible for twelve annual reports, including some from Quebec and others from the Wendat mission. This makes him the second most prolific author of the series, but his writings have not received the same kind of sustained attention as those of Le Jeune, perhaps because they are generally less rich in descriptions of Indigenous cultures than many of the other *Relations*, focusing instead on the functioning of the mission itself and the Jesuits' efforts to win conversions.[12] Ragueneau was responsible for just five of the texts, but is nonetheless worthy of careful attention as an extraordinarily skilled writer. One of his reports, the account of events in the Wendat mission in 1649, is among the best-known and most frequently studied of the series due to its sensational account of the dispersal of the Wendat and violent deaths of two missionaries at the hands of Haudenosaunee adversaries. But the author himself is often overshadowed in scholarship by these events. This book does not offer a comprehensive account of the lives of Paul Le Jeune, Jérôme Lalemant, Paul Ragueneau, or any of the others whose work is examined here, a task that is best reserved for volumes dedicated specifically to these individual writers. But its focus on these three writers nonetheless allows some sense to emerge, over the course of this study, of how the *Relations* were shaped by the characteristics and preoccupations of the individual Jesuits who were charged with preparing them.

Second, this book accounts in more detail than ever before for how people other than Jesuits in New France shaped the *Relations* in various ways. Scholars tend to understand the texts as the work of the missionaries alone, for reasons that are, at least superficially, entirely understandable. They are full of fascinating accounts of the trials and triumphs of individual priests, whether in French settlements or while working in isolation among Indigenous people, passages that leave no doubt about who were the protagonists and scribes of these reports. And their basic characteristics seem to confirm the impression that the Jesuits alone were responsible for their contents. Each instalment is explicitly framed as high-level communication between the Jesuit superior in New France and the provincial of the Society of Jesus in Paris, both of whom are mentioned in the full title of most of the *Relations*.[13] Well-grounded in the texts themselves though it may be, the common focus on the New France missionaries alone leaves little room to consider the surprising ways in which others could sometimes play a significant role. Despite being credited to a single Jesuit missionary, most of the texts were in reality the products of many hands, not all of them Jesuit. This book shows how others in both New France and France – female religious, the Jesuits' lay assistants, Indigenous people, editors, and even readers in both Quebec and Paris – were involved in various ways in the creation of the *Relations*. Accounting for such figures allows the emergence of a more nuanced understanding of how these texts came to exist, one that does not cast them only as the result of the solitary toil of Jesuit missionaries.

Finally, this book casts a critical eye not only on the published *Relations* themselves, but also on the little-studied relationship between these texts and the large body of other writings produced in New France at the same time, including letters, preliminary reports, journals, mission registers, and contracts, especially but not exclusively those written by Jesuits. The missionaries' published reports now overshadow all other texts written in New France, but it is clear that the Jesuits wrote constantly, and for many different reasons. To get a sense of the scale of this corpus, it is necessary only to consult the tables of contents of the volumes that make up Lucien Campeau's massive edited collection of Jesuit writings from New France, *Monumenta Novae Franciae*. The volumes covering 1610 to 1650 alone catalogue some 963 texts in addition to the published *Relations*.[14] Campeau reproduced many of these. Others have disappeared in the centuries since their creation and are only known to have existed thanks to references to them in other surviving texts. Many scholars are aware of at least some of this material and have occasionally used it to good effect to illuminate specific events in the history of Indigenous-French contact or the mission itself. It has generally not, however, been examined as a potential source of information about the Jesuits' annual reports.[15] As this book will show, careful comparison of this material to the published texts affords precious glimpses of various aspects of the *Relations* that are otherwise impossible to see. The same is true of the writings of non-Jesuits that some of the following chapters examine alongside the missionaries' annual reports.

This book's examination of the Jesuit *Relations* along the lines traced above employs an unapologetically eclectic set of techniques instead of applying a single method or theoretical approach from start to finish. There are passages in the following chapters that perform close readings of the texts, of the kind most often found in works of literary criticism, to bring to light the patterns and subtle meanings to be found in the Jesuits' writing. Other parts of this book more closely resemble the kind of narrative normally offered by historians, based on the careful assembly and evaluation of details about situations or events that took place long ago, drawn from a variety of sources. Still others bring to bear on the texts the insights of book history or the perspectives offered by Indigenous scholars. This flexible and varied approach to telling the story of the New France Jesuits' annual reports is necessitated, at least in part, by the kinds of sources or objects of analysis that are available for the cases examined in each of the following chapters. Much preliminary or complementary material that could shed light on the published versions of the texts has been lost, and so it is necessary in each case to draw on whichever tools and approaches are available and seem most fruitful. But it is also fitting that a study of the *Relations* would use a variety of approaches, since scholarly interest in the texts has not been restricted to any one discipline. The result, it is hoped, is that this book will resonate with and be useful to the texts' various readers, regardless of the disciplinary or methodological distinctions that usually divide them.

Chapter 1 examines Paul Le Jeune's 1632 *Relation* for what it reveals about how the Jesuits who were charged with preparing each year's report went about doing so. This particular text is usually understood to mark a starting point, both of the Jesuits' second attempt to establish a mission in Quebec after France temporarily lost control of the settlement in 1629 and of the forty-year series of published annual reports that followed it. Chapter 1 considers it instead as a result of the Jesuit tradition of edifying letters that had already been in place for nearly a century by the time Le Jeune arrived in Quebec. Comparison of Le Jeune's 1632 report to its predecessors both from around the world and from earlier Jesuit attempts to establish missions in North America – Pierre Biard's 1616 *Relation* from the Society's short-lived mission in what is now Nova Scotia and Charles Lalemant's 1626 letter from Quebec to his brother Jérôme – bring into relief how the New France annual reports were shaped from the beginning by this broader Jesuit tradition. The chapter pays particular attention to a little-remarked alternative version of the 1632 *Relation*, a letter that was written scarcely a week earlier and that seems to have been sent to Rome at the same time as the text that would be published was dispatched to Paris. It recounts the same events as the published report, sometimes in the same language, but with differences that make clear that Le Jeune must have known the letter he sent to Paris would likely be published, and adjusted his writing accordingly. Together, the two versions of the 1632 report provide a precious glimpse of a writer at work in New France on a text that was simultaneously the start of something new and a result of his particular religious order's well-established standards and expectations for annual reports.

Chapter 2 considers the Jesuits' annual reports in relation to a different tradition of writing within the Society of Jesus: the recording of events day by day, as they occurred. It focuses on the journal entries made by Jérôme Lalemant during his two stints as mission superior in Quebec from 1645 to 1650 and from 1659 to 1665. These entries are contained in a manuscript journal kept by the Jesuits who served in this role for the twenty-three years following Lalemant's arrival in Quebec. This is the only journal kept by the New France superiors that has survived, but there is good reason to believe that more once existed and that rank-and-file missionaries also kept such records as a matter of routine. This seems, in fact, to have been a major part of the writing performed by New France missionaries, albeit one that is easy to overlook because few examples have survived. Many scholars are aware of the journal that contains Lalemant's entries and some have drawn information from it about life in New France or specific events there, but it tends to be treated only as a complementary source that confirms what is reported in the *Relations* and in some cases adds useful details. Chapter 2 shows that attention to Lalemant's journal sheds useful light on how he prepared his annual reports. His entries sometimes overlap with the content of his *Relations* but also frequently differ from them on points of fact and emphasis. Comparing parts of the journal to corresponding passages in the published texts reveals how Lalemant shaped his material for presentation to a metropolitan French readership. And attention to news that is reported in the journal but not the published texts, or vice versa, brings into focus the factors that determined what Lalemant included in the reports that he knew would be published, and what he left out.

The third, fourth, and fifth chapters consider the relationship between the New France Jesuits' annual reports and three people who were not members of the Society of Jesus, but whose own compositions nonetheless intersected with the *Relations* in various ways. Chapter 3 traces how Paul Ragueneau prepared his account of the violent deaths in the Wendat mission of his colleagues Jean de Brébeuf and Gabriel Lalemant – Jérôme and Charles Lalemant's nephew – on the basis of a preliminary report prepared by a layman named Christophe Regnaut. Both accounts of this sensational event are commonly cited in efforts to reconstruct the priests' final hours and understand their significance, but this chapter shows that the texts also provide a rare glimpse of how New France missionaries could compile the *Relations* not only by revising their own previous writings, as in the cases of Le Jeune and Jérôme Lalemant, but also on the basis of the work of others. Whereas the two previous chapters show, respectively, how Jesuit authors could frame their comments about Indigenous cultures differently when writing for publication and carefully choose which of a given year's noteworthy events to include in the annual report and which to leave out, chapter 3 shows the extent to which these texts could also be deliberately composed to elicit emotional responses in readers, at least in cases when a particularly skilled writer like Ragueneau was charged with preparing the text. It also begins a discussion of the oft-overlooked ways in which the Jesuits' writings were sometimes shaped by the actions of Indigenous people, in this case the informants whom Regnaut credited with providing his information and whom Ragueneau scarcely mentioned.

This book's consideration of the contributions of non-Jesuits to the *Relations* continues in chapter 4, which shows how attending to Indigenous ways of preserving and transmitting knowledge, and not just the alphabetic writing of European settlers, can shed light on French-Indigenous encounters. It examines the case of a Wendat man named Joseph Chihoatenhwa, who is well known as a particularly faithful early convert to Christianity. He sought lessons in reading and writing from the Jesuits and reportedly learned enough to write some letters, none of which are known to have survived. This effort on Chihoatenhwa's part is usually understood as another sign of his extraordinary faith and desire to emulate the Jesuits, but this chapter uses it instead to develop a more nuanced understanding of Indigenous participation in the writing practices of French missionaries, one that accounts for the pre-existing knowledge and use of various methods of preserving and transmitting information among the peoples the Jesuits attempted to convert to Christianity. It argues that writing ought, in colonial contexts, to be understood to include not only the Jesuits' practices of alphabetic encoding but also how they intersected with the analogous systems used by Indigenous Peoples. Conceiving of writing in these terms allows Joseph Chihoatenhwa – and other Indigenous people, for that matter – to be thought of as having contributed deliberately to the Jesuits' texts for their own reasons that were not limited to faith or a desire to please the missionaries. And it also casts the Jesuits' comments about the enthusiasm of Indigenous people for alphabetic writing in a new and revealing light, one that does not take at face value missionaries' claims that their ability to preserve and transmit information was an entirely new phenomenon to Indigenous people. Finally, this chapter briefly traces the involvement of Indigenous people like Joseph Chihoatenhwa in the circulation of information that served as raw material for the Jesuit *Relations* and argues that this too ought to be considered among the factors that shaped the texts.

The various ways Marie de l'Incarnation interacted with the Jesuits' reports – as contributor, reader, and witness to their publication and reception – are examined in chapter 5. This Ursuline nun is a well-known chronicler of seventeenth-century New France in her own right. She wrote thousands of letters and various other texts over the course of more than thirty years in Quebec, where she served as superior of her order's convent and school. These writings have usually been studied in isolation from those of the New France Jesuits, or occasionally as a complementary source of facts about particular events, but this chapter shows the degree to which her correspondence in particular was related to the Jesuits' annual reports, in three ways. First, for a few years after her arrival in Quebec, she wrote annual letters specifically for inclusion in the *Relations*. The way these letters were presented to readers testifies to a special relationship between the Jesuits and their female counterpart, a cooperative if unequal arrangement in which the male missionaries at least for a time specifically sought to draw their own readers' attention to the work of the Ursulines. Second, Marie de l'Incarnation's occasional comments in her other letters on her own status as a reader of the *Relations*, both before and after they were published, intimated to her own readers that she enjoyed a privileged relationship to the Jesuits, and that their reports were not only the products of individual feats of writing but also of an atmosphere of exchange and cooperation between religious leaders in Quebec. She at least sometimes mined the Jesuits' annual texts for material to include in her own letters, and thereby extended the reach and renown of the Jesuits by trumpeting her sources and referring her readers to the Jesuits' reports for more information. And finally, her letters, which are generally more conversational and focused on personal experiences than the Jesuits' annual reports, offer testimony about what it was like to keep up with an annual flood of correspondence during the season when ships were in port in Quebec. This was a challenge that Marie de l'Incarnation's male counterparts also had to confront, but that they did not usually describe in such vivid detail, making her letters a useful window on the experiences of the Jesuit writers. More broadly, this chapter contributes to the work undertaken in the previous two chapters of showing how non-Jesuits – including women, who have been almost entirely left out of studies of the *Relations* – were more involved in the creation of those texts than has generally been assumed. It also begins an examination of the texts' preparation in Paris and reception by readers that is continued in the final two chapters of this book.

Chapter 6 examines the path of the *Relations* to publication upon the arrival in Paris of the manuscripts prepared in Quebec – or, on occasion, the raw materials that were sent in place of an annual report. It focuses in particular on three figures who seem to have had a role in this work: the provincials who led the Society of Jesus's province of France headquartered in Paris, the procurators who served as the mission's agent there for the final three decades of the published series, and the bookseller who was charged with bringing most of the texts into print, Sébastien Cramoisy. Drawing on the published *Relations* themselves as well as an array of other sources, the chapter assembles the available evidence about decisions made in Paris to omit material from the texts or alter it in various ways, additions that procurators in particular sometimes introduced, and, in the case of Paul Le Jeune during his more than ten years in this role, instalments in the series that were assembled in France instead of in Quebec. Numerous significant changes made in Paris to the manuscripts prepared in Quebec are plainly visible to anyone who cares to look for them, and there are reasons to think that there were many other alterations that are impossible to see in the absence of surviving manuscript versions of most of the reports. Scrutiny of the surviving clues about how the *Relations* could be changed in Paris and by whom shows that this was a more significant step in the process than has sometimes been assumed, and that any full understanding of the New France Jesuits' annual reports must reckon with the role of Paris as an important site in their preparation. More broadly, the significant roles played by various figures in Paris, apparently as a matter of routine during at least some portions of the series' history, shows that the *Relations* may best be understood not as the work of various individuals in New France, but rather as the result of the collaborative production of institutional knowledge in which it was well understood at the time that the New France Jesuits did not have the last word.

Finally, chapter 7 examines the long history of readers' encounters with the *Relations*, from the seventeenth century to the present. It focuses on how the form in which the texts have been available at various times since their initial appearance in France has influenced how they have been perceived and used. First, it examines the New France Jesuits' readership in seventeenth-century France, drawing primarily on comments in the texts themselves since there is little external record of who read them and why, with the notable exception of Marie de l'Incarnation's letters that are discussed in chapter 5. The earliest readers of the reports, who experienced them one at a time as they came off the press each year, could contribute to shaping subsequent instalments in the series by corresponding with Jesuits both in New France and elsewhere in Europe or otherwise making their interest known. They asked questions or complained about particular aspects of the texts, prompting decisions on the part of the missionary authors about both the form and content of the following texts in the series. Second, a new surge of interest in the *Relations* in nineteenth-century North America resulted in efforts to define the corpus and to collect full sets of the texts, which by this time were scattered in private and institutional hands and generally not as available to interested parties as they are now. Understandably, this climate of scarcity and keen interest in the texts eventually led to the texts' republication. And third, readers today usually consult the missionaries' annual reports in one of three major modern editions that appeared in the nineteenth and twentieth centuries. The final part of chapter 7 traces how each of these editions presents the texts differently – both from each other and from the ways in which they were available to readers at earlier times – and how these differences have shaped scholarly characterizations and uses of them. The conditions of readers' access to the texts have changed dramatically more than once since their initial publication, and this is as much a part of the story of the creation and enduring legacy of the Jesuit *Relations* from New France as any of the steps in their preparation that are examined in the first six chapters of this book.

It is necessary to comment briefly on some of the decisions that have shaped practically every page of the chapters following this introduction. The collection of texts related to the mission prepared by the late Canadian Jesuit Lucien Campeau, *Monumenta Novae Franciae*, which appeared between 1967 and 2003, has served as the starting point for the analyses offered in these chapters. This edition is not without flaws. It presents texts related to the New France mission in their original languages only – French, Latin, and occasionally Italian – limiting its usefulness for many scholars. And Campeau's own interpretations in footnotes and prefatory materials sometimes appear to be rooted more in faith than in scholarship. Still, this is the most rigorously prepared and trustworthy edition of the textual record of the mission, including the *Relations*, that is available. It accounts for textual variants, offers clarifying footnotes, and provides useful cross-references, all features that no other edition can match. The regrettable fact that Campeau's edition stops, due to his death in 2003, with the 1661 annual report forces recourse to another edition for the last decade of the published series. Reuben Gold Thwaites's *Jesuit Relations and Allied Documents*, which despite its flaws remains the most popular and widely available option more than a century after its appearance, serves as the edition of reference for these later years.[16] For the readers' convenience, English translations of the *Relations* and of other texts written in

French are provided in the body of the following chapters. The original versions of the seventeenth-century texts upon which the analysis in this book is based can be found in the notes. Thwaites's edition is the major but not exclusive source of the translations offered here. These translations are often generally adequate, but in many cases leave something to be desired in accuracy. Corrections to Thwaites's renderings – and to published translations of other texts, for that matter – are indicated in brackets and explained in the notes, when necessary.

A word about the names used in this book for the various Indigenous Peoples the Jesuits described: the names preferred by the modern descendants of such peoples are used here instead of those used by the French – Wendat instead of Huron, Haudenosaunee instead of Iroquois, Innu instead of Montagnais, etc. Names imposed by outsiders still appear in quotations from the *Relations* or from the work of other scholars. "Indigenous people" is used here as a generic term, having come in recent years to be preferred in scholarship to common alternatives like Amerindian, Native American, American Indian, and First Nations, some of which are specific to modern national contexts. The generic term used by the Jesuits and appearing throughout this book in quotations, *sauvage*, presents its own challenges. The Thwaites edition consistently translates this term as "savage," a plainly offensive term in modern English that does not, in any case, align perfectly with the original French *sauvage*. As Gordon Sayre has pointed out, "the adjective *sauvage* means wild as opposed to domesticated, which also gives an idea of its meaning as a noun."[17] It is a lack of cultivation that this word most clearly designates in French, not, as in the similar English word, barbarity, cruelty, or ferocity. Thwaites's translations have therefore been adjusted throughout this book to retain the original French word. This is a matter of accuracy, in acknowledgment that words that resemble each other in two languages are not always good translations for each other, but also of respect, to avoid wherever possible the use of an offensive term that was not, in any case, the one used by the Jesuits.

In many ways, this book is intended to offer not only a far more detailed account of the Jesuit *Relations* than the version of the story that currently prevails, but also a more inclusive one. The following chapters acknowledge the various kinds of work performed by missionaries in preparing these texts, but also make room for the many people who were involved in less-obvious ways. Lay assistants to the Jesuits, female religious, and Indigenous people in New France are all shown to have more to tell us about the Jesuits' annual reports than has previously been suspected, as are the various figures in Paris who were charged with ushering them into print. It is debatable whether the way scholars now tend to talk about the Jesuits' texts allows for a full accounting of their relationship to the colonization of North America, particularly now that that story tends to be regarded not as one of great men planting the seeds of a nation but as one of exchange, exploitation, and domination. Including people other than New France missionaries in this life story of the Jesuit *Relations* from New France, it is hoped, will clarify how these texts might also contribute to better understandings of settled Canada's earliest history.

1

"I Come Here Like the Pioneers"

Paul Le Jeune's Briève Relation *and the Jesuit Tradition of Edifying Letters*

Paul Le Jeune was the forty-year-old superior of the Jesuit residence in the French seaside town of Dieppe when, on the last day of March 1632, he was appointed to lead the Jesuit mission in New France. As he later reported, "the joy and happiness that I felt in my soul was so great that I believe I have experienced nothing like it for twenty years, nor has any letter been so welcome to me."[1] But Le Jeune had no time to bask in this favourable turn of events. He left Dieppe the next day for Rouen, where he joined his Jesuit brethren Anne de Nouë and Gilbert Burel, and the three then proceeded on to Le Havre as quickly as possible. Having crossed the Seine to Honfleur, Le Jeune boarded a ship on 18 April, less than three weeks after learning of his new assignment. Two months and eighteen days later, he was in Quebec. He professed himself thrilled by his new assignment, and yet he also insisted it was an unexpected development in what had until then been a quiet life, and not one he was actively seeking. He had entered the Society of Jesus at the age of twenty-two, after converting from Protestantism when he was sixteen.[2] Before his arrival in Dieppe in 1630, he had spent his adult life studying the requisite philosophy and theology at the Jesuit colleges of La Flèche and Clermont, respectively, and teaching rhetoric in the colleges in Nevers, Rennes, Caen, and Bourges. As Le Jeune reflected after the fact, "I [was not thinking] of coming to Canada when I was sent here; I felt no particular affection for the [Sauvages], but the duty of obedience was binding, even if I had been sent a thousand times further away."[3]

Perhaps not surprisingly in light of the sudden, strange turn his life had taken, Le Jeune's account, in the first of the Jesuit *Relations*, of the treacherous Atlantic crossing and his arrival in Quebec is full of vivid descriptions of new experiences. He wrote that he had seen rough seas from the safety of the shore in Dieppe but had never before felt the ocean's fury beneath him; that he had contemplated death, alone in his room, but never with the immediacy inspired by massive waves battering his ship; and that he had never seen anything at all like the cruelty he witnessed Indigenous people meting out to captured enemies, despite probably having at least some knowledge or experience of judicial practices in Europe that were arguably just as violent.[4] Le Jeune also emphasized the novelty of his mission work, which consisted of re-establishing the Jesuit mission in Quebec after the settlement had briefly fallen into British hands between 1629 and 1632.[5] Wrote the new mission superior upon saying mass for the first time after reaching land, "It is my opinion that I come here like the pioneers, who go ahead to dig the trenches; after them come brave soldiers, who besiege and take the place."[6] This comment has frequently attracted scholars' attention as an example of the militaristic or adversarial rhetoric Jesuits sometimes used to describe their work in New France, but it is also notable for how Le Jeune presented his own situation, as the initiator of something new.[7] In some ways, Le Jeune's characterization of his own status as that of a pathbreaker was prescient. Dozens of his fellow Jesuits followed him to New France in the ensuing decades, and his written account of his experiences inaugurated a series of published reports that appeared annually for the next forty years.[8]

And yet, it is also true that both Le Jeune's mission and his 1632 *Relation* were part of the Society's traditions and practices that were already well established by the time he put quill to paper in New France. Starting in the previous century, Jesuits had fanned out across the globe, establishing missions of varying size and durability in India, Japan, China, Mexico, Brazil, Paraguay, and other places. These missions, along with the efforts of Jesuits working closer to home in Europe, produced voluminous written records that are not all that different from Le Jeune's 1632 report. The regular submission of letters was a requirement from the earliest days of the Society of Jesus. As explained in the Society's *Constitutions*, it was intended to facilitate members' "learning frequently about one another and hearing the news and reports which come from the various regions."[9] Although initially conceived solely for circulation among Jesuits, such letters were sometimes shared with outsiders from the earliest days of the

Society, and many were published by Le Jeune's time.[10] This chapter examines the inaugural New France report in relation to this long history of Jesuit letter writing – which is often mentioned in studies of the *Relations*, but has never been brought to bear as a tool for interpreting the texts – instead of following Le Jeune's own rhetorical framing of it as the start of something new.[11]

Approaching Le Jeune's first *Relation* as a result of many decades of Jesuit practices and traditions sheds new light on Le Jeune as a writer, on the origins of the series of reports from the New France mission, and on a unique text within that series. Le Jeune's 1632 report has often been characterized as fundamentally different from those that followed, as a private letter hastily composed by a newly minted missionary who did not yet know his words would be published. Lucien Campeau, for example, wrote that "the *Relation* of 1632, written without the preoccupation of an audience to satisfy, is a simple travel account, in which events and descriptions come one after the other according to chronological order."[12] Similarly, Léon Pouliot claimed that this first annual report had an audience of just one: "he was not writing, to start with, for the general public. He was fulfilling a duty: he was informing his Superior of the journey's incidents and of the state in which he had found the mission."[13] And Joseph Donnelly saw "more orderliness and ... more detail" in the *Relations* starting in 1633, and concluded that Le Jeune's inaugural text was "not written with a public audience in mind."[14] Particularly in comparison to the 1634 report, which was organized into thematic chapters and seems to have served as a model for subsequent texts in the series, Le Jeune's letter has appeared to many scholars to give an unvarnished view of one missionary's writing choices, unaffected by any expectation that it would be read widely.[15] In this version of events, Le Jeune launched the forty-year series of *Relations* from New France more or less accidentally, while believing himself to be writing a private letter, and subsequently altered his writing practices to appeal to a broader readership of which he only became aware after the publication of his first report. This chapter will show, however, that Le Jeune was certainly aware of the writings of his brethren around the world, and that his first published account of his time in New France is best understood in relation to this longstanding and public-facing Jesuit tradition.

* * *

From the earliest days of the Society of Jesus, its founders counselled members to take great care in crafting the letters they were expected to send to the Jesuit hierarchy in Rome, in terms of both content and style. Such correspondence was intended not only to create a sense of solidarity and mutual inspiration among the far-flung Jesuits, but also to represent their activities to outsiders in the best possible light.[16] In a 1542 letter to the Society's co-founder Peter Faber, which he indicated would be copied and sent to all Jesuits, Ignatius Loyola instructed that "members of the Society should, when they write to us here, write out a *principal* letter which can be shown to others; that is, to anyone at all." Such letters were to report "what each one is doing in the way of preaching, hearing confessions, giving the Exercises, and other spiritual activities, as God makes use of each for the greater edification of our hearers and readers. If the soil you are working be unproductive and there be little to write about, put down briefly something about health, your dealings with others, or such matters." Lamenting the lack of care he had so far observed in letters from his fellow Jesuits, Loyola urged the adoption of a specific method for preparing them: "I beg and beseech you in our Lord to write out the main or principal letter as I have here indicated then, after looking it over, rewrite it; that is, it should be written twice, as I do with mine. In this way I am convinced that the letters will show greater order and distinction."[17]

Jesuits working far from Europe received similar advice on the importance of sending to the Society's leadership well-written letters that would not only entertain anyone who might read them, but also impart lessons that were consonant with the faith. In a 1549 letter to his fellow Jesuit Juan de Beira, who was then working in the Maluka Islands, the Jesuit co-founder Francis Xavier wrote that his colleague should "write a very long letter to Father Master Ignatius and Father Master Simão, giving them a detailed account of the fruit which you are all producing there. It should contain matters of edification; and be careful not to write of things that are not ... keep in mind the fact that many will read it. It should therefore be written in such a way that no one is disedified."[18] Three years later, Xavier wrote a set of letters to Gaspar Berze upon the latter's appointment as vice provincial and rector of the Jesuit college in Goa, India. Among Berze's duties, Xavier wrote, was the collection of news from the missionaries under his supervision, wherever they may have been working in India: "These letters should be well composed, and no scandalous things should be reported in them, nor any evil said of anyone."[19] In sum, the Society's early leaders were consistent in instructing that letters – whether from Jesuits in Europe or on the other side of the world – be crafted with great care in order to please sympathetic readers and to avoid giving critics anything to complain about.

The consequences of ignoring the advice of the Society's leadership on the form and content of letters could be serious, as the case of the Spanish Jesuit Nicolás Bobadilla illustrates.[20] Bobadilla found himself at risk of punishment when he failed to heed Loyola's repeated pleas that he include only edifying news in his principal letters, and report all other matters separately. After initially complying, Bobadilla reverted to including in his letters material that Loyola did not feel comfortable sharing widely with outsiders. Wrote Loyola in a 1543 letter to his recalcitrant fellow Jesuit, "The fact that you were suffering from a touch of skin irritation which was tormenting you should have been put on a sheet by itself, as we had often agreed, so that we could give to each a morsel according to his taste, and everything be for the good."[21] Bobadilla also refused Loyola's requests to write his letters twice to ensure their quality, and instead sent only brief summaries. For the Jesuit founder, these were no small matters, but rather aspects of Bobadilla's letters that limited their usefulness and could even sour relations with the Society's supporters. Wrote Loyola to Bobadilla, "Many friends and acquaintances who know we have letters from some of the Society wish to see them and find a great delight in them. If we don't show the letters when they ask, we estrange them; if we show them a disorderly letter, they are disedified." Loyola employed the tone of a supervisor attempting to reason with a resistant subordinate, but he also threatened Bobadilla with a direct order to obey. As Paul Nelles has observed, this was an extraordinary exercise of Loyola's authority: "Few direct orders are to be found in Jesuit letters ... Though the self-image and structure of Jesuit governance was sharply hierarchical, communication was dynamic. Cohesion rather than obedience was the goal."[22] Loyola's willingness to threaten ordering Bobadilla's compliance with norms for correspondence demonstrates the importance the early Society placed on the production of well-written, edifying letters that could be shared widely.

The processes that enabled the writing, editing, and dissemination of letters were a matter of constant evolution from Loyola's time to Le Jeune's. The flow of letters to Rome increased along with the Society's size, making copyists' task increasingly onerous and time consuming.[23] In response to these challenges, the frequency with which letters were to be written was gradually reduced until they became annual reports. The copying or summarizing of reports to facilitate their circulation among Jesuit houses and colleges was replaced in 1581 with printing, allowing a faster and farther-reaching circulation, with the bulk of this work oscillating between Rome and local Jesuit hubs in Europe over the decades, as those charged with the task sought to increase its efficiency and reduce its burden on members. Already by 1581, many Jesuits were clamouring for changes to the system that would simplify it, characterizing the annual flood of long and detailed reports from various corners as repetitive and exhausting. And in 1593, the rector of the Jesuits' Roman College, Robert Bellarmine, proposed to end the practice altogether, or at least to impose strict limits on length. Even though his proposal was rejected, it attests to the waning enthusiasm among Jesuits and other readers for long, tedious reports – especially those emanating annually from the Society's members in Europe – as well as the cost and logistical challenges of disseminating them. As Markus Friedrich has observed of reports from within Europe, "By around 1600 it seems to have been clear that the annual letters ... were not necessarily meant to be circulated without restriction."[24]

Mission reports, in contrast, grew only more popular over the course of the Society's early history, and in time came to be treated differently from the intra-European edifying letters. Reports from both contexts always tended to emphasize the work of individual Jesuits, facts, and events instead of abstract theological commentary, but by Le Jeune's time other differences had developed.[25] Mission reports tended to be written in the vernacular instead of Latin, perhaps in recognition of their public appeal, and often included information about the unfamiliar people, flora, and fauna Jesuit missionaries were encountering in parts of the world far from their European homes, subjects that understandably arose less often in the letters prepared within Europe. And by 1559, it was already clear that Jesuits working in distant corners of the globe would not always be able to submit reports on the prescribed schedule, as they were at the mercy of local conditions and the availability of merchant ships to carry their news back to Europe. A set of instructions for the Society's writing practices prepared that year advised that missionaries working overseas should do their best to send news regularly within the constraints imposed by the comings and goings of ships.[26] By Le Jeune's time, despite the ways in which they differed from the reports of European Jesuits, mission reports remained, in Friedrich's words, "rooted in Ignatius' original ideas concerning Jesuit communication [and] a systematic conveying of information," and continued to find readers in Europe.[27] What began as a trickle of overseas mission reports published in Europe in the mid-1500s became a flood by the end of the century, holding steady between sixty-five and ninety texts per decade all through Le Jeune's early life and career as a student and teacher in Jesuit colleges.[28]

Despite the longstanding tradition of Jesuit letter writing, well established by Le Jeune's time, and the apparent popularity of reports from foreign missions in particular, the above-mentioned common conclusion that Le Jeune's first *Relation* was not intended for publication is not unreasonable. As Loyola himself suggested in instructing Bobadilla on the proper way to write about his rash – on a separate sheet that could be kept private instead of circulated along with his letter – not every piece of Jesuit writing was necessarily expected to find its way into the hands of multiple readers. Private letters and separate sheets of paper accompanying the principal letter, but not intended for distribution, were a part of Jesuit correspondence from the earliest days of the Society of Jesus. Loyola encouraged this practice in the above-mentioned letter to Peter Faber and wrote that such missives did not necessarily have to meet the high standards of writing and content he set for the principal letters that might reach a broad audience: "In these sheets one may write hurriedly out of the abundance of the heart, with or without a predetermined order."[29] So too did Jesuits exchange letters to manage the affairs of their rapidly growing organization. These administrative letters pertaining to governance or business were not intended for circulation outside the Society, but were often read by many Jesuits even if formally addressed to just one.[30] Letters of this kind were certainly still part of the Society's correspondence by Le Jeune's time, and form an important part of the textual record of the New France mission. The superiors there frequently wrote letters to the provincial in Paris or to the superior general of the Society of Jesus in Rome in addition to the *Relations*, the content of which could overlap with the year's annual report in French. Missionaries in New France also frequently corresponded with Jesuit leaders or rank-and-file members in France, their family members, and various others on the other side of the Atlantic Ocean, ranging from brief and unpolished notes to long letters that were as intricate and carefully composed as any of the published annual reports, even if they were not expected to be read widely.[31]

In some ways, Le Jeune's first *Relation* looks more like a private letter than one meant for a wide readership. It is framed from the beginning as correspondence between two people, opening "My Reverend Father" and closing with a personalized valediction: "Of Your Reverence, The very humble and obedient servant, in God, Paul le Jeune."[32] The text's content strayed far from the recommended strict focus on edifying news, narrating in detail Le Jeune's reception of the news of his appointment and voyage to Quebec, including descriptions of the sea life he saw during his Atlantic crossing, the weather, and the vexatious insects he encountered upon reaching Canada. And Le Jeune also characterized it as something quite different from the kind of polished and well-organized letter that Loyola and Xavier had urged their fellow Jesuits to produce. As the new superior himself conceded in bringing his letter to a close, "[This is enough], we are in such a hurry that I have not observed any order in this narrative."[33]

And yet, it is difficult to square the notion that Le Jeune simply did not realize that his letter would find its way to readers other than his official correspondent with the longstanding Jesuit practices traced above, of which the New France superior certainly must have become aware during his long career as a student and instructor in the Society's colleges. Such places were incubators for future missionaries, where idealistic young members could meet Jesuits who had returned home from distant lands full of stories to inspire them to seek appointments overseas. While a student in the Jesuit Collège in La Flèche, Le Jeune must have come into close contact with a veteran of the Society's earlier missions in North America. Énemond Massé returned from the mission in what is now Nova Scotia and took up a post as the school's boarding school minister during Le Jeune's time there. It is perhaps little wonder that so many of Le Jeune's fellow pupils went on to become missionaries in New France, including Charles Lalemant, Barthélemy Vimont, Anne de Nouë, Jacques Buteux, Charles du Marché, and Alexandre de Vieuxpont.[34] Even without meeting a former missionary, however, Le Jeune surely would have seen many written reports from distant missions. Such texts were regularly received in Jesuit colleges, read aloud over meals, and included on approved reading lists for students.[35] The Jesuit Louis Le Grangier's *Lettres envoyées du Levant* was published in Paris in 1615, when Le Jeune was studying philosophy at the college in La Flèche. He was still there a year later when Pierre Biard's *Relation* from the Acadian mission appeared. Ten years later, Le Jeune was a professor of rhetoric at the Society's Collège de Nevers when Charles Lalemant's letter from Quebec to his brother Jérôme Lalemant was scandalously printed, a case that will be discussed later in this chapter. And Francis Xavier's letters from Asia were published in French translation in 1628, when Le Jeune was undergoing a year of probation at the Collège de Bourbon in Rouen before taking his final vows.[36] Le Jeune may have been caught by surprise when informed of his posting to New France in 1632, as mentioned above. But there is reason to believe that he was, at least at one time, interested in an overseas appointment, probably having been moved to volunteer by the news from various missions to which he must have been exposed in the Jesuit colleges. In 1625, around the time he was finishing his formal studies, Le Jeune followed many of his contemporaries by writing to the Jesuit superior general Mutio Vitelleschi to request an overseas posting.[37]

There are signs in Le Jeune's 1632 *Relation* that he was well aware of the activities of Jesuits in places he had never visited. The priest justified his opinion that winning the conversion of the Wendat was within reach by referencing the earlier experience of Society of Jesus missionaries working to convert the Guaraní in Paraguay: "I can say of the Hurons all that was written to us a while ago by the Father of a young Paraguayan: to wit, that much suffering must be endured among them, but that great results may be expected; and that, if the consolations of the earth are lacking there, those of Paradise may already be enjoyed."[38] It is regrettably unclear to which letter Le Jeune referred, and whether he meant father in the familial or ecclesiastical sense, but it seems clear that he was referencing written news of the settlement Spanish Jesuits had established among the Guaraní in 1610. Soon after, Le Jeune suggested that Christianizing the Indigenous people among whom he was just beginning to work might be relatively easy, by again pointing to the apparently more difficult challenges Jesuits had encountered in other corners of the globe: "Great fruits have been obtained in the East Indies and in south America, although there have been found in those countries not only vices to combat, but also strange superstitions, to which the people were more attached than to their lives. In new France there are only sins to destroy, and those in a small number; for these poor people, so far removed from all luxury, are not given to many offenses."[39] The New France superior's references to two regions – remote from each other – in which the Society's missionaries were active and to the broad patterns of belief and behaviour they found there suggests familiarity with Jesuit activity around the world. Surely, the fact that such information was available to him must have suggested to Le Jeune that his own words might also find an audience beyond the Jesuit provincial to whom they were addressed.

The above-mentioned case of Charles Lalemant's 1626 letter to his brother Jérôme, who was later to become a prominent New France missionary in his own right, would have made Le Jeune aware that his words could end up being public even if he wished them to be private. The elder Lalemant, who served as superior during the Society's brief stint in Quebec from 1625 until the English takeover of the colony in 1629, sent a letter in August 1626 to his younger brother, who was then teaching at the Collège de Clermont. Jérôme Lalemant loaned the letter to a fellow Jesuit, with an explicit request to do nothing with it except read it. While the letter was in the possession of this other Jesuit, it seems someone copied it and then had it published without the permission of either Lalemant.[40] There can be little doubt that Le Jeune, who had recently requested an overseas posting and was either at the Collège de Clermont studying theology or freshly departed to begin a two-year teaching post in Nevers, was familiar with this letter. Even if, as seems likely, he had left for Nevers by the time the letter arrived at Clermont, he surely would have caught wind of the scandal it quickly provoked. Charles Lalemant's letter included a stinging comment about the influence in Quebec of the Protestant trader Guillaume de Caen, whose company then held a monopoly on New France trade and frustrated the Jesuits and the Franciscan Recollets with his organization's half-hearted efforts to encourage the settlement and Christianization of New France.[41] Wrote the elder Lalemant to his brother, "The help which has reached us from France is a good beginning for this Mission, but things are not yet in such a condition that God can be faithfully served here. The heretic holds as complete dominion here as ever, and therefore I send back Father Noiroit, according to the permission that I have received from the superiors, in order that he may finish what he has begun; he is the most capable one for this affair."[42] Lalemant's letter amounted to a smoking gun, certain proof that the Jesuits – and more particularly Philibert Noyrot – were actively working to undermine and even overthrow the Caen group. The letter provoked Caen's fury, leading him to denounce Noyrot as a schemer in a confrontation before Henri de Lévis, Duc de Ventadour and then-viceroy of New France. The incident was sufficiently well known to be mentioned in Samuel de Champlain's 1632 collection of his own writings about New France, making it difficult to imagine that a Jesuit like Le Jeune, who was already interested in the activities of his brethren in distant lands, would not have heard of Lalemant's text – and perhaps even sought to read it.[43]

Indeed, there are passages in Le Jeune's 1632 and 1633 *Relations* that confirm his familiarity with the news and opinions related in his predecessor's illicitly published letter. Charles Lalemant wrote, for example, of what he saw as the importance of building seminaries to keep nomadic Indigenous children in one place in order to isolate them from their parents' influence and facilitate their conversion, a sentiment Le Jeune repeated in 1632. The resemblance between the two texts on this point is all the more striking because both writers expressed this opinion immediately after enthusiastic comments on the apparently easier prospects of converting the more sedentary Wendat.[44] Lalemant also reported in 1626 on the Jesuits' efforts to clear land and erect lodgings, work that Le Jeune knew about, to judge from his report that the English, who had newly lost control of the colony in 1632, had burned "a greater part of the detached buildings which Father Charles Lallement had had erected," leaving the newly arrived French with a dearth of shelter.[45] And in his second *Relation*, covering events in 1633, Le Jeune repeated Lalemant's story about his efforts to enlist the trading company's interpreter, Nicolas Marsolet, in his own efforts to learn the Innu language. In Lalemant's account, this was no easy task due to negative impressions of the Jesuits that were then prevalent in New France, and because Marsolet had already refused to help others. Against all expectations, Lalemant succeeded in securing the interpreter's help, a story Le Jeune repeated in recounting his own efforts to learn the language.[46] Le Jeune's familiarity with the deeds and opinions of his predecessor shows that he likely read Charles Lalemant's letter before his own arrival in New France. But even if he knew only of the scandal surrounding its publication, this episode would have shown Le Jeune that he could not expect his own letter in 1632 to remain private, regardless of whether that was his intention.

Perhaps the most certain sign that Le Jeune was aware that his words would likely reach far beyond the provincial to whom they were superficially addressed is that he appears to have followed the advice of the Society's founders and the various figures who revised and reaffirmed its standards for correspondence, in at least two ways.

First, the *Relation* suggests that supplementary information was being sent separately. Of his efforts to learn the language of his new Indigenous interlocutors, Le Jeune wrote, "In truth, any one who knew their language could manage them as he pleased. Therefore I will apply myself, but I shall make very little progress this year, for reasons which I shall write [privately] to your Reverence."[47] The fact that Le Jeune felt the need to justify disappointing news in a different letter – apparently what Loyola had characterized in the previous century as a "separate sheet" that could be withheld from circulation – shows that the new superior was already attuned, in 1632, to the necessity of distinguishing between interesting and edifying news that could be shared widely, and the more tedious, discouraging, or disedifying news that was best kept private.

And then there is the little-remarked fact that Le Jeune appears to have written his 1632 text twice, albeit not – or not only – for the precise reasons Loyola had given nearly a century earlier. A manuscript recounting events in the mission in 1632 lurked undetected in the Jesuit archives in Rome for centuries, having been misfiled with obituaries for the Society's province of France for the years 1591 to 1652, until researchers finally noticed it in the mid-twentieth century.[48] The most obvious conclusion yielded by its comparison to the published *Relation* is that the two texts were not written independently of each other. Both cover the same period of time, from the last day of March 1632 until mid-August of the same year, during which Le Jeune learned that he was being sent to New France, made the treacherous Atlantic crossing, and began to settle in to life in his new, unfamiliar home. They recount many of the same events, usually in the same order. And most striking of all are the multiple passages that they share word for word, or nearly so. The manuscript, for example, reports on Le Jeune's observations of the land after disembarking for the first time in North America: "After Mass we went into the woods with which this land is entirely covered; the snow was still very deep, and so strong that it bore our weight."[49] The published annual report closely echoes this language, eliminating only Le Jeune's comment on the extent of the land's woods: "After Mass we went into the woods; the snow was still very deep, and so strong that it bore our weight."[50] Le Jeune's account in the *Relation* of his first glimpse of the land's Indigenous inhabitants includes a line that is even more similar to one in the manuscript, omitting only the word "but" (*mais*) at the beginning of the sentence: "They are like the Grecian Philosopher who would wear nothing that he had not made."[51] And to cite just one more case, the missionary begins a passage describing the Innu's treatment of captured Haudenosaunee enemies in practically identical terms in both texts. The manuscript reads, "When we arrived at Tadoussac the Montagnards were coming back from a war against the Hiroquois, and had taken nine of them; those of Quebec took six, and those of Tadoussac three," varying from the *Relation* only in punctuation and in the substitution in the published text of the generic "Sauvages" for the specific reference to the Innu whom Le Jeune called the Montagnards.[52]

One possible explanation for the close resemblance between the manuscript and the 1632 *Relation* is that one served as the direct basis for the other, that Jesuits in Paris copied and adapted the manuscript for publication before sending it on to Rome. As the sixth chapter of this book will show, it was more common than scholars have typically acknowledged for various figures in Paris to alter the New France reports before publishing them. But there are good reasons to doubt that the differences between the two versions of Le Jeune's letter were solely the work of editors in France, and to conclude instead that the published text was based on a second manuscript that has since been lost. The surviving manuscript is dated 16 August 1632, twelve days prior to the date recorded at the end of the published *Relation* for 1632. And the two texts appear to be addressed to two different people. Le Jeune mentions the Jesuit provincial in Paris in his manuscript in the third person, but in the *Relation* addresses him directly using the second-person pronoun *vous*.[53] Campeau speculated, on the basis of the manuscript's presence in the Jesuit archives in Rome, that Le Jeune had sent this letter to Étienne Charlet, who was then the French Jesuit assistant in Rome.[54] And finally, the published text is substantially longer, containing more than a dozen paragraphs that do not correspond to anything in the manuscript. This material both expands on the news reported in the manuscript and includes events that took place after 16 August, when Le Jeune closed his first report on his activities. It is unlikely this material could have been added by an editor in Paris. Since the Jesuit mission in New France had only just resumed after a three-year hiatus, no one in the French capital could have had sufficient knowledge of events there to add so much material to the manuscript. It is much more likely that Le Jeune finished writing his first report – a letter to Rome – on 16 August 1632, and then, while this initial version was close at hand and awaiting dispatch on the autumn ships, used it as the basis for a second, longer manuscript that would in turn serve as the basis of the published *Relation*.

Le Jeune's earlier manuscript may not have been precisely the kind of first draft that Loyola expected Jesuits to write before producing the final version of an edifying letter, but it nonetheless provides a precious glimpse into how Le Jeune revised his own text in preparation for its publication. Many passages of the manuscript are more awkward and wordier than what eventually appeared in print. Describing a perceived commitment on the part of Indigenous people to avenge all insults and injuries, Le Jeune wrote in his manuscript letter that "so enraged are they against every one who does them an injury, that they even eat the lice on their heads – in a word all their vermin, not because they like them, but only, they say, to eat those that eat them."[55] The *Relation* echoes this language closely: "So enraged are they against every one who does them an injury, that they eat the lice and other vermin that they find upon themselves, – not because they like them, but only, they say, to avenge themselves and to eat those that eat them."[56] The two passages are identical except for the published text's identification of the motivation for this behaviour – vengeance – and the manuscript's clumsy identification of the enemy. The manuscript's "even the lice on their heads – in a word all their vermin" becomes more direct in the *Relation*: "lice and other vermin they find upon themselves." Le Jeune's above-mentioned comment on his own status as a kind of pioneer underwent a similar modification. In the manuscript, he wrote, "It seems to me that I am like those pioneers, who go ahead to dig the trenches; then the brave soldiers come after, who besiege and take the place."[57] The published text echoes this comparison, but sharpens and smooths the language. "But it is my opinion that I come here like the pioneers, who go ahead to dig the trenches; [and afterward] come brave soldiers, who besiege and take the place."[58]

Sometimes, passages of the *Relation* not only read more smoothly than the corresponding parts of Le Jeune's manuscript, but also extend a clearer invitation to the reader to imagine being in the priest's shoes as he endured the trials of his voyage and arrival in an unfamiliar place. The manuscript's account of the storms that threatened to sink Le Jeune's ship during the Atlantic crossing, for example, reports, "We had some great storms. Every moment we feared the winds should snap our masts, or that the sea's blows, which threw themselves against our ship with fury, would break it open. And, in fact, there was a leak, which would have sunk us if it had been lower down."[59]

The published text closely echoes the final two sentences of this passage, but introduces them in more harrowing terms, as the manuscript's simple declarative sentence about severe weather gives way to a more poetic description of winds battering the ship without restraint: "You would have said that the winds were unchained against us."[60] And the shift in subject from the first-person we (*nous*) to the second-person you (*vous*) implicates the reader directly in assessing the seriousness of the storm, inviting vicarious engagement in the perils faced by Le Jeune and his companions.[61]

There are also substantive differences between the two versions of the text that show that Le Jeune and whoever else may have had a hand in bringing the 1632 *Relation* into print understood that it was important to shape the contents of mission reports carefully. The published text often seems to subtly suggest a greater degree of rusticity or barbarism on the part of Indigenous people than the manuscript does, even when closely echoing its language. Le Jeune's account in the manuscript of his first glimpse of the inhabitants of the St Lawrence Valley, for example, reports that "it was here that I saw [Sauvages] for the first time. As soon as they saw our vessel, they lighted fires, and two of them came on board in a little canoe very neatly made of tree bark. The next day, twelve of them came with their captain. When I saw them enter our captain's room, where I happened to be, it seemed to me that I was looking at those maskers who run about in Carnival time."[62] Here, Le Jeune marks Indigenous people as culturally different from the French by highlighting the curious vessels they used to reach the French ship and the colourful face painting that the new missionary found as disconcerting as a carnival mask. But he also suggests that other aspects of Indigenous culture were analogous to the more familiar practices of home, by using the same word to designate the leadership of both the French and the Innu: *capitaine*. Later in the manuscript, Le Jeune put a version of this word directly in the mouth of an Indigenous interlocutor: "One of them approached me and said: *Ania Kir Capitana?* 'My brother, art thou Captain?' They were asking for the superior of the house."[63] Coupled with Le Jeune's earlier use of this term to describe an Indigenous leader, this passage suggests a certain resemblance between French and Indigenous cultures, even as much of the surrounding text in the manuscript highlights the unfamiliar cultural practices of the land's inhabitants.

The published *Relation* includes a somewhat altered version of the first of these passages. "[Now,] It was here that I saw [Sauvages] for the first time. As soon as they saw our vessel, they lighted fires, and two of them came on board in a little canoe very neatly made of bark. The next day a Sagamore, with ten or twelve [Sauvages], came to see us. When I saw them enter our Captain's room, where I happened to be, it seemed to me that I was looking at those maskers who run about in France in Carnival time."[64] The small differences between the two versions of the passage aside – the opening addition of "Now" (*Or*) in the published version, a few spelling variations, and the deletion of the superfluous precisions that the bark of which the canoes were made came from trees and that the offending carnival mask wearers Le Jeune had in mind were in France – it is clear that the *Relation* here borrows heavily from the manuscript report Le Jeune had already written.

One notable difference between the two passages, however, is the replacement of the word Le Jeune had initially used to designate the leader of the Indigenous group, *capitaine*, with *sagamo*. This is a Mi'kmaq word recorded in French texts written earlier in the seventeenth century in Acadia, in what is now Nova Scotia. Le Jeune and anyone else who came in contact with Pierre Biard's aforementioned 1616 *Relation* from the Acadian mission could have learned in a chapter on the government of the Mi'kmaq that a *sagamo* was "the eldest son of some powerful family, and consequently also its chief and leader."[65] The word is out of place in Le Jeune's report on his work among the Innu, both geographically and linguistically. The second manuscript passage mentioned above was altered to explicitly claim that Innu leaders were called *sagamos*: "one of them approached me and said: *Ania Kir Capitana?* 'My brother, art thou Captain?' They were asking for the superior of the house. They call their Captain 'Sagamore,' but by associating with the Europeans they have come to use the word *Capitana*."[66] Instead of leaving unexplained the notion that the Innu called their leaders captains just like the French did, as he had done in the manuscript, the *Relation* clarified that they only did so due to French influence, and actually had their own term. These differences between the manuscript and the published version of the text are all the more striking because Le Jeune never used the term *sagamo* in his manuscript letter, whereas it appears several more times in the published version dated just days later.[67] Particularly in passages that are otherwise nearly identical, the substitution of *sagamo* for *capitaine* stands out. Perhaps Le Jeune used this Indigenous word in the version of his text that was destined for publication in an effort to lend authenticity to his account, a touch of local colour that would give readers some taste of what he was learning. Or maybe he substituted *sagamo* for captain as a way of diminishing the manuscript's suggestion of cultural similarity between the French and the Indigenous people they encountered, to present his own missionary task in the starkest terms possible. Either way, it is clear that he made different choices about how to characterize Indigenous leadership structures in his private letter and in the one he must have known would be public.

It is possible that someone other than Le Jeune – perhaps an editor in Paris – introduced these differences between the two versions of the texts, but the mission superior's own comments on the subject in his 1633 *Relation* suggest that he likely did so himself. Le Jeune apparently realized the inaccuracy of the term *sagamo* for describing leaders among the Innu after dispatching his 1632 report to France and before writing the following year's instalment, in which he reported that this word was rarely used among the Innu: "the word *Sagamo* is used by only a few here to say 'Captain.' The correct word is *Oukhimau*; I believe this word, *Sagamo*, comes from Acadia; there are many others like it. When a person first visits a country, he writes a great many things upon the word of others, believing them to be true; time reveals the truth. I have been told many different things about the customs of these [nations]; we shall have time enough to learn how true they are."[68] Although it is possible that this correction was added in Paris, the grounds on which an editor could have realized the mistake are unclear, since the most recent information from the colony – Le Jeune's own *Relation* from the previous year – had reported that the Innu called their leaders *sagamos*.

There are other differences between the manuscript and the *Relation* that suggest the second version of the text intentionally emphasizes the supposed barbarity or rusticity of Indigenous people in a way that the manuscript does not. In Le Jeune's explanation of Indigenous warfare, for example, barbarity replaced vengeance as the motivation for violent conflict as the material moved from manuscript to published text. In the manuscript, Le Jeune wrote, "Now, as there are a great many nations in the wide stretches of territory in this country and they are very prone to vengeance, they very often make war upon each other."[69] If perhaps still not easy to condone, such violence may have been more palatable to French readers if framed as a matter of righting past wrongs. After all, Europe's own judicial torture, cruelty in punishing witchcraft, and inhumane prisons surely ceded nothing in brutality to the Indigenous practices Le Jeune and his colleagues witnessed in

North America.[70] It is striking, then, that the published *Relation* alters Le Jeune's initial report of Indigenous violence to attribute it not to vengeance, but to the absence of civilization: "Now, as in the wide stretches of territory in this country there are a great many wholly barbarous tribes, so they very often make war upon each other."[71] Attributing such practices to barbarism instead of a perhaps relatable impulse to balance out past wrongs insists forcefully on Indigenous Peoples' otherness while also helping to make the case for French intervention in their lives. In both its original Greek and French usage, *barbare* signalled an absence of civilization.[72] The word itself is the result of onomatopoeia in Greek, mimicking the unintelligible noises of foreigners attempting to make themselves understood. Since language was at the centre of Greek culture and identity, such inarticulate outsiders were considered not only insufficiently eloquent, but also deficient in the attributes necessary for inclusion in the *polis*.[73] In short, the violent behaviour of Indigenous people passes, between the manuscript and the published version of the text, from a lamentable if perhaps understandable practice borne of a desire to punish wrongdoing to a sign of deep cultural difference from the French, but one that need not be permanent and that could be remedied through the Jesuits' efforts to convert Indigenous people to their own religious worldview.

To cite just one more example, a similar change differentiates the two texts' descriptions of Indigenous dwellings. Le Jeune's manuscript describes a shelter in which he and his companions were received as "made of poles surrounded by bark, open at the top for the purpose of letting in light and of leaving an opening for the smoke to go out."[74] The published version of the same passage adds a comment on the structure's quality, noting that it was "made of poles, clumsily covered with bark, the top left uncovered for the purpose of letting in light and of leaving an opening for the smoke to go out."[75] The two passages convey the same basic information about Indigenous dwellings, but the published version's addition of the word clumsily – *grossièrement* – introduces an element of judgment that is absent from the manuscript.

This example and the others discussed above show that one key difference between the *Relation* and the letter is that the latter text often described the Innu people whom Le Jeune was attempting to convert to Catholicism in more sympathetic and familiar terms, as if to minimize their otherness. The published annual report, in contrast, sharpens the differences between them and casts Indigenous people in a less favourable light, even when borrowing language from the earlier version. In light of the standards for Jesuit correspondence traced above, with their emphasis on good writing and edifying content, it is not difficult to understand why this should be the case. The *Relation* was carefully crafted to make the case for the mission as persuasively as possible. It portrays Indigenous people not only as different, but as deficient in ways that were helpful in making the case for missionary intervention.[76]

Le Jeune's 1632 *Relation* was not only, then, the hastily prepared personal account of its author's unexpected Atlantic crossing and frenzied first days as superior of the New France mission for which it has often been taken; the text was also deeply influenced by the long tradition of Jesuit mission reports that had come before it. Just as the founders of the Society of Jesus had counselled in the previous century, the published version of the Le Jeune's letter reflects care for clarity and style, as well as signs that he deliberately described at least some of what he saw differently than when writing a letter that was not meant to be public. The very fact that Le Jeune appears to have written two versions of his text, and his apparent awareness of the fact that mission reports were often published, leaves little doubt that he knew the text he sent to France would find its way to readers other than his official correspondent. This understanding of the text, which emerges only through close examination of the published *Relation* in comparison to the manuscript Le Jeune had written shortly beforehand, invites reconsideration of longstanding ideas about the inaugural annual report and about Le Jeune as a writer. Le Jeune himself has sometimes been characterized as a particularly fluid writer, who could scarcely stop his quill from filling page after page with words that came to him easily and practically unbidden.[77] It is certainly true that Le Jeune was a prolific writer. And yet this vision of him is plainly not the whole story. There can be no doubt that Le Jeune was also a deliberate and careful writer, who kept a close eye on how his words would be received by readers as he crafted – and at least sometimes rewrote – the report he must have known would find its way into the hands of readers in France, and that he did not mind contradicting things he had said elsewhere when it suited his needs.[78] More broadly, the case examined here shows that Jesuit missionaries' initial accounts of their work could be significantly different from what eventually made it into print, even in the case of published texts that, like Le Jeune's inaugural *Relation*, appear to have been hastily composed.

The fact that Le Jeune wrote two versions of his 1632 *Relation* also hints at a possible step in the preparation of the New France annual reports that has so far not been included in scholarly accounts of the process. Could the various New France superiors who were charged with preparing the text over the years have systematically written two drafts, as Ignatius Loyola had originally counselled in the previous century? It is not possible to say with any certainty, since none of the original manuscripts sent from New France seem to have survived, let alone in two versions.[79] But there are tantalizing clues that they may have done so, at least sometimes. In 1643, the year's report from the Wendat mission was stolen by a group of Haudenosaunee while it was in transit to Quebec in the care of their Wendat adversaries.[80] The published *Relation* for the following year included the year-old report from the Wendat mission, but an explanatory letter from then-superior Barthélemy Vimont clarified that it was not based on the manuscript that had been lost, but instead on a second copy that had arrived in Quebec too late the previous year to be sent to France and published on time. Explained Vimont, "The first copy of the Relation of our Fathers among the Hurons for last year was taken by the Iroquois; and the second reached me too late to send it to your Reverence, as the ships had already sailed. I send it this year, with a new Letter that has come from them respecting what has since occurred in connection with their affairs generally."[81] The availability of a second copy of Jérôme Lalemant's report so soon after it had been lost – albeit not quite soon enough to make it to Quebec before the ships departed that autumn – suggests that this must have been a relatively simple matter of producing a new copy of a preliminary version, and not rewriting the text from scratch.

Comments in other *Relations* suggest that such rewriting was understood to be the norm – or at least a desirable practice – even if circumstances sometimes prevented it. Le Jeune's second annual report, recounting events in 1633, concludes with the priest's apology for the haphazard nature of his writing: "It was not my intention to write so much; the pages have insensibly multiplied and I am so situated that I must send this scrawl, as I am unable to rewrite it and to make a clean copy of it, such as I think ought to be presented to Your Reverence. I shall write another time more accurately, and with more assurance."[82] Remarks like this one have probably contributed to some scholars seeing Le Jeune as a fluid and unstoppable writer instead of a careful and methodical rewriter. But such comments also reflect his understanding that the sloppy character of his text was not what was expected of him, and that failing to make a clean and improved copy was something for which he ought to apologize. A similar comment appeared in the 1648 *Relation*, when the shipping schedule forced Jérôme Lalemant – by then superior for all of New France, in Quebec – to send his manuscript to Paris without having a chance to revise some parts of it. Explained Lalemant, "The haste that the departure of the Ships causes us does not permit me to review the Chapter in which I have spoken of the sickness of a second Job as regards patience; so I must set down here some sentiments with which God blessed his death."[83] By occasionally making excuses for slipshod or hastily prepared material, the various New France missionaries who prepared the annual *Relations* made clear that they knew they were expected to carefully revise their reports before sending them to France.[84]

If Le Jeune's inaugural *Relation* is more like those that followed it than scholars have tended to suggest, it was still atypical in at least one way. Unlike most of the texts in the series, it was written from start to finish by a single priest, whereas most of them are well understood to have been compiled on the basis of letters and other materials that came into the hands of the superior, or his designee, who was charged with preparing it. Later chapters of this book explore how some of this material, whether initially drafted by Jesuit missionaries or by others, was revised by the superior in Quebec for publication. But Jesuit revision practices did not consist solely of improving prose and sharpening messages in order to meet longstanding standards of the Society of Jesus, or – as in the case of Le Jeune's first *Relation* – adding material. Just as studies of the texts have paid little attention to the importance of rewriting as a part of the work of the mission superior in Quebec, they also have not accounted for how much news the mission superior opted not to include. The leaky pipeline from preliminary record to published text is the subject of the following chapter, taking as its prime example the relationship between Jérôme Lalemant's journal and his published *Relations*.

2

"What Occurred Most Noteworthy"

Jérôme Lalemant's Journal and the Preparation of Annual Reports from New France

On 21 November 1646, New France mission superior Jérôme Lalemant learned of what he called "the greatest disaster which had yet happened in Canada": the accidental sinking of a small ship that was on its way from Quebec up the Saint Lawrence River to the French settlement of Trois-Rivières. Nine men perished, including an apothecary in the service of the Jesuits named Gaspar Gouaut, who had just arrived from Poitiers. "A very good fellow," in Lalemant's estimation, Gouaut was bound for Sainte-Marie, the Jesuits' mission headquarters among the Wendat in what is now Midland, Ontario.[1] It is easy to see why Lalemant saw this as a particularly lamentable loss, even by the standards of life in a place where violent conflict with Indigenous people, accidental fires that sometimes threatened to destroy entire French settlements, and other disasters large and small were far from uncommon. A valuable would-be contributor to the Jesuits' efforts among the Wendat had been lost along with eight other settlers at a time when New France was struggling to grow its population.[2] And the loss of the ship's cargo caused Lalemant and his colleagues in Quebec to scramble to find an alternative means of delivering supplies for mass that were desperately needed in Trois-Rivières. Wrote Lalemant, "As 3 rivers lacked Candles more than anything else, we availed ourselves of a Canoe which was leaving, to send thither two dozen Yellow Tapers taken from the parish church of Quebek, and two dozen white wax Candles taken from my cupboard."[3]

Such an unfortunate loss – and particularly one that the mission superior himself singled out as the worst disaster New France had yet seen – might be exactly the sort of news one would expect to find in one of Lalemant's annual reports from around this time, all of which billed themselves in their full titles as *Relation[s] of What Occurred Most Noteworthy in the Missions of the Fathers of the Society of Jesus in New France*.[4] But he never shared this news with French readers. His report for 1646 had already been sent to France three weeks before he learned of the ship's loss, when the merchant ships bearing a season's bounty in furs departed Quebec on the last day of October.[5] And he chose not to mention it in the following year's *Relation*, despite belatedly including some other events that had occurred around the same time, including the death of the Quebec Augustinian Hospitaller nun Marie Guenet de Saint-Ignace and the Haudenosaunee ambush of a small group of Wendat on 5 and 17 November, respectively.[6] Lalemant instead wrote about the loss of this ship and its passengers in a notebook where he kept track of events during his two stints as New France mission superior, from 1645 to 1650 and from 1659 to 1665, and to which his successors in the role and occasionally other missionaries – Paul Ragueneau, François-Joseph Le Mercier, Jean de Quen, Gabriel Druillettes, Pierre-Marie-Joseph Chaumonot, and Simon Le Moyne – contributed entries up to the middle of 1668, halfway through Le Mercier's second stint as superior.

Lalemant's omission from his *Relations* of this as-yet unsurpassed disaster is a striking reminder that the Jesuits' annual reports from New France constitute only a partial record of events, and that even incidents that the Jesuit authors considered significant and that might have been of interest to readers in France – or to modern readers, for that matter – could be left out. Preparing the annual report was not only a matter of rewriting preliminary material to make it rhetorically pleasing and to emphasize the urgency of missionary intervention in New France, as Le Jeune had done in 1632. It also required sifting through a full year's worth of news to decide what should be reported to readers and what need not be mentioned, a process that scholars have scarcely examined so far and that Lalemant's journal can help illuminate.[7] This chapter traces the relationship between Lalemant's journal entries and his published annual reports, and, more broadly, between the Jesuit tradition of regularly reporting news for dissemination throughout the Society of Jesus and beyond that was examined in the previous chapter and another recommended practice that has been generally overlooked in studies of the New France mission reports: the routine keeping of daily records of events.[8] As an account of life in Quebec and the New France mission that sometimes overlaps with Lalemant's *Relations* but just as often diverges from them both in content and in how particular events were presented, the journal offers a glimpse of how one mission superior performed the work of selecting news to report to readers in France each year.

* * *

Unlike Paul Le Jeune, who may have long dreamed of an overseas posting but whose appointment as Quebec mission superior was apparently sudden and unanticipated, Lalemant was extraordinarily well prepared when he took up the job in 1645 and already had a reputation for competence. His early career as a Jesuit had comprised a series of stints studying philosophy and theology in Jesuit colleges, after which he took a variety of teaching and administrative roles in those institutions, accruing a broad set of experiences that seem to attest to a perception among his superiors that he was a capable leader.[9] By this time, the New France mission was practically the Lalemant family business. Jérôme's brother Charles Lalemant had occupied the post of superior in Quebec during the Jesuits' first tenure there, from 1625 to 1629, and had returned to serve as a missionary under Le Jeune from 1634 to 1638. He shared his news from the mission directly with his younger brother more than once, in private letters that may have given Jérôme Lalemant a more intimate and unvarnished understanding of what it was like to serve as a missionary in New France than he could have found in Le Jeune's *Relations* intended for a broad readership.[10] Jérôme Lalemant was serving as a spiritual advisor at the Jesuit College of Clermont when he was sent across the Atlantic Ocean to become superior of the Wendat mission, between Lake Huron's Georgian Bay and Lake Simcoe in what is now southern Ontario. He served in this role for six years before being appointed to lead the mission in Quebec, writing reports that were published along with the Quebec *Relations* prepared by Le Jeune and Vimont. By the time Lalemant arrived in Quebec, then, he was already a seasoned mission leader and writer of annual reports.

He also was known to sometimes behave in an imperious, angry, or sullen manner toward those around him. In letter to Lalemant dated 25 January 1643, the Society's superior general Mutio Vitelleschi reported that news of his correspondent's disagreeable nature had reached him in Rome, and exhorted him to reflect on his treatment of others.[11] Vitelleschi's letter and others between Jesuits in New France and Rome allude to Lalemant's difficult personality, but only in vague terms. And Lalemant's *Relations* understandably enough do not shed much light on unpleasant aspects of his personality, carefully crafted as they were to cast the mission in the best possible light for French readers.[12] His journal entries, on the other hand, bear unmistakable traces of an exacting and unforgiving disposition, particularly when others failed to live up to his high standards. In July 1647, for example, he recorded the death of a man in the Jesuits' service named Bastien, who had died after passing out drunk in a building that caught fire. Far from expressing any compassion for the unfortunate death of a man with whom he was doubtless in frequent contact, Lalemant's remarks on the demise of this servant were harshly critical: "They took out what was left of his body, which we did not Judge proper to bury in Consecrated ground, since he was an open and public drunkard, – Incorrigible, and one who had in his drunkenness, died without a sign of penance; consequently, no public prayer was said for him."[13] This critical and unforgiving attitude can also be seen in Lalemant's comments on the perceived faults of his fellow religious labourers. In April 1649, for example, he reported in his journal that "the Ursulines made a remarkable mistake in that, during the *tenebræ* of the 3 Days, they had no Triangular candlestick or Taper lighted on the Altar, – save, on the 1st or 2nd Day, two white tapers."[14] And eleven years later, he had harsh words for the execution of the Jesuits' own Good Friday service, which he found to be "very badly performed" because his colleague Claude Dablon had not had adequate time to prepare himself and others.[15] Still, letters to Vitelleschi in 1644 from two other Jesuits in the Wendat mission, Paul Ragueneau and Charles Garnier, argued that Lalemant should continue in his leadership role there instead of rotating out as was customary because he had done nothing so egregious as to merit removal and because of his many strengths as an administrator.[16]

Whatever his personal shortcomings may have been, Lalemant had established a track record as an exceptionally innovative and detail-oriented leader by the time he became superior in Quebec. His first *Relation* from the Wendat mission began by providing basic facts about the mission – its size, location, distance from Quebec, personnel, etc. – that neither of his two predecessors had thought to share with readers.[17] He presided over the construction, beginning in 1639, of the above-mentioned permanent Wendat mission headquarters of Sainte-Marie, marking a profound change from the previous strategy of embedding individual priests with groups of Wendat more or less permanently. Establishing the Jesuits' own settlement would, Lalemant reasoned, make the mission more efficient by centralizing certain functions, allow the cultivation of food so missionaries could be less reliant for sustenance on the good will of Indigenous people, and give individual members opportunities to regularly rotate out of Indigenous settlements for rest and spiritual renewal in Sainte-Marie.[18] He also had a census conducted of those he hoped to convert not long after his own arrival in Wendat territory, reporting in the 1640 *Relation* that some twelve thousand Indigenous people resided in thirty-two settlements.[19] And he was responsible for the introduction of *donnés* – literally "given men," evoking the gift of their own labour such men made to the mission – to the Jesuits' efforts in North America. These men pledged their service to the Jesuits in return for food and shelter, but no pay, significantly expanding the Wendat mission's workforce and allowing the priests to spend less time on menial chores unrelated to their missionary work. It was Le Jeune who had re-established the New France mission in Quebec after the colony passed back into French hands in 1632, but it may have been Lalemant whose unconventional ideas and organizational skills, honed during his time as superior at Sainte-Marie, did the most to favour its success. The Ursuline nun Marie de l'Incarnation, whom Lalemant served as spiritual director while they both resided in Quebec, claimed in a 1650 letter to her adult son in France that "it was he ... who brought the good order that is seen in the Quebec Church with as much majesty as in the middle of France."[20]

Lalemant's journal has occasionally been seen as one more innovation in a career full of innovations. Its first editors, in the nineteenth century, concluded that it was the Jesuits' first regularly kept journal in New France, on the basis of an inscription on the page where daily entries began that reads "journal begun, 1645."[21] In truth, however, daily writing about matters large and small was already a well-established practice among Jesuits around the world, and likely also in New France. Ignatius Loyola himself maintained a spiritual diary for approximately thirty-five years, with entries sometimes limited to a single word and other times offering a detailed account of his experiences.[22] And in the Society's missions worldwide, Jesuits wrote as a matter of daily routine, in what Paul Nelles has called a "culture of habitual observation and notation."[23] The Society's leadership had long recommended that Jesuit leaders in mission settings keep a preliminary record of events to facilitate the writing of their periodic reports to Rome. In a 1594 order reaffirming the Society's commitment to the practice of preparing and circulating annual letters, in part in response to calls for its abolition mentioned in the previous chapter, the Society's superior general Claudio Acquaviva wrote that each Jesuit house and college should appoint an "investigator" to keep track of noteworthy events, day by day, with the purpose of facilitating the task of writing the annual letter.[24] Daily journals produced by missionaries are now scarce compared to reports like the *Relations* that were published – and certainly are overshadowed by them in scholarship – but there are nonetheless many surviving traces of this practice that suggest it was common among members of the Society in its early decades. The missionary to China Matteo Ricci's *History of the Introduction of Christianity into China*, for example, was completed by colleagues after his death on the basis of his daily notes, and Antonio Monserrate mentioned in a 1591 letter to Acquaviva that he recorded the events of each day every night for two and a half years while serving as a missionary in India.[25]

In the seventeenth-century Jesuit mission in New France, keeping a journal appears to have been a common practice among mission superiors from the beginning. Le Jeune's *Relations* for 1632 and 1633 are organized chronologically, recounting a year's worth of events in detail and citing precise dates, often without any thematic thread tying one item to the next. And from 1634 until 1640, each of Le Jeune's reports included a final chapter, variously labelled journal or collection (*ramas*), that presented events that had not been included in any of the previous, thematic chapters. These basic characteristics of Le Jeune's annual reports seem to attest to the existence of a preliminary record made day-by-day throughout the preceding year that served as a source for the *Relations* and that has been lost at some point in the intervening centuries.[26] Le Jeune himself suggested that writing was part of his daily routine in a passage of his 1634 annual report describing his effort to communicate indifference to an Innu spiritual leader whom Le Jeune believed to be trying to frighten him, or perhaps preparing to kill him: "But in order to show him that I was not at all astonished at these devilish acts, I continued, in my usual way, to read, write and say my little prayers; and when my hour for retiring came, I lay down and rested as peacefully through his orgies, as I would have done in a profound silence."[27] Even if he did not specify in this case what, exactly, he wrote as a matter of routine, other passages of the same *Relation* suggest that he and his colleagues kept close track of events as they occurred. He reported, for example, that a strange, pulsating light had lit up the windows of the Jesuits' residence in Quebec shortly after the death of an Indigenous convert on 28 January 1634, which the Jesuits took as a favourable sign from God of the condition of the man's soul. Le Jeune himself was forty leagues away from Quebec at this time, but knew that "this light appeared there at the same time and at the same hour, as we have since observed, Father Brebœuf and I, by comparing our notes."[28]

Traces of the existence of at least two additional volumes containing journal entries by Jesuit superiors in Quebec as late as 1755 have survived even if the manuscripts themselves have not. The Society of Jesus in Canada was extinguished for more than forty years after the last Jesuit there, Jean-Joseph Casot, died in 1800, having been prevented from replenishing its ranks by the 1759 English takeover of Canada and the worldwide suppression of the Society by the Church in 1773. Upon Casot's death, the Crown seized everything that had been in his possession and prepared an inventory that includes a book that apparently did not have a title, but that is identifiable as the journal for 1645–68 by its description as starting "*si varat annales, etc.*"[29] These are the first few words of a poem in Latin that precedes Lalemant's journal entries for 1645, marred by an apparent misreading of the letter c for an r in the word *vacat* on the part of the inventory's writer.[30] Also listed in the inventory is "a parchment folio book, the first sheet beginning, 'Continuation of the previous Registers, in which all the Rectors of this College wrote the most considerable things that happened in this country,' etc."[31] This inscription, which is regrettably truncated in the inventory of Casot's possessions, was fortunately recorded in some excerpts made around this time by the historian William Smith: "Continuation of the previous Registers in which all the Rectors of this College wrote the most considerable things that happened in this country during the time of their Superiority, except R.P. Vincent Bigot, who recorded nothing in all his six years, so that the R.P. Bouvar to whom he immediately succeeded is the last who wrote in the previous book, covered in Red, and we will begin to write in this one, covered in Parchment, on the 10th day of September 1710."[32] Not only does this description confirm that this was a volume of the journal kept by mission superiors, it also indicates that a third volume between the two that are listed in the inventory also must have once existed. The reference to "preceding registers," plural, makes clear that there were more than one, and the mention of Bigot's silence could not have been a reference to the journal for 1645–68 or an even earlier one, because this Jesuit did not arrive in Canada until 1680. It is not known what happened to this second volume after its seizure by the Crown, or any others that may have once existed without leaving such clear traces.[33] But it seems certain on the evidence traced above that Jesuit leaders in New France almost always engaged in this kind of record keeping, from the earliest years of the mission.[34]

Although the journal was not among Lalemant's unique or innovative contributions to the New France mission, his entries do reflect a particularly serious approach to maintaining a regular record of events. Despite serving as superior for only eleven of the nearly twenty-three years the manuscript covers, Lalemant was responsible for writing nearly two-thirds of it. He filled page after page with brief records of matters both important and trivial, preserving for posterity fascinating glimpses of what life was like for the Jesuits and other French residents of Quebec. Lalemant frequently recorded marriages between French settlers in Quebec or between Frenchmen and converted Indigenous women, while his successors only infrequently bothered to mention such unions in their portions of the journal.[35] He was the only author of the journal to pause, not infrequently, to comment on candles – the size of the remaining stock, when they were made, how they were distributed, and the conservative standards he established for their use – reflecting both the importance of these objects in a time before electric light and Lalemant's own keen attention to even the smallest details.[36] And he was far more likely than his successors to record the regularly occurring moments in the rhythms of life in Quebec, including the yearly arrival of spring and winter, the comings and goings of ships from France, and how feast days and other important occasions were observed. He sometimes simply reported that ceremonies or celebrations had been exactly the same as the previous year, a bit of record-keeping his successors never bothered with.[37]

In light of the Society of Jesus's formal advice linking the keeping of daily records to the preparation of regular reports and the apparent use of earlier journals for this purpose in New France, it is understandable that the relatively few scholars who have commented on the purpose of the surviving journal have characterized it primarily as a source of information for the annual *Relation*.[38] And it is easy enough to identify passages in Lalemant's annual reports that he could have written on the basis of entries in his journal. The death of the veteran

Jesuit missionary Énemond Massé in the early hours of 12 May 1646 not surprisingly warranted several paragraphs of commentary on his life and career in the year's *Relation*.[39] The annual report Lalemant sent to Paris in the fall of 1648 opened with a chapter entitled "Of the Arrival of the Ships" that discusses the news and people brought to Quebec by the merchant ships that year, and ends on an incongruous note by reporting the death on 23 May of two French settlers who perished when a storm arose while they were crossing the Saint Lawrence River near Trois-Rivières.[40] And Paul Le Jeune's 31 October 1649 departure for France, where he would take up his new post as the mission's Paris-based procurator, was reported in the following year's *Relation*.[41] In each of these cases, Lalemant had already noted the dates and bare details of these events in his journal when they first occurred.[42] It is, of course, possible that a detail-focused person like Lalemant was simply able to keep basic facts about important events fresh in his mind for months or even a year before it was time to write the next annual report. But it is just as plausible that he would have consulted a previous record like the journal in order to be sure of the dates of one colleague's demise and that of another's departure for France. And the awkward addition of the unfortunate drowning death of two settlers to the end of a chapter on an unrelated topic could have been the result of the mission superior reading through his journal one last time after drafting his annual report in search of noteworthy events he had neglected to mention, and then tacking on whatever he found as best he could. This is unavoidably speculative, in the absence of any direct testimony from Lalemant about his own writing process, but it is not difficult to imagine the mission superior thumbing through his journal while at work on each year's *Relation*, jogging his memory of particular events and perhaps also being reminded of some he had all but forgotten.

At the same time, there are many signs that Lalemant's journal and annual report were more loosely connected than might be expected if one was intended primarily to serve as a source for the other. In some of the cases in which particular events were recorded in both places, there are factual discrepancies. Lalemant noted in the journal, for example, that his colleague Isaac Jogues departed for a planned winter among the Haudenosaunee on 29 September 1646, in the company of a *donné* named Jean de Lalande, a Wendat man named Otrihouré who had been adopted by the Haudenosaunee, and a few other Wendats.[43] The *Relation*, which must have been sent to Paris no more than one month later, when the last of the season's ships departed, included a different account of the cultural identities of the Indigenous people who accompanied Jogues, and placed his departure on a different date.[44] Jogues, wrote Lalemant, "started from three Rivers on the 24th of that month, in company with a young Frenchman, and some Iroquois and other [Sauvages]."[45]

There are also cases in which the journal does not mention events that are reported in the year's annual report despite being the sort of news Lalemant usually included there. Lalemant opened his 1663 *Relation* with a chapter devoted to strange atmospheric phenomena that had been seen in the preceding year in New France, including a particularly remarkable one in which mist rising from the river caused the sun to appear to be three separate objects, each "crowned by a Rainbow." This was first observed on 7 January 1663, and again for a shorter period one week later.[46] In light of Lalemant's above-mentioned habit of including observations on weather and the climate in his journal – the arrival of snow, the beginning of spring, etc. – the strange appearance of the sun is just the sort of thing one might expect to find recorded there. But the annual report, written many months after the fact, appears to be the only place where Lalemant mentioned it.[47] Such cases show that while Lalemant may well have used his journal at least occasionally as a source for his *Relations*, he did not necessarily always consult it closely or allow the details it contained to override his own memory or what may have been written down elsewhere.

It may be best, then, to think of the journal as a separate record, one that was not necessarily related to the preparation of the *Relations* even if it could sometimes be useful for this purpose. Lalemant's particular preoccupations in the journal – weddings, candles, the comings and goings of the ships, etc. – do not seem to have been noted specifically in preparation for writing his report for publication because these routine aspects of life frequently went unmentioned in the annual reports. And it seems unlikely that Lalemant would have bothered to add to the journal events that took place just before the departure of the ships, like Jogues' above-mentioned departure from Trois-Rivières, if the only reason to do so would be to make a record to facilitate the preparation of the annual report. In such cases, he could have simply bypassed the journal and added the late-breaking news directly to the *Relation* that he must have then been finalizing.

The rest of this chapter examines two kinds of cases in which Lalemant's journal seems particularly disconnected from his annual reports. First, events that are reported in both places, but with substantial differences and apparently on the basis of information transmitted and preserved elsewhere, bring clarity to the different purposes of the *Relations* and the journal. And second, matters like the drowning of Gaspar Gouaut, mentioned at the beginning of this chapter, that are described only in the journal offer insight into how Lalemant decided what to include in his annual reports destined for readers in France and what to leave out. In both cases, attention to differences between the New France superior's private record and the one he created for the public brings into focus how the authors and editors of the *Relations* understood the promise in the titles of these texts that they contained news of the "most noteworthy" events of the year.

* * *

Comparison of Lalemant's treatment of events that are recorded in both his journal and annual reports shows the degree to which the *Relations'* particular purpose – transmitting to readers in France edifying information about the mission – could shape the way news was presented there. In such cases, Lalemant's *Relations* often focus on different details than those that are noted in the journal and deploy the basic facts of particular episodes in ways that supported the fundamental premises of the Jesuit mission in New France: Indigenous people were in need of intervention to ensure their salvation, they were entirely capable of converting to Christianity, and the Jesuits' methods of inducing them to do so were effective. In one representative case, Lalemant wrote a relatively long entry in his journal to mark the death, in November 1646, of the mother superior of the Hôtel-Dieu hospital in Quebec: "On the 5th, mother Marie de St Ignace, first Superior of the hospital at Quebek, died about 5 o'clock in the morning; she was not buried until the next day. I said high mass in their Church, at which monsieur de St Sauveur and other choristers made the responses. After the Gospel I spoke, for the space of two or three *misereres*, upon death, on the occasion of that of this good mother; we entered their Choir, – 5 priests and a lay chorister, St Martin, – to perform the Burial office."[48] In some ways, this entry is quite vague, limited to recounting the series of events following the death of this notable personage without mentioning the cause of her death or pausing to memorialize in any way her contributions to New France's spiritual or civic life. At the same time, it reflects

Lalemant's usual keen attention to seemingly small details, including how many cantors participated and naming the figures who played a prominent role in her memorial. On the whole, it is a just-the-facts accounting of the day's events, a record of who participated and what transpired, without any reflection on its context or significance.

The account of the mother superior's death in the next *Relation*, on the other hand, focuses squarely on other details and leaves out many of those recounted in the journal. The subject of her death is raised only incidentally, after a report of the deathbed baptism of an Indigenous person in the hospital. The 1647 *Relation* reports that the Augustinian nuns who operated the hospital were very pleased at this event because it preserved their unblemished record of managing to baptize Indigenous people before they passed away. In Lalemant's words, the mother superior "who has blessedly passed from this life into the other, had so especial a care for this, that she could not sleep soundly, if the souls of these patients were not in safety, so far as charity can place them therein."[49] Having raised the fact of this nun's death while recounting another event, Lalemant reported believing himself obligated to say more. He noted some details of the health problems that culminated in her death, the difficulty breathing that she had experienced even before departing France and that only got worse after her arrival in Canada, and the violent stomach aches that tormented her constantly for the last fifteen months of her life. But he also insisted that her own ill health did not prevent her from caring for and ministering to the sick and dying persons in her charge. By Lalemant's account, she sometimes had her bed placed in the rooms of particularly ill patients in order to watch over them and redirected to her sickest patients the fresh meat that had been allotted to her on account of her own illness. In sum, Lalemant wrote, "She lived only six years and a half in New France; but in that short time she greatly suffered and toiled here for the good of the French Colony and of the [Sauvages]."[50] Whereas the journal simply marks the date of this nun's passing and details some of the usual rites and ceremonies that followed her death, the published record of her death offers an unmistakable portrait of a dedicated and zealous evangelical labourer, focusing on her accomplishments and faith, and how these were made all the more remarkable by her own poor health.

Another notable death recorded in both the journal and the corresponding annual *Relation*, that of a notorious Algonquin apostate in December 1646, offers a striking example of how the annual reports were crafted to emphasize what the Jesuits saw as Indigenous Peoples' receptivity to Christianity. The death of this man – who is identified in the missionaries' annual reports by two names, Chibanagouch and Abdon – brought an end to his long and turbulent relationship with the French missionaries.[51] He had been baptized while deathly ill at Trois-Rivières on 19 April 1639 and was apparently a faithful convert for a time, or at least a willing follower of the Jesuits, enough so that he had his child baptized two years later. Conflict arose, however, when Chibanagouch, whom the Jesuits named Joseph upon his baptism, took the name Oumasatikoueie and its associated nicknames *La Grenouille* (the frog) and *Le Crapaud* (the toad). These names had previously belonged to dead Algonquin leaders and were passed on in hopes of causing their best qualities to manifest in someone new.[52] This name change, Lalemant claimed, made the man proud and insolent and changed his relationship to both the Jesuits and to his adopted faith. Despite his own conversion to Christianity and baptism, he reportedly began hindering the Jesuits' efforts to convert others at every opportunity.[53] Matters came to a head in the fall of 1646, when La Grenouille's people were stricken with a deadly illness. Lalemant claimed that many had been healed after accepting Christianity and praying for health, but La Grenouille insisted to his fellow Algonquin that the illness itself was caused by the Jesuits' religion and any healing that occurred was owed to traditional practices. When he fell ill himself, he demanded that his dreams be carried out by his countrymen, in accordance with the pre-existing customs of his people, after which he declared himself healed. But the *Relation* reports that he was struck with a violent fever as he was declaring his triumph over the Jesuits' faith-based healing, "foamed like one possessed," and then died.[54] Lalemant's journal marks La Grenouille's passing in a terse and harshly judgmental entry containing only the bare facts of the matter: "This month we received news of the death of a wretched Apostate at three rivers, named Abdon, or la grenouille."[55]

The *Relation*, in contrast, not only recounts the history of the Jesuits' association with this man, but also highlights the value they found in his death – the way it helped secure the conversions of other Indigenous people. The chapter recounting this event begins by putting it in a broader context, the apparent divine punishment of various men who were preventing the widespread adoption of Christianity in their Algonquin community. "Three men of influence among the [Sauvages] were placing some obstacles against the expansion of the Faith, by their polygamy, – openly retaining two wives. A thunderbolt hurled from Heaven, – I mean to say, an extraordinary punishment, – has killed their bodies, and, perhaps, wretchedly destroyed their souls."[56] After recounting the demise of two other men, named Kapimichats and Chichiontibik, and describing how their fate led some other Indigenous people to ask God for forgiveness, Lalemant turned to the story of La Grenouille, noting that the two earlier deaths had not been enough to touch the hardest of hearts: "Some [Sauvages] were touched by it; but as the ears are not as near to the soul, so to speak, as the eyes, it was necessary that some Apostates and some hardened Pagans should see another blow, in order to be shaken."[57] This final blow came in the form of La Grenouille's public death after so vehemently choosing his culture's traditional healing practices over his former Christian faith. Wrote Lalemant, "This thunderbolt, while killing one man, raised several to life; the good Christians gave a thousand blessings to God, the lukewarm ones became warm, the Apostates became reconciled to the Church; and the Pagans, honoring Jesus Christ, asked his holy Baptism. No one dared longer open his lips against the Faith; it was now spoken of only with a dread and respect that altogether pleased us."[58] Whereas Lalemant's journal had simply reported, in what could be seen as a tone of relief or even satisfaction, that this "wretched apostate" had died, his *Relation* emphasized how this event helped open additional hearts to the Jesuits' message.

It was not only deaths that could be reported briefly in the journal but amplified in the *Relations* to make a point about spiritual conditions or evangelical progress in New France. In an entry for July 1648, the journal records the story of the capture by the Haudenosaunee of two Frenchmen, Pierre le Febvre and an unnamed nephew of the prominent settler and occasional deputy governor of Trois-Rivières Jacques Leneuf de La Poterie, during a confrontation that also saw the kidnapping and killing of some Wendats who were allies of the French, as well as the death of two Haudenosaunee attackers.[59] The version of the story in the year's *Relation* largely follows this account, but adds details and also omits facts that may not have been useful in conveying the edifying nature of this news to French readers.[60] According to the published account, the Haudenosaunee attacked two Frenchmen who were watching over livestock, and five Wendats, hearing the disturbance, rushed to the aid of the French. Before French reinforcements could arrive, one unnamed Frenchman had already been killed and two others were taken prisoner, along with two of their Wendat rescuers. One of these two French captives is identified, as in the journal, as a nephew of La Poterie, but the other is not named, as if there was simply no point in naming a relatively obscure figure like Pierre Le Febvre to French readers for whom the name would probably have been meaningless. The *Relation's* account of this attack notes instead that the slain Wendat man was a good Christian and that some Haudenosaunee men who were then being held by the French in Trois-Rivières asked to be instructed in Christianity upon hearing news of this attack, apparently because they expected the French to retaliate by putting them to death. Whereas the journal reports this incident as the worrisome kidnapping of two French settlers and the violent deaths of some Wendat and Haudenosaunee people, the *Relation* finds positive news for the mission: the edifying death of a Wendat convert and the consequent opening of the possibility of converting some representatives of the group that killed him. The basic facts recounted in Lalemant's two versions of the story are not in conflict, but they are deployed to support strikingly different messages.[61]

In each of these cases – the deaths of Marie Guenet de Saint-Ignace and La Grenouille and the Haudenosaunee attack on a pair of French settlers – Lalemant's journal does not seem to have been the primary source for the account in the corresponding *Relation*. On the subject of the death of the hospitaller nun, the two texts contain such different information that they seem scarcely related. Lalemant's journal itself indicates that he possessed a separate record of the death of La Grenouille. It reports that "we received word" of the man's death, presumably in the form of an oral or written report of events in Trois-Rivières, no trace of which seems to have survived, that may have served as the basis of both the journal entry and the annual report. And news of the attack on Le Febvre and La Poterie's nephew similarly must have reached Lalemant in Quebec in written or oral form, or perhaps both, since this incident occurred in Trois-Rivières. Indeed, the journal indicates that more information could be found "in the letters among the Archives or in the relation."[62] The apparent independence of Lalemant's two records of each of these events means that each can be viewed as a reflection of the particular purpose of the journal and the *Relations* – and not, in the case of the annual report, as an echo or adaptation of what he had already written in his notebook. As a record made day by day as events unfolded, Lalemant's journal is made up of spare entries on particular events that occurred at specific times, generally omitting context like the long-standing spiritual excellence of Marie de St Ignace or the troubled history of the Jesuits' relationship with La Grenouille, information with which Lalemant would already have been very familiar. His *Relations*, in contrast, consistently reflect their purpose as texts intended to communicate edifying news to readers in France, including context on these subjects that may have been less closely associated with particular events or dates, and never failing to emphasize how they were related to the progress of efforts to convert Indigenous people. These differences between Lalemant's journal and annual reports are a useful reminder that even when the published texts seem to simply report events in the New France mission, they probably do not much resemble what their authors would have written if making only a private record for themselves. In the *Relations*, events that might reasonably be seen as bad news were used as opportunities to show how the mission was winning Indigenous hearts and minds.

* * *

Finally, the many events that are recorded in Lalemant's journal but not in his *Relations* bring into relief the kinds of news that tended to go unmentioned in the annual reports destined for French readers. Examples are numerous and range from mundane activities like the start of construction on an oven in the Jesuits' lodging in Quebec to more intriguing occurrences such as the preparation of several items of Indigenous clothing for transport to France to satisfy a desire expressed by the child king Louis XIV, both of which took place on 19 October 1645.[63] In many cases, the omission from the annual report of events that are mentioned in Lalemant's journal is understandable enough. Events like the construction of an oven were significant in the daily lives of the Jesuits and other residents of Quebec, but might not have been particularly interesting to readers in France. And the king's apparent curiosity about Indigenous clothes may be an intriguing detail for modern readers, but an understandably lower priority for inclusion in the *Relation* than news more directly related to the mission's progress in converting Indigenous people. It would not be possible, of course, for the annual reports to include everything that happened in an entire year without quickly becoming very tedious. And so, much was simply left out. In some cases, however, Lalemant's journal testifies to the exclusion from the *Relations* of particularly significant or curious events, and these collectively give some sense of how he decided what to include and what need not be mentioned. The rest of this chapter examines three such cases: a bout of drunken excess on the part of some French settlers and its consequences in Quebec in 1645, the performance in 1646 of a play that may have been Pierre Corneille's famous tragicomedy *Le Cid*, and the demonic possession of a settler named Barbe Hallay in 1660.

In December of 1645, Lalemant recorded in his journal an incident in which two French people drank too much and caused a public scandal. Wrote Lalemant, "Two of our french having begun to drink, while waiting for the midnight mass, became intoxicated, with much scandal to some frenchmen and [Sauvages] who saw them."[64] This incident was not particularly unusual in itself. Drunkenness among French settlers in Quebec was a particular preoccupation of Lalemant, as least to judge by the way he periodically mentioned it in his journal and his successors' almost complete silence on the topic in their own entries.[65] In July 1647, for example, he noted that a sailor named Charles drank four cupfuls of brandy and then threw himself into the sea when refused any more.[66] And in 1648, he reported that four or five people were put on the rack for having been intoxicated on Easter.[67] The incident before midnight mass in 1645 took on particular significance, however, because of what it implied to witnesses about the unequal punishment of similar crimes committed by Indigenous people and French settlers. Continued Lalemant in his journal, "We preached vigorously against it, because the [Sauvages] said: 'They make us take the discipline when we get drunk, and they say nothing to the french.' Nothing further was required than this public expression; Monsieur the governor had them put on the [rack], exposed to a frightful Northeast wind."[68] This incident appears, in the journal, as a case of justice being meted out not only to punish public drunkenness but also to respond to charges of hypocrisy levelled by Indigenous observers whose own inebriation, they charged, would not have been overlooked.

This particular incident went unmentioned in Lalemant's next *Relation*, but the superior did include a similar comment about French hypocrisy in punishing inebriation, in the context of a discussion of Indigenous – not French – abuse of alcohol in nearby Sillery in November, 1645.[69] Lalemant described several events in which Algonquin people who indulged in alcohol sought punishment from the missionaries or punished themselves. In one case, a group of people who had drunk to excess whipped themselves and each other in view of the Jesuits as an act of penance. As one of them exclaimed, according to the *Relation*, "Let us repay to God what we have stolen from him by our offense. I know well that those who do not believe will mock us, but their jeerings must not prevent us from atoning for our offenses."[70] An unconverted man who presented himself for the same penalty was reportedly turned away, and Lalemant wrote that "this consoled the Christians, who believed that God preferred them to the Infidels, by accepting their penance."[71] One of those in attendance reportedly asked why French people who drank too much were not similarly punished, to which the Algonquin converts replied that the settlement's civil authorities sometimes did punish them, but that the new Christians themselves preferred to do penance before the Jesuits. The *Relation* does not suggest that French settlers were entirely innocent. It acknowledges that they sometimes faced consequences for drinking, reported that some "base soul" traded brandy to Indigenous people for furs, and referenced "irregularities which the vessels usually occasion by their liquors … while they are anchored in our ports."[72] But Lalemant's *Relation* omitted any specific details about French settlers who drank too much, of the kind he reported in his journal, and instead included stories about the contrition and efforts to make amends of Indigenous Christians who drank. The same pattern holds for Lalemant's reports for 1647 and 1648, which do not mention the drunk sailor named Charles and the handful of people punished for being drunk on Easter, and instead focus on the remorse of Indigenous people who drank and their zealous efforts to prevent others from making the same mistake.[73]

The same dynamic that operates in the case of drunken misbehaviour in December 1645 – a worrying incident involving French settlers going unreported in the *Relations*, which focused instead on good news for the mission to be found in the similar conduct of Indigenous people – can also be found in the surviving records of theatrical performances in Quebec. On New Year's Eve of 1646, Lalemant recorded in his journal that "on the last Day of the year, they gave a performance at the warehouse, Enacting the *sit.* Our Fathers were present, – in deference to Monsieur the governor, who took pleasure therein, as also did the [Sauvages], – that is, fathers de Quen, Lalemant, and defretat: all went well, and there was nothing which could not edify. I begged Monsieur the governor to excuse me from attendance."[74] It has often been speculated that this was a performance of Pierre Corneille's *Le Cid*, particularly since the journal contains a clearer reference to a performance of this play in 1652.[75] Lalemant did not condemn this performance outright, even if his journal entry betrays a certain level of unease that appears to be typical of how New France's religious authorities regarded theatrical performances throughout the century.[76] It reports that other missionaries attended the play not because they wanted to, but out of consideration for the governor. And Lalemant's report that nothing unedifying occurred betrays a contrary fear or expectation. It is perhaps not surprising, then, that the mission superior chose to omit this event from the year's *Relation*, even though a performance of one of the most popular plays from the metropolitan stage might have been a remarkable enough occurrence to have merited mention in a report on life in the colony, even one focused on religious matters. Lalemant was not the only Quebec mission superior who noted theatrical performances in the journal, but opted not to mention them in the annual reports that were destined for publication. His immediate successor, Paul Ragueneau, noted in the journal performances of Corneille's *Héraclius* in 1651 and *Le Cid* 1652, both of which go unmentioned in the corresponding *Relations*. Even the anonymously authored and religiously themed *Le Sage visionnaire*, which apparently was such a hit in Quebec in February 1668 that it was performed twice in a three-day period – as then superior François-Joseph Le Mercier reported in the journal, "with great success and to every one's satisfaction" – was apparently not worth mentioning in that year's annual report.[77] A reader of the *Relations* alone would be left with the impression that theatrical performances were almost unheard of in Quebec.

The only exception to the *Relations'* general silence on this topic involves a performance during Barthélemy Vimont's term as superior, in which the Jesuits were invited to add content to an unspecified tragicomedy staged by then-governor Charles du Hault de Montmagny, as part of the settlement's celebration of the birth of an heir to the French throne. As Le Jeune described this event in the 1640 *Relation* that he prepared at Vimont's request, the performance had an immediate and positive impact on the missionaries' efforts to convert Indigenous spectators:

> Sieur Martial Piraubé, who had charge of this performance, and who represented the chief personage, succeeded excellently; but in order that our [Sauvages] might derive some benefit from it, Monsieur the Governor, endowed with uncommon zeal and prudence, invited us to put something into it which might strike their eyes and their ears. We had the soul of an unbeliever pursued

> by two demons, who finally hurled it into a hell that vomited forth flames; the struggles, cries, and shrieks of this soul and of these demons, who spoke in the Algonquin tongue, penetrated so deeply into the hearts of some of them, that a [Sauvage] told us, two days afterward, that he had been greatly frightened that night by a very horrible dream. "I saw," said he, "a hideous gulf whence issued flames and demons. It seemed to me that they tried to destroy me, and this filled me with great terror."[78]

In Le Jeune's telling, this was not a potentially morally damaging event of the kind Lalemant would nervously remark on in the journal several years later. It was instead an opportunity to present an edifying message to potential converts – in their own language, no less – that might induce them to convert, an activity that was harmonious with longstanding Jesuit pedagogical tradition. The performance of tragedies and comedies treating subjects like the martyrdom of saints and the passion of Christ was specifically recommended to Jesuit colleges in the 1599 *Ratio Studiorum*, the Society of Jesus's educational regulations.[79] It became a common practice both in Europe and in the Society's sixteenth- and seventeenth-century missions around the world.[80] In this particular case, the performance of a play to which the Jesuits added their own material served their goals, at least as Le Jeune reported it to readers of the *Relation*. He closed his account of this curious event by remarking on the progress he and his colleagues believed themselves to be making in Christianizing the Indigenous people around them: "In brief, these poor peoples are giving themselves up to Jesus Christ from day to day; the help that is given them in clearing and cultivating the land encourages them so greatly, that it is a blessing to see them praying and working, each in due time."[81] The pattern is clear: plays staged by secular authorities always went unmentioned in the *Relations* regardless of who was serving as superior. But the one case in which the Jesuits were invited to harmonize a theatrical performance with their own message received fulsome commentary for its effect on potential converts.

Similarly omitted from the annual *Relations* is the particularly sensational case of the demonic possession of a French settler named Barbe Hallay, which Lalemant mentioned in his journal in December 1660.[82] According to a much fuller account of Hallay's ordeal in a 1661 letter from the Ursuline nun Marie de l'Incarnation to her son in France, this young woman was the victim of a miller named Daniel Vuil, who had been forced to renounce his Protestantism upon arrival in New France. He sought to marry Hallay, who had crossed the ocean from France with her parents on the same ship that brought him to Quebec, but was refused due to the family's concerns about his character. In the nun's telling, "He summoned Demons or crazy spirits to the girl's house with specters which gave her much pain and fright." The bishop of Quebec sent priests to attempt to drive out the demons, and even attempted to do so himself, all to no effect. "Phantoms were seen there, the playing of the drum and the flute was heard, stones were seen to come loose from the walls and fly here and there, and all the while the Magician was there with his companions to worry the girl."[83] Both Hallay and the miller were transported from their remote homes to Quebec, where the first was imprisoned and eventually executed and the second was entrusted to the care of the Augustinian Hospitaller nuns. It was Hallay's arrival in Quebec in December 1660 that prompted her inclusion in Lalemant's journal: "In this month, barbe Halé was brought from beauport. She had been possessed with a Demon of lunacy for 5 or 6 months, but only at intervals. At first she was placed in a room in the old hospital, where she passed the night, in the company of a keeper of her own sex, a priest, and some servants. [A long story, which I will discuss elsewhere]."[84] The surviving accounts of this incident report that Hallay's demons were eventually driven out through the miraculous intercession of Jean de Brébeuf, the famous Jesuit martyr whose 1649 death is discussed in the following chapter, and whose rib bone was furnished for use in this exorcism by his fellow missionary Paul Ragueneau.[85] Despite the Jesuits' own involvement in attempting to exorcise Hallay's demons, the role attributed to their fallen comrade Brébeuf, and the undeniably sensational nature of the story, this episode goes unmentioned in Lalemant's published accounts of events in New France.

He did not hesitate, however, to highlight in the *Relations* other cases of apparent harmful supernatural interference in the religious mission, particularly when he believed they inspired impious behaviour on the part of Indigenous people.[86] Lalemant's *Relation* for 1659–60, for example, includes the following advice for would-be missionaries: "A Missionary destined for this great work must make up his mind to lead a very strange kind of life, and endure unimaginable destitution of all things; to suffer every inclemency of the weather, without mitigation; to bear a thousand impertinences, a thousand taunts, and often, indeed, blows from the Infidel [Sauvages], who are at times instigated by the demons, – and all this without human consolation."[87] The following year, he reported that "although our enemies prevent our free passage in all directions for gathering fruit of such sweetness and ripeness, we have not failed, despite all the Iroquois and all the Demons, to extend our Missions this year to the four quarters of this New World, and to go almost everywhere in search of these poor wandering sheep."[88] It seems, then, that the omission of the case of Barbe Hallay from Lalemant's annual reports reflects not a general aversion to the topic of demonic influence over human life, but rather a narrower preference to avoid painting too unflattering a picture of the spiritual condition of French settlers and to focus instead on Indigenous potential converts.

One pattern that unites the three disparate examples above – drunken behaviour, theatrical performances, and demonic possession – is that Lalemant was more likely to highlight inharmonious aspects of life in the mission and the French settlement in his journal than in the *Relations*. The Jesuits occasionally complained of French excesses in their published annual reports – Lalemant did lament, as mentioned above, the drunkenness and other poor behaviour that often accompanied the presence of merchant ships.[89] But, in general, Lalemant's journal and *Relations* give different impressions about who was drinking excessively in New France and whether this was ultimately productive for efforts to win converts, what sorts of occasional secular entertainments were available to settlers, and who was summoning malevolent spirits or falling victim to their influence. Reading Lalemant's journal entries alongside his published reports makes clear the extent to which the published reports constitute a highly selective account of events in French settlements and the New France mission, curated to cast the Jesuits' mission and its prospects for success in the most favourable possible light. This selectivity was no doubt at least partly intended to hide unsavoury or disedifying news about the behaviour of French settlers from French readers, but it also served to support a long-articulated Jesuit vision of New France as a particularly harmonious and religiously observant place. Scholars have long pointed to rhetoric in the *Relations* that insisted on New France's status as a kind of budding spiritual utopia, a place free of France's vices and imperfections.[90] In his first report as New France superior, for example – the same one that reported the drunken spectacle that caused Indigenous people to raise questions of fairness – Lalemant listed "the piety and good example of the habitans" among the factors contributing to what he saw as the dawning of Christianity in the land.[91] Lalemant's omissions from his *Relations* show that it was not only explicit commentary or rhetorical framing that served to make this case in the published texts, but also the very stories and facts that were selected for inclusion. Incidents that threatened to undermine the Jesuits' favourable portrait of the French settlement frequently went unmentioned in the Jesuits' published annual reports, making way for stories that presented Indigenous people as both in need of and susceptible to the Jesuits' religious message.

* * *

The act of compiling the Jesuit *Relations* from New France has typically been understood as a once-per-year chore performed by the mission superior in the late summer or early autumn, after reports from missionaries in the field made their way to Quebec, as part of the Society of Jesus's long-standing tradition of edifying letters discussed in the previous chapter. This chapter has shown that other traditions and schedules are also important parts of the story of how the *Relations* were created, or at least that they provide useful context for understanding the process. Jérôme Lalemant did not write only once a year when it was time to assemble his annual report and answer letters from France. Nor did his predecessors or successors, for that matter. The task of documenting events was instead carried out daily or nearly so, a Jesuit tradition that had existed for just as long as the mandate to submit regular reports discussed in the first chapter of this book, but that has typically not been understood as part of the story of how the New France *Relations* came to exist. As this chapter has shown, Lalemant's habitual writing in his journal sheds light on the process by which he wrote his annual reports. There are passages in his reports that might well have been crafted on the basis of entries he made in the journal. And differences between Lalemant's journal and his *Relations*, both in content and in the way he characterized particular events, bring into relief the degree to which the published texts were never intended to give an unvarnished view of the mission and of life in the colony. In addition to providing a glimpse behind the scenes of Jesuit efforts to present a particular image of New France to readers, this chapter's close examination of Lalemant's journal shows how accounting for Jesuit writing practices other than their annual reports, and the distinct purposes of the various kinds of texts produced by missionaries, can enrich scholarly understandings of the

Relations themselves. It is not only factual differences or differing points of emphasis between the *Relations* and other records of events in New France that can provide insight into the Jesuits' annual reports. As the following chapter shows, such texts also sometimes show how the missionary authors took care to frame the news they prepared for readers in France in the most emotionally affecting way possible.

3

Paul Ragueneau, Christophe Regnaut, and the Making of a Tale of Martyrdom in the *Relation* of 1648–49

On 16 March 1649, Haudenosaunee warriors captured two French Jesuits in the village of Teanaostataé (known to the French as Saint Louis), near Lake Huron's Georgian Bay in what is now Ontario. This was just one small part of a broader campaign to subdue their Wendat economic and territorial rivals once and for all.[1] Jean de Brébeuf was a seasoned mission veteran who had spent most of the preceding fifteen years among the Wendat, including a stint as mission superior from the founding of the mission in 1634 until 1638. His companion, Gabriel Lalemant – thirty-eight years old to Brébeuf's nearly fifty-six – had been in Wendat territory for just six months after working for two years in Quebec alongside his uncle Jérôme Lalemant. He bore his ordeal no less stoically than his more experienced colleague, at least according to subsequent accounts, and this would have been no easy task.

The captors stripped the pair naked, tore out some of their fingernails, and led them to the settlement of Taenhatentaron, which the French called Saint Ignace. There, Brébeuf and Lalemant were beaten with clubs all over their bodies as a prelude to even worse torments. Collars of red-hot axe heads placed around their necks severely burned their upper bodies; their torsos were enclosed in belts made of bark and filled with burning pitch and resin; and they were doused repeatedly with boiling water in what the year's *Relation*, prepared by then-superior of the Wendat mission Paul Ragueneau, characterized as a mock baptism. Finally, the Haudenosaunee stripped flesh from the priests' still-living bodies to be roasted and eaten, and forced them to witness their own consumption before removing and eating their hearts. The worst of Brébeuf's suffering lasted three hours on the afternoon of his capture, ending with his death. Lalemant endured some fifteen hours, through the night, before expiring mid-morning on the seventeenth day of March. Within a year, the Wendat had been dispersed and the Jesuits had burned their mission headquarters of Sainte-Marie to the ground to keep it from falling into Haudenosaunee hands.[2]

This eruption of violence was sensational news among French settlers and the Jesuits' readers in Europe, and has remained an object of intense interest ever since, at least in part because the surviving accounts of it offer unusually detailed descriptions of the violence Jesuit missionaries sometimes experienced in New France, as well as their steadfast faith in the face of death.[3] The *Relation* describing the last hours of Brébeuf and Gabriel Lalemant seems to have been the single most popular in the entire series, immediately appearing in four distinct editions to meet what must have been unusually strong and widespread demand.[4] The story is now often regarded as a prime example of Jesuit missionaries' extraordinary faith and as evidence that Brébeuf and Lalemant died as martyrs.[5] It is also seen as part of a rich vein of hagiographical writing that runs through all of the *Relations*, itself part of a broader trend in French literature during the Wars of Religion and the Catholic Reformation in the sixteenth and seventeenth centuries.[6] Scholars have also read accounts of this incident against the martyrological grain, attempting to understand what it might have meant to Indigenous witnesses and participants. James Carson's provocatively titled article "Brébeuf Was Never Martyred," for example, argued that the missionary died in a political conflict between Indigenous rivals instead of as a result of hatred of the faith, as martyrdom requires. And Emma Anderson has examined the story from three different points of view: those of the Jesuits, the Haudenosaunee who tortured them, and the Wendat apostates who had previously been captured and adopted by the Haudenosaunee, and who participated in torturing the Jesuit captives. Such readings have revealed this incident to be much more complicated than the simple if gruesome narrative of faithful suffering for which it was long taken.[7]

This chapter uses surviving accounts of the incident not to examine once again the significance of Brébeuf's and Lalemant's deaths, but rather to shed light on the *Relations* themselves, and how they were composed in New France before being sent to Paris for publication. The previous chapters of this book examined cases in which two mission superiors drew on their own earlier writings – or chose not to do so – while preparing their annual reports, but the Jesuit mission leader's task also frequently involved the collation and adaptation of material penned by others. As Lawrence W. Wroth described the process in a classic article on the *Relations*, the published reports were based on "reports in the form of letters or journals, coming fresh from the field of action and composed under circumstances of the greatest difficulty," and "the Canadian Superior ... edited the original reports, removing portions here, altering the language there, and welding the several pieces before him into a concise and comprehensive story of the year's mission in Canada."[8] Wroth was describing the work of the superior in Quebec, but this is also an apt description of how the reports from the Wendat mission were prepared, at least in some cases. These were published in the same volume as the Quebec reports for most years between 1635 and 1650, and frequently contain the same blend of the mission superior's own words and those of his colleagues.[9] Wroth's characterization of how mission leaders made use of their colleagues' writings has often been echoed in scholarship, but very little attention has been devoted to examining how this work could shape the contents of the *Relations*.[10]

Brébeuf's and Gabriel Lalemant's last hours offer a unique glimpse of this process because, as a subject of understandably intense interest among French missionaries and settlers, they were described in writing multiple times. Ragueneau put versions of the story to paper at least twice in the immediate aftermath of his colleagues' deaths: once for the annual *Relation* and once in a letter to Vincenzo Carafa, who in 1645 had replaced Mutio Vitelleschi as the Jesuit superior general in Rome.[11] There is also a report by a *donné* named Christophe Regnaut that was written around the same time, and a letter the Quebec Ursuline nun Marie de l'Incarnation sent to her order's convent in Tours in September of the same year.[12] The Jesuit historian François du Creux's 1664 *Historia Canadensis* reports the existence of yet another version of the story, now lost, that was apparently prepared in New France soon after the fact by the Jesuit Jacques Bonin, who arrived among the Wendat at the same time as Gabriel Lalemant.[13] New versions of the story would continue to appear in subsequent years. Ragueneau wrote about it a third time in a 1652 report for the archbishop of Rouen on all of the Jesuits who had been killed in New France, and the Italian Jesuit missionary to the Wendat, Francesco-Giuseppe Bressani, offered his own version of the story in 1653, in the only published account of the Society of Jesus's missions in New

France to appear in Italian.[14] This chapter draws on three of the surviving accounts of the event in particular – Ragueneau's two versions of the story from 1649 and Regnaut's report – because of the way they are related to each other. Together they provide a precious window into how the Wendat mission superior produced the version of the story in his *Relation*, and also bring attention to the role in this process of a non-Jesuit, a line of inquiry that will be further developed in the following two chapters.

Regnaut's report and Ragueneau's published account are certainly not unknown. Both are frequently cited by scholars who examine Brébeuf and Lalemant's fatal ordeal. Regardless of their particular perspective on these events, researchers have tended to treat these two accounts as overlapping collections of facts, alternate sources that mostly confirm each other and add up to a richly detailed record of what happened to the two missionaries. This equivalence has occasionally been stated explicitly, in the form of the erroneous assertion that Regnaut's account, like Ragueneau's, was published in the seventeenth century or otherwise intended for France's reading public.[15] More frequently, however, it is simply implied by an absence of commentary on the texts' different purposes and narrative characteristics.[16] Studies of the death of Brébeuf and Lalemant that use the texts this way have brought welcome nuance to scholarly understandings of one of the most sensational events in the history of the Jesuit mission, showing that it is more than the terrifying tale of Christian martyrdom for which it was long taken. But they also testify to the fact that the relationship between the Jesuits' published reports and other mission records remains to be accounted for. The rest of this chapter traces how the version of the story in Ragueneau's *Relation* came to exist, beginning with the work of a voluntary labourer in service of the Jesuits in Sainte-Marie.

* * *

Christophe Regnaut arrived in Quebec in or around 1635, when he was twenty-two years old, and by 1638 had committed himself to serving the Jesuits in their mission to the Wendat.[17] He was one of the four *donnés* whom Jérôme Lalemant enlisted to work in the Wendat mission that year, as mentioned in the previous chapter, having secured permission for this practice from the Society's provincial in Paris, Étienne Binet.[18] This was a solution to a problem that mission leaders in New France had identified more than a decade earlier, the way progress in winning conversions was seemingly delayed by the necessity of devoting precious time to meeting basic material needs and handling day-to-day chores.[19] Hired workers were in short supply in the Wendat mission, at least in part due to the real or perceived dangers of working in a remote settlement like Sainte-Marie. And Jesuit brothers (*frères coajuteurs*) were generally better suited to spiritual and evangelical work of the kind undertaken by the priests than the sort of manual toil that was so desperately needed to meet the basic needs of the Jesuit community. The addition of *donnés* to the mission's workforce must have seemed like an ideal solution. Lalemant never explained where he got the idea to use these volunteers as a way to expand the mission's workforce. French people had occasionally gifted their own lives and labour to religious communities since the tenth century, but this practice seems to have been rare in France in Lalemant's time.[20] A plausible, if uncertain, source of inspiration is the Spanish missions of other Catholic orders in South America, where faithful volunteers had already been serving as lifelong domestic labourers, especially in Peru.[21] Wherever he got the idea, Lalemant pursued it with his characteristic vigour. By the time Brébeuf and Lalemant died, some two dozen such men had joined the Wendat mission. They grew crops and tended livestock, carried supplies from Quebec on their backs or paddled them along rivers and lakes, built and defended chapels and other essential infrastructure, staffed the mission's medical facility, and saw to the provision of the firewood necessary to keep the winter cold at bay, among other routine tasks.[22]

Regnaut, for his part, is listed in the mission registers as a sort of all-purpose handyman (*ad omnia*) and later as a shoemaker (*sutor*).[23] How he came to write an account of the violent death of Brébeuf and Lalemant is unclear. The labour performed by the *donnés* was usually of the manual variety and did not typically include documenting events in the mission. Many of them – perhaps most – may not have been sufficiently literate to write detailed reports, although at least one other, the Sainte-Marie surgeon François Gendron, was also able to write. Several of his letters from the Wendat mission during his time there from 1643 to 1650 were published in 1660, a decade after he had returned to France to become a priest.[24] Regnaut may have found himself penning an account of this violent incident because he appears to have been among the members of the mission best positioned to gather information about it in its immediate aftermath. In his account of the violent treatment of the two priests, he reports that he was part of a team sent to recover their bodies.[25] Despite Regnaut's apparently exceptional usefulness to the Jesuits' efforts in Wendat territory, very little is known about him – or, for that matter, most of his fellow voluntary labourers in the mission. A small number of the *donnés* achieved lasting notoriety, including Jean de Lalande and René Goupil, who are now counted among the famous Canadian martyrs due to their violent deaths while in the Jesuits' service. Many others are scarcely known at all, being mentioned in the surviving textual record of the mission by only a first or last name or by the tasks they performed.[26]

A general sense of how such men understood their roles in the mission can be gleaned from the contracts they signed upon offering themselves to the Jesuits, two of which have survived. An agreement signed at Sainte-Marie in December 1639 records the pledge made by a man named Robert Le Coq "to serve and assist with all my power and diligence the Fathers of the said Society ... and particularly those who are employed in the conversion of the poor [Sauvages] and barbarians of New France among the Hurons ... without claiming anything else whatever except to live and die with the said Fathers in whatever part of the world I am required to be with them."[27] A second document, signed by Lalemant and a man named Jean Guérin in March 1641, formalized a similarly broad gift of all of the latter man's labour for the benefit of the Jesuits. It also suggests that such gifts were sometimes presented as the result of deep faith, and that the Jesuits' part of the bargain – life-long material support – was conditional on the *donné's* virtuous conduct. Guérin was reportedly motivated by his "desire to consecrate himself to the Service of God and of our Society," and intended his gift of his own labour to last the rest of his life. In recognition of Guérin's demonstrations of faith, the Jesuits promised for their part "to maintain him according to his condition with food and clothing, without other wages or claims on his part, and to care for him kindly in case of sickness, even to the end of his life, without being able to dismiss him in such case, except with his own consent; provided that, on his part, he continue to live in uprightness, diligence, and fidelity to our service, even as by these presents he promises and binds himself to do."[28]

Some of the *donnés* did end up devoting their rest of their lives to the Jesuits, like Joseph Boursier dit Desforges, who served in the Wendat mission until its dissolution not long after Brébeuf and Lalemant died, and then became a member of the Society of Jesus and lived out his days at the Jesuit college in Quebec. Another, the aforementioned Jean Guérin, was killed by an accidental gunshot after nearly twenty years of service.[29] Others left the Jesuits' service when other opportunities or desires presented themselves. Guillaume Couture, for example, was working for the Jesuits as a volunteer carpenter when he found himself captured by the Haudenosaunee. When released, he asked to be freed of his contractual obligation to the mission, nonetheless maintaining ties with the Jesuits and aiding their westward explorations in later years.[30] Another carpenter, Jean Guiet or Guay, must have separated from the Jesuits at some point after 1650 for reasons that are not clear, judging by his 1652 marriage to a woman in Quebec.[31] Eustache Lambert seems to have asked to be released in order to avoid hazardous duty patrolling the Saint Lawrence River for Haudenosaunee raiders, and René Ouré requested release in 1658 after participating in the Jesuits' first, ill-fated attempt to establish a mission among the Onundagaono (Onondaga) Haudenosaunee at Gannentaha.[32]

Regnaut does not appear to have left any written explanation of his own choice to serve the Wendat mission with no pay, and the contract he must have signed has not been found, but he does seem to have been sincerely devoted to the Jesuits.[33] Whatever his initial motivations, it is clear that by the time he found himself in Quebec after the destruction of the Wendat mission, he had already decided to attach himself even more closely to the Society of Jesus. The journal kept by the superiors in Quebec discussed in the previous chapter records Regnaut's departure for France in November 1650 in the company of another *donné* from Sainte-Marie named Joseph Molère, describing the pair in Latin as perpetual household members who hoped to become members of the Society of Jesus.[34] Upon his arrival in France, Regnaut entered the Society's novitiate and eventually became a Jesuit brother. Molère, who had entered the Wendat mission's service at the same time and served as an apothecary at Sainte-Marie, also joined the Society upon his arrival in France and later became a missionary in the Antilles.[35] Other *donnés* followed the same path, becoming either brothers or priests after working in the Wendat mission, including François Gendron, Joseph Boursier dit Desforges, Guillaume Lauzier, and René Goupil, who reportedly took his priestly vows before the Jesuit Isaac Jogues shortly before his own death, while the pair was held captive by the Haudenosaunee.[36] Some of the *donnés* were apparently not permanently committed to giving their lives to the Society of Jesus. But it seems that others were, including Regnaut.

The fragmentary nature of the surviving information about Regnaut and most of the other *donnés* is likely a result of the strong disapproval that met Lalemant's introduction of this practice once it became known in Rome. Superior General Mutio Vitelleschi expressed his grave concerns about it, at least in part on the basis of what he saw as the Society's negative experiences with it elsewhere in the world. He specifically objected to having the *donnés* take vows and wear uniforms to mark them as different from paid labourers, and also expressed concern that the entire Society of Jesus might end up financially responsible for these men instead of only Sainte-Marie or the broader Jesuit mission in New France.[37] After several years in which Lalemant corresponded with Vitelleschi to answer his concerns, the superior general in 1643 even went so far as to ban the practice outright and order Regnaut and his fellow *donnés* freed of their commitments.[38] He relented after Lalemant and his colleagues protested the following year, but only as long as such men were no longer distinguished from other groups of labourers in any way, and as long as the Jesuits' commitment to them could be cancelled if their behaviour warranted it.[39] These limits placed on the practice, coupled with lingering anxiety due to Rome's strong reluctance to allow it, likely account for the fact that the *Relations* do not use the word *donné* even when discussing the actions of these men, whereas the journal discussed in the previous chapter and administrative records like mission registers do use the term.[40] As a distinct group of labourers who lived and worked with the Jesuits at Sainte-Marie, the *donnés* are nearly invisible to readers of the annual reports. But it is clear that their labour was essential to the mission and even, as discussed below, to the creation of the *Relations*, at least in the case of Ragueneau's effort to tell the story of the violent final hours of Jean de Brébeuf and Gabriel Lalemant. Regnaut's text is a succinct summary of all he had been able to learn of the last hours of the priests' lives spanning thirteen manuscript pages in the surviving copy. It is stylistically simple, narrating events chronologically and taking care to specify how particular information was learned, as if written by someone who was scrupulously gathering every shred of information he could, not knowing or wanting to assume what might be important.

Paul Ragueneau's versions of the story, in contrast, were the work of the practised hand of an experienced mission leader, one recognized by his contemporaries as extraordinary in many ways, but who is now overshadowed by his better-known colleagues like Paul Le Jeune and

Jean de Brébeuf. Unlike his predecessor Jérôme Lalemant, who took up leadership of the Wendat mission immediately upon his arrival from France, Ragueneau had spent years growing into this role. After a few years teaching at the Jesuit college in Bourges and then studying theology at La Flèche, he disembarked in Quebec on the last day of June 1637 and made his way to the Wendat mission later that summer.[41] He served as a rank-and-file missionary there for eight years under two different leaders, Brébeuf and Jérôme Lalemant, before becoming superior at Sainte-Marie himself in 1645 upon Lalemant's appointment to head up the mission in Quebec. By this time, it seems Ragueneau had established a reputation for effectiveness among his fellow missionaries, with none of the difficult personality traits they had found in Jérôme Lalemant. The 1644 letter by Charles Garnier that is cited in the previous chapter, which praises Jérôme Lalemant's leadership of the mission, presented Ragueneau as a worthy candidate for the role of superior in the future. Wrote Garnier of Ragueneau, "He is endowed with unusual graces of virtue, talent, providence, and learning; and, in many respects, he [exceeds] him whom we now have for superior, Reverend Father Jerome Lallemant."[42] Four years later, Brébeuf reported Ragueneau's exceptional gifts and his success in meeting his potential in a letter to the Jesuit superior general Vincenzo Carafa: "He has not his counterpart here, and I know not whether he will have in the future. The mission owes very much to him, for he has up to this time governed it most prudently, most benignly, and most vigorously. Such, moreover, is the condition of affairs and circumstances, that I regard him as the one and only man who can govern it now, as befits its dignity. For there are many men here, and among ours there are certainly men who are most devout, and illustrious for many gifts of both nature and grace; nevertheless, they are all, in my judgment, far inferior to him in many respects, – in all other things, indeed, but most of all in the matter of administration."[43]

One of Ragueneau's particular gifts, and the one that is most relevant here, was his extraordinary ability as a writer in both Latin and French. He was responsible for five of the annual reports, including three from Sainte-Marie and two from Quebec. He also published a spiritual biography of the Quebec Hospitaller nun Catherine de Saint-Augustin in 1671, after her death three years earlier. And when his correspondence and various other writings in New France that were not intended for publication are factored in, the nineteenth-century Jesuit historian Camille de Rochemonteix may have been right to assert that "no Jesuit of Canada wrote as much as or better than he."[44] Zachary Yuzwa has examined five letters Ragueneau wrote in Latin, finding them "self-consciously literary" and rich in allusion to the Latin literary canon that would have been familiar to the superior general and any other Jesuit with whom he chose to share them, even if not intended for a wide audience.[45] In Lucien Campeau's opinion, one of these – the above-mentioned report to Carafa on the torture and death of Brébeuf and Lalemant – was written with great emotion and in Latin unequalled by any of Ragueneau's peers. Wrote Campeau, "It would probably be difficult to find a letter of this quality among the letters addressed to the General by the superiors."[46] Even though Ragueneau's writing abilities are occasionally recognized as exceptional, he has received substantially less attention than some of the other New France missionaries and authors of the *Relations*, especially Le Jeune and Brébeuf.[47] Close scrutiny of Ragueneau's accounts of the torture and death of two of his colleagues in the Wendat mission shows not only how he skilfully crafted his public version of the story to be as emotionally affecting as possible, but also how even this exceptional writer at least sometimes made liberal use of the work of others in preparing his annual reports.

As mentioned above, Ragueneau wrote two versions of the story of Brébeuf and Gabriel Lalemant's last hours in the weeks after their deaths. The first is the letter to Carafa in Rome, dated 1 May 1649.[48] Written in Latin, it is a clear example of the particular kind of internal Jesuit letter mentioned in the first chapter of this book, written to communicate important matters within the Society of Jesus and not necessarily intended for further circulation. The second version, contained in the fourth chapter of Ragueneau's *Relation* for 1649, is undated, but the letter he sent to Quebec to accompany the text on its journey there and thence to Paris is dated the same day as his letter to Carafa, suggesting the two texts must have been prepared around the same time.[49] And yet, they do not contain precisely the same information. The report destined for readers in France is, for example, more specific about how the torture with red-hot axe heads worked. Whereas the letter reports only the essential characteristics of this form of torment – burning axe heads were hung around the neck, causing excruciating pain as they burned the skin – the published version of the story describes its mechanics: leaning forward caused the axe heads to burn the back and shoulders more acutely, leaning back caused more intense burning of the chest, and standing perfectly erect caused both front and back to burn simultaneously.[50] Ragueneau's two versions of the story also recount the three main forms of torture endured by the priests – hot axe heads, burning belt, and mock baptism – in a different order, the mock baptism being mentioned first in the letter to Carafa, and last in the annual report.

At the same time, the story as recounted in the *Relation* bears an unmistakable resemblance to the version in Regnaut's manuscript account. The *donné* described how the hot axe head torture worked the same way Ragueneau did in the published text, albeit in mostly different words, with the exception that both accounts referred to standing directly upright as a "double torture."[51] There are also other, longer sequences of words that appear verbatim in the two texts. Both reports, for example, claim that Brébeuf continued to preach the faith while being beaten even though he was "overwhelmed under the burden of these blows."[52] Both also say that the Jesuits and their French associates went to retrieve the bodies of their slain brethren "as early as the next morning, when we had assurance of the departure of the enemy."[53] In other cases, passages in the two texts vary by only a few words. The published *Relation*, for example, describes the greeting Brébeuf and Lalemant received upon their entry into the village of Saint Ignace as "a hailstorm of blows with sticks upon their shoulders, their loins, their legs, their breasts, their bellies, and their faces, – there being no part of their bodies which did not then endure its torment."[54] Regnaut's manuscript describes the same treatment in nearly identical terms: "[a hailstorm of blows with sticks upon] the shoulders, the loins, the belly, the legs, and the face, – there being no part of their body which did not endure this torment."[55]

These points of resemblance make clear that Regnaut's manuscript and Ragueneau's published account of the incident are related to each other, but how? One obvious possibility, in light of the fact that the only surviving copy of Regnaut's manuscript is dated 1678, nearly thirty years after Ragueneau's *Relation*, is that the *donné* wrote his version of the story long after the fact and borrowed liberally from the published account. This is the conclusion Lucien Campeau drew in his massive collection of documents related to the New France mission. Noting a small difference between Regnaut's account and the version of the story in Marie de l'Incarnation's September 1649 letter to her son, Campeau speculated that "Brother Regnaut, writing thirty years later, may have forgotten this detail."[56] This theory is at least superficially plausible, but it leaves unexplained the factual discrepancies between Ragueneau's version of the story and that of Regnaut. For example, Regnaut claims that the priests were first captured in the village of Taenhatentaron (Saint Ignace) where they were tortured and killed, instead of in the nearby village of Teanaostataé (Saint Louis). Regnaut also appears to suggest that only Brébeuf suffered the mock-baptism with boiling water and subsequently had his heart eaten, while the *Relation* indicates that both priests suffered these torments. And Regnaut reports that just one person administered the boiling water baptism, instead of the multiple actors suggested by Ragueneau's published version of the story. If Regnaut's report amounted to simply retelling a story that had long before been told by Ragueneau, and was dependent enough on the *Relation* to copy some of its language verbatim, it seems he also would have deferred to its account of the basic facts.[57]

It is more likely that the influence between the two texts flowed in the opposite direction, that Regnaut's manuscript and Ragueneau's published version of the story resemble each other because the mission superior borrowed from the *donné's* account as he was preparing the *Relation* – or from an earlier copy of it than the one that has survived. Most scholars who have considered the question of when each of these accounts was written have concluded that Regnaut's work predates the initial composition of Ragueneau's annual report. Reuben Gold Thwaites sees the manuscript's relatively unpolished style and urgent tone as clues that "it was written not long after the event" and that it served as the basis of Ragueneau's version of the story in the *Relation*.[58] Similarly, Guy Laflèche points out that Regnaut's text is a personal and minutely detailed account of an attempt to gather all available information about this event as quickly as possible after it occurred, including participating in the excursion to recover the priests' bodies and the examination of their wounds, whereas the *Relation* reads more like a subsequent synthesis.[59] Certainty on this question is out of reach, but the available clues suggest that the most plausible scenario is that Regnaut wrote his account first and that Ragueneau borrowed from it when preparing his annual report. But Ragueneau's verbatim copying or close paraphrasing of language from Regnaut's manuscript was not the full extent of his engagement with it. Instead, as the rest of this chapter will show, comparison of the superior's *Relation* to the *donné's* manuscript suggests that he calibrated the material he borrowed for maximum emotional impact on its readers in France.

One challenge of comparing these two versions of the story is that in both cases, modern readers do not have access to the original versions prepared before Ragueneau sent his manuscript off to be published in the spring of 1649, not long after Brébeuf and Gabriel Lalemant died. In the case of Regnaut's account, it is not clear when the surviving copy was made, or who made it. It appears to have been signed only with the well-spaced initials C.R. At some point afterward, someone writing in a different hand and with different ink added an excerpt of Ragueneau's 1649 *Relation*, filled in the rest of Regnaut's name, and added more details about his identity: "Brother coajuteur with the Jesuits of Caen, 1678, companion of Fathers Brébeuf and Lalemant above."[60] The fact that this material was added to the manuscript separately from its composition raises a tantalizing possibility: perhaps the surviving manuscript was actually written much earlier than the date belatedly added to it, while Regnaut was still a *donné* in New France and not long after the events it describes. The place and date of its composition will have to remain a mystery in the absence of any other clues. But those who have examined the manuscript closely have concluded that it is too neatly written to be a first draft.[61] It cannot be ruled out, then, that whoever made the surviving copy also introduced changes. Still, the fact that the extant manuscript does not always align with the details recounted in the *Relation* suggests that whoever copied it must have sought to preserve its unique qualities instead of bringing it into perfect alignment with Ragueneau's published version. As for Ragueneau's *Relation*, whatever he wrote at Sainte-Marie could have been altered in Paris prior to publication. As the sixth chapter of this book will show, the manuscripts sent from New France could sometimes be changed significantly before being printed. If any such changes were made to Ragueneau's manuscript of the 1649 *Relation*, they would be invisible now due to the lack of a surviving manuscript to which the published version could be compared. Still, since both Regnaut and Ragueneau were in the Wendat mission when they composed their texts and there is no evidence of the *donné's* account having been immediately sent to France, it seems reasonable to conclude that it was the superior himself who was responsible for including the *donné's* language discussed above.

Even allowing for the possibility that either or both of these texts may have been changed somewhat between their initial composition and the form in which they are now available, there are several broad patterns of difference between them that show how Ragueneau used the *donné's* account but also departed from it intentionally in significant ways. Regnaut frequently commented on the relationship between various torments visited upon Brébeuf and Lalemant and the typical practices of Indigenous people toward their enemies, but Ragueneau's *Relation* was entirely silent on such correspondences. Ragueneau also omitted all of Regnaut's careful chronological precisions that made clear when various parts of the ordeal occurred in relation to each other and, as noted above, even went so far as to change the order in which he recounted them. And the mission superior also opted not to borrow Regnaut's detailed information about how practically every aspect of what he had written was known. The *donné* consistently credited either Indigenous people or the Frenchmen who had been sent to retrieve Brébeuf and Lalemant's bodies as the sources of the various facts he recorded, whereas Ragueneau almost never did so. It is worth exploring each of these three patterns in detail.

First, Ragueneau chose to omit from his *Relation* information that Regnaut had included in his report about how particular torments were related to Indigenous customs or common practices, even as he borrowed material from the *donné's* text. In the case of the hot axe heads, Ragueneau echoed Regnaut's description of how a person's posture affected the torment of the hot axe heads, as noted above, but omitted contextualizing information included by the *donné*. Regnaut had not been present to witness Brébeuf and Lalemant's suffering or the preparations leading up to it, and was careful to specify that his knowledge of this particular form of abuse came from observing its use on previous occasions. Wrote Regnaut, "This is the fashion in which I have seen the collar made for other prisoners: They make six hatchets red-hot, take a large withe of green wood, pass the 6 hatchets over the large end of the withe, take the two ends together, and then put it over the neck of the sufferer."[62] This reference to previous uses of this torture device alerts the report's readers to its precise construction, helping them understand why it would be so unpleasant, but it also suggests that what the priests endured was not unique or unusual, but instead typical of the way Indigenous Peoples behaved toward captured enemies. Since Ragueneau echoed the part of Regnaut's account that described what made this instrument of torture so terrible, it is clear that he must have deliberately chosen not to include the *donné's* comments about its general place in the violent treatment of captives. Ragueneau also could have opted to include Regnaut's suggestion about the particular significance of the consumption of the priests' hearts to their captors, but did not. Regnaut wrote that the captors explained that "Father de Breboeuf had been very courageous to endure so much pain as they had given him, and that, by drinking his blood, they would become courageous like him."[63] Ragueneau omitted any hint of the alleged significance to the Haudenosaunee of this particular action, writing instead that the captors drew Lalemant's and Brébeuf's hearts from their bodies with "sacrilegious hands" and fed on them "inhumanly."[64]

Ragueneau also, in one case, opted not to include Regnaut's observation that a particular violent act was to his knowledge entirely unique, even as he otherwise followed closely the *donné's* remarks. On Brébeuf's mock baptism with boiling water, Ragueneau's initial letter reported only that boiling water was thrice poured over Brébeuf's and Lalemant's bodies.[65] Regnaut offered considerably more detail, most notably by quoting the words of the person who he said performed this act, a Wendat man who had converted to Christianity previously but had strayed from the faith by the time he came to participate in Brébeuf's torture after having been captured himself by the Haudenosaunee. This unnamed man reportedly reminded the priest of his own claim that baptism was necessary for access to heaven, and tauntingly claimed to be sending him there by dousing him with boiling water.[66] Aside from its mention of multiple torturers instead of just one and the different words attributed to them, the version of this incident in Ragueneau's *Relation* resembles that in Regnaut's manuscript, in that Brébeuf's tormentors express the same mocking sentiments in both texts.[67] And the fact that both versions of the story specify that this particular torment was done "in derision of holy baptism" and was accompanied by "biting gibes" confirms the influence of the *donné's* manuscript on the published report in this instance.[68] Absent from the *Relation*, however, is anything resembling Regnaut's comment that the boiling water baptism was a novel form of torture. As Regnaut summed up the priests' ordeal, "I have seen the same treatment given to Iroquois prisoners whom the huron [sauvages] had taken in war, with the exception of the boiling water, which I have not seen poured on any one."[69] Whereas Regnaut frequently either commented directly on or alluded to the relationship – or lack thereof – between the events he was reporting and pre-existing Indigenous practices or beliefs, the published text did not, even in cases in which its contents are traceable to Regnaut's manuscript.

Second, Ragueneau omitted practically all of Regnaut's chronological precisions, which provide clarity on when each part of the priests' ordeal occurred in relation to the others. In the description of the burning belt, for example, Regnaut devotes two sentences to describing this torture device and Brébeuf's reaction to its use: "After that they put on him a belt of bark, full of pitch and resin, and set fire to it, which roasted his whole body. During all these torments, Father de Breboeuf endured like a rock, insensible to fire and flames, which astonished all the bloodthirsty wretches who tormented him."[70] The published *Relation* goes well beyond the single-sentence description in Ragueneau's preliminary letter and echoes Regnaut's language closely, confirming the mission superior's reliance on the *donné's* manuscript. It also suggests that both priests were tortured in this way, not only Brébeuf: "They put about them belts of bark, filled with pitch and resin, to which they set fire, which scorched the whole of their bodies. At the height of these torments, Father Gabriel Lallement lifted his eyes to Heaven, clasping his hands from time to time, and uttering sighs to God, whom he invoked to his aid. Father Jean de Brebeuf suffered like a rock, insensible to the fires and the flames, without uttering any cry, and keeping a profound silence, which astonished his executioners themselves."[71] Whereas Regnaut specifies that this stage in Brébeuf's suffering came "after that" – *that* referring to the hot axe heads that he had described just before – and indicates that the priest's stoicism was simultaneous to it ("during"), the *Relation* transitions abruptly from its description of the axe heads to the burning belt, and then begins a new paragraph with the chronologically vague observation that Brébeuf's rock-like suffering came "at the height of these torments." Lost in Ragueneau's adaptation of Regnaut's description of this method of torture and the priest's reaction to it are the clear indications of chronology and simultaneity that make explicit when the three principal events reported in this portion of the text – the axe heads, the burning belt, and Brébeuf's stony suffering – occurred in relation to each other.

Regnaut's care to provide chronological clarity in this instance is typical of the rest of his account. The second sentence of the manuscript starts the clock in an unambiguous way: "It was on the 16th Day of March, in the morning, that we perceived a great fire at the place to which these two good Fathers had gone."[72] The *donné's* description of the ensuing ordeal ends with Brébeuf's death, which is marked in the text at the moment it occurred, "the same day as his

Figure 3.1 Brébeuf and Gabriel Lalemant occupy the centre of Grégoire Huret's famous illustration of the martyrdom of Jesuits and their allies in New France, published in François du Creux's 1664 *Historiae Canadensis*. Brébeuf, the larger of the two, is depicted here wearing the collar of axe heads while boiling water is poured over him and his flesh is cut off and eaten.

capture, about 4 o'clock in the afternoon."[73] Regnaut specifies that his mission to recover the bodies took place the next morning, that he examined their remains for more than two hours, and that they were buried on 21 March, a Sunday.[74] In between these chronological precisions that bookend Regnaut's account, the details of Brébeuf's suffering are presented in sequence, and without any advance hint of torments to come. This linear approach to recounting the event is marked in the text by repeated use of transitional expressions linked to the passage of time. "After that" (*après cela*) appears twice in addition to the example cited above, including as a transition between the mock baptism and the axe heads. And expressions indicating simultaneity – during and while (*pendant que* and *pendant*) – are also prevalent. In short, Regnaut's text shows consistent care to signal how the various stages of priests' ordeal unfolded in relation to each other.

In the published *Relation*, in contrast, Ragueneau seems to have intentionally avoided giving a chronological account of the priests' torture and death. Instead of preserving the order of events as presented in his letter to Carafa and confirmed by Regnaut's manuscript – mock baptism with boiling water first, axe heads second, and then the burning belt – the version of the story in the published report first tells of the hot axe heads, then the burning belt, and finally the mock baptism, without any explicit acknowledgment that this was not how two previous versions of the story had situated these events in relation to each other. There are, however, many moments when the text makes clear that events are being recounted out of order, such as the flashback that the *Relation* inserts between the boiling water torture and the removal of priests' hearts to Brébeuf and Lalemant's prayers and joy at the very beginning of the torture, at the prospect of their impending death and presumed ascent to heaven.[75] It also sometimes announces key events in the story before they arrive in the narration. The published version of the story, for example, signals the outcome of the priests' ordeal before it has even begun to tell the story: "Having had, before that, certain news, through some escaped captives, of the deaths of Father Jean de Brebeuf and of Father Gabriel Lallement, – we sent one of our Fathers and seven other Frenchmen to seek their bodies at the place of their torture."[76] And the eventual removal of Brébeuf's heart is likewise announced ahead of time, when Ragueneau writes that even though his lips had been removed, Brébeuf, "his heart not being yet torn out," continued to praise God and motivate the Christians around him.[77] A series of violent acts recounted at the end of Ragueneau's account in the *Relation* are narrated in the pluperfect, indicating that they had occurred some unspecified time prior to the most recently related events, the roasting and eating of the priests' flesh before their very eyes. The passage begins, "They had slashed their bodies in various parts; and, in order to increase the feeling of pain, they had thrust into these wounds red-hot hatchets. Father Jean de Brebeuf had had the skin which covered his skull torn away; they had cut off his feet and torn the flesh from his thighs, even to the bone, and had split, with the blow of a hatchet, one of his jaws in two."[78] Perhaps not surprisingly, in light of his deliberate choice to tell the story out of order, Ragueneau omitted entirely the clear indications of chronological order – after that, while, and during – that Regnaut used repeatedly in describing the mock baptism, the axe heads, and the burning belt. And it was not until after telling most of the story that Ragueneau specified the dates and times of the priests' capture and death, all at once instead of at the corresponding moments in the story, as Regnaut had done.[79]

Finally, Ragueneau's *Relation* almost never shared with readers the source of any particular piece of information, whereas Regnaut nearly always did so. One striking fact about the priests' violent deaths is that they were not witnessed by any of the French people who were nearby at the time. To be described in writing at all, Brébeuf and Lalemant's final hours had to be reconstructed after the fact, on the basis of whatever information could be gathered. Regnaut made no effort to disguise this fact, beginning the story of Brébeuf's torture by crediting his Indigenous sources: "This is what these [Sauvages] told us of the taking of the Village of St Ignace, and about Fathers Jean de Breboeuf and Gabriel L'Allemant."[80] And he ended it in similar terms: "This is what we learned of the Martyrdom and blessed death of Father Jean de Brebœuf, by several Christian [Sauvages] worthy of belief, who had been constantly present from the time the good Father was taken until his death. These good Christians were prisoners to the Iroquois, who were taking them into their country to be put to death. But our good God granted them the favor of enabling them to escape by the way; and they came to us to recount all that I have set down in writing."[81] He also sometimes acknowledged Indigenous sources of specific pieces of information. He introduced the boiling water torture, for example, by saying "[they] told us further," in reference to the Wendat captives who had escaped the Haudenosaunee and fled to safety among the French, whereas the *Relation* makes no mention of how this specific piece of information was obtained.[82]

Regnaut's text is also peppered with instances of *nous* and *je* that record what the *donné* and his countrymen saw with their own eyes, both from the safety of the nearby Jesuit settlement of Sainte-Marie and upon reaching the site of the priests' death. The manuscript's first paragraph alone, consisting of seven sentences, has twelve instances of we (*nous*) and our (*notre*), foregrounding from the very start the role of the French in gathering information about what had happened to the two Jesuits. Perhaps most remarkably, the manuscript's description of Brébeuf's torments concludes with a series of sentences detailing the damage done to his body that can be seen as a deliberate echo of Thomas the Apostle's famous incredulity in the Gospel of John.[83] In that biblical story, Thomas refuses to believe the word of his fellow apostles that Jesus had been resurrected from death without first personally examining his wounds: "Unless I see the mark of the nails in his hands and put my finger in the mark of the nails and my hand in his side, I will not believe" (John 20:24, New Revised Standard Version). Regnaut's report on Brébeuf's demise concluded with a sequence of eight evocations of the same kinds of proof Thomas demanded – seeing and touching wounds himself rather than relying on the reports of others. Wrote Regnaut, in part, "I saw and touched a large number of great blisters, which he had on several places on his body, from the boiling water which these barbarians had poured over him in mockery of Holy Baptism. I saw and touched the wound from a belt of bark, full of pitch and resin, which roasted his whole body. I saw and touched the marks of burns from the Collar of hatchets placed on his shoulders and stomach. I saw and touched his two lips, which they had cut off because he constantly spoke of God while they made him suffer."[84] In the context of Regnaut's care to make clear how he knew everything he reported about the Jesuits' final hours, this description of the damage done to Brébeuf's body amounts to further evidence of the truth of his account, even if he had not personally witnessed the violence. But the *donné's* evocation of Doubting Thomas also would have served to remind anyone reading his report of the virtues of belief in the absence of direct personal experience. When Thomas encounters the resurrected Jesus a week after expressing his doubts, Jesus offers him the proof he sought: "'Put your finger here and see my hands. Reach out your hand and put it in my side. Do not doubt but believe.' Thomas answered him, 'My Lord and my God!' Jesus said to him, 'Have you believed because you have seen me? Blessed are those who have not seen and yet have come to believe'" (John 20: 27–29). By casting himself in the role of Thomas and relying on his own eyes for proof, Regnaut seems to suggest that the testimony of the faithful Indigenous eyewitnesses he highlighted earlier in his account ought to be enough to establish the truth of what happened, even as he also took care to document every detail he could.[85]

In contrast to Regnaut's careful accounting for the sources of his information while also offering a subtle reminder of the virtue of belief in the absence of personal experience, the version of the story in Ragueneau's *Relation* recounts Brébeuf's ordeal mostly in the third person and cites only "persons worthy of credence, who have seen it, and reported it to me personally, and who were then captives with them, – but who, having been reserved to be put to death at another time, found means to escape."[86] It appears that Ragueneau intentionally omitted Regnaut's scrupulously recorded information about sources, even as he drew heavily from the substance and language of the *donné's* account. Among the significant ways in which Ragueneau's writing choices shaped the version of the story presented to French readers, the erasure of the indispensable contributions of Indigenous people to gathering the information it contains should not be overlooked. It serves to make his version of the story a more focused confrontation between Jesuit martyr and Indigenous martyr maker than Regnaut's more complicated tale, at the expense of giving the Indigenous Christian witnesses their due. As the following chapter of this book will show, this would not be the only time when the actions of Indigenous people had a significant impact on the content of the *Relations*, albeit one that is not immediately obvious upon reading the published texts. And Ragueneau's decision to sharply curtail indications of how particular pieces of information were known also entailed omitting even the pious reminder offered by his *donné* source about Jesus's own words on the value of belief in the absence of personally experienced evidence, since it came in the context of a direct personal account of the nature of Brébeuf's wounds.[87]

The differences between the versions of the story in Ragueneau's *Relation* and in Regnaut's manuscript discussed above are less a matter of the texts' content than of how it was presented to readers. The factual discrepancies concern relatively minor points such as whether both priests were tormented in a particular way or only one and the number of Indigenous participants in particular acts of violence.[88] And since neither Ragueneau nor Regnaut – nor any other Frenchman, for that matter – was present to actually witness the events they described, it is easy to understand why some confusion about the details would persist. Nor are the basic facts of the incident used to advance different arguments about its significance. Both Regnaut's manuscript and Ragueneau's *Relation* make the case for the priests' status as martyrs. This is not particularly surprising in light of the missionaries' preoccupation, reflected in their annual reports, with the possibility of their own deaths. Even before Brébeuf and Lalemant were killed, the texts had long presented martyrdom as a possibility and perhaps even a desirable outcome for the missionaries in New France because spectacles of faithful suffering might be expected to help win converts.[89] Regnaut refers to the priests' ordeal as martyrdom more than once and insists on the hatred of the faith that allegedly motivated the attackers, describing them as pouring boiling water over Brébeuf's body "in derision of Holy baptism" and as "enraged against him for constantly speaking to them of God and of their conversion."[90] Ragueneau, meanwhile, expressed more reluctance to explicitly draw such a conclusion – one that, in any case, could only be drawn after an official investigation by Church authorities – but does admit that "I would gladly call them, if I were allowed, by that glorious name" and attributes the violent actions of the Iroquois to "hatred for the Faith and contempt for the name of God."[91] Whatever differences exist in the details recounted in the two texts and how explicitly each of them makes the argument that the priests were martyrs, a more significant difference is that at every turn Ragueneau took care in his *Relation* to frame the story to be as emotionally engaging as possible to its readers, even when copying material directly from Regnaut's more matter-of-fact manuscript.

Indeed, the ways in which Ragueneau adapted Regnaut's material traced above systematically invite the reader to feel closer to the action. First, the absence of any contextualizing comments about the use of hot axe heads and the consumption of enemies' hearts as part of the way Indigenous Peoples treated their captives – and, for that matter, of any mention of the apparent originality of the mock baptism – draws attention squarely to the events being described, providing no opportunity to consider them in relation to customary behaviour or other instances of violence against captured enemies. Then, the decision to tell the story non-chronologically instead of maintaining the order used in the initial letter to Rome and confirmed by Regnaut's manuscript adds suspense, announcing the priests' violent death before it happens and then alternating scenes of violent torture with quieter moments, creating a sense of building to a climax that would have been particularly resonant to anyone reading the story as the last hours of a pair of martyrs: the mock baptism with boiling water. And finally, the absence of references to sources, whether Wendat survivors or the *nous* of the French, eliminates the impression of distance created by the *donné's* account, which reminds readers at every turn that their own access to events came only through an intermediary who himself had only indirect information about what happened to the priests in the hours leading up to their deaths. Even Regnaut's allusion to Thomas the apostle's doubts about Jesus's resurrection and its implied admonition to prefer faith over proof, of which Ragueneau presumably could only have approved, makes way in the published account for a version of the story that focuses closely on its events. To the common scholarly observation that the mission superior drew material from others' writings while compiling the annual *Relation*, it can be added that this was at least sometimes not a simple matter of stitching individual reports together and smoothing out rough edges to create a maximally informative and coherent narrative. Ragueneau's use of Regnaut's manuscript involved making writerly choices that would enhance readers' experience of the material, even when the changes that resulted from such an approach caused a loss of context, chronological precision, and clarity about how particular facts were known. He deliberately made his account less factual than it could have been, but undoubtedly more apt to stir readers' emotions.[92]

In addition to providing a glimpse of how initial reports of events could be transformed into a text for the French reading public, this analysis points to an aspect of the Jesuit *Relations* of which it is easy to lose sight when they are used primarily to reconstruct historical events. Not only did they transmit facts and opinions about life in New France and the Jesuit missions there – selectively and framed carefully to support the Jesuits' perspectives and goals – they also specifically sought to induce a reaction in readers, an affective response that could fan the flames of faith. This was undoubtedly a useful feature of the texts in the context of the Catholic Reformation and its concern for shoring up French Catholicism and combatting the perceived threats posed by various forms of otherness, whether Protestantism or the example of Indigenous Peoples far from Europe who were often depicted as having no religion at all.[93] The affective weight of the *Relations* has received some attention from scholars, but has not been as appreciated as their undeniable documentary richness.[94] The Jesuit historian Léon Pouliot even went so far as to claim that they were not crafted with the intention of eliciting an emotional response, but only to convey facts about the year's events: "What they offered to the public was not an effort or an effect of their imagination, it was not a composition, intended to move people at all costs, it was the story of the year's most memorable events, the result of their own observations or the testimony of credible persons."[95] This chapter's analysis of how Ragueneau calibrated the story of Brébeuf and Lalemant's death for maximum emotional impact on readers shows that the *Relations* are the result not only of rhetorical choices or the careful selection of facts, as shown in the two previous chapters, but also of a deliberate effort to make readers feel a certain way.

The question, then, is what precisely readers of the published *Relation* were being invited to feel when they read Ragueneau's account of Brébeuf's and Lalemant's violent deaths. One answer might be found in how his characterization of the audience of Brébeuf's demonstrations of faith during the worst parts of his ordeal – the burning belt, the hot axe heads, and the mock baptism with burning water – differs from the one offered by Regnaut. Both accounts use identical language, reporting that he "suffered like a rock, insensible to the fires and the flames."[96] Regnaut reported that during these torments "his zeal was so great that he preached continually to these infidels, to try to convert them."[97] Ragueneau, in contrast, acknowledged the suffering priest's message to the unconverted Haudenosaunee, but put greater emphasis on his efforts to reassure those who already believed. According to the published version of the story, Brébeuf "preached to those Infidels, and still more to many good Christian captives" and, later, that "his tongue did not fail to render him service until the last sigh, for blessing God for these torments, and for animating the Christians more vigorously than he had ever done."[98] The *Relation* even includes the purported words of Brébeuf to the Christians who had been captured at the same time he was: "My children, let us lift our eyes to Heaven at the height of our afflictions; let us remember that God is the witness of our sufferings, and will soon be our exceeding great reward. Let us die in this faith; and let us hope from his goodness the fulfillment of his promises. I have more pity for you than for myself; but sustain with courage the few remaining torments. They will end with our lives; the glory which follows them will never have an end."[99] Ragueneau also included words he claimed were uttered by the Christian converts suffering alongside Brébeuf, who reportedly reaffirmed their faith and pledged to follow him to heaven.[100] In Regnaut's account, the priest only addressed these captured Christians at the beginning of his ordeal, upon being beaten with clubs. Wrote Regnaut, "He did not cease continually to speak of God, and to encourage all the new Christians who were captives like himself to suffer well, that they might die well, in order to go in company with him to Paradise."[101] In the *donné's* telling, Brébeuf's attention during the worst of his ordeal was reserved for potential new converts, not those he and his colleagues had already won. Not only did Ragueneau tell the story in such a way as to stir the emotions of his readers as much as possible, then, he also seems to have adjusted the content to make the message as clear as he could without spelling it out explicitly: the value of Brébeuf's suffering was not, as Regnaut had seemed to suggest, that it represented a final opportunity to win Indigenous converts to Christianity, but rather its capacity to inspire renewed faith in believers, whether those who witnessed it in the territory of the Wendat or those who subsequently read about it in France.

4

Indigenous Literacies Meet Alphabetic Writing

The Case of Joseph Chihoatenhwa

In the winter of 1637, a Wendat Christian man of approximately thirty-five years named Joseph Chihoatenhwa approached the Jesuits who were then working to convert his people to Christianity and made an unusual request: he wanted to learn how to read and write, as he had seen the missionaries do.[1] This request was recorded by François-Joseph Le Mercier in the annual report he prepared on behalf of mission superior Jean de Brébeuf. Le Mercier attributed several motives to the would-be scribe, who had only recently recovered from a near-fatal bout with one of the epidemic diseases that killed more than half of the Wendat between 1634 and 1639.[2] He first claimed that Chihoatenhwa was motivated by a desire to fully absorb the religious instruction he had been receiving and to keep track of his own adherence to lessons about pious behaviour: "Before and after the instructions that are given him, it is a pleasure to see him on his knees asking grace of the divine Spirit; even going so far as to force himself to learn to write, this winter, that he may remember and repeat what was said to him; but, above all, to indicate more clearly, he said, the number of his sins."[3] Later in the same text, Le Mercier added two more explanations, admiration of the Jesuits and a desire to create a record of events in his homeland: "The esteem in which he holds us inspired in him a strong desire to learn to read and write, as he saw us do ... with such purity of motive that he recently asked us if there would be any sin in wishing to know how to write, so that he could set down in writing not only what concerned the progress of his soul, but also the affairs of the country."[4] Charmed by what they understood to be Chihoatenhwa's pious motivations and desire to imitate their own habits, the missionaries agreed to teach him to use the written form they had devised of the Wendat language, and Le Mercier reported that he spent much of the winter diligently and patiently studying their lessons.

It is not clear how fully Chihoatenhwa mastered the art of putting words on paper and deciphering the marks made by others. Le Mercier, for his part, was optimistic that the Wendat man would easily gain the first of these skills, but reported that the second – reading – would take longer due to the pupil's difficulty grasping the very concept. Wrote Le Mercier, "This labor has not been in vain; as for the writing, it will be very easy for him, but the reading will cost him a little more effort. The difficulty we had in explaining to him the secret has somewhat delayed him; nevertheless, we hope that in a short time he will succeed."[5]

Chihoatenhwa was a fixture of the missionaries' annual reports for several years following his conversion due to his apparently staunch faith and willingness to assist the missionaries in bringing their message to the Wendat. But the Jesuits who were charged with compiling the annual *Relation* during this period never again returned to the subject of his efforts to learn to write before his sudden death in 1640, and rarely mentioned him thereafter. The only trace of the writing he did under their tutelage is a brief mention, in the same text in which his interest in learning to write was first reported, of a letter he had composed, and which Le Mercier apparently sent to Quebec for the Jesuits there to admire. Wrote Le Mercier in his report, which was superficially addressed to Quebec mission superior Paul Le Jeune but like all of the *Relations* prepared with full knowledge that it would reach a larger audience, "You will be comforted by receiving one of his letters; I give you my word, at the outset, that it is all written by his own hand."[6] This fleeting mention of Chihoatenhwa's letter indicates that it was not the only one he had written, but there is very little else that can be said with certainty about his efforts to inscribe words on paper. None of his letters appear to have survived, and their contents are not described in Le Mercier's annual report except, in the case of the letter that was sent to Quebec, as a source of cheer or solace to its Jesuit reader. The missionary's focus was on assuring his readers of the authenticity of the letter, as if he expected the news that an Indigenous person could write to be surprising enough to strain credibility. It was not anything in particular that Chihoatenhwa wrote that Le Mercier seems to have expected readers – whether Jesuits in Quebec or mission supporters in France – to find remarkable, but rather the fact that he had written at all.

Chihoatenhwa's effort to learn to put words on paper points to a generally overlooked aspect of the relationship between Indigenous people and the Jesuit *Relations*. For most of the twentieth century, scholarship drawing on these annual reports tended to treat Indigenous people as objects of analysis, scrupulously and carefully described by Jesuits who were understood to be the early forerunners of scholarly participant observers, if also obviously influenced by their own pre-existing beliefs.[7] More recently, scholars have understood the texts' portrayals of Indigenous people as strategic representations whose words, beliefs, appearance, and cultural differences or familiarity were deployed intentionally by the Jesuits in the service of the messages they were attempting to transmit to readers in France.[8] Others have treated the texts as the missionaries' record of reciprocal cultural exchange with Indigenous people – biased, to be sure, but also a precious account of how European and Indigenous cultures influenced each other.[9] Indigenous people are present in each of these points of view, whether as passive objects of study or as conversation partners, but all active roles in the creation of the *Relations* themselves have always been reserved for the Jesuits alone.

The interest Chihoatenhwa showed in learning to put words on paper is a useful reminder that Indigenous people frequently witnessed missionaries engaged in this activity, that they were sometimes curious about it or suspicious of it, and that they at least occasionally sought to participate in it. Taking Chihoatenhwa's experiences in the Wendat mission as its prime example, this chapter examines Indigenous involvement with the Jesuits' writing practices. It begins with the Jesuits' own account of the interest Chihoatenhwa and his fellow Wendat showed in writing, but also seeks to probe beyond the missionaries' point of view to account for how Indigenous people may have understood this way of preserving and transmitting knowledge. It argues that people like Joseph Chihoatenhwa ought to be understood as among the actors who shaped the annual *Relations*.

* * *

It is not known when Chihoatenhwa first noticed and took an interest in French settlers' ability to put words on paper.[10] He is believed to have been born in or around 1602, and therefore would have been an adolescent when the French explorer and colonial administrator Samuel de Champlain arrived in Wendat territory in 1613 and again in 1615. Chihoatenhwa also could have seen a French person write in his early twenties, when the Franciscan Récollet missionary Gabriel Sagard arrived to attempt to convert the Wendat in August 1623. Sagard's account of his relatively brief stay, until May of the following year, reports that he took notes to keep track of what he was learning about the Wendat language, and that his interlocutors even urged him to do so, saying "take up your quill and write" before answering his questions.[11] Chihoatenhwa could have been present for such sessions with Sagard, or heard about them from those who were, but since he is not mentioned by name in the Recollet missionary's text, it is impossible to know. Nor is he named in either of the first two of the Jesuits' annual reports from the Wendat mission, describing events in 1635 and 1636 and prepared by Brébeuf. Only when the Jesuits began to perceive an intense interest on Chihoatenhwa's part in their religious message did he finally appear in the French record of contact with the Wendat. Le Mercier's above-mentioned 1637 *Relation* devotes three full chapters and part of another, out of ten, to describing Chihoatenhwa's conversion, and mentions that his interest in Christianity had been sparked the previous year, when he heard Brébeuf explain the rudiments of his own faith. Le Mercier wrote that after this event, Chihoatenhwa quickly took a profound interest in the Jesuits and their religious message. He offered one of his sons to be baptized, took up prayer on his own initiative, and, when the Jesuits established a residence in his village of Ossossané (which the Jesuits called La Conception) not long afterward, became a frequent visitor in their cabin.[12] He was baptized on 16 August 1637 while deathly ill, which seemed to the Jesuits to prompt a miraculous recovery. His wife and children followed soon after, making them the only converted family in the village for nearly a year. Chihoatenhwa was not the first of the Wendat to be baptized and to convert to Christianity. But what the missionaries saw as his keen interest in their religious lessons, steadfast faith, and constant willingness to aid them in matters both spiritual and temporal made him a special case, and one they took care to describe in detail in the *Relations*.

Chihoatenhwa's faith remained the focus of Jesuit comments about him in the *Relations* for the remainder of his life, serving as the lens through which the missionaries interpreted his every action and characteristic.[13] Many of his fellow Wendat had sought baptism in desperation, when ill with one of the diseases that were killing so many of them and perhaps perceiving it to be a healing ritual. Chihoatenhwa, however, reportedly remained more steadfast in his faith than most after recovering his health.[14] Le Mercier and Jérôme Lalemant devoted long passages of their annual reports for the years between 1638 and 1641 to chronicling his pious behaviour. As noted at the beginning of this chapter, Chihoatenhwa's request to learn to write was interpreted mostly along the same lines, as a consequence of his desire to remember religious lessons, tally his sins, and keep a record of his own spiritual progress. The missionaries believed him to be extraordinarily intelligent, and focused their descriptions of his intellectual ability on how they heard it reflected in what he said about Christianity. While introducing Chihoatenhwa to readers and simultaneously reporting his conversion, Le Mercier wrote that "he is a man of superior mind not only as compared with his countrymen, but even, in our judgment, he would pass as such in France. As for his memory, we have often wondered at it, for he forgets nothing of what we teach him, and it is a satisfaction to hear him discourse upon our Holy Mysteries."[15] Unlike what Le Mercier understood to be the usual practice among the Wendat, Chihoatenhwa had been married to the same woman since his youth.[16] And he also seemed to the missionary to refrain from all of the Wendat pastimes and beliefs that the Jesuits believed to be frivolous or downright morally objectionable: he never gambled, smoked tobacco, used charms to enhance his luck, or engaged in what Le Mercier called "diabolical feasts."[17]

Chihoatenhwa is still remembered primarily this way, as a particularly devout early convert among the Wendat, even if scholars have increasingly taken an interest in his story for how it can illuminate Wendat beliefs about the intervention of supernatural forces in everyday life, Jesuit strategies to induce conversion to Christianity, and Indigenous responses to colonization.[18] This enduring legacy is due at least in part to the intense focus of Le Mercier and later Jérôme Lalemant on Chihoatenhwa's spiritual status, and also to the mysterious circumstances surrounding his death. He died alone while cutting wood near his home on the second day of August 1640, murdered by unseen attackers whom his village's leaders declared to be Onödowá'ga (Seneca) Haudenosaunee raiders. Lalemant's account of Chihoatenhwa's death in his 1641 *Relation* did not question this claim, but some modern observers have suggested with varying degrees of conviction that he may instead have been struck down by his own people who had lost patience with his complicity with the Jesuits' suspected disease-inducing witchcraft or his conversion to Christianity.[19] It is little wonder, then, that Chihoatenhwa has been seen as a holy figure at various times since his death.[20] Brébeuf's private spiritual journal, for example, described a vision the priest had immediately after Chihoatenhwa's burial in which a dome descended from the heavens and settled on the deceased convert's grave before it was drawn back upward. Brébeuf took this vision as a sign of Chihoatenhwa's special spiritual status, writing that "the sentiment that I felt from it is that God wanted to make understood the state of the soul of this good [Christian]."[21] And in the present, as Emma Anderson has observed, some North American Catholics continue to advocate for Chihoatenhwa's recognition as a martyr and saint.[22] Perhaps understandably, in light of these longstanding perceptions, the few of Chihoatenhwa's biographers who have commented on his interest in learning to record his thoughts with quill and paper have mostly taken it for exactly what the Jesuits said it was: first and foremost, a sign of his faith.[23]

It is not surprising that writing and faith were closely associated in the missionaries' descriptions of Chihoatenhwa, nor that they have remained so among modern writers who are particularly interested in his spiritual status. *Relations* from the end of the decade occasionally reported that some of the Wendat and neighbouring peoples viewed writing and other Jesuit practices and objects to be potential sources of illness that were best avoided.[24] But the earliest reports from the Wendat mission prepared by Brébeuf and Le Mercier between 1635 and 1638 are full of comments suggesting that writing was a new and exciting concept to the Wendat, and highlighting its usefulness in winning converts. In his first *Relation* as the inaugural leader of the mission, for example, Brébeuf touted writing as even more effective in this regard than any of the curious objects he and his colleagues showed potential converts, like magnets, magnifying lenses, and prisms: "They could not conceive how, what one of us, being in the village, had said to them, and put down at the same time in writing, another, who meanwhile was in a house far away, could say readily on seeing the writing. I believe they have made a hundred trials of it. All this serves to gain their affections, and to render them more docile when we introduce the admirable and incomprehensible mysteries of our Faith; for the belief they have in our intelligence and capacity causes them to accept without reply what we say to them."[25] The following year, Brébeuf indirectly suggested that writing must have frequently been a topic of conversation between the missionaries and the Wendat in a chapter of the 1636 *Relation* devoted to describing the Wendat language. He offered an example of one of the two kinds of verb conjugations he had identified, and the verb he selected was *ahiaton* – to write.[26] When Le Mercier took over preparing the annual report in 1637, he too linked the interest of the Wendat in writing to the prospect of their conversion, putting "the art of inscribing upon paper matters that are beyond sight" at the top of a list of things that he believed made the Wendat inclined to accept the Jesuits' religious message.[27] As the missionaries saw things, the Wendat at least initially perceived writing as a curious new tool, one that enhanced the Jesuits' credibility as sources of truthful information around the time Chihoatenhwa apparently began to show interest in Christianity.

The missionaries also reported deliberately taking advantage of Wendat interest in writing to convince them of the truth of their religious message. Brébeuf wrote in 1636 that he had shown some letters from New France's civil authorities to an assembly of Wendat leaders who would not have been able to read them, effectively using these texts as a prop, a guarantor of the truth of what he was saying.[28] And in his 1637 *Relation*, Le Mercier quoted Brébeuf's words while instructing a group of Wendat leaders on the tenets of the Christian faith, in which the mission superior similarly appealed to the authority of the written word: "Another one asked him how we knew there was a Hell, and whence we obtained all that we told about the condition of the damned. The Father replied to this that we had indubitable proofs of it, that we possessed it through divine revelation; that the Holy Ghost himself had dictated these truths to certain persons, and to our Ancestors, who had left them to us in writing, and that we still carefully preserved the books containing them."[29] At least in the earliest years of their mission among the Wendat, when Chihoatenhwa was becoming familiar with the French settlers and noticing their ability to jot down information to use it later or transmit it to someone else verbatim, the Jesuits consistently characterized writing as a concept that was new to the Wendat, and that they presented to potential converts as linked to certain knowledge about the past. From the perspective of the Jesuit missionaries, the story of Chihotenhwa's interactions with their writing practices ends here. Like his fellow Wendat, he probably saw demonstrations of writing and heard missionaries associate it with certain knowledge of the truth of their religious message, and therefore sought to learn how to do it himself as part of his broader embrace of Christianity.

Expanding the story to include Chihoatenhwa's fellow Wendat who learned to write – or even to other Indigenous Peoples with whom the French were in contact – likely would not change its basic characteristics. Despite Brébeuf's suggestion that the Wendat were deeply curious about the missionaries' writing abilities, the Jesuits only infrequently reported that any of them attempted to learn how to do it themselves, and when they did, it was always as a sign of a convert's faith or favourable disposition to the mission. Le Jeune's second *Relation* from Quebec, recounting the events of 1633, reported that he was sending to the Jesuit provincial some letters written by a Wendat convert named Louis Amantacha, also known as Louis de Sainte-Foi, who had spent time in France after the Jesuits' earlier stint in New France. These letters reportedly testified to the man's positive feelings toward the notion that missionaries might again be deployed to attempt to convert the Wendat and pledging his own services to lead them from Quebec to the distant mission field, should the Society's provincial in Paris prove willing to send the necessary personnel.[30] In another case, Barthélemy Vimont's 1642 report from Quebec reports that young Wendat girls who had been taken there and placed in the Ursuline convent were passionate about learning to write in their own languages, using the system of spelling developed by the Jesuits. Included in the *Relation* is a short note written by one of them, Chihoatanhwa's niece Thérèse Oionhaton, who had travelled to Trois-Rivières: "My good Mother, I am about to leave. I thank you for having taken such care of me, and for having taught me to serve God well. Do I thank you for a trifling matter? I shall never forget it."[31] Cases like these show that Wendat people other than Chihoatenhwa at least occasionally learned to write and that their compositions could even find their way into print, where the missionary authors consistently treated the phenomenon as a positive sign for the mission's prospects and nothing more.[32]

To end the story here, however, would be to assume that Chihoatenhwa, his fellow Wendat, and other Indigenous Peoples were truly as astonished and impressed by writing as the missionaries claimed they were, and that they understood it in exactly the same way the Jesuits reported presenting it to them in the pages of the *Relations*. In recent decades, scholars occasionally have taken at face value the Jesuits' claims about Indigenous reactions to writing.[33] But many others have expressed skepticism about the texts' portrayal of Indigenous reactions to colonization, both in general and on the specific subject of writing. More than one Indigenous scholar has pointed out that the *Relations*' role in justifying and promoting the Jesuit mission to French readers calls into question the accuracy of their accounts of what Indigenous people did, said, and thought in their encounters with the French. The Kanien'kehaka (Mohawk) Haudenosaunee scholar Susan M. Hill, for example, has written that "sources such as the *Jesuit Relations* are full of ... biased portrayals, written to help justify the presence of the missionaries in New France as they waged a spiritual battle against 'pagan' beliefs of the unconverted."[34] There is undoubtedly much about how Indigenous people understood and related to Jesuit writing that was omitted from the texts as irrelevant or damaging to the Jesuits' rhetorical purposes, or that the missionaries simply were not able to perceive as outsiders who were only recently acquainted with Indigenous languages and cultures and were primarily focused on inducing change. There is no consideration in the *Relations* of the possibility, for example, that Chihoatenhwa's admiration of writing may have been less a result of the Jesuits' habit of linking it to truth and faith than of his own efforts to negotiate as advantageously as possible the challenges and opportunities presented by the arrival of the French in his homeland. Scholars have occasionally argued for motivations for the apparent cooperation of Indigenous people with settlers that are not explicitly accounted for in the *Relations*. Lisa J.M. Poirier, for example, pointed out that Chihoatenhwa may have sought a close relationship with the French in order to enhance his own prestige or to be able to rely on their help during times of scarcity or conflict as much as for any spiritual motivations.[35] And John H. Pollack has made a similar point about Chihoatenhwa's effort to learn to read and write.[36] It is not difficult to imagine that the Wendat convert had his own particular reasons, unrelated to matters of faith, for interacting with the Jesuits in the way he did, and that these reasons are simply not visible in the absence of any surviving explanation in his own words, unfiltered through the Jesuit missionaries' world view.

Chihoatenhwa's individual and private reasons for taking an interest in the Jesuits' writing practices and seeking to learn the skill himself can only be a matter of speculation, but glimpses of how his understanding of this tool may have differed from what the Jesuits reported can be had by comparing it to pre-existing Wendat record-keeping systems with which he must have been familiar. Despite Brébeuf's above-noted comment emphasizing the novelty of writing among the

Wendat – their confusion, and the excitement with which they made repeated trials of it – he and his fellow Jesuits also acknowledged that their potential converts had their own ways of preserving and transmitting knowledge, even if the missionaries stopped short of recognizing such methods as fully equivalent to alphabetic writing. Describing in his 1636 *Relation* preparations for the ceremonial reburial of the remains of a former Wendat leader as part of the periodic feast of the dead, Brébeuf wrote that the man's daughter "put beside him his *Atsatonewai*, that is, his package of Council sticks, which are all the books and papers of the Country."[37] Brébeuf did not pause to describe these sticks in any detail, but this fleeting reference suggests he knew they had a role in documenting important knowledge or events, even as his dismissive description of them as the Wendat's only books and papers marks them as unequal to those objects.

Sticks or straws are reported elsewhere in the *Relations* to have been used for a range of communication and record-keeping activities among the Wendat and other Indigenous Peoples.[38] Jérôme Lalemant's 1646 *Relation* from Quebec – his first upon becoming superior there – records a conversation with an unnamed convert to Christianity who had strayed from the Jesuits' teachings about monogamy and was seeking to repent and re-enter the Jesuits' good graces. "This poor man draws forth a little bundle of wood, like a bunch of matches, and showing it to the Father, said to him: 'There are all my sins, I have written them upon these pieces of wood, after our fashion, for fear of forgetting them.' He confesses with great remorse, his eyes filled with tears, his utterance choked with sobs, and his heart full of regret and grief. After his confession, he related to the Father how he had fallen into the abyss of his sins."[39] The same year, Paul Ragueneau reported from the Wendat mission that a similar tool helped storytellers remember the content of their tales and pass them to younger generations:

> They are accustomed, on such occasions, to relate the stories which they have learned regarding their ancestors, even those most remote, – so that the young people, who are present and hear them, may preserve the memory thereof, and relate them in their turn, when they shall have become old. They do this in order thus to transmit to posterity the history and the annals of the country, – striving, by this means, to supply the lack of writing and of books, which they have not. They offer, to the person from whom they desire to hear something, a little bundle

> of straws a foot long, which serve them as counters for calculating the numbers, and for aiding the memory of those present, – distributing in various lots these same straws, according to the diversity of the things which they relate.[40]

These passages compare sticks or straws to alphabetic writing, but they also suggest that this way of communicating and preserving knowledge was not equivalent to the more familiar ways the Jesuits' brought with them from Europe. This was only, in the terms the missionaries attributed to their interlocutors, writing after a fashion, useful to make up at least in part for the absence of the real thing. Indeed, the Jesuit missionary Francesco-Giuseppe Bressani, who had spent five years working among the Wendat, claimed explicitly in his 1653 Italian-language account of the mission that "they have neither books nor any writing, as we have said."[41]

Bundles of sticks or straws were, to judge by the above testimony, still in use among the Wendat in the 1630s and 1640s, but these devices had already begun to wane in popularity across the Indigenous cultures with which the Jesuits were in contact as the availability of wampum increased.[42] Wampum, which the French called *porcelaine*, are small white and purple beads made by segmenting and hollowing out cylindrical pearls found inside various species of shellfish on the Atlantic coast.[43] Such beads were mostly, though not exclusively, made by Indigenous Peoples living near the ocean, including the Narragansett, Pokanoket, and Massachusetts, who were able to dramatically increase production following the introduction of metal tools through exchange with Europeans.[44] Wampum beads were an important trade good throughout large stretches of the continent, and the Jesuits often described their function among the Wendat as akin to money or precious metals.[45] But they were also woven into belts or strings in particular patterns that had a mnemonic function, to aid in preserving the memory of particular events or agreements. According to the Wendat scholar Georges Sioui, such belts "accompanied and sealed most agreements between Amerindians, or between them and the Whites" starting in the early seventeenth century.[46]

The Jesuits recognized the function of wampum belts as a form of record keeping but, as with the sticks and straws discussed above, stopped short of explicitly identifying this as equivalent to alphabetic writing. In his 1653 *Relation* from Quebec, then-superior François-Joseph Le Mercier recorded a diplomatic visit by an Onundagaono

Figure 4.1 Wampum belts, such as this example made by unknown members of an Eastern Woodlands Indigenous group during the eighteenth century, were constructed by stringing together hollowed-out purple and white shells.

(Onondaga) Haudenosaunee leader to a Wendat village near Quebec, where he sought peace with the French. Wrote Le Mercier, "This Captain displayed his presents, which, among all these Barbarous tribes, have the same use that writings and Contracts have with us ... These presents consisted of beaver-skins and porcelain; and each of them had its name, and testified the desire of the speaker and of those who had delegated him."[47] Wampum is identified here not as writing, but only as being used in a similar way. Le Mercier was chronicling a Haudenosaunee – not Wendat – use of wampum as a form of contract or text, but he also claimed that this was a common practice across the Indigenous cultures with which the French were in contact.[48]

The Jesuits consistently differentiated writing, which they always took to mean alphabetic script of the kind they used, from the Indigenous forms of record keeping discussed above, but this is increasingly recognized as an unjustifiable distinction. Indigenous cultures throughout the Americas had their own ways of keeping track of information and communicating it. Gordon Sayre has noted that the bundles of sticks like those used by the Wendat and similar methods of keeping track of information are a consistent motif in early writings about Indigenous cultures in the Americas.[49] And examples like Mayan pictographs, the birch bark scrolls of the Ojibwe, and the Incan knotted cords known as *quipus* also attest to the ability of Indigenous Peoples to preserve and transmit knowledge before the introduction of alphabetic writing.[50] The exclusion of such systems from studies of the textual record of colonial encounters is now often understood to perpetuate colonial power structures. As Birgit Rasmussen has put it, "As long as literary scholars continue to think about writing predominantly as the alphabetic system used by Europeans, we uphold that legacy by defining other forms of recording knowledge and narrative out of existence."[51] In recognition of this challenge, Indigenous literacies are increasingly considered alongside those of European settlers, including wampum but not, it seems, the comparatively less-studied sticks and straws discussed above. Onödowá'ga (Seneca) Haudenosaunee literary scholar Penelope Kelsey, for example, has used wampum as a lens for interpreting contemporary Haudenosaunee texts and art, drawing on the way "these belts record international agreements, key historical events, and original instructions from various epochs of Iroquois history."[52] Rasmussen has examined the confrontation between wampum and alphabetic writing in the context of a particular French-Haudenosaunee diplomatic council.[53] And Angela M. Haas has traced the conceptual connections between Wampum and digital hypertext.[54] Instead of taking at face value the Jesuits' claims that the Wendat had no writing, then, efforts to understand how Chihoatenhwa and his countrymen understood the missionaries' ability to record knowledge word-for-word and then read it back later ought to account for the fact that they already had their own ways of preserving and communicating knowledge. When Chihoatenhwa and his fellow Wendat observed Jesuit alphabetic writing for the first time, they were not, contrary to what the Jesuits suggested, confronted with an entirely new concept, but rather a different method for performing a task that their friends, family members, and leaders had been doing all along.

It is reasonable to think that Chihoatenhwa would have at least initially understood alphabetic writing through the lens of his own culture's systems for recording knowledge, just as Brébeuf seems to have understood the *atsatonewai* (packet of council sticks) in relation to the closest comparator he could find in his own culture – books and papers. Jérôme Lalemant reported that Chihoatenhwa evaluated other things that were introduced by the French this way, in comparison to the equivalents offered by his own culture. Lalemant's 1639 *Relation* reported that Chihoatenhwa urged his fellow Wendat to adopt Christianity by pointing to all the ways in which various tools introduced by the French had been accepted as superior to the local equivalents, and reproached them for rigidly adhering to their own ways in matters of spirituality: "I ask you, when at first you saw their hatchets and kettles, after having discovered that they were incomparably better and more convenient than our stone hatchets and our wooden and earthen vessels, did you reject their hatchets and kettles, because they were new things in your country, and because it was the custom of France to use them and not yours? Now if they urge us to believe what they believe, and to live conformally to this belief, we are under great obligations to them; for indeed, if what they say is true, as it is, we are the most miserable people in the world if we do not do as they tell us."[55] It is easy to understand why Lalemant included this material in his report: he characterized this argument in favour of conversion as among the "flashes of the spirit of God" that he believed he frequently saw in Chihoatenhwa's words and actions. But it is also possible to see Chihoatenhwa's purported words as the sign of a relatable impulse to evaluate unfamiliar objects and practices in light of those that were already known. And there are signs that the Wendat, at least eventually, did not understand their own practices to necessarily be completely separate phenomena from alphabetic writing. François-Joseph Le Mercier's *Relation* for 1653–54 describes a gift Wendat Christians prepared for Jesuits in Paris: a wampum belt that used beads to spell out *Ave Maria gratia plena* (hail Mary, full of grace).[56]

As mnemonic media for recording information, devices like sticks and wampum do not, of course, operate exactly the same way as the method used by the Jesuits. Alphabetic writing involves recording words letter by letter in the form of marks on a page or similar medium, such that any person who sees them and knows how to decipher them can receive the message as initially composed, no matter how far away or how long in the past and despite not having been present at the moment of composition. Wampum, in contrast, does not constitute a verbatim record of a particular message, and its meaning is not encoded in particular marks that always signify the same words to any reader. Instead, it works as a visual tool to help a speaker specially trained for this purpose call to mind a particular message that had previously been transmitted orally into the wampum. More specifically, as Angela Haas has explained this process, "In order to memorize the belt and its story, the trained individual would impress in the mind the visual representation of the belt and subsequently forge mnemonic associations between the visual representation of the belt and the accompanying story."[57] Unlike alphabetic writing, this system depends on the memory and skill of a trained interpreter who is present at both the moment of composition and the moment of interpretation to fulfill its function as a record of an event or agreement. But like alphabetic writing and despite its reliance on the presence of an interpreter, the wampum belt itself is understood to be where this knowledge resides, as opposed to the memory of the speaker.[58] Composition, in this system, is the work not of the person who makes the wampum belt or the person charged with associating its features with the knowledge it is intended to record for later repetition, but with the person who first speaks words over the wampum, transmitting the message into the belt. Less specific information is available about how bundles of sticks or straws functioned as mnemonic devices, but it seems these too were sometimes a way of preserving and communicating words that had been spoken aloud, at least to judge by Paul Ragueneau's above-cited description of their use in storytelling among the Wendat.

Reconsidering the above-cited passages, in which Jesuits described their efforts to introduce writing to potential converts, in light of the role of oral composition in Wendat communication and record-keeping systems suggests that Chihoatenhwa and others must have found something very familiar about alphabetic writing when they first encountered it. The passage from Brébeuf's 1636 *Relation* discussed earlier in this chapter as an example of the Jesuits' frequent claim that writing was entirely new to the Wendat and a source of excitement to them shows that by the priest's own account, the repeated trials the Wendat made of alphabetic writing all began with the oral composition of a message. Brébeuf wrote that the missionaries who participated in these trials spoke words aloud, while recording them on paper, just as the information recorded in a wampum belt was spoken aloud. Another passage cited earlier, in which Le Mercier reported assuring the Wendat of the accuracy of his religious message by pointing to its presence in books, also links writing to speech. These books had been written, of course, but Le Mercier also told the Wendat that their contents had been dictated by the Holy Spirit. When the Wendat learned about alphabetic writing, then, they did so in a context in which their own practices for recording information and the lessons of the Jesuits were seemingly aligned on at least one point: the act of composing material to be preserved for later communication was, or at least could be, oral. This could explain, at least in part, Le Mercier's above-noted observation that Chihoatenhwa was making fast progress in learning to write, but was struggling to comprehend the very concept of reading. And it also suggests that although the Wendat may have been excited by alphabetic writing, as Brébeuf claimed, their excitement may have been more a reflection of the differences they could observe between this method of recording knowledge and their own practices, instead of a sign that the very concept of communicating or preserving knowledge in a form other than word-of-mouth was entirely new to them. One of the key features of wampum belts as a way of preserving and transmitting information mentioned above is their reliance on the presence of an interpreter at both the moment of composition and the moment of repetition to a new audience. The trials of alphabetic writing described by Brébeuf relied on no such interpreter. There was no oral communication at all between the priest who sent the message and his colleague who received it, and the Wendat who witnessed each step in the process played no active role aside from perhaps carrying the paper from one Jesuit to the other, although even this much is unspecified in Brébeuf's account. And so, it is understandable that the Wendat may have been surprised by the successful transmission of a message this way, even if the oral act of composition must have seemed at least somewhat reminiscent of their own practices.

Viewed in this light, Chihoatenhwa's frequent dictation of material to Jesuits who diligently wrote it down, an action that bears a resemblance to the act of speaking words into wampum, might be considered among the ways he could have understood himself to be engaged in alphabetic writing, even if he was not putting quill to paper himself. Wrote Le Mercier in the 1638 *Relation*, "We have profited greatly, for, in serving him as Instructors in reading, we have made for ourselves a good Master in the language. When we ask him the initial or final letters of the words, which are sometimes hardly distinguishable, he utters them for us very distinctly; so he will be of great service to us, with the help of God, in the conjugations. He has even dictated to us several excellent speeches upon our Holy Mysteries, in a very logical sequence; but he speaks so distinctly that you do not lose a syllable."[59] The *Relations* contain many utterances on pious topics that are attributed to Chihoatenhwa and other Indigenous people, but the missionaries who were responsible for these texts do not always specify which of these were the result of dictation and which may have been reconstructed from memory after the fact.[60] This is probably because the missionaries understood Indigenous Peoples' participation in these exchanges not as a way of writing, but rather as an act of assistance to their own linguistic efforts and, at least in the case of Chihoatenhwa and other converts, a sign of their successful conversion to Christianity. It is understandable that Le Mercier would perceive Chihoatenhwa's oral production of information to Jesuits with quill at the ready in this way, through the lens of his own linguistic and evangelical projects, but it is also possible to think of these encounters as participation in writing broadly conceived to include not only the alphabetic encoding practised by a Jesuit jotting down information as he learned it, but also the transfer of a familiar practice – speaking information aloud as a first step in recording it for later use – to a newly introduced way of communicating and preserving knowledge.

Chihoatenhwa's best-known and longest composition in the Jesuits' annual reports is an example of the "excellent speeches" Le Mercier reported the Wendat man dictated to the missionaries. Lalemant included it in his 1641 *Relation* – that is, the year after the Wendat man's sudden death. A substantial text, covering four pages in Lucien Campeau's edition, it includes both the original version in Wendat and a French translation prepared by the Jesuits. It takes the form of a prayer, describing God's status as master of all he had created, including human beings, the relative weakness of other supernatural entities and of humans, Chihoatenhwa's gratitude to God, his anticipation of a happy afterlife and consequent lack of fear of death, and many other themes that are recognizable echoes of the Jesuits' own accounts of their message to the Wendat.[61] Lalemant explained that he chose to include Chihoatenhwa's prayer to satisfy readers' curiosity about the language of the Jesuits' would-be converts, and added that it could also serve as persuasive evidence of the man's faith: "Certain persons have desired to see a specimen of the Huron language, in order to ascertain its structure and their methods of expression. I cannot select anything better than one of the most ordinary communions which Joseph Chihwatenhwa, that excellent Christian whom we have mentioned, had with God toward the end of his days; by the same means can be recognized the Spirit of God which animated him."[62] There is no reason to doubt that conversing with Chihoatenhwa and writing down what he said was a great help to the missionaries' efforts to learn the Wendat language. But the prayer also stands as a particularly clear example of how Indigenous people could be thought of as having participated in writing.[63] Chihoatenhwa was echoing the missionaries' religious lessons when he spoke these words, or perhaps telling them what he knew they wanted to hear.[64] But he was also knowingly speaking so the Jesuits could write down his words, an act that he surely must have noticed bore an unmistakable resemblance both to the above-described missionary method for demonstrating writing – by jotting down something someone said out loud – and to his people's own mnemonic systems of record keeping.

Thinking of Chihoatenhwa as consciously engaged in composing words for distant readers when he dictated material to Jesuit scribes unfortunately does not mean that understanding his contributions to the *Relations* is as simple as performing a close reading of passages in the texts that the missionaries identified as having come out of his mouth, in the same way previous chapters of this book have examined other passages of the annual reports. The Jesuits who wrote such passages down were not only scribes, but also translators, constantly working between languages as they sought to communicate both with Indigenous people and with French readers. With the help of people like Chihoatenhwa, they rendered their religious message and everything else they needed to say into local languages in order to communicate with potential converts, as had been the custom of the Society of Jesus from its very founding.[65] And they also, selectively, translated the words and ideas of their interlocutors into French for inclusion in the annual reports. It is no exaggeration to say that lurking behind every pious utterance attributed to an Indigenous person in the Jesuit *Relations* is a double translation: from French to an Indigenous language in order to introduce European and Christian concepts to a would-be convert in their own tongue, and then from the Indigenous language back into French in order to report the results to readers. It is easy to see how this process would obscure from view the imprecisions and compromises in meaning that were necessary for the Jesuits to communicate their message, as well as their undoubtedly imperfect mastery of their interlocutors' languages.[66] And it also means that there is unfortunately no opportunity to probe the nuances of Indigenous Peoples' rhetorical choices, since the features of their speeches in the *Relations* may be just as much the result of the Jesuits' translation choices as of what was actually said. If the words that Indigenous People dictated to the Jesuits therefore resist close analysis, it can at least be said that Chihoatenhwa and some of his fellow Indigenous people created material that appears in the *Relations*. He *wrote*, from a perspective that accounts for his culture's own practices and for the place of oral composition in the Jesuits' demonstrations of alphabetic writing, even if it must be acknowledged that his contributions were always subject to the approval of the Jesuits who translated his words and decided what to include in their annual reports.

* * *

There is one other way in which Chihoatenhwa likely interacted with Jesuit writing practices that is worth briefly exploring: he may have at least occasionally delivered letters on behalf of the Jesuits, facilitating the process by which material for the annual *Relation* was gathered. In the summer of 1639, Chihoatenhwa travelled from Sainte-Marie to Quebec in the company of the Jesuit François-Joseph Le Mercier. He floated down rivers, navigated dangerous rapids, and, when necessary, carried his canoe and its contents overland. Chihoatenhwa's journey has most commonly drawn attention for what Jérôme Lalemant wrote about it in his 1640 report from the Wendat mission, describing Chihoatenhwa's reaction to the close relationships he witnessed between Christians in Quebec and the charitable behaviour of newly arrived female religious orders, and reporting his words of astonishment upon noticing differences between his own culture's practices and those of the French: "Ah! but we are very far from such friendship!"[67] The journey itself is not discussed in detail in the year's *Relation* except to note that Chihoatenhwa carried a heavy load on behalf of the Jesuits, both ways – yet another sign, for the Jesuits, of his faith: "Last Summer, on his way to and from Kébec, at the rapids and portages he made three or four trips, laden almost above his strength; and all that for God. At the beginning of the portage, he offered his labor to our Lord; on the way, he continually conversed with him; and at the end, he thanked him for having given him the strength to do something for him."[68] There is regrettably no surviving account of exactly what Chihoatenhwa carried for the Jesuits, either on this occasion or on any other. The only specific item mentioned in the *Relation* was a bundle of holy objects he reportedly carefully protected: "In the bundles which he brought back for us, there were among other things some precious Relics of some Saint; that was his consolation, and he would never allow that another than he should charge himself with a burden so holy, though heavy; and his most usual discourses, at the height of his toils, were with those whom he knew not even by name, but whom he loved and honored, inasmuch as they were friends of God."[69]

The contents of Chihoatenhwa's bundles go unspecified, but it would not be surprising if they contained correspondence, whether administrative letters of the Society of Jesus or the personal mail of individual missionaries. There are many instances in the *Relations* of priests relying on Indigenous people, both Wendat and others, to transport letters on their behalf. To mention only a few examples, in his 1637 report from the Wendat mission addressed to Paul Le Jeune in Quebec, Le Mercier assured his distant colleague that "we received a package of letters from your Reverence through the medium of a [Sauvage]."[70] The following year, Le Mercier reported that Brébeuf, with his own assassination on suspicion of causing disease seemingly imminent, had taken Wendat allies up on their suggestion that he write a letter for them to carry to Quebec in the event of his death.[71] And Jérôme Lalemant's 1647 *Relation* reports that the Jesuits in Quebec entrusted a packet of letters to a large group of Atikamekw who were on their way to trade with the Wendat, so that the latter could then deliver the letters to the Jesuits who were labouring among them. At the same time, the *Relation* reports that the Jesuits among the Wendat had taken advantage of the same trade mission to have letters delivered to Quebec via the Atikamekw traders.[72] Cases like these abound throughout the Jesuits' published reports. News circulated among the missionaries and their colleagues elsewhere largely thanks to the willingness to carry them of people like Joseph Chihoatenwha and even those of his countrymen who were reputed to be less committed to the faith, so much so that in his first *Relation* from the Wendat mission, Le Mercier acknowledged how dependent he and his colleagues were on the help of Indigenous porters, as "both spiritual and temporal help come to us here only through the medium and the hands of the [Sauvages]."[73] Chihoatenhwa himself had been expected to carry Lalemant's final letter of the year to Quebec in 1640 before his untimely death scuttled that plan. Wrote Lalemant, "I was preparing to write to Your Reverence for the last time in this current year, by the hand of Joseph Chihouatenhoua, our good Christian; and now the same paper of which he should have been the bearer is used to carry to Your Reverence the news of his death."[74] The *Relations* do not report that Chihoatenhwa transported letters to and from Quebec on behalf of the Jesuits or even from village to village within Wendat territory, but the frequency with which news was transmitted this way, coupled with Chihoatenhwa's apparent desire to please the Jesuits, makes it seem all but certain.

There is no reason to think Chihoatenhwa was ever less than fully cooperative in transporting items, including correspondence, that the missionaries may have entrusted to him, but other Indigenous people sometimes did not deliver the news as expected. The *Relations* record cases in which Indigenous people intentionally prevented information from reaching its intended recipient. Barthélemy Vimont's 1642 report from Quebec, for example, lamented that a shipment of supplies bound for the Wendat mission had been intercepted by a group of Haudenosaunee, who deliberately destroyed a batch of letters.[75] Letter carriers also sometimes accidentally failed to deliver the mail, as in the case recorded in Paul Ragueneau's 1648 *Relation* from Sainte-Marie of a Wendat man who had been entrusted with two letters to carry to the mission superior, but lost one of them along the way.[76] And sometimes Indigenous people were simply unavailable to carry letters when the Jesuits wished to send news in one direction or another. Le Mercier's 1638 *Relation* reports, for example, that when a rumour that Brébeuf had been killed proved unfounded, "we could not impart the news of the Father's safety to the settlement of saint Joseph until a week afterward, for lack of a messenger; the letters that they wrote us show plainly that the rumor passed for the truth among those of their village."[77]

Since the authors of the *Relations* usually did not specify which items of news had been brought to them by Indigenous hands, the impact of faithful delivery, wilful obstruction, or accidental loss are not always obvious in the published annual reports. Still, there are enough clues to conclude that Indigenous people inevitably – whether consciously or not – shaped what was available for inclusion in the texts when they carried letters for the Jesuits or opted not to do so. In the 1641 *Relation*, for example, Lalemant lamented the sparseness of the information he was able to report about the Jesuits' new efforts among the Chonnonton, whom the Jesuits called the Neutrals. He explained that the Wendat who acted as couriers sometimes intentionally threw letters away out of malice or fear at the prospect of the Jesuits seeking other alliances.[78] And there is at least one clear case in which Indigenous Peoples' service carrying a letter clearly shaped the Jesuits' annual report. The 1643 Quebec *Relation* prepared by Barthélemy Vimont contains a long letter written by the Jesuit missionary Isaac Jogues, who had been taken captive by a group of Haudenosaunee the previous year.[79] Jogues apparently wrote four different letters, entrusting them to Haudenosaunee men who were setting out in search of their Indigenous enemies, and instructing them to tie the letters to poles along the banks of the Saint Lawrence River. Whether directly or through one or more intermediaries, one of these letters was found by a Wendat man, who then carried it to Quebec where it was included in the *Relation*.[80] It is striking that Jogues's communication with other Jesuits was entirely dependent on not one, but at least two Indigenous people – who were in conflict with each other, no less – to carry his letter to its destination. This letter certainly could not have been included in the published report if Indigenous people had not delivered it to its intended recipient. In light of Jogues's particular circumstances, held captive instead of being more-or-less comfortably ensconced in a community of converts, this is an extreme example. But these circumstances may also be why the Jesuits in this case bothered to account for the extraordinary path Jogues' letter had to travel to be included in the annual report.

* * *

Describing the process by which the Jesuit *Relations* from New France were created, Sara Melzer wrote that "each report began with the priests in the field who would write up their experiences. These reports were then taken by summer canoe to the superior in Quebec, who could compile them. He would copy some verbatim, rewrite others, and then send the whole package to the Jesuit headquarters in Paris."[81] Conspicuously absent in this characterization of the process and others like it is any agency attributed to Indigenous people.[82] All active roles in the creation of the Jesuits' annual reports are typically reserved in scholarship for the missionaries themselves. This chapter has shown that this common understanding of the texts is not the full story. Chihoatenhwa and others participated in writing, whether by learning to use alphabetic script or by speaking words for the Jesuits to put on paper – an act that resembled both their own, more familiar practices and the missionaries' method of demonstrating alphabetic writing. It is not difficult to understand why Le Mercier chose to highlight Chihoatenhwa's desire to learn alphabetic writing or his enthusiasm for dictating words and even whole speeches to priests with quill at the ready. These activities contributed to a flattering portrait of what the missionaries took to be a whole-hearted embrace of Christianity, as well as of the general prospects of the mission. Such messages surely would have been welcome news to readers of the annual report who may have been curious about the Jesuits' progress in effecting conversions. But they also can serve to make a more straightforward and overlooked point: just as the Jesuits could draw from and adapt manuscript reports written by people like Christophe Regnaut or their own preliminary records of events while composing the annual *Relation*, they also sometimes incorporated material composed out loud by Indigenous people, and there are good reasons to suspect those people at least sometimes understood themselves to be participating in writing, even if the missionaries did not.

Similarly, willingness to carry letters across long distances for the Jesuits appears in the texts as an encouraging sign of good will toward the French and toward the faith, with the intentional interruption of the flow of raw material conversely serving as notice to readers of the challenges the Jesuits faced. Whatever the Jesuits' particular reasons for including this material, it amounts to a consistent picture of the indispensable role the Wendat and other Indigenous Peoples played in moving information from place to place on behalf of the Jesuits. This aspect of the way news circulated across large swathes of land has always been visible to anyone who cared to observe it in the *Relations*, but scholarly descriptions of the process by which the texts were compiled have tended to obscure the involvement of Indigenous people. Joseph Donnelly, for example, wrote that the superior "received from various missionaries accounts of their work." And Melzer, as noted above, wrote that the *Relations* "were taken by summer canoe" to the superior, without specifying who was doing the taking.[83] Masked by such formulations is the pivotal role often played by Indigenous people in moving the raw material of the annual reports from one place to another in New France. It is not an exaggeration to say, on the basis of the *Relations'* own testimony, that the availability of the writings of missionaries scattered across a large geographical area for inclusion in the published reports frequently depended on the willingness of Indigenous people to deliver their letters. And their occasional interference or failure to deliver the news as expected caused material that otherwise may have been included in the annual reports to be unavailable.

This chapter has sought to account for actions of Indigenous people that are related to the process by which the *Relations* were created, but it should not be understood to suggest that this was truly a collaborative endeavour. As the Kanien'kehaka (Mohawk) Haudenosaunee scholar Scott Manning Stevens has pointed out, scholarship in recent decades that has emphasized reciprocal influence between Indigenous Peoples and settlers in their historical interactions may succeed in casting the former as actors instead of mere objects of ethnographic description, potential converts, or passive victims of colonization. But it also risks suggesting that they were empowered by their interactions with the French. According to Stevens, "Unwittingly, this position obscures the overwhelming pressures placed on Native communities to convert or assimilate to European cultural norms, including emotional ones, in the period of conquest as well as the continuation of these pressures down to this day."[84] This chapter should not be taken as an argument that Chihoatenhwa or any other Indigenous people were complicit in the way the perspectives of the Jesuits as expressed in the published annual reports came to dominate understandings of historical events. Since the Jesuit missionaries controlled what was in the manuscript that was sent to France each fall, this was certainly not a relationship in which the two parties had equal power, even if Indigenous people at least sometimes sought to participate in the Jesuits' writing practices in ways that can bring important nuance to scholarly understandings of the *Relations*.

5

Writer, Reader, Colleague

Marie de l'Incarnation and the Jesuit Relations *from New France*

A long account of the life and works of an Ursuline nun known in religion as Marie de Saint-Joseph, who had died in Quebec in April 1652, appeared in the Jesuits' *Relation* of events in the New France mission for 1651–52. It was composed not by mission superior Paul Ragueneau but by Paul Le Jeune, who had returned to France and begun serving as the mission's procurator in Paris, a role that will be examined in detail in the following chapter. This chapter of the Jesuits' annual report amounted to a reworking of a text written in Quebec by an Ursuline nun named Marie Guyart, who is better known by her religious name Marie de l'Incarnation. Her tribute to her fellow long-time evangelical labourer in New France had made its way across the ocean and into Le Jeune's possession. Le Jeune acknowledged that this text had not been intended for readers of the *Relation*, but he explained that he simply could not resist passing it along to this audience: "Mother Marie de l'Incarnation, Superioress of the Ursuline Seminary of Kebec, in New France, wishing to console her Sisters in regard to the death of Mother Marie de saint Joseph, sent them a short account of her life, her death, and her virtues. As these Memoirs have fallen into my hands, I thought it would be wronging the public to confine the enjoyment of this treasure exclusively to the Houses of the Ursulines. Accordingly, I have extracted therefrom the greater part of the facts which I shall relate in this Chapter."[1] Le Jeune borrowed very little of Marie de l'Incarnation's language, but his debt to her is clear. His chapter closely follows the structure and subject matter of her text.[2]

As Marie de l'Incarnation described her own discovery of Le Jeune's use of her work, this was a rude surprise. In a 1653 letter to her adult son, a Benedictine priest named Claude Martin, she described sitting down to read a copy of the previous year's published *Relation* that had made its way back to Quebec, as appears to have been the norm.[3] At least as she reported them to Martin, her feelings about this use of her text were decidedly mixed: "He much obliged me by doing it, but he [would have] given me [a] singular pleasure [by] not publishing my name. Knowing nothing of all that, as the reader in the refectory I found myself just about to begin with this story. I was embarrassed about it and put it aside to make someone else read it."[4] Her expression of unease upon reading her name in the published text may have been a gesture of pious self-effacement or adherence to the expectation of her time that female letter writers present themselves as of service to others, rather than as writers worthy of attention in their own right, as much as it was an expression of genuine discomfort.[5] Indeed, her misgivings do not seem to have outweighed her appreciation of Le Jeune's role in spreading the word about her fellow Ursuline's remarkable life. In a 1653 letter to an erstwhile colleague, the Tours-based Ursuline nun Françoise de Saint-Bernard, Marie de l'Incarnation reported of Marie de Saint-Joseph that "people have written to me about her from various places in France in a manner that shows the love and devotion they feel for her. This is an effect of our letters and of the account of her life that the reverend Father Le Jeune gave in the *Relation*."[6]

How exactly Le Jeune had come to possess this Ursuline nun's tribute to her deceased colleague was initially something of a mystery to her. In the above-referenced letter to her son, she could say only that it had somehow gone astray from its intended recipients and that Le Jeune's use of it was not what she had intended. "I had ordered that someone send you a copy of the account I made for our Mothers about the life and death of our dear departed. I have been told that this has not yet been done, because this writing fell into the hands of the Reverend Father Le Jeune. This good Father took what he wanted from it to put into the *Relation*, without me having asked him to do so."[7] By the time she revisited this episode years later, in a 1669 letter to the mother superior of the Ursulines in Tours, she had apparently learned some further details: an unnamed friend of the Ursulines in Paris opened a package that was expected to contain the account of Marie de Saint-Joseph's life and took it upon himself to deliver the text to Le Jeune instead of to its intended recipients.[8] It is only thanks to Marie de l'Incarnation's letters that we know anything more specific about the events leading to Le Jeune's use of her account of the life of her fellow nun than his own vague comment that it had fallen into his hands.

This episode is emblematic of Marie de l'Incarnation's unique relationship to the New France Jesuits' annual reports. The obituary for Marie de Saint-Joseph that Le Jeune appropriated unexpectedly was not the only time the Ursuline nun's words served as a source for the *Relations*. On at least a few occasions, Le Jeune and his successor as leader of the Quebec mission, Superior Barthélemy Vimont, solicited news of the Ursuline community's activities for inclusion in their own accounts of the year's events. And her encounter with the *Relation* for 1651–52 was not the only time she read the Jesuits' annual reports. She was an avid reader of them both before and after her arrival in Quebec, and frequently used them as a point of reference in her own letters from New France, pointing to the existence of a mutually supportive community of writers in the French settlement. And she was also a uniquely well-placed witness to the process by which the Jesuits' annual reports were produced, commenting in her letters not only on specific cases like Le Jeune's use of her tribute to a deceased colleague, but also more broadly on the challenges of reporting news of the New France mission and settlement year after year. Her comments on what it was like to keep up with an annual flood of correspondence offer a glimpse of the similar task that confronted the Jesuit mission superior each year, about which their annual reports say comparatively little.

This chapter examines Marie de l'Incarnation's correspondence for what it shows about the Jesuit *Relations*, focusing in turn on her contributions to these texts, her reactions to them recorded in her letters, and her descriptions of her own writing life in New France. It continues the consideration begun in the two previous chapters of how the work and perspectives of non-Jesuits are useful for understanding how the *Relations* were created, and also begins an examination of the texts' publication and reception that is further developed in the final two chapters. But mostly, it seeks to make room in scholarly understandings of the Jesuits' annual reports for the contributions, reactions, and perceptions of a woman. The story of how the Jesuit *Relations* came to exist is typically understood to be one of the actions of men alone. This is understandable enough in light of the status of the Society of Jesus as an all-male religious order, but this chapter shows that accounting for the case of a woman who was also writing in New France at this time can bring into view aspects of the Jesuits' annual reports that are not otherwise visible.

* * *

Marie de l'Incarnation's life in New France began in 1639, when she travelled from her lifelong home in the western French town of Tours to Quebec and established a convent and school for young girls there, in the company of her aforementioned colleague Marie de Saint-Joseph and a third Ursuline, Cécile Richer de Sainte-Croix, from Dieppe. This was the culmination of a long and improbable personal journey begun years earlier. She was born in 1599 to a family of modest means in the baking business, and in 1617 married a silk maker named Claude Martin.[9] In April 1619, she became mother to an infant son also named Claude Martin, and six months later became a widow. For approximately ten years, she and her son lived with her sister's family amid the hustle and bustle of a thriving business transporting goods throughout France, which she helped manage. As she later recalled of this period, she could easily have ventured further into the world of commerce, and with strong backing: "God had given me talent for business, and there were many people who offered to give me advances for that."[10] But her spiritual life was pulling her in a different direction. She had always been very observant, attending church daily during her brief marriage. But her faith intensified as the years went by, blossoming into mysticism characterized by ecstatic visions and spurred on by mortification of her own flesh with hair shirts, chains, and nettles. She wrote an exhaustive account of her owns sins, and would have fastened it to the door of the cathedral in Tours as an act of mortification if not for the intervention of her spiritual advisor, Dom Raymond de Saint-Bernard, a member of the Congregation of the Feuillants.[11] In 1631, she left her eleven-year-old son in the care of family and entered the convent of the Ursulines, a female religious order founded in Italy in 1572 and dedicated to the education of girls.[12] This abandonment of her already fatherless child – shocking in our time and at least unconventional in hers, if for no other reason than her deliberate decision to take no steps to ensure his future material comfort – earned her the stern reproaches of her family.[13] Claude Martin himself made a series of desperate and fruitless bids to extract his mother from the convent. In one episode, as she later remembered it, he stood outside the convent shouting "give me back my mother, give me back my mother," egged on by other children.[14]

Not long after permanently joining the Ursulines in 1633, Marie de l'Incarnation began to take an interest in New France, with the encouragement of various members of the Society of Jesus. She dreamed of walking with an unknown laywoman in an unfamiliar place surrounded by deep valleys and towering mountains, and encountering a beautiful church shrouded in fog upon which was perched the Virgin Mary with the infant Jesus in her arms.[15] The Jesuit priest Georges de La Haye, who had become her spiritual director not long after she entered the Ursuline convent and who must have been aware of the *Relations* Paul Le Jeune had begun sending back from New France, suggested to her that the land in this vision was the one on the other side of the Atlantic Ocean and along the Saint Lawrence River, where his colleagues were labouring to convert Indigenous people to Christianity.[16] This revelation seems to have ignited in her a fervent desire to travel to New France despite, by her own account, scarcely being aware of its existence until then.[17] Her correspondence from her time in the Ursuline convent in Tours shows that she read Le Jeune's earliest annual reports with rapt attention, drawing from them both inspiration for her own blossoming desire to establish a school for Indigenous girls in New France and practical information that would be useful for her journey. In the Jesuits' reports she found clues about the best time of year to depart Europe in order to be able to settle in to life in Quebec before the arrival of winter, tantalizingly optimistic assessments of the prospects of converting Indigenous people to Christianity, and the courage necessary for her own eventual voyage.[18] She also seems to have written to Le Jeune in the spring of 1636, while he was still serving as superior in Quebec, at least in part to express her wish to join him there.[19] Finally, the Jesuits were instrumental in connecting her with the means to realize her long-held desire. Members of the Society in Paris in 1639 mentioned her to a wealthy widow named Madeleine de la Peltrie, who had vowed when gravely ill to travel to New France to build a school for Indigenous girls there if she recovered her health.[20] The same year they met, the pair boarded a ship bound for Quebec along with the two other Ursulines mentioned above and a small group of Augustinian nuns who were on their way to establish a hospital in the French settlement. This first contingent of female religious settlers arrived in Quebec on the first day of August 1639, and Marie de l'Incarnation spent the rest of her life there, dying in 1672 after complaining of increasing fatigue, weakness, and failing eyesight.

Throughout the various stages of her life, Marie de l'Incarnation wrote, producing accounts of her spiritual life and visions, letters, and a variety of other texts, many of which do not seem to have survived.[21] This chapter examines in particular her correspondence during her time in Quebec because this is the part of her oeuvre that is most directly comparable to the Jesuit *Relations*. Like the annual reports that are the subject of this book, her letters were sent to France on the merchant ships that departed Quebec each autumn. And at least some of them seem to have reached a wider readership than might be expected since they were usually addressed to a single correspondent in France – family members, friends and former colleagues, and supporters of the Ursuline convent in Quebec.[22] In one of two 1642 letters to a noble woman named Mademoiselle de Luynes, who had withdrawn to the Ursuline convent in Saint-Denis, for example, she specified that only the other letter should be shared with others, suggesting that she understood her words would be passed along absent a specific request to the contrary: "This is a letter from my heart; my other one which relates what has happened in this new Church of God can be made public and communicated to others."[23] Like other well-known French women practitioners of the epistolary genre to whom she has sometimes been compared, such as Jean-Françoise Freymot (also known as Sainte Jeanne de Chantal) or her granddaughter Marie de Rabutin-Chantal, Marquise de Sévigné, Marie de l'Incarnation knew that the audience for her letters was larger than the single person to whom they were addressed, and that they could serve as a way of disseminating her writing as much as a means of staying in touch with friends or family.[24] Unfortunately, the vast majority of Guyart's letters do not seem to have survived. The most complete collection includes 278 letters, but her own comments about the scale of her communications with people in France make clear that many more must have existed. In a 1644 letter to Martin, she reported that she had written more than two hundred letters that year alone, only fourteen of which have survived. Three years later, she told the same correspondent that she had written some 120 letters, but just eleven are still known to exist. Scholars who have attempted to extrapolate the full extent of Marie de l'Incarnation's correspondence from the portions that have survived have offered estimates ranging from 3,000 to 13,000 letters.[25]

Marie de l'Incarnation is now mostly remembered as a mystic, missionary, and problematic mother, a rich seventeenth-century example of a woman charting her own course and acting independently of men not only in New France, but also in the wider French and European contexts.[26] She persisted in her ardent desire to travel to New France, even when her male religious mentors regarded this as an unseemly ambition in a person of her sex.[27] Once in Quebec, she and her

Figure 5.1 Claude Martin's 1677 spiritual biography of his mother, Marie de l'Incarnation, includes a portrait that fittingly shows the nun, an avid and life-long reader and writer, standing in front of a shelf full of books, with another on the table in front of her.

colleagues withstood pressure from the male clergy to conform to restrictive notions of their duties in New France, and ultimately enjoyed more independence than their counterparts in France. Whereas Ursulines in Europe found themselves by the mid-seventeenth century increasingly limited by Church authorities to convent life and to educating day students, despite their origin as an uncloistered order, the community in New France engaged in missionary work beyond the education of young girls from the time of their arrival, including catechizing adult Indigenous people.[28] And they also resisted a plan by the Jesuit leadership in New France to subject them to the practices and rules of the Ursuline community in Paris, instead of those of Marie de l'Incarnation's own convent in Tours. The earliest Ursulines instead worked out a compromise among themselves, whereby all would wear the habit preferred in Tours and take a vow that was particular to the congregation in Paris.[29] Later, in 1659, they successfully resisted an effort by the first bishop of Quebec, François de Laval, to replace the community's governing document – authored by Jérôme Lalemant with input from the nuns themselves – with a more restrictive set of rules of his own device.[30] These and other aspects of Marie de l'Incarnation's story have made studies of her writings an important counterpoint to decades of scholarship that subordinated the history of women's participation in New France's civic and religious life to the stories of men like the Jesuits, Samuel de Champlain, Gabriel Sagard, and others.[31]

It is easy to understand, then, why scholars who have taken note of the fact that Marie de l'Incarnation's letters sometimes appeared in the published *Relations* have tended to focus on her own intentions and choices in preparing them. Natalie Zemon Davis, for example, observed that "when she wrote for the *Jesuit Relations* ... she knew she was going right into print."[32] And Marie-Florine Bruneau has written that the Ursuline nun's ability to adapt her writing for specific readers included bowing to Jesuit expectations about the proper place of female religious: "The Jesuits represented Marie de l'Incarnation as they wanted women to be: obscure, serving, humble, and silent. And when writing for the *Relations*, Marie de l'Incarnation complied with their desire."[33] Such characterizations of this Ursuline nun as a thoughtful and careful writer who tailored her letters for their expected audience are undoubtedly accurate within their limits. But as the preceding chapters of this book have already shown, the various texts the Jesuit superiors drew on in crafting their annual reports generally did not find their way into print entirely unaltered. It is worth examining in more detail how two Jesuit superiors, Paul Le Jeune and Barthélemy Vimont, made use of Marie de l'Incarnation's writings. They did so selectively, and in ways that resulted in their own voices dominating or becoming indistinguishable from hers. At the same time, however, the Ursuline nun was at least for a time specifically credited in the

Relations as the author of particular words or the source of certain information, whereas some others who made similar contributions, like the *donné* Christophe Regnaut discussed in chapter 3, would be entirely unknown if their own texts had not survived. The prominence the Jesuits gave Marie de l'Incarnation in their annual reports attests to her special status as a contributor to those texts, even if the New France superiors nonetheless tightly controlled her words.

Indeed, even in cases in which the *Relations* directly attribute language to Marie de l'Incarnation – a relatively infrequent occurrence, judged against the series' full four-decade span – it is clear that the Jesuits were deliberate and selective in their use of her words. Paul Le Jeune's 1640 report, for example, contains a chapter specifically devoted to reporting the activities of the Ursuline community over the preceding year. It includes excerpts of two of her letters, but frames them in such a way that her voice is dominated by that of the Jesuit. The chapter begins with Le Jeune's narratorial I – *je* – declaring that he had never seen mothers more protective of their children than the Ursulines and Madeleine de la Peltrie were of their young pupils, before briefly describing their living conditions. The rest of the chapter comprises excerpts of letters from several women connected to the Ursulines' efforts: the nun Cécile de Sainte-Croix, Madeleine de La Peltrie, and Marie de l'Incarnation. In all cases, these letters are fully embedded in Le Jeune's own account of events in the Ursuline seminary, stripped of the usual salutations and valedictions, and, presumably, any other portions that Le Jeune did not feel the need to include. The first excerpt of a letter from Marie de l'Incarnation, for example, is introduced by a sentence linking it to a subject Le Jeune had already been discussing for several paragraphs, both in an excerpt from a letter by Cécile de Sainte-Croix and in his own account of the work one of his colleagues had been doing to prepare young Indigenous girls for first communion: "But let us see what mother Marie de l'Incarnation wrote me, concerning the first communion of these children."[34] Even though Le Jeune explicitly cited the words of the Ursuline superior and her colleagues throughout the chapter, the impression is less one of a deliberate effort to showcase the words of female missionaries than of a conductor calling on various instruments in turn and assembling their contributions into a coherent tune of his own, just like any other passage in which a mission leader cobbled together various letters and reports for inclusion in the *Relation*. Le Jeune himself alerted readers to the highly selective nature of his use of the Ursulines' words that appeared in his chapter: "Let us hear them speak of their treasure, – that is to say, of their children. If I were to copy here all the joyful letters they have written me upon this subject, I would almost make a book instead of a chapter."[35]

The 1642 *Relation* prepared by Barthélemy Vimont at least superficially presents one of Marie de l'Incarnation's letters more completely, in a chapter devoted to the work of the Ursuline school. It begins with a customary salutation – "My Reverend Father" – and continues for several paragraphs, giving the impression of allowing the nun to speak for herself more fully than Le Jeune had done two years earlier.[36] On closer examination, however, it is sometimes difficult to distinguish between the nun's words and those written by Vimont. In the original seventeenth-century edition of the text printed by Sébastien Cramoisy in Paris, material drawn from the letter is not set apart from Vimont's prose by quotation marks or any equivalent sign. In some cases, language in the middle of the letter is attributable to Vimont with certainty. The first paragraph's final two sentences, for example, only make sense as an addition made by the person who inserted this material in the *Relation*, rather than its original author: "This letter has seemed worthy of being inserted here. Let us enter into details."[37] Similarly, the following paragraph contains a third-person reference to Marie de l'Incarnation and the goals of her order's evangelical efforts among Indigenous girls that must have been written by Vimont: "There is no doubt that if the means were at hand to lodge a number of them, they would be made as dextrous and as well-mannered as our Europeans. It is not this that is sought at present, but rather to write upon their hearts the Love and fear of him whom they now know. It is to that end that the efforts of these good mothers are directed, to whom our Lord seems to have given his blessing."[38] Other passages seem certainly attributable to the Ursuline superior, such as a paragraph recounting the insistence of two young girls that they be allowed to prepare for first communion that refers to Vimont in the third person and contains first-person pronouns referring to the Ursuline: "Two of our Girls, aged about eight or nine (says the Mother) pressed their Teacher for nearly a year to prepare them for Communion. When they were refused, they came to me and begged me, with many endearments, to grant them that favour. I told them that they were too young, but they did not lose courage. When Reverend Father Vimont came to see them during Advent, to give them some instruction, they threw themselves at his feet, and prayed him to give Our Lord to them at least at Easter."[39] The fact that Vimont's voice occasionally intrudes in what otherwise seem to be passages taken directly from Marie de l'Incarnation's letter is not necessarily surprising. The New France Jesuits did not always make the boundaries of quoted material completely clear in their reports, and it was not uncommon for them to sometimes interject when presenting someone else's words.

In this particular case, however, several substantial passages cannot be attributed with certainty to either Vimont or Guyart. Lucien Campeau and Guy Oury disagreed over which parts had been written by whom in their editions of Jesuit texts related to the mission and the nun's correspondence, respectively. Oury reproduced two paragraphs of the chapter in his reconstituted version of the letter, neither of which Campeau enclosed within quotation marks in *Monumenta Novae Franciae*, as was his general practice for indicating borrowed passages. And one paragraph that Campeau did mark as coming from the letter is omitted from Oury's reconstructed version.[40] These paragraphs describe the desire of the Ursulines' pupils to avoid contact with men, their diligence in confessing sins, and their imitation of the Ursulines in fasting and mortifying their own flesh – subjects that could have been described by either Marie de l'Incarnation or Vimont. None of these passages includes any grammatical clues as to the writer's identity, making it easy to understand how two well-informed modern observers could reach such different conclusions. Despite the appearance of this portion of Vimont's chapter as a letter from the Ursuline superior's own hand, then, it is impossible to be sure what she actually wrote. In both 1640 and 1642, her words were tightly controlled by the Jesuit superiors who included them in the *Relations*.

At the same time, the Jesuits' use of Marie de l'Incarnation's words was different from their occasional unacknowledged use of others' texts, like Ragueneau's borrowings from Regnaut's manuscript several years later. It was common at this time for male religious figures who served as spiritual directors or confessors to nuns and other devout women to also oversee their writings, disseminating them and even sometimes publishing them after revising or editing them as they saw fit.[41] And it is well known that Marie de l'Incarnation's own son – despite not serving as her formal spiritual director – took charge of her writings in this way. Martin made many changes while preparing his mother's letters and other writings for publication, particularly in order to ensure adherence to Church doctrine, protect his mother's reputation as a trustworthy mystic, and rid her language of expressions that were either outdated or too informal for French literary standards – sometimes amounting to completely rewriting her compositions.[42] This is regrettable for modern readers, as it has left very few of Marie de l'Incarnation's texts that can be said with certainty to have not been altered by the men who brought them into print. But there was nothing out of the ordinary about Martin's alterations to his mother's words in his own time or, for that matter, the way the Jesuits who inserted her letters into their *Relations* adapted them and presented them selectively.[43] Understood as an act of publicity and preservation, the Jesuits' inclusion of a female missionary's words in their annual reports must be viewed as a success. In four cases, including those examined above, a letter composed by Marie de l'Incarnation has only survived – albeit in partial and potentially edited form – thanks to its inclusion in the Jesuits' annual reports.[44] To the portrait of the *Relations* this book has so far offered, as selective and polished final versions of material drafted earlier by missionaries or sometimes by others, can now be added another, overlooked aspect of the texts: they also, at least sometimes, served in part to draw attention to and disseminate the words of a female colleague of the Jesuits in New France.

The regular incorporation of Marie de l'Incarnation's words into the *Relations* was a short-lived aspect of the texts' annual compilation. In addition to the two cases examined above, the reports for 1641, 1643, and 1644 contain chapters dedicated specifically to accounting for the Ursulines' work, and two of these include signs that they were based at least in part on written reports by the Ursuline superior. Like Le Jeune's 1640 *Relation*, his 1641 report attributed a few sentences to a report (*mémoire*) she had prepared, without reproducing it in its entirety.[45] And Vimont's 1644 *Relation* includes words attributed to her, praising the preparation of Indigenous girls for their first communion, that seem as if they could have been drawn from a written account: "'I admit,' said the Mother Superior, 'that, when I questioned them to see whether they were fit to receive that celestial bread, they surpassed my expectations; I found them instructed and impressed, beyond my hopes.'"[46] The Jesuit's verb choice in this case – *dire*, to say – makes it possible that this was an oral report, but it seems just as likely to have been a letter or written report of the kind she certainly prepared in 1640, 1641, and 1642. After 1644, sustained reports on the Ursulines' activities were much less frequent, suggesting that the Jesuits' appetite for including news about their female colleagues waned around this time, perhaps due to the 1645 appointment of the famously mission-focused Jérôme Lalemant as superior in Quebec. Marie de l'Incarnation's career as a regular contributor of material for inclusion in the Jesuits' reports was quite brief, lasting only five years from 1640 to 1644. She nonetheless continued to write to the Jesuits, including her spiritual director Jérôme Lalemant. The Quebec superior's journal, discussed in the second chapter of this book, records Lalemant's receipt of a letter from her on the first day of January 1647, and a letter to him on an unspecified date in 1648 is among her surviving correspondence.[47] The last of the published *Relations* devoted an entire chapter to material she had written, in the context of reporting her death and that of Madeleine de La Peltrie.[48] Remarks on the Ursulines' activities continued to appear in the Jesuits' texts after 1644, but they tended to be more fleeting and cursory than the full chapters that were included for the first five years after the nun's arrival.[49]

The handful of letters Marie de l'Incarnation wrote specifically for inclusion in the *Relations* constitute a very small part of her total correspondence. As noted above, nearly three hundred other letters have survived, and these have served scholars as a precious resource for efforts to understand her spirituality and what was surely her most confounding and well-documented relationship, her familial, spiritual, and editorial ties to the son she abandoned and then corresponded with for decades. Perhaps less appreciated is these letters' status as an invaluable point of comparison for the Jesuits' texts. As the rest of this chapter shows, Marie de l'Incarnation's correspondence provides insight into the Jesuits' annual reports in at least two ways. First, her presentation of herself as a reader of the *Relations* brings to light the degree to which the preparation of these texts was at least sometimes a collaborative affair and shows how she worked to promote the missionaries' texts to her own readers. And second, her vivid remarks on the extreme difficulty of keeping up with an annual flood of letters from France in the short interval between the arrival of merchant ships in the spring and their departure in the fall casts the Jesuit mission superior's similar work in a new if admittedly speculative light, providing a glimpse of how difficult it must have been to produce a report for publication year after year. In both cases, her letters illuminate aspects of the process by which the Jesuits' annual reports were created that are not explicitly accounted for in the texts themselves.

* * *

In addition to writing material for the *Relations*, Marie de l'Incarnation is known to have read them with interest. As noted above, she began doing so while still living in Tours, after concluding that the land she had seen in a vision was New France. And her above-mentioned discovery of her own name in the 1652 text is just one example of the references she sometimes made in her letters to Jesuit reports that had made their way back to Quebec in published form.[50] Perhaps more surprising is that she also sometimes referenced the content of Jesuit texts that had not yet been published. In a letter dated 4 September 1641, for example, she wrote to her son that "Monsieur our Governor drove the Iroquois away in an offensive undertaken to save our good neophytes. The *Relation* will tell you about it."[51] This event is indeed described in Paul Le Jeune's annual report for that year, in a full chapter about the ongoing conflict between the two parties.[52] It is worth examining Marie de l'Incarnation's presentation of herself as aware of the contents of annual reports yet to be published because it brings to light a previously overlooked aspect of the way the Jesuits' texts were prepared by the superior and also points to an apparently deliberate effort on the part of the Ursuline nun to claim for herself a measure of authority and knowledge by promoting the Jesuits' texts and linking her own letters to them.

In one particularly detailed reference to a *Relation* that had not yet been sent to Paris for publication, Marie de l'Incarnation wrote to one of her brothers on 4 September 1640 that "sorcerers are seen to become apostles and courageously preach the Gospel to their compatriots. The Relation will tell you about it, because the letters arrived so late that I do not have the leisure to go on about it. As you are protective of the glory of the King of Nations, your heart will be filled with joy to learn that twelve hundred people have been baptized. These are the effects of the almighty arm, which through the works of his life and his passion, has acquired all these peoples. We have again discovered some new ones for whose conversion we will work."[53] The news she mentioned briefly in this passage bears a striking resemblance to several passages of Le Jeune's 1640 report dated 10 September, less than a week after her letter, on at least three points. The Jesuit described in this text the actions of two Indigenous spiritual leaders to whom he referred as sorcerers (*sorciers*), one who had already become a vocal Christian and another who had signalled a new openness to converting.[54] Marie de l'Incarnation's report of the number of baptisms performed over the course of the preceding year matches Le

Jeune's triumphant declaration in the first sentence of a paragraph he devoted to this topic: "We have baptized this year about twelve hundred [Sauvages], including those among the Hurons as well as those down here."[55] And the Ursuline's reference to Indigenous Peoples of whom the French missionaries had only recently become aware corresponds to a chapter of Le Jeune's *Relation* that enumerates the various peoples in the areas around where missionaries were already established, including some he had never mentioned before.[56] She did not use any of Le Jeune's language in her condensed summary of these points, but her prediction that her son would find more information about them in the report that Le Jeune must then have been actively working to finalize was entirely accurate.

One day earlier, on 3 September 1640, Marie de l'Incarnation penned a letter to an unnamed woman in France that resembles the contents of Jérôme Lalemant's *Relation* from the Wendat mission that would soon be sent to France and published with Le Jeune's report from Quebec, on two points in particular. It opens with an expression of appreciation for a letter she had received from her correspondent, and framed her own response as related to a fuller account of events to be found in the Jesuits' text: "Even if your occupations prevent you from writing to me, or if accidents on the sea deprived me of so precious a letter, I would not have neglected to send you tidings of this dear land, while waiting for the relation to give you more ample ones."[57] Although the letter mostly describes events in the Ursulines' own school, it also touches briefly on news of the Jesuits' efforts, including among the Wendat: "There was a great persecution at the Hurons, where one of the Fathers thought he would be martyred with an axe. A stick was broken on him in detestation of the faith he preached."[58] The first of these attacks is described in a letter written by Paul Ragueneau that was included in a chapter of Jérôme Lalemant's *Relation* recounting events in the village of Ossossané, which the missionaries called La Conception. Ragueneau wrote about his efforts to tell a Wendat man about Christianity, and the violent response he received: "This young man whom we had instructed forcibly seizes the Crucifix which I wore about my neck, takes a hatchet in his hand, and says that positively I should die ... He lifts the hatchet directly above the middle of my head, – then uncovered, – and deals his blow so steadily that Father Chaumonot and I think to see at that moment what we have so long desired; I know not what stopped the blow, unless the greatness of my sins, but, short of feeling the hatchet cleave a head in twain, one cannot see one's self closer to death."[59] The following chapter of Lalemant's *Relation* mentions the second incident to which Marie de l'Incarnation referred, which had been reported separately from Ragueneau's letter describing his near death experience, in which a Wendat man resorted to violence to prevent the priest from baptizing his dying wife: "He seized a large stick, for want of a hatchet, which he could not find. He mightily discharged his anger on the Father, giving no other response to all that he could say, except to redouble his blows; and his stick was broken in two, after five or six good strokes, he continued with what was left in his hand."[60]

To judge from the points of correspondence between Marie de l'Incarnation's letters and the *Relations* that were awaiting dispatch to France in the cases mentioned above – Le Jeune's 1640 and 1641 reports and Lalemant's account of events in Wendat mission in 1640 – the Ursuline nun genuinely knew what her correspondents would find in these texts, but she did not specify how she had gained this knowledge. There does not appear to be any surviving private correspondence between her and missionaries in Quebec and Sainte-Marie that could have given her this information, but this does not mean it never existed. Perhaps Le Jeune or one of the other Jesuits had simply told her about the contents of the annual reports in progress, in enough detail to explain her own knowledge of their contents. This would have had to be a long conversation to touch both on specific events in various places and bird's-eye assessments of the mission. As discussed later in this chapter, it is difficult to imagine that either party would have had time for such a wide-ranging discussion of the year's events in the weeks before the ships departed for France, when they were scrambling to finish writing letters to be dispatched across the ocean. Perhaps, then, she had access to the draft *Relations* themselves or to an assortment of letters and other materials that had been used in their preparation. Claude Martin asserted in a foreword to his 1681 edition of his mother's correspondence that she was frequently privy to such materials: "Often ... the Reverend Father who was charged with working on the Relations gave his Memoirs to her, to draw from them what she deemed appropriate, in order to inform her Friends and the Benefactors of her House in France about it."[61] It is regrettably unclear what Martin meant, exactly, by *mémoires*. Perhaps the Jesuits shared with his mother the internal letters and private notes that were normally kept within the Society of Jesus. Or perhaps it was the manuscript *Relations* themselves that were the source of her knowledge, as Oury concluded on the basis of Martin's comment in the introduction to his edition of her letters.[62] It is not difficult to imagine that Le Jeune might have been more willing to share texts that he knew would soon become public than letters that were intended for Jesuit eyes only. It cannot be said with any certainty how Marie de l'Incarnation sometimes knew what would be included in the published texts, but the simplest answer is that she must have read the manuscripts before they were sent to Paris.

Whether she frequently had advance knowledge of the contents of the *Relation*, as Martin suggested, is not clear. There are cases in which her advice to readers about what they would find in the Jesuit report was incorrect. In an 8 October 1648 letter to a Benedictine nun in France, for example, Marie de l'Incarnation wrote that "the Iroquois massacred a good Dogic in hatred of the Faith. He is a second martyr whose story the Relation will tell you, and all the affairs of this Church."[63] But there is no mention in the year's report of the murder of a dogic, a Christian Indigenous religious teacher or catechist. Assuming such an incident occurred, it seems the Ursuline nun may have made an incorrect assumption about the contents of a text she had not actually seen. Or it could be that she got the details of the story wrong. The *Relation* records the killing of a French domestic servant named Jacques Douart – who was a *donné* but was not identified explicitly as such, probably for the reasons explained in chapter 3 – but makes clear that the unknown attacker was Wendat, not Haudenosaunee.[64] This incident inflamed tensions among the Wendat between Christian converts and the traditionalists who were blamed for orchestrating Douart's murder, and put Sainte-Marie into a state of crisis in anticipation of further attacks on the French. Whether she was referencing an incident that was entirely absent from the *Relation* or simply misstating the facts, Marie de l'Incarnation's claim that the *Relation* contained news of the murder of a dogic suggests that she may not have read Ragueneau's manuscript report, or at least did not have sufficient access to it to fully absorb its contents.[65]

In another case, Marie de l'Incarnation directed her readers to the year's *Relation* for more information on an event of particular interest, but evidently drew her own information from at least one other source. In a September 1649 letter addressed to the Ursuline community in Tours, she described the violent deaths of Brébeuf and Gabriel Lalemant that are examined in the third chapter of this book: "I have been happy to give you an abbreviated account while waiting for you to see it at greater length in the relation, where you will also see the great calamities of this Church and the great risks that the workers of the Gospel run."[66] Her summary is fragmentary, containing no mention, for example, of the belt made of bark and filled with burning resin. But it includes features that are particular to at least two of the accounts written in the immediate aftermath of the priests' death. Like Ragueneau's published report, Marie de l'Incarnation's letter described the mock baptism with boiling water after the collar of red-hot axe heads instead of near the beginning of the priests' ordeal. But like Regnaut's manuscript, on the other hand, her letter claimed that the Haudenosaunee tormentors cut out Brébeuf's tongue to stop him from preaching, whereas Ragueneau's preliminary letter and *Relation* both claim that it was not the priest's tongue that was removed, but his nose and lips. In short, none of the surviving sources align perfectly with the version of the story she told, and so it seems that her information must have come either from another account entirely – either oral or written, but in either case no longer known – or from more than one of the surviving sources, but certainly not from the Jesuits' annual report alone. It is possible that factual discrepancies between the Ursuline's letters and the Jesuits' reports are the result of changes made by the *Relations'* editors in Paris and not of Guyart's reliance on other sources that she opted not to mention. But this seems unlikely since the changes to the Jesuits' annual reports that were made in Paris do not seem to have altered such basic details about events in New France, as the following chapter will make clear.

What, then, to make of Marie de l'Incarnation's self-presentation as a devoted reader of the Jesuits' annual reports, and even as knowledgable about the contents of texts in the series that had not yet been published? There can be no doubt in light of the cases examined above that she at least sometimes did have this knowledge, and so it is understandable as a practical matter that she might choose to direct her correspondents to the Jesuits' annual report for more information on particular subjects in order to save herself the labour of writing out what would soon enough be available in print. But cases in which she apparently only speculated about the *Relations'* contents or drew on at least one other source suggest that her references to the Jesuits' texts were not only a matter of giving credit where it was due, helping her readers find more information, or avoiding the task of writing detailed accounts of some events. A better answer might be found in how Guyart characterized the relationship between her own letters and the

Relations in the cases examined above, in both accurate and inaccurate references to the latter texts. The Jesuits' reports contained, she wrote, "more ample" news explained "at greater length" than her own letters, which were mere "abbreviated accounts" by comparison. By such characterizations, Marie de l'Incarnation relegated her own summaries of events to a less significant, supporting role, a small foretaste of the year's news to tide her readers over until they could get their hands on the Jesuits' fuller, definitive account. In light of the above-mentioned expectation of her time that women who wrote letters present themselves as of service to others instead of as serious writers in their own right, as well as the submission and self-effacement expected of women religious who wrote, her references to the contents of past *Relations* and intimations of knowledge about those not yet published may best be understood not primarily as testimony to her own reading habits, but rather as a deliberate effort to promote the Jesuits' reports as the premier source of information on New France, while also signalling her own apparently privileged connection to them. She sometimes pointed her readers to the *Relations* for news on the New France mission in general, without even mentioning a particular event or precise topic about which they might want to know more. In a 4 October 1658 letter to her son, for example, she wrote, "In the letters I wrote you about what has happened, I did not speak to you about this new Church. I don't want to let this ship leave without saying a word about it, as you await the *Relation* which will discuss it at greater length."[67]

This aspect of Marie de l'Incarnation's letters points to a cooperative approach to reporting the year's news among religious leaders in New France. The process by which the *Relations* were created has often been understood as one of solitary toil on the part of the mission superior, who collated and adapted material prepared by his colleagues, wrote sections of his own, and assembled these various pieces into a coherent narrative of the year's events. It is now possible to add that this process at least sometimes also involved conversation, the sharing of drafts or preliminary material to inform the accounts of another writer, or maybe both. Marie de l'Incarnation, for her part, corresponded with the Jesuits and sometimes contributed directly to their annual reports, but also used her letters to draw attention to their work, apparently regardless of whether she knew with certainty what readers would find there, reminding her own correspondents of her status as a knowledgable and dedicated participant in the evangelical effort, even if the norms and expectations of the time demanded that she assign herself a subordinate role. The result is that the two corpuses – the Jesuit *Relations* and Marie de l'Incarnation's letters – can be thought of as more related to each other, in a variety of ways, than might be expected from the largely separate bodies of scholarship devoted to each of them. Writing the year's news in Quebec was, it turns out, an endeavour that was at least sometimes carried out in a context of exchange, cooperation, and mutual promotion.

* * *

Marie de l'Incarnation's correspondence was not, of course, limited to – or even primarily composed of – the two kinds of letters examined above, those that were written specifically for inclusion in the *Relations* and those that referenced those texts, past or forthcoming. On the whole, her surviving letters are quite distinct from the Jesuits' annual reports in both substance and style. It has often been remarked that she was less systematically ethnographic in her writings than her male contemporaries, more focused on describing the experiences of women and girls, and much more inclined to describe her own interior life.[68] She remarked in a 1668 letter to her son that the Jesuits' reports "only discuss the progress of the gospel and what relates to it," omitting much of interest about life in New France and leaving her to share news about the activities of her own community.[69] And whereas the Jesuits wrote in a formal style that often echoed the Latin works they had studied for years and then taught in the Society of Jesus's colleges, Marie de l'Incarnation composed her letters to be fluid and conversational. In this way, the tone of her letters is not much different from what was specifically recommended to women writers of letters later in the seventeenth century, inspired more by reading literature in French and by oral exchanges than by the norms of classical rhetoric.[70] Hers were often intimate letters, intended not only to share news of New France and the Ursulines' school but also to inform friends and family members about her personal experiences and to maintain those relationships, most particularly with her son.[71] These qualities of her letters perhaps not surprisingly led her to comment on practical aspects of writing news for readers in France in more vivid detail than her Jesuit counterparts, who knew they were writing for publication on behalf of all of their colleagues in the mission and mostly focused on sharing news of their own evangelical efforts and the characteristics of the people they were attempting to convert. Because of these differences, the Ursuline nun's words are useful in shedding light on one experience in particular that she shared with her male counterparts: the difficulty of keeping up a brisk transatlantic correspondence year after year.

Marie de l'Incarnation raised this subject frequently in her surviving letters. In an August 1650 letter to one of her sisters, for example, she reported that time to dedicate to her writing was in short supply due to the many other demands on her attention: "I cannot tell you how many interruptions I have. This letter is short and yet it was necessary for me to write one line now, another line later."[72] Answering her various correspondents was made all the more difficult by the fact that she had only a few months each summer to do so. Letters from France arrived in Quebec each spring or summer on ships transporting supplies, trade goods, and new settlers. If her correspondents were to have replies in less than a year and a half, she had to finish writing them before the ships departed in the autumn. By her own account, this compressed writing schedule cost her sleep, forced her to write until her body ached, and resulted in letters that were less polished than she would have liked. In September1644, she complained to her son about her own exhaustion due to having written approximately two hundred letters in preparation for the ships' departure: "I am extremely tired by the quantity of letters that I have written."[73] And she had already described the discomforts of keeping up with her correspondence to the same correspondent the previous year: "I am writing you at night on account of the number of the letters and the ships that are about to leave. My hand is so weary that I can hardly guide it, and because of this, I finish by begging you to excuse me if I do not reread my letter."[74] Such comments acknowledging that her letters were not as polished as may have been ideal are understandable as a manifestation of the above-mentioned expectation that women adopt a tone of self-effacement and service to others in their writing, instead of presenting themselves as serious writers. But in Marie de l'Incarnation's case they seem to have been at least as much the result of a real struggle to accomplish her task in the short time available as of any rhetorical strategy. At least once, in 1651, the compressed writing season prevented her from responding to all of her correspondents, forcing her to defer some letters to the following year.[75]

The circumstances of the Jesuit superiors who crafted the annual *Relations* from New France were not all that different from those of their Ursuline counterpart. They were subject to the same shipping schedule that dictated Marie de l'Incarnation's frantic pace of writing, and sometimes pointed to this fact when acknowledging that their reports were less polished than they may have liked. Le Jeune closed his 1634 report, for example, by announcing, "It is time to sound the retreat; the vessels are ready to depart, and still I have not yet read over nor repunctuated this long Relation, which ought to be enough for three years. Your Reverence will understand ... that I have not all the leisure I could desire. I do not know how it happens that news is always written in haste."[76] The Jesuits also sometimes mentioned in their annual reports receiving many letters from France, at least some of which presumably required a reply. Paul Le Jeune reported in the 1633 *Relation*, for example, that his newly arrived colleague Jean de Brébeuf had carried with him across the ocean a startling number of letters from readers in France.[77] And like the Ursuline leader Marie de l'Incarnation, the Jesuit superiors had to keep up with their writing – essentially writing an entire book for publication each summer and also preparing other letters for the autumn ships – and still manage to handle the routine tasks of their position: providing leadership to the mission, seeing to the spiritual needs of French settlers, and actively participating in efforts to convert Indigenous people.

The Jesuit superiors who wrote the *Relations* tended not to describe in detail the physical demands associated with their writerly obligations, but there are reasons to think that Marie de l'Incarnation's descriptions of her frenzied and fatiguing efforts to keep up with her correspondence also give some idea of what her male counterparts must have endured.[78] Even when compiled partly on the basis of letters prepared by others, this was an enormous amount of work to accomplish in a short period. It required writing original passages, copying and adapting the words of others, writing transitional material, and ideally, as discussed in the first chapter of this book, revising the entire report at least once. It is perhaps little wonder that the mission superiors occasionally suggested in passing that preparing this text was more of an onerous chore than a pleasant pastime. Le Jeune called the 1640 text an annual payment (*rente annuel*) to Jesuit authorities and other readers, and Lalemant referred to his 1648 *Relation* as a tax or tribute (*tribut)* owed to the same audiences.[79] Marie de l'Incarnation's descriptions of her late-night writing sessions, her hand being so weary from wielding her quill that she could scarcely move it, and the general difficulty of trying to keep up with correspondence while also meeting her other obligations provide a glimpse, if only a speculative one, of a Jesuit superior who must have been thoroughly exhausted and perhaps even suffering physically by the time the ships departed for France each autumn.

* * *

As this chapter has shown, Marie de l'Incarnation's correspondence has much to show scholars about the Jesuit *Relations* in addition to the letters she occasionally wrote specifically for inclusion therein. It is true that she was, for at least a few years after her arrival in Quebec, a kind of protégé of the Jesuits when it came to reporting the results of efforts to convert Indigenous people to Christianity. They deliberately drew attention to her words, albeit in the selective fashion typical at the time of male spiritual directors who oversaw the dissemination of the writings of female religious. But the leader of the Ursulines in Quebec also seems at least sometimes to have been a privileged and trusted early reader of the missionaries' manuscript reports – among the very first non-Jesuits granted access to the texts. She drew material from them before their publication and shared it with her own readers, and also frequently mentioned the texts after they had been published.

By her own account, this was not a relationship of equals. Her letters frequently strike a tone of deference to the Jesuits, presenting her own accounts of important events as mere summaries or condensed versions for her readers to enjoy until they could get their hands on the fuller account in the *Relations*, even as her self-presentation as knowledgable about the Jesuits' texts can be read as a claim to her own status as a key figure in efforts to bring Christianity to New France. Despite the way Marie de l'Incarnation consistently positioned the Jesuits' texts as a more authoritative source than what she could offer, her own letters are of great value in illuminating the context in which her male contemporaries assembled their annual reports. They attest to the existence of a cooperative relationship with the Jesuits in which both parties, at least at times, willingly enriched and promoted the contributions of the other while also accruing benefits of their own. And they also offer glimpses of what the physical experience of compiling the annual report may have been like, a topic on which the Jesuits' themselves did not offer such vivid commentary.

None of this is to say that Marie de l'Incarnation's only or even primary value is as a point of comparison for the Jesuit *Relations*. As the rich body of scholarship devoted to her texts cited throughout this chapter amply attests, this corpus is incontestably of great value for efforts to understand the lives of female religious in seventeenth-century New France, French efforts to convert Indigenous Peoples to Christianity, and the reactions of those peoples. But it is nonetheless true that among her legacies is a closer relationship to the Jesuits' annual reports than has typically been acknowledged. Marie de l'Incarnation's letters testify to one woman's involvement in the creation of the Jesuit *Relations* as a writer and a reader, and also as a rare witness to the process.

Marie de l'Incarnation's correspondence is without equal as a point of comparison for the writings of her male contemporaries in the middle decades of the seventeenth century, even if the surviving letters are only a small part of what once existed. But it is also true that she was far from the only woman who interacted with the New France Jesuits and their annual reports in the ways traced above. As noted earlier in this chapter, the same part of the 1640 *Relation* that contains excerpts of her letters also attributes words to Madeleine de La Peltrie, Cécile de Sainte-Croix, and Marie de Saint-Joseph, and there are excerpts of letters written by other women in Frances both new and old scattered throughout the Jesuits' texts.[80] And the mutually beneficial writerly relationship between Marie de l'Incarnation and the Jesuits that is traced above is in some ways similar to Paul Ragueneau's long association with the Hospitaller nun Catherine de Saint-Augustin. Ragueneau's *Vie de la Mère Catherine de Saint Augustin*, mentioned in chapter 3, was the result of his close ties to this well-known mystic, to whom he acted as confessor.[81] And finally, New France female religious other than the Ursuline superior whose story is examined in this chapter also read the *Relations* and sometimes specifically referred their own readers to those texts, including cases in which they seem to have seen the manuscript version of volumes that had not yet been published. Like Marie de l'Incarnation, Catherine de Saint-Augustin is known to have read and drawn inspiration from the *Relations* before departing France.[82] The Ursuline nun Cécile de Sainte-Croix wrote a letter to the superior of her former community in Dieppe one month after her arrival in Quebec in August 1639, and reminded her correspondent that an Indigenous convert whose enthusiasm for the violin she described was already a familiar figure: "This is a man named Nouel who is spoken of in the *Relations*." She also reported that news of how the settlement marked the birth of the future king Louis XIV would be included in the as-yet unpublished report that Le Jeune would soon send to Paris.[83] Similarly, a 1641 letter from two other members of the Ursuline community in Quebec to a nun in Paris described that year's text in terms that suggested they had read it before it was sent to France: "It is a lively relation that will be able to give you all kinds of consolation."[84] And the superior of the Augustinian nuns who operated the hospital in Quebec similarly endorsed a forthcoming text in a letter to the Jesuits' publisher in Paris: "You will learn from the Relation how the great courage of Monsieur our Governor prompted him to conduct a campaign against the Iroquois during last winter's severe cold."[85] This chapter has shown how accounting for one woman writer in New France can enrich scholarly understandings of the *Relations*. This should not, however, be understood as the full extent of what attention to the experiences and words of women– whether missionaries themselves or supporters of the mission – might have to tell us about the Jesuits' annual reports.

6

Provincial, Procurator, Printer

From Manuscript to Book in Paris

The *Relation* of events in New France in 1651–52 opens with a letter from mission superior Paul Ragueneau to the Jesuit provincial in Paris recounting a particularly tragic event. On the tenth day of May 1652, the Jesuit missionary Jacques Buteux was ambushed and killed by a group of fourteen Haudenosaunee while travelling along the Saint Maurice River in the company of a French soldier named Pierre Fontarabie and a young Wendat convert, Thomas Tsondoutannen.[1] Buteux had departed Trois-Rivières on the fourth day of April and was making his way north in the company of a group of Atikamekw in hopes of expanding the Jesuit mission into new territories and perhaps reaching the body of water that is now known as Hudson Bay. There were initially about sixty people in this party, but they eventually decided to separate when hunting along the way proved insufficient to feed so many at once. Buteux and his two companions proceeded in a canoe of their own making, following the others who had already departed. On the day of their death, the trio pulled this vessel from the water to carry it around rapids and suddenly found themselves surrounded by enemies. In what must have been a disorienting explosion of violence, the attackers immediately seized Buteux's Wendat companion and fired their rifles at the two Frenchmen. The Jesuit priest was hit three times, with two musket balls striking his chest and a third breaking his right arm. If he was not yet dead after this initial assault, he soon would be. His attackers "immediately threw themselves upon him, to stab him with their javelins, and to kill him and his companion with strokes of their hatchets."[2] Finally, Buteux's killers stripped his body of clothing, along with that of his fellow Frenchman, and dumped both in the river. Part of Fontarabie's body was eventually found, crow pecked and otherwise disturbed by wild animals, but Buteux's remains were never recovered.

This was not the kind of news that was normally discussed at length in the mission superior's opening letter to the provincial. It was common for the *Relations* to begin with prefatory *lettres d'envoi*, short, bird's-eye accounts of the year's successes and setbacks that often also contained expressions of gratitude to supporters and correspondents in France and expressions of joy inspired by receipt of news upon the arrival of merchant ships from France. Ragueneau's comparatively long opening text – nine pages in the original seventeenth-century edition – and its detailed comments on what was surely the year's most important and sensational news are probably explained by the fact that this was the only portion of the year's report that he actually wrote. As he explained in closing the letter, "I have been unable to prepare anything but this letter for the Relation. The Fathers, who are only just returning from their Missions, furnished me their memoirs too late, and I send them to Father Paul le Jeune, [procurator] of our Missions, who will present them to Your Reverence for such disposition as you shall choose to make of them."[3] Apparently realizing he had to say something about a significant event like the violent killing of one of his colleagues, but finding himself unable to compose the full account of the year's event as usual, Ragueneau made do with a letter. He shared details about what, exactly, had happened to the two Frenchmen that he learned from Tsondoutannen, who managed to escape his Haudenosaunee captors and arrived back in Trois-Rivières on 28 May, as well as the reports of some Indigenous converts who subsequently searched for the pair's bodies. And he also summarized the life and works of his fallen colleague, emphasizing how such seemingly unhappy news would ultimately "redound to the glory of God in the death of those who lay down their lives for the salvation of souls."[4]

It was Le Jeune, who had taken up residence in Paris in 1649 to serve as the mission's agent there, who shaped these raw materials into an annual report, added his own adaptation of Marie de l'Incarnation's account of her colleague's life that is discussed in the previous chapter, and placed Ragueneau's letter at the beginning of the resulting manuscript as its first chapter. Circumstances forced this particular annual report from New France to be composed in a very different manner from most of the others – and for a priest's violent death and life's work to be described in a prefatory letter instead of across several chapters, as in the case of Brébeuf and Gabriel Lalemant examined in chapter 3 – but its full title nonetheless followed the usual format, identifying it as an account of the year's events in New France prepared by the mission superior in Quebec.

Scholars have long understood that various hands in Paris had a role in preparing the annual New France *Relations* for publication, but have tended to stop short of examining this phenomenon as a significant part of the texts' annual journey to publication. Classic overviews of the Jesuits' annual reports by Lawrence Wroth and Joseph Donnelly attributed this work to the provincial alone.[5] More recently, Catherine Desbarats and Bronwen McShea have suggested that this Jesuit leader was joined in the task by the mission's agent in Paris – its procurator – and even the publisher Sébastien Cramoisy or someone working for him.[6] Others have pointed to an unspecified committee or unidentified individuals at the headquarters of the province of France in Paris.[7] With few exceptions, however, such acknowledgments of the work of various figures in Paris have tended to be fleeting and vague, saying very little about what kinds of changes could be made at this stage and who made them, and giving the impression that this work generally consisted of the small adjustments and polishing that any text bound for the printing press undergoes in the final stages of preparation.[8] It has sometimes been suggested or even directly asserted that the changes made to the *Relations* in Paris were only superficial, and of no significance to efforts to understand them.[9] And yet, Le Jeune's assembly of the 1651–52 *Relation* was not the only time the work performed in Paris amounted to much more than merely tidying up a text that had been written on the other side of the Atlantic Ocean. Several other reports were compiled in France when no manuscript arrived from Quebec, and in many other cases the draft prepared by the mission superior was substantially changed before being sent to its publisher. Focusing in particular on two figures Ragueneau suggested had a role in the editorial fate of the report for 1651–52 – the Jesuit provincial and the mission's procurator – as well as one he did not mention, the printer, this chapter shows that the work of editors in Paris was a key step in the process by which the *Relations* were prepared.

* * *

Perhaps surprisingly, in light of the editorial control the Society of Jesus normally exercised over members' books, Rome scarcely figures in the story of how the New France *Relations* came to be published. From the very founding of the Society of Jesus, the publication of books by

Jesuits had been strictly controlled by its leaders there. The Society's *Constitutions* required that "one who has talent to write books useful for the common good and who has written them ought not to publish any writing unless the superior general sees it first and has it read and examined, so that if it is judged apt to edify, it may be published, and otherwise not."[10] Another section of the *Constitutions* specifies that "at least three persons of sound doctrine and clear judgment about the field in question" would be charged with examining book manuscripts prior to publication, and that "differing doctrines" were not to be tolerated by these examiners.[11] More specific rules for the approval of books were established in 1601, in which five revisors general in Rome were to review and approve all books written by Jesuits after an initial review at the provincial level by three censors or revisors. Criteria for approval included the conformity of any given work to the standards set out in the *Constitutions*, the degree to which its content was edifying in nature, and its care to avoid including anything that could cast the Society of Jesus in an unflattering light. Books on relatively non-controversial topics might be read in full by only two revisors, whereas books on more delicate subjects concerning philosophy or theology would be scrutinized by at least three before the superior general of the Society made a final determination about their suitability for publication. This system proved unwieldy as the Society grew and sent missionaries far and wide, and so approval came to be granted or denied solely on the basis of the reports of local reviewers.[12]

In many cases, the Society of Jesus's process for reviewing and approving manuscripts written by individual Jesuits seems to have been quite rigorous. The Spanish Jesuit Pedro de Ribadeneira struggled for years to meet demands for changes to his late-sixteenth-century biographies of Loyola's successors as Jesuit superior general, Diego Laínez and Francis Borgia.[13] The surviving records pertaining to the review, revision, and final approval of the German Jesuit Athanasius Kircher's three-volume *Oedipus Aegyptiacus*, published between 1652 and 1654, show that censors reproached him for not going far enough in condemning the pagan, Jewish, and Muslim beliefs he described in his manuscript, and demanded removal of everything Kircher had included about the cult of Priapus. They also addressed matters that today might be recognized as questions of sound scholarship and good writing, pointing out factual errors, repetition, and what they took to be an immodest tone.[14] Texts prepared in the Society's overseas missions were not necessarily exempt from this kind of scrutiny. Censors' notes prepared in 1631 on a report from Brazil by the Jesuit Conrado Arrizzi called for improvements to its style, increased emphasis on edifying readers instead of merely satisfying their curiosity, and a clearer distinction between converted and unconverted Indigenous people in order to better highlight the mission's results, among other changes.[15] Compliance with the demands of the censors was not always perfect. Kircher, for example, seems to have simply ignored much of what was asked of him.[16] And publication of works without permission did occur, a transgression that appears to have been regarded as fairly minor.[17] But the review and approval of books was nonetheless a requirement that left clear marks on many books written by Jesuits that found their way into print in early modern Europe.

Despite this robust tradition of pre-approval, the New France *Relations* benefited from an expedited review process, a byproduct of the particular relationship between the Church and the French Crown that had been set in motion long before the first of the New France annual reports was written. Upon becoming king in 1589, Henri IV sought to establish France's religious autonomy, putting French Jesuits at odds with the Crown due to their close relationship to Church and Society leadership in Rome. At least partly as a consequence of these tensions, Jesuits were falsely blamed for an attempted assassination of the king in 1594, prompting their banishment from most of France before returning at Henri IV's own invitation in 1603. When a second attempt on the king's life in 1610 was successful, the Jesuits in France responded to renewed hostility and suspicion directed toward them by drawing closer to the Crown and even explicitly supporting claims that the Church in France enjoyed a special independent status. Taking this position earned them the rebukes of both the Jesuit superior general in Rome and Pope Gregory XV, but it also set the stage for the warm relationship members of the Society would enjoy with the French Crown for decades to come.[18] This context explains at least in part how the *Relations* could appear year after year, without any sign of the permission of Society of Jesus leadership in Rome. And it is also worth noting that Jesuit superior general Mutio Vitelleschi acknowledged, in a brief letter to Paris-based provincial Étienne Binet dated 1 January 1638, that delaying publication of the *Relations* until Rome had a chance to pass judgment on them might cause the mission's ardent supporters to lose interest. He nonetheless cautioned that Binet should not neglect to have the texts reviewed by local censors lest the Jesuit leadership in Rome decide to assert its right to prior approval.[19]

The work of reviewing each manuscript *Relation* and making any pre-publication alterations deemed necessary, then, was carried out exclusively in France. Ragueneau's above-mentioned comment about what he expected would happen to the raw materials he sent to Paris in place of a finished manuscript for 1651–52 makes clear that he expected two figures in particular to play a role: the provincial and the mission's Paris-based procurator. Provincials were, and still are, members of the Society of Jesus appointed by the superior general to lead one of the Society's geographic divisions, usually for a three-year term. During the time the New France annual reports were published, France was divided into five provinces – France, Aquitaine, Lyons, Toulouse, and Champagne – and the New France Jesuits reported to the leader of the Province of France, in Paris. It is not difficult to understand why some observers have concluded, as mentioned above, that this person was responsible for editing the manuscript *Relations* before sending them to be printed. The provincial formally sanctioned each year's report and his explicit permission to publish it was recorded at the beginning or end of most of the printed books.[20] The provincial was also mentioned as the intended recipient of the texts in their very titles, in most cases, sometimes by name and other times only by office. The report for 1642, for example, was entitled *Relation of What Occurred in New France in the year 1642. Sent to Reverend Father Jean Filleau, Provincial of the Society of Jesus in the Province of France. By Reverend Father Barthelemy Vimont of the same Society, Superior of the Residence of Kebec.*[21] And the various Jesuits who occupied this post in Paris over the years were also frequently mentioned in the texts, in the form of comments addressed to "your reverence" (*vostre révérence*).

The administrative post of procurator – *procureur*, in French – had existed within the Society of Jesus long before Jesuit missionaries arrived in New France. Appointed by provincials, these officials were charged with overseeing the Society's worldly affairs: managing finances and establishing and maintaining networks through which information, people, and supplies could be moved throughout the world.[22] As this role was originally conceived, there was to be only one procurator in each of the Society's provinces and one in Rome, who served as an advisor to the society's superior general and oversaw legal and financial matters.[23] But more such positions were created as the Society grew over the course of the mid-sixteenth century from an initial small circle in Rome to a network spanning much of the globe, with increasingly complex affairs to manage. Individual colleges, missions, and residences soon came to have procurators of their own.[24] Scholars who have commented on the contributions of these Jesuits have tended to focus primarily on their oversight of financial matters within the Iberian sphere of influence. But they have also sometimes highlighted procurators' work to ensure reliable communication, including editing the written reports prepared by individual houses and then sending them to Rome.[25]

The appointment of a Paris-based procurator dedicated to New France was something of a bone of contention from the beginning of the mission, one that pitted Jesuits in Quebec and the Society's leadership in Rome against the leaders of the province of France. As discussed in the first chapter of this book, the Jesuit Philibert Noyrot had scarcely arrived in Quebec, where he apparently served as the on-site procurator for the mission, when superior Charles Lalemant sent him back across the Atlantic Ocean in 1626 to protest the influence of Protestant traders in the fledgling settlement.[26] While he was in Paris, he also saw to the New France mission's material needs, recruiting labourers and artisans to populate and help build the French settlement, purchasing a year's worth of provisions, and chartering a ship for the voyage back to Quebec.[27] In a 1 August 1626 letter to Superior General Mutio Vitelleschi, Charles Lalemant wrote that he hoped another Jesuit could continue Noyrot's work on behalf of the mission once he returned to Quebec, since support from their brethren in Paris was not forthcoming: "Our own Fathers at Paris, for some reason, put difficulties in our way, and seem rather unfriendly to our mission ... As Father Noyrot is to return at the beginning of spring, another of our members will be absolutely necessary at Paris, or at Rouen, to fill his place and to look after our interests, sending us yearly what supplies we need, and receiving our letters, if Your Paternity so decide."[28] Vitelleschi responded later the same year by recommending to then-provincial Jean Filleau the appointment of a procurator for the New France mission, in a letter dated 15 December 1626.[29] But even this well-placed support for the idea does not appear to have yielded results, since Vitelleschi repeated the request two years later, in a letter to Filleau dated 2 November 1628.[30] The question was rendered moot when English privateers blockaded Quebec and took over the settlement in 1629, bringing a temporary end to the Jesuits' mission there.

When France regained control of Quebec in 1632 and the Jesuits resumed their mission, Charles Lalemant became the mission's de facto procurator, albeit with no formal appointment to the role and while also serving as the rector of the college in Eu and then in the same role at the college in Rouen. In a letter dated 1 May 1632 and addressed to Étienne Charlet, the French Jesuit assistant in Rome, Lalemant reported on the departure of Le Jeune to resume the mission that had been interrupted in 1629, lauded the trading company leader Jean de Lauson as a staunch supporter of the mission, and requested his own return to Quebec the following year as he was "only languishing" after three years in his college posts. He also asked for Charlet's help to ensure that funds donated to the mission were spent only on its needs and suggested that he needed the superior general's intervention to persuade the provincial in Paris to properly support the Jesuits' efforts in New France:

> For us, my Reverend Father, we need two things: the first, freedom to receive what is offered to us. It suffices for Your Reverence to obtain the consent of our Reverend Father and take the trouble to make me know. Otherwise we are extremely limited financially. Secondly, that Monsieur and Madame de Gamaches's money be used for the mission and that it not be diverted elsewhere, and that permission be given to use it every year. And on this second point, it would be necessary for our Reverend Father to write to the Reverend Father Provincial and for me to know something about it. And truly, I do not see why anyone would want this mission to be in worse condition than that, for example, of Constantinople, that of the Indies, which use the income they have. If it pleased Your Reverence to work for that, he would greatly oblige the mission.[31]

This letter confirms that Charles Lalemant was well informed about the newly revived mission, the resources made available by its supporters, and the factors in France he believed were standing in its way. But he was not officially the mission's procurator at this time, and whatever work he did in Paris on behalf of the mission came to an end in 1634 when his wish to return to Quebec for a second stint as a missionary there was finally granted.

Not until Lalemant returned to France in 1638 did the mission finally have a dedicated and formally appointed procurator in Paris, and former New France superiors would continue to occupy this role in the following decades. Paul Le Jeune succeeded Lalemant in 1649 and passed the torch in turn to Paul Ragueneau in 1662.[32] The *Relations* themselves do not provide many explicit accounts of the work performed by these men, but three comments in the first five years of Lalemant's term in this role – only one of which mentions the role of procurator by name – give some sense of how it was understood by the mission superiors in New France. In the 1638 report, then-superior Paul Le Jeune reported Lalemant's return to France and described his work there as both the management of the mission's unspecified business in Paris and the facilitation of the flow of information related to the mission. Lalemant, he wrote, "is going to France to look after our little affairs ... [and] will relate verbally what I cannot record upon paper without tediousness."[33] Two years later, the *Relation* – attributed on its title page to then-superior Barthélemy Vimont but actually written at his request by Paul Le Jeune – pointed to Lalemant as a source of information for anyone who wished to support the mission: "I dare not specify what several are doing in this matter, because they have given me to understand that they wish God to be their only witness. Those who have the devout wish to imitate these have over yonder Father Charles Lalemant, [procurator] of all our missions, who can very well tell them what will be most advisable, when he is informed of their good intentions."[34] And Vimont's 1643 *Relation* mentioned his receipt of a letter from Lalemant, in which the procurator reported using the contents of the annual reports to secure financial support for a mission settlement at Tadoussac from a well-placed benefactor, the Duchesse d'Aiguillon: "Father Charles Lalemant writes to me from France that, hearing the tears and the complaints of the [Sauvages] of those quarters, because they so seldom had persons to instruct them, she has furnished means for supporting, this year, the Fathers necessary to that mission."[35] The relative silence of the *Relations* on the role of procurator, especially as compared to the provincial who was frequently mentioned or addressed directly, probably explains why the work of this administrator has received so little attention.

In many cases, it is impossible to know for sure who – provincial, procurator, or a censor of the kind Vitelleschi mentioned in his 1638 letter – actually performed or ordered specific revisions to the manuscript annual reports received from New France. There does not appear to be any independent account of this process by anyone who witnessed it or was involved in it, and the changes that can be identified by closely examining the *Relations* themselves do not always clearly indicate who was responsible. It seems most likely, however, that the procurator did most of this work, for at least three reasons. First, as discussed below, clear differences can be observed in how the work of editing and revising the texts was handled depending on whether anyone was serving in this role, and who. Second, the three Jesuits who served as procurator each did so for at least a decade, making this the office where knowledge and institutional memory of the process of preparing the manuscripts for publication most likely resided. In contrast, the provincials generally rotated out of their position after three years, during which time they had many other duties and may not have had much time to devote to New France.[36] And finally, it was the procurators who may have had the most to gain by ensuring that the *Relations* were as exciting and informative as possible, as their job included raising funds for the mission.

The following pages reconstruct, as best as possible, the editorial work performed on the missionaries' annual reports in Paris during four stages of their history: the initial period from 1632 to 1638 when no Paris-based procurator was in place, Charles Lalemant's time in this role from 1638 to 1649, Paul Le Jeune's tenure from 1649 to 1662, and Paul Ragueneau's term, which lasted through the end of the published series. No complete record exists of what was done to each of the New France reports in Paris before being sent to the printer. The manuscripts sent from Quebec could be compared to the published versions of the texts to assess how Paris-based editors shaped the texts, but they do not seem to have survived, as noted in the first chapter of this book. The effort below to reconstruct the work done by the procurators in Paris therefore relies on other clues, fragmentary glimpses of the process that do not represent its full extent. The printed *Relations* themselves frequently identify material that was added in Paris. Variant printings of some of the texts reveal the hand of an editor or censor at work altering or eliminating some of the New France superior's words. And other works, including a contemporaneous handwritten copy of one of the reports, a letter written by Marie de l'Incarnation, and a book about the life of a Hospitaller nun in Quebec that Ragueneau wrote after his return to France, also offer insights into the kinds of changes that could be made in Paris, and by whom.

* * *

There are signs that someone paid close attention to the manuscript *Relations* from New France between 1632 and 1638, when the New France mission had no formally appointed procurator in Paris to oversee its affairs there, deleting some material, adding other information, and keeping a close eye on both politics and propriety. A contemporaneous handwritten copy of Le Jeune's report for 1634 includes a number of passages that do not appear in the printed version of the text, including a complaint about mistakes in the typesetting of Indigenous words in the previous year's text and descriptions of various aspects of Innu daily life and culture: food, jewellery, tattooing, body painting, piercing, and the addition of decorative touches to their clothing.[37] Whether these passages were left out to avoid burdening readers with tedious detail, as Campeau suggested, or because this information risked undermining the *Relation's* explicit claims about the Innu's exclusive focus on survival and lack of interest in aesthetics, their omission from the printed version of the text testifies to the hand of an editor at work that is only visible thanks to the fortunate existence of the manuscript copy.[38] Additions to the texts were also made in Paris during this time. The report for 1635 contains news from the Jesuit missionary Julien Perrault, who was then working in the settlement of Sainte-Anne on Cape Breton Island. The ships that carried news and goods to and from this island were not the same ones that serviced Quebec. As Paul Le Jeune noted in the first chapter of his 1635 *Relation*, "we have no communication with our Fathers who are in the Residences of Sainte Anne and of Saint Charles, except by way of France; hence neither letters nor other things should be sent to us to hold for them, but they should be given to those Vessels which go to these French settlements. It follows also that I can say nothing of the things which take place in these Residences, on account of their remoteness and the little commerce we have with them."[39] Le Jeune's comment shows that his manuscript report did not include Perrault's news, which therefore could only have been added to the year's *Relation* in Paris, and also that the Quebec mission superior did not know ahead of time that an editor would do so.

Changes were also made to the 1633 and 1635 *Relations* during printing, apparently both to flatter the powerful and to avoid offending readers. A variant printing of the first edition of Paul Le Jeune's 1633 report omitted the expressions of gratitude to the Jesuit provincial, to Samuel de Champlain, and to unnamed people who supported the mission in various ways that appeared in the earliest printed copies, apparently to make room for an effusive expression of gratitude to Cardinal Richelieu for his wisdom and vision in supporting the settlement of New France. This new material was written in the first person, making it appear to be Le Jeune's own words despite the fact that it could only have been added to the text in France. Wrote an anonymous editor in Paris, "It occurs to me sometimes that this great man, who, by his admirable wisdom and peerless conduct of business, has acquired such renown on earth, is preparing for a very brilliant crown of glory in heaven, for the care that he shows himself to have for the conversion of so many souls that faithlessness causes to be lost in these wild lands. I pray affectionately for him every day, and our company, having by his means occasion to glorify God in this so noble initiative, will have for him an eternal obligation."[40] Two years later, the name of one of Richelieu's favoured allies, the lieutenant governor of France's settlement in Acadia, was added to the *Relation* during the printing process, at the end of a passage recounting the arrival of ships from France and which settlements they were expected to visit before returning across the ocean: "On the fourth of July, a shallop sent from Monsieur du Plessis Bochart, commandant of the fleet, gladdened all our French, – assuring us of his coming, and that he was followed by eight strong ships, six for Tadoussac and two for Miscou, not including the one sent to Cape Breton and the coast of Acadia, to Monsieur the Commandant de Razilly."[41] Another change to the same *Relation* removed a reference to a muskrat's testicles as the source of its distinctive odour, attributing it instead to "a part of its body," apparently to avoid the potentially offensive mention of this specific anatomical part.[42]

There is nothing particularly unusual about the notion that small corrections could be introduced to a text during the printing process. Variant printings of *Relations* throughout the series show that typos, punctuation errors, faulty pagination, and other small blemishes were often corrected while the texts were still rolling off the press, as was common at the time.[43] But the changes made to the 1633 and 1635 *Relations* were more significant, altering the meaning of the New France superior's words by thanking different people; explicitly acknowledging an ally of Richelieu who had gone unnamed in the first printed version of the text, and who in any case had nothing to do with Quebec at this time; and making an observation about a particular animal's anatomy less precise than it apparently had been in the Quebec superior's version of the text. That changes like these were made while printing was already in progress suggests that the process by which the manuscript reports were reviewed was not yet working smoothly enough, in these early years of the series, to identify every substantive editorial intervention that was needed before pages started coming off the press. More importantly, they show that the manuscripts prepared by the New France mission superior were not viewed in Paris as the work of an individual whose intent as expressed in his report ought to be respected in all cases. It was acceptable to omit some of his words and even to make him appear to say things he had not said.

None of the above-mentioned departures from the Quebec manuscripts in these earliest years of the published series – additions, deletions, and substitutions midway through the printing process – can be attributed with any confidence to anyone in particular. Charles Lalemant could have inserted the expression of gratitude to Richelieu in the 1633 *Relation*, but he was in Quebec when the rest of the above-mentioned changes were made. It is easy enough to imagine a Jesuit censor deciding that testicles need not be mentioned, or even that descriptions of Innu tattooing, body painting, and fashion did not count as edifying news. But it seems unlikely that a person charged with reviewing the texts for adherence to Jesuit standards would add material like Perrault's report from the Sainte-Anne mission or, once printing had already started, the names of well-connected figures in France. The two provincials who served during this initial period, Barthélemy Jacquinot and Éstienne Binet, may have been responsible themselves for all of these changes, as they presumably would have been able to recognize opportunities to please powerful figures in France, to include information that had arrived separately from the manuscript *Relation*, and to identify parts of the New France superior's text that might not be fit for publication. And it is possible, of course, that some other person – or more than one – was designated by the provincials or by the mission superior in New France to perform this work.[44] What is certain is that whoever was responsible for editing the *Relations* during this time before the formal appointment of a procurator avoided drawing attention to their own work. The changes mentioned above are visible to anyone who takes the time to closely examine the variants of the printed texts and the 1634 manuscript copy, but none of them are explicitly signalled in the texts themselves. At this earliest stage of the series' history, it seems that a premium was placed on preserving readers' impression that the New France *Relations* were the simple, direct accounts of missionaries in the field.

This pattern continued, for the most part, during Charles Lalemant's term as procurator beginning in 1639. Most of the *Relations* that appeared between this date and 1648 contain no explicit sign that they had been edited in Paris, and there are no manuscript copies or substantive variant printings that reveal any significant changes. The sole exception came in the annual report for 1643. The opening letter of Barthélemy Vimont's report on this year's events in Quebec contains a warning that readers should not expect to find in its pages any news about his colleagues' work among the Wendat because it had been intercepted and stolen by adversaries: "Your Reverence will not this year find your usual satisfaction in the Relation; for the best part of it, which is that concerning the Hurons, was taken by the Hiroquois, together with our Fathers' correspondence."[45] The thirteenth chapter of the printed text, however, is entirely devoted to news from this mission. Its opening paragraph explains the discrepancy: "some Frenchmen, and some [Sauvages] of our allies, – marching afterward in the footsteps of those Barbarians, our enemies, – picked up some papers which they had thrown into the woods, or which had escaped from their hands; and, they having caused us to receive these in France, we have collected from them what follows, in order to console those who interest themselves with so much love in the conversion of those poor peoples, and to give them a little knowledge of what our Lord continues to effect in that extremity of the world."[46] France is explicitly identified here as the location where news of the Wendat mission had been added to the *Relation*. And the fourteenth chapter of Vimont's annual report also must have been added in Paris, since it was composed mostly of letters to Charles Lalemant and another unspecified person from the Jesuit missionary Isaac Jogues that he had composed in a Dutch settlement in what is now New York and in Rennes, France after escaping from Haudenosaunee captors.[47]

These two chapters seem to have been added to the 1643 *Relation* not on the initiative of Charles Lalemant, but rather of Paul Le Jeune. The former superior of the Quebec mission had been dispatched to Paris that year to lobby for resources to defend the French settlement from Haudenosaunee adversaries.[48] His involvement in adding chapter 13, on events in the Wendat mission, is practically certain thanks to a passage it contains that recounts the arrival in Quebec of an unnamed surgeon who was on his way to take the place at Sainte-Marie of René Goupil, who had been captured and killed by Haudenosaunee the previous year: "Another young Surgeon, well versed in his art, and well known in the Hospital at Orleans, where he has given proofs of his virtue and of his competence, has chosen to take the place of his comrade; he has crossed into New France; and I who write this last chapter, seeing him on the point of going up to the Hurons, represented to him all the perils into which he was about to plunge."[49] This surgeon is recognizable as François Gendron, who, as noted in chapter 3, served as a *donné* at Sainte-Marie.[50] This passage, then, could only have been written by a Jesuit who had been in New France when the ships arrived in the spring or summer of 1643, but who was in Paris later that year when the material used to write chapter 13 was received and added to the manuscript *Relation*. These details do not match Charles Lalemant, who had been in France for several years by this point, or any other Jesuit except Paul Le Jeune. There is no such smoking gun to indicate Le Jeune's involvement in the addition of the fourteenth chapter of the 1643 *Relation*, which mostly comprises excerpts of Jogues's letters, but his involvement seems all but certain given the lack of any visible sign that Charles Lalemant ever intervened in the texts in this way and Le Jeune's unabashed insertion of himself into the previous chapter.[51] Still, it seems that Lalemant must have been involved in at least some way because two of the three letters that formed the basis of chapter 14 had been addressed to him personally. Whatever the case, it can be said that, with the sole exception of the 1643 *Relation* that was prepared while Le Jeune was temporarily in France, the annual reports from the New France mission that appeared during Charles Lalemant's time as procurator scrupulously preserve the texts' appearance as having been written entirely in Quebec.

Perhaps not surprisingly, in light of Paul Le Jeune's transparent addition of at least one chapter to the 1643 *Relation*, his own term as procurator starting in 1649 marked the beginning of a new approach to preparing the text for print, in at least three ways: the frequency with which material was added to the manuscripts in Paris increased dramatically, the kind of news that could be added at this stage expanded to include events that had not taken place in North America, and Paris came to be presented in at least some cases as a site of composition of the texts in its own right. It is worth briefly examining each of these points.

First, many of the *Relations* that appeared during this period – including those recounting events in 1648–49, 1650, 1650–51, 1653–54, 1655–56, 1657–58, and 1660–61 – contain material that was explicitly acknowledged to have been added to the manuscripts in Paris.[52] Le Jeune did not always leave clues to his own identity as the person responsible for these additions, as he had in the 1643 report, but he did at least once provide enough information to rule out the involvement of another possible editor mentioned above, the provincial. The addition to the 1650 text of a letter from the missionary Jérôme Lalemant to then-provincial Claude de Lingendes was preceded by a sentence appended to what had been the final chapter of the manuscript sent from Quebec: "I thought that this Chapter would conclude the Relation for this year; but – Father Hierôme Lallemant having returned from new France by the last vessel, and not having met at Paris our Reverend Father Provincial – we will insert here the letter which he sent to the latter in order to render an account of the missions which he has for so long a time directed at this end of the world."[53]

Second, some of Le Jeune's changes during his time as procurator concerned events that had taken place in France or on ships at sea, and therefore could not have been known to any of his Jesuit colleagues on the other side of the Atlantic Ocean. To the second edition of the report for 1649 that he prepared immediately upon his return to France, for example, Le Jeune explicitly acknowledged adding a story about the sinking of a ship bound for New France, the reluctant rescue of its crew by an English vessel, and their eventual arrival back in France – all without ever reaching Quebec.[54] The following year, he added an account of the unhappy experiences of a Haudenosaunee man who had travelled to France in Le Jeune's company in 1649, after it was concluded that it was unsafe to allow him to return to his people because he had observed Quebec closely enough to spot its vulnerabilities. The man, whose name Le Jeune did not mention, slipped on the ice and injured his foot in Dieppe, prompting the Jesuit to leave him there to heal and continue on to Paris. When the man eventually arrived in Paris on 20 January 1650, he had a fever that proved fatal. Le Jeune reported these facts along with some details of the man's reactions to France – his astonishment at seeing the port of Le Havre full of ships, his aversion to French shoes – and also included letters written by those who had cared for him after his injury and during his illness.[55] And the 1650–51 *Relation* contains a letter addressed to the procurator and written in France by the Jesuit Martin Lyonne, who had just returned from Quebec carrying the year's manuscript report, recounting the frosty reception his ship received upon its arrival, apparently due to strife between France's nobility and the Crown that was unrelated to the mission.[56] It is easy to understand how Le Jeune could have concluded that each of these episodes would be interesting to readers of the *Relations*. But none of them could have been included in the manuscript prepared in Quebec, since they concerned events that had taken place on the other side of the Atlantic Ocean. They would have been entirely unknown to the Jesuits whose names appeared as authors on the title pages of the annual reports for 1648–49, 1650, and 1651–52. In these cases, news was carried by the *Relations* not only from Quebec to Paris, but also vice versa, since the texts seem to have been routinely sent back to Quebec after publication, as mentioned in the previous chapter.

Finally, Paris was often presented in the *Relations* during Le Jeune's term as procurator as a key site in the texts' preparation. This is the cumulative effect of all of the above-mentioned additions made in France to manuscripts prepared in New France, but it is especially true of the small number of texts that Le Jeune composed entirely or nearly so during his time in this role. He did so at least four times, including the 1651–52 report mentioned at the beginning of this chapter, when circumstances left the Jesuits in Paris with no annual report from New France to send to the printer. The 1652–53 *Relation* opens with a letter from the Quebec Superior – François-Joseph Le Mercier, by this time – reporting that "we send to Father Paul le Jeune, Procurator of our Missions, the account of both our good and our ill fortunes, in order that he may present it to Your Reverence."[57] The first chapter of the text, however, tells of the loss of whatever Le Mercier had sent at the hands of English raiders who boarded the ship that was transporting it to Europe, and of the consequent composition of the year's report on the basis of recovered scraps of letters and reports.[58] The 1654–55 *Relation* prepared in New France was stolen from the messenger who had been charged with carrying it from La Rochelle to Paris after its arrival from New France. The thief scattered its pages, causing Le Jeune to publish two letters he had received from Le Mercier in its place, along with some material he wrote himself on the basis of "what we have learned from some Letters, and from the mouths of those who have recently returned from New France."[59] And finally, a prefatory letter Le Jeune wrote for the 1656–57 *Relation* explained of the Quebec superior's manuscript report that "the Ship to which it had been confided was taken by the Spaniards, and all the Letters on board were thrown into the Sea; and this has compelled me to gather together, in the little Book which I present to Your Reverence, all that could be recovered of those Letters and of some other Memoirs which reached us too late last year."[60] All four of these texts, then, explicitly identify themselves as having been prepared in Paris by Le Jeune due to the unavailability of a manuscript *Relation* from New France.

Among the annual reports that Le Jeune composed in Paris, the 1652–53 report stands out for how clearly it reflects the unusual circumstances of its preparation, and how frequently the procurator reminded readers thereof. Reporting on the capture of the Jesuit Joseph-Antoine Poncet de La Rivière by the Haudenosaunee, for example, Le Jeune explained the fragmentary nature of his information: "The Father was bidden, upon his return, to commit to paper his capture and all his adventures; he obeyed with reluctance, desiring that his Crosses be known only to the King of the crucified; but a part of his account was torn up by the English. After citing two or three short passages from a letter written on this subject, we shall follow, in this Chapter, what has come into our hands [after having reported two or three little notes from a letter written on this subject]."[61] On the subject of Poncet's eventual deliverance from captivity among the Haudenosaunee and reappearance in Quebec, Le Jeune again reminded his readers that the disastrous loss of the ship carrying the year's news from Quebec limited what he could say: "The letters and memoirs which told of his arrival and of the councils held for the establishment of peace, were lost in the vessel taken by the English."[62] And acknowledging the lack of news in the *Relation* about the Jesuits' efforts to bring about religious conversion, Le Jeune explained that "I have not sufficient information to speak in detail of all these peoples and all these Nations. I will relate a little circumstance, taken from what has come into my hands."[63] There are more examples of this kind, and also many passages in which Le Jeune simply reminded readers that his knowledge came only from what he had read.[64] Of the danger posed by the Haudenosaunee to settlers in Montreal, for example, Le Jeune wrote that "I have read in a letter that the routes taken by them in their flight were found all covered with their blood; and that, a considerable time after their departure, the dogs kept bringing back fragments of human bodies to the French settlement. 'There has not passed,' say the memoirs which have reached us, 'a single month of the year in which these Hunters have not visited us by stealth and tried to surprise us.'"[65]

Le Jeune's frequent references to the limitations he faced in composing the 1652–53 *Relation* are understandable as an honest explanation of his inability to say as much as he might have liked about some of the year's most sensational events, like the captivity of his Jesuit colleague. But it is worth noting that these remarks also run counter to the expectation set in the very title of this annual report which, like most of the others in the series, specifically presented it as a text prepared in Quebec that had been "Sent to the Reverend Father Provincial of the Province of France. By the Superior of the Missions of the same Society."[66] This *Relation* superficially resembles most of those prepared in Quebec, but there is no mistaking its text as having been prepared anywhere but France. By frequently describing himself reading the scraps of information that had found their way to him in Paris and reminding readers of the toll the capture of ships had on his ability to share the year's news, Le Jeune rhetorically distanced the *Relation* from events in New France in a way that is unusual, both compared to his own earlier reports and to the series as a whole. He could have simply summarized the news he had received as best as possible, without so much commentary on his own work or the quality of his raw materials. This case is an interesting counterpoint, then, to Paul Ragueneau's account of the torture and death of Jean de Brébeuf and Gabriel Lalemant examined in the third chapter of this book. Whereas Ragueneau avoided signalling how he knew particular pieces of information as part of a broader effort to draw readers as close to the action as possible, Le Jeune in the 1652–53 *Relation* acknowledged at every turn his own distance from and imperfect knowledge of events, thereby reminding his readers that they also were far away from and poorly informed about what had happened in New France. This is perhaps a surprising choice in a text intended to foster readers' interest in and connection to the New France mission, and one that can be explained as a result of the abnormal circumstances. But it can also be seen as a manifestation of personal style. Le Jeune was not inattentive to the need to craft his texts to send the right message to his readers, as shown in chapter 1, but it seems he also sometimes could not resist placing his own experiences in the foreground when narrating events in which he did not participate, even from his perch in Paris.

That Le Jeune's approach to his work on the *Relations* in Paris was unique is confirmed by the way the three aspects of his work explored above – the frequent addition of material, the insertion of news that would have been entirely unknown in New France, and the decision not to rigorously preserve the texts' appearance as reports from New France – did not continue during the term of Paul Ragueneau as procurator starting in 1662. Several substantial passages were added to the texts after this date, but they were limited to material that had been prepared in New France and silent or enigmatic on the question of who had inserted them. The final chapter of the 1662–63 *Relation*, for example, is an anonymous account of a journey along the primary riverine corridor for the movement of goods, people, and information in New France, the opening lines of which make clear that it had been added to the Jesuits' annual report in Paris: "While this Relation was being printed, there fell into our hands the account of a journey performed by a person of merit expressly to reconnoiter the country of New France, from the entrance of the Gulf of Saint Lawrence up to Montreal. Some persons have thought it fitting to make an extract from this narrative, and publish it in this Relation."[67] Similarly appended to the report for 1663–64, although not afforded its own chapter, is a short account of a Guyohkohnyoh (Cayuga) Haudenosaunee diplomatic visit to Quebec, billed as an "Extract from a Letter Written at Quebec on the 22nd of September." Its opening sentence identifies the place of its composition as Quebec and specifies that it was written after the manuscript annual report had already been sent to France, leaving no doubt that this material was added to the manuscript in Paris even if this is not made explicit: "Since dispatching the Relation by the Ship which sailed from here on the 31st of August, the Onionenhronnons have come on an Embassy, reaching Quebec on the 18th of September."[68] There is no mistaking where either of these texts was added to the *Relation*, but there are no clear signs of the identity of the person responsible of the kind that Le Jeune had sometimes included.

There is, however, a third case that can be attributed with near certainty to Paul Ragueneau, on the basis of clues external to the *Relations*. The annual report for 1667–68 ends with a letter from the superior of the Hospitallers in Quebec, Marie de Saint Bonaventure de Jésus, reporting the death of her colleague Catherine de Saint-Augustin in May 1668.[69] It is addressed to "My Reverend Mother," indicating that it was not sent directly to any of the Jesuits who were involved in preparing the text, and a note at the end of the letter explains where it came from: "This Circular Letter was sent for the Convents which are in France, belonging to the Institute of the Hospital Nuns of Dieppe. He who was charged to have it printed, having received many authentic Memoirs on the life and death of that blessed deceased, has deemed it proper to add here the following particulars."[70] It is not clear from the way this note is phrased who, exactly, had been charged with printing the letter, or if the publication in question was meant to come in the *Relation* or separately. But attentive readers could have solved the mystery several years later, when Ragueneau's book on the life and works of the deceased nun – whom he knew intimately, having served as her confessor and spiritual director while in New France and corresponded with her after his return to France – appeared in print in Paris.[71] A chapter of this book recounting the nun's death begins with an acknowledgment of its source, the same circular letter that had appeared in the *Relation*, and reprints much of it.[72] Ragueneau wrote in his dedicatory epistle that he had been charged with writing the biography of this distinguished nun by bishop of Petra François de Laval, who also then served as vicar apostolic of New France and furnished the Jesuit procurator with unspecified memoirs approved by his own hand for the task.[73] These clues point to Ragueneau as the person who added the letter to the published report and who wrote the above-mentioned "particulars" that followed the letter. These amount to approximately twenty pages in the seventeenth-century edition, detailing various aspects of the deceased nun's life and career, followed by two pages lauding the contributions of both the Ursulines and the Augustinian hospitaller nuns – in short, a substantial text about the contributions of women religious that otherwise would not have appeared in the year's *Relation*.

The three former missionaries who served as Paris-based procurator for the New France mission approached their responsibilities differently, at least as regards the *Relations*. Charles Lalemant either did not add anything to the texts at all or disguised his interventions so thoroughly that they are indistinguishable from the material composed in Quebec. There is no obvious explanation in the textual record for Lalemant's apparent restraint, but it may not be a coincidence that he was the only one of the mission's procurators who had never prepared an annual report of his own for publication while serving as superior in Quebec. Perhaps he simply felt less licensed by his own experiences to intervene in the texts the way Le Jeune and Ragueneau did. Paul Le Jeune, for his part, was a prolific author of annual mission reports long before his departure from Quebec and continued to take an active role once installed in Paris. As shown above, the published texts themselves testify to his intervention in all those that appeared during his term as procurator except those of 1658–59 and 1659–60, whether by adding material to a manuscript prepared in Quebec or by fashioning the entire report himself. And this accounts only for cases in which there is clear evidence of Le Jeune's work. There are other passages that attentive readers have attributed to him on the basis of a feeling of recognizing his particular style of writing.[74] Even excluding such uncertain cases, the examples presented above make clear that Le Jeune actively shaped the New France *Relations* from his post in Paris, sometimes explicitly identifying himself as the person responsible for introducing material to the texts in Paris, adding news about events that had taken place far from New France, and sometimes even drawing focus away from the mission by foregrounding his own work and perceptions. Ragueneau was more self-effacing in his additions to the texts, but nevertheless explicitly signalled them to readers. It would not quite be accurate to say that it was a matter of routine for material to be added to the texts in Paris. There are many *Relations* from before 1649 and after 1665 that contain no obvious evidence of editorial intervention after the manuscripts were received in France. But the cases discussed above show that this was at least possible no matter who was procurator or provincial, and that Paris was an especially important site in the creation of the New France Jesuits' annual reports during Le Jeune's term in the former role.

The examination above of the work of three Paris-based procurators focuses on the additions they sometimes made to the texts, but there are reasons to think they – or perhaps censors or the provincial – also decided not to print many things that had been included in the mission superiors' manuscript reports. Direct evidence of this is limited to the above-described passages of Le Jeune's 1634 report that are preserved in a handwritten copy and the changes made during the printing process in 1633 and 1635, but Marie de l'Incarnation reported in a 1668 letter to her son that the omission of material in Paris was a common occurrence. She mentioned that she had received complaints two years in a row from one of her correspondents about decisions made in Paris to leave certain unspecified news out of the Jesuits' texts. Wrote the Ursuline nun, "Many things are edited out of the *Relations* once the copies sent from here arrive in France. Madame la Duchesse de Senneçay, who has given me the honour of writing to me all these years, told me last year how displeased she was about something that had been edited out, and she told me something similar this year."[75]

As discussed in the previous chapter, Marie de l'Incarnation was positioned as well as any other non-Jesuit to be aware of how the missionaries' published texts differed from the manuscripts prepared in Quebec. And the fact that her correspondent also knew of the contents of the manuscripts in enough detail to notice how they were altered upon publication suggests the degree to which it was once well known – if now often forgotten or ignored – that the text prepared by the New France mission superior could at least sometimes be quite different from what eventually found its way into print.

* * *

No matter who edited them or where they were composed, nearly all of the *Relations* eventually made their way into the hands of Paris's leading bookseller. Sébastien Cramoisy had inherited a modest bookselling business from his grandfather Sébastien Nivelle in 1606, when he was in his early twenties, and swiftly made himself, in Henri-Jean Martin's estimation, "the undoubted leader of the Paris book trade."[76] He benefitted in this endeavour from the ways in which the political and religious disputes of the Wars of Religion had weakened the publishing houses that had dominated the sixteenth-century French book trade. Their leaders disappeared or left Paris for the countryside or Protestant-friendly places like Geneva.[77] More than any other bookseller in Paris, Cramoisy thrived in this context. By 1621, he was the official printer to the Duke of Lorraine, the first in a series of prestigious appointments. He served as syndic of the printing guild from 1628 to 1630 and again in 1643, won a monopoly on the printing of financial records in 1629, became the king's printer in 1633, and took the directorship of the *Imprimerie Royale* in 1640, also serving in leadership roles for hospitals and religious organizations.[78] But above all, he published and sold books: more than 2,500 titles between 1606 and 1669, amounting to one in ten books published in Paris and more than any other bookseller of the time, whether French or foreign.[79] When he handed over the business to his grandson Sébastien Mabre-Cramoisy in 1669, after seven years working together, he had already indelibly linked himself to the Jesuit *Relations* by publishing all but one of them over the previous four decades, the sole exception being the 1637 report brought forth by Jean Le Boullenger in Rouen, perhaps as a gesture of gratitude to the mission supporter Madeleine de la Peltrie for her pledge to establish a religious school for young girls in Quebec.[80]

Even aside from Cramoisy's status as Paris's leading publisher, it is not surprising that he was entrusted with bringing the *Relations* into print due to his already longstanding interest in New France and close relationship to the Society of Jesus. He was a member of the Company of the Hundred Associates, which held a monopoly on trade in New France starting in 1627, and began serving as its agent in 1633, taking an active role in promoting the affairs of the distant settlement in the French capital.[81] He was also a member of the Congrégation des Messieurs, a Jesuit-lay fellowship in Paris.[82] And his track record of bringing forth Jesuit texts was already well established, making him practically, if not by formal designation, the Society of Jesus's official bookseller in Paris. By the time the New France *Relations* began to appear, he had already published translations of missionary letters from Japan and other sites in Asia, textbooks for use in Jesuit colleges, and scholarly tomes written by individual members of the Society.[83] He also maintained a correspondence with the Jesuit leadership in Rome, apparently receiving more letters from superiors general of the Society than any other non-Jesuit in France between 1628 and 1666.[84] His specific interest in the New France mission led him to become the single largest donor of books to the Jesuit college library in Quebec, at least to judge by the inscriptions in books once held in that collection that are now housed in various Canadian libraries.[85] Cramoisy's largesse also extended to meeting the needs of the Jesuits and Augustinian Hospitaller nuns for medical supplies out of his own pocket.[86] In sum, his involvement and interest in the New France mission extended well beyond a simple commercial arrangement between client and bookseller.

Even though Cramoisy held various titles as official printer, in truth he printed nothing himself. Booksellers at this time acted as publishers, and the two roles were not distinct in the way they usually are now. Printing was for the most part carried out in separate shops by master printers who were paid by the job, with the help of the wage earners they employed. There were seventy-five such operations in Paris in 1644, with 176 presses between them, and Cramoisy alone is known to have used seven of these shops.[87] The feverish pace of work when a book was being printed probably explains some of the characteristics of the printed *Relations*. It took at least two workers to operate a press, one who pulled the handle to press the machine's plate against the type and a second to add ink to the forms when necessary, put blank sheets of paper in place, and remove them after printing.[88] An apprentice would normally be charged with dampening the paper before printing and hanging it to dry when it came off the press. These three workers could print one sheet every ten seconds, a pace that would be maintained for up to fourteen hours per day. While these men were working, another was typically nearby setting type into forms in preparation to print the next page. This step in the process was the most prone to causing delays. A 240-page, octavo-sized book printed in 1,350 copies would take two weeks to print, but thirty days to be composed in the forms. Work would have been much slower in some shops, in which the compositor himself also operated the press. The pressure to set type quickly into the forms, coupled with the varying levels of education of the men who did so – in particular, the inability of some to understand Latin, Greek, and, presumably, Indigenous languages – and the fact that most printers could not afford to hire a dedicated corrector, explains the large number of typos and other small errors that afflicted many printed books during this time, including the *Relations*.[89]

Cramoisy's lack of personal involvement in the manual labour of printing the New France Jesuits' annual reports does not mean he left no mark on them. There are five texts that he seems to have had at least some role in adding to the *Relations*. Appended to the end of the 1650 report, in its second edition, is a short letter from the mother superior of the Augustinian nuns in Quebec to an unnamed "bourgeois de Paris." It describes how the destruction of the Wendat mission had increased the burden on her community's hospital as Wendats fleeing the violence settled near its doors.[90] Some copies of the published text for 1664–65 contain a letter from the same nun to "Monsieur * * * *, Citizen of Paris."[91] This letter and a list of needed supplies that follows it had been printed and distributed before the *Relation* was published, to judge by its separate pagination and page signatures. McCoy speculates plausibly that the copies that remained after the letter's initial distribution were inserted between the printed pages of the Jesuits' annual report as a way of extending the reach of the nun's request for help, which would explain why it is not present in every surviving copy of the *Relation*.[92] The following year, another letter from the Augustinian superior also bears its own page numbers and appears to have been printed and distributed separately initially, but this time it was listed in the *Relation's* table of contents and bound with the annual report instead of merely being inserted between its pages. The letter in this case was printed twice, perhaps so there would be enough copies for the entire print run of the Jesuits' text once the first edition of the letter was exhausted.[93] After the full integration of the nun's letter in this case, the following two annual reports reverted to what had been done the year prior, distributing surplus copies as inserts only.[94]

The *Relations* themselves do not include any explicit indication of who inserted this nun's letters – or in two cases, 1650 and 1665–66, incorporated them into the published text – but there are good reasons to believe Cramoisy was involved. He had long been a supporter of this religious community in Quebec and corresponded regularly with its superior.[95] On this basis, he has sometimes been identified as the recipient of the 1650 letter, although this is speculative.[96] A stronger case can be made for the four letters incorporated or inserted into *Relations* in the 1660s. The list of supplies needed by the Hospitaller nuns that follows each of the letters includes a request that readers wishing to support the hospital send their contributions to Cramoisy to be forwarded to New France, pointing to the printer's involvement in making the community's needs known.[97] Additional evidence of Cramoisy's involvement comes in the above-referenced 1668 letter from Marie de l'Incarnation to her son. Wrote the nun, "M.C. who prints the *Relations* and who has a strong affection for the Hospitallers here, inserted therein upon his own initiative a letter that the superior had written him, which caused quite a commotion in France."[98] She did not specify which of the cases she had in mind or the precise reason for the commotion it caused. Perhaps this commotion was related to the content of the letter, its plea for support for the Augustinians' efforts. Or maybe the one-year promotion of the superior's letter to an integral part of the *Relation* in 1665–66 was seen as too great a liberty on the part of the printer. Whatever the case, the subsequent return to the previous year's less-intrusive insertion of the letter between the printed pages suggests that this method of using the Jesuits' text to spread news about the efforts of their female colleagues must have had at least the tacit approval of Jesuit authorities in Paris.

* * *

The clues assembled in this chapter by no means constitute an exhaustive record of how the manuscript *Relations* were shaped in Paris prior to publication. The cases of the annual reports for 1633, 1634, and 1635 and the 1668 comments of Marie de l'Incarnation discussed above suggest that in all likelihood many changes to the texts were made before printing began. Barring the discovery of more pre-publication manuscripts to which published reports could be compared, it is unlikely that it will ever be possible to fully account for what, exactly, was written in Quebec and how it was changed in Paris. The cases examined in this chapter nonetheless are sufficient to show that editors in Paris could play a more significant role in the process by which the annual reports on events in New France were created than scholars have tended to acknowledge. Without their work, the texts would look quite different in many cases – and in others would not exist at all. The fact that this aspect of the *Relations'* production has usually received only fleeting attention reflects the way their stature as a trove of information about a place and its inhabitants far from France now overshadows characteristics of the texts that do not fit this reputation. The value of the texts as a rich source of details about the past is incontestable. But the ways in which they were shaped in Paris make clear that the modern perception of them as reports created by missionaries in the field, perhaps with some editorial and mostly inconsequential adjustments in Paris, is a poor reflection of how members of the Society of Jesus themselves understood them. Both in this particular mission and in others throughout the world, texts like the *Relations* were understood first and foremost as the production of institutional knowledge. Scholars examining Jesuit mission writings from other parts of globe – particularly Brazil and China – have shown how such reports were altered in Europe prior to publication, and have argued that their authors well understood that they represented collective knowledge instead of the work of individuals that ought to be respected as such.[99]

There are signs that the New France Jesuits also understood this. In his 1638 *Relation*, written before New France had its first procurator in Paris, Paul Le Jeune provided a window into how he understood his own work as author in relation to the editorial process on the other side of the Atlantic Ocean when he complained of the printing errors that plagued the previous year's report, and commented in particular on one amusing mistake. Wrote Le Jeune, "In chapter 8, on page 145, – where some quarrel I had with a sorcerer is in question, – the Printer makes me, in place of employing exorcisms against the devil, use a sword. This is what I wrote in the original: 'In fact, I intended to employ a sort of exorcism'; the printer made it: 'In fact, I intended to use a sword hereafter.' I must confess that this pretty witticism made me laugh." For Le Jeune, this was not only a humorous mix-up, but also an opportunity to reflect on his own status as author and the ways in which his control over his own text was limited. Continued Le Jeune, “When one speaks from so great a distance, [one does not make one’s thoughts so well understood]. Writing is a mute language, which [changes as easily as] it is easy to take one Character for another; a child is made to say whatever one wishes, when its father is absent.”[100] Le Jeune understood himself to be an active creator – the metaphorical father of a child – but also at the mercy of unnamed others who could make his child/*Relation* say something other than what he had intended.[101]

7

Reading the Jesuit *Relations* from the Seventeenth Century to Today

A set of seventy-three volumes collectively titled *The Jesuit Relations and Allied Documents*, published under the supervision of Reuben Gold Thwaites between 1896 and 1901, fills most of a section of shelves in practically every North American research library. Its matching dull-gold tomes, or the digital reproductions that present them as items on a long online list, give even a casual observer the impression of an enormous, uniform corpus.[1] With this set of volumes continuing to serve as the standard edition of the New France Jesuits' annual reports more than a century after its appearance, it is perhaps little wonder that scholars often describe the texts in terms that suggest coherence and unity, calling them, to mention just a few examples, "an important document," a "voluminous and important written source," and a "documentary mass."[2] This chapter examines how this common perception arose, how texts that appeared individually over the course of forty years and that sometimes do not much resemble each other came to be widely understood and treated as a unit. This process, in which Thwaites's edition was only one factor, is as much a part of the story of how the Jesuit *Relations* came to occupy a prominent place in scholarly understandings of the past – and on library shelves and in digital repositories, for that matter – as any of the various steps in their creation during the seventeenth century that are considered in the first six chapters of this book.

In tracing the *Relations'* journey from individual yearly reports to voluminous corpus, this chapter attends in particular to the conditions of readers' access to the texts in various times and places since their initial publication. As more than one scholar has observed, the way any text is perceived and used depends not only on factors like the particular choices of its author or its readers' preoccupations and interpretations, but also on external circumstances and the form in which interested parties encounter it. Changes to the context of a book's reception or to the material qualities of the text itself inevitably also influence how readers understand it.[3] As this chapter will show, the ways in which readers have experienced the *Relations*, and their reasons for doing so, have more than once changed dramatically since their initial publication. While these annual reports were still coming off the press each year in the seventeenth century, readers in religious communities and among France's cultural and political elite consumed them one at a time, year by year, and could even shape subsequent reports by corresponding with the missionary authors or their counterparts in France. In nineteenth-century North America, descriptive essays appeared that defined the corpus in detail for the first time, albeit variously. And bibliophiles and antiquarians competed to collect copies of the individual instalments in the series that were by then difficult to find, assembling the previously scattered texts into complete or nearly complete sets. Researchers throughout the world now have easy access to the Jesuits' annual reports in three large-scale modern editions, each of which presents the *Relations* differently and leaves unmistakable marks on the way the texts tend to be presented in scholarship. The New France Jesuits' annual reports have certainly been read by audiences other than these, in other times and places, but this chapter focuses on these three moments in the history of readers' engagement with the *Relations* because they collectively show how the perceptions and experiences of earlier readers can inform understandings of the texts in the present.

***

It has often been asserted that each of the Jesuit *Relations* was greeted by a large and enthusiastic readership upon its publication in Paris, at least in part on the basis of the large number of editions and variant printings that have been identified in collections in North America and Europe.[4] No precise information about the size of the annual press runs has survived, but it is clear that at least some of the texts were printed repeatedly, apparently to keep up with public demand.[5] As mentioned in the third chapter of this book, the 1649 *Relation* that includes the harrowing story of the torture and death of Jean de Brébeuf and Gabriel Lalemant immediately appeared in four distinct editions, including a bootleg version printed in Lille and a Latin translation in Innsbruck. Many others – including Le Jeune's inaugural text in the series, most of the reports for the 1640s, and various others – appeared in just one edition, albeit sometimes in several variants due to corrections made during the printing process, apparently testifying to a more modest reception.[6] The size of the *Relations'* readership at the time of their publication seems on this evidence to have varied more than is sometimes acknowledged. The very fact of their publication nonetheless indicates a larger audience than the Jesuit provincial in Paris to whom most of them were at least superficially addressed.

In the absence of much independent commentary, the *Relations* themselves are the best source of information on who read them as they appeared year by year during the seventeenth century, and why. The missionaries who prepared these annual reports often made clear whom they understood their audience to be. The first chapter of Paul Le Jeune's 1637 report, for example, catalogues powerful figures in France who apparently had shown keen interest in New France and in the *Relations*, including King Louis XIII, Cardinal Richelieu, the grand master of Malta, the pope, and the French queen Anne of Austria.[7] Also sometimes mentioned, albeit usually not by name, are the wealthy and socially connected ladies and gentlemen of France's polite society, as in Le Jeune's 1633 appeal to such readers for material support for the mission: "There are Ladies in Paris who yearly spend over ten thousand francs in [their petty pleasures]; if they would apply a part of this to gather in the drops of blood that the Son of God shed for so many souls that are going astray daily for want of help, then they would not be put to shame when they appear before God, and must give an account of the goods of which he has made them stewards."[8] And it is clear that potential future missionaries – who, as mentioned in chapter 1, could have encountered the texts in Jesuit colleges – were also among their readers. Jérôme Lalemant's *Relation* for 1647–48 includes an excerpt of a letter from a newly arrived missionary who reported, on the topic of Indigenous converts to Christianity, that he "read the Relations on this subject over and over again, and always with admiration and satisfaction" before becoming a New France missionary himself.[9] The texts' audience could not, however, have included everyone who may have been supportive of the mission or interested in crossing the Atlantic Ocean themselves. Estate inventories show that artisans and merchants were much less likely at this time to own books than members of the clergy, nobility, and legal and medical professions, and that even when they could read they primarily owned devotional works or texts related to their trades.[10] After offering advice to poor people who might want to settle in New France, Le Jeune acknowledged in his 1636 report that such people were unlikely to read his words: "But to whom do I speak? To people who cannot know what I am writing, unless more capable ones than they tell it to them."[11]

The *Relations* also found their way into the hands of people who were not particularly supportive of the Jesuits' efforts in New France.[12] The Franciscan Recollet missionaries who had shared the mission field with the Jesuits from 1625 until both groups were expelled by the British in 1629, for example, seem to have suspected their erstwhile colleagues of working to exclude them when France regained control in 1632.[13] They mounted a vigorous campaign to be allowed to resume work there, and in the process sometimes revealed that they were paying close attention to the Jesuits' annual reports. Former Recollet missionary Gabriel Sagard, for example, wrote his 1636 *Histoire du Canada* as a counterpoint to the Jesuits' texts, in the context of what Marie-Christine Pioffet has recently called a "duel of quills" between the two groups on the subject of the New France mission.[14] While preparing his book between 1634 and 1635, Sagard borrowed material from the *Relations* as they became available, even as he argued for his own order's return to New France. He drew news of a Haudenosaunee attack that killed two Frenchmen in Trois-Rivières from Le Jeune's 1633 *Relation*, content and language about the physical characteristics of beavers from the Jesuit's 1634 report, and an entire sentence, word for word, on the peculiar odour of muskrats from the 1635 text, among other examples.[15] Le Jeune's texts in particular reflect an awareness that people like Sagard were reading his words, and take special care to respond to criticisms, both actual and anticipated.[16] To cite just one example, he directly addressed an unspecified reader's negative assessment of the Jesuits' progress in winning conversions in his 1636 *Relation*: "Among various propositions that have been made to me from Old France, some one asks me how it happens that in so many years so few persons have been baptized. It seems to me that the proposition ought to be reversed, and stated, 'How happens it that in so few years so many persons have been baptized?'"[17] Many readers – powerful decision makers, well-heeled potential financial backers, and would-be future missionaries – apparently awaited the Jesuits' annual reports with enthusiasm, but the mission leaders responsible for compiling them understood that rivals and critics of their work read them too.

The way these various readers encountered the Jesuits' reports – one at a time, as they became available each year – allowed them to react to the news they contained in time for their responses to be accounted for in subsequent texts in the series. There is evidence that the Jesuit authors paid close attention to the questions and criticisms of at least some of these readers. In one particularly clear example, Gaston d'Orléans, brother of King Louis XIII and first in line for the throne in the absence of an heir, complained to Jesuit officials that he found the *Relation* for 1637 too long and repetitive. This criticism is mentioned in a brief 1638 letter from Jesuit superior general Mutio Vitelleschi to the Paris provincial Étienne Binet urging that care be taken to remedy this problem lest a powerful figure and benefactor of the Jesuit college in Blois be angered.[18] It is little wonder, then, that the 1638 report was extremely concise in comparison to its predecessor. It was less than 150 pages long, approximately one-fourth the length of the 1637 *Relation*, and riddled with comments reflecting a new concern for brevity. The opening letter, for example, explains that "people are already so full of the customs of our [Sauvages], and of our little labours for them, that I fear disgust; hence I shall say little of many things – omitting whole chapters, lest I be accused of tediousness."[19] The Jesuit superiors who were charged with preparing each year's text never again wrote such a long report, even when detailing particularly sensational or tragic events such as the capture and torture of missionaries or the dispersal of the Wendat. The longest *Relation* to appear in the following decade came in 1644. At just over four hundred pages, it was nearly two hundred pages shorter than the report that had drawn the ire of Gaston d'Orléans. And years after this incident, missionary authors still shied away from comprehensive accounts of even their most important evangelical work, reporting that they feared a negative reaction from unspecified readers. Barthélemy Vimont's 1645 report, for example, recorded his own concern to avoid displeasing his readers: "We will not say anything in particular of the various residences, or of the various Missions of our Society, for fear of repetition; the new events that occur are so similar to those which have already been written of, that the fear of causing distaste will make us more and more concise."[20]

The *Relations* record numerous other cases in which the reactions of unspecified readers influenced their contents. Le Jeune's 1636 report devoted an entire chapter to answering questions received from readers in France, ranging from the colony's agricultural prospects and whether Spaniards were present to navigational information and what goods the land might offer for export.[21] In the 1639 *Relation*, Jérôme Lalemant justified expanding on his earlier description of the geography of the Wendat territory, where he was then leading the Jesuits' mission, by explaining that someone had asked to know more: "It is not my intention to repeat here what can be found in the preceding Relations, or in other Books which have already treated of this subject, but only to supply the lack of certain particulars, regarding which I have discovered that some information is desired."[22] Three years later, Lalemant responded to readers' requests for information on the eclipses the Jesuits had observed by describing a lunar eclipse that had taken place on 14 April 1642.[23] The missionary authors sometimes also acknowledged readers' questions, but declined to answer them, as in Le Jeune's response to a reader's letter from which he quoted in the 1637 report: "There is reason for great edification in all that has been inserted in the Relation which has been sent. We would ask, however, for some enlightenment as to what we may hope for the establishment of the Christian Religion, and then communication with the countries contiguous to the [Sauvages], their frontiers and boundaries."[24] Le Jeune answered the first of these questions at some length, but offered only a terse reply to the second, reasoning that "as to communication with the neighboring countries, this has been fully answered in the other Relations, and in the books which treat of these lands."[25]

In addition to cases like those discussed above, in which readers' complaints or questions shaped the form or content of the texts, there are also signs that the Jesuits' mere awareness of their readers could influence their writing choices, even in the absence of specific feedback. Examples include material in the texts that was specifically addressed to the potential missionaries who were apparently avid readers of the texts, including full chapters in the 1634 and 1636 *Relations*. Le Jeune's 1634 report from Quebec includes a chapter filled with practical information intended as "weapons necessary for the combat" in which new missionaries would be expected to engage.[26] It explains the hardships such men would encounter if they found themselves wintering with the Innu, as Le Jeune himself had just done, including the discomforts of temporary shelters, unappealing or scarce food, and the behaviour of those hostile to the Jesuits' religious message – in Le Jeune's case, a particularly antagonistic Innu spiritual leader named Carigouan, whom the Jesuit labelled a sorcerer (*sorcier*).[27] Two years later, a similar chapter of Brébeuf's 1636 *Relation* described the Wendat mission's particular difficulties, including the poor state of the Jesuits' accommodations, the constant threat Indigenous enemies of the Wendat posed to the missionaries, and the inescapable torments of insects during the summer months. Wrote Brébeuf, explaining the inclusion of this material in his *Relation*, "We have learned that the salvation of so many innocent souls, washed and made white in the Blood of the Son of God, is stirring very deeply the hearts of many, and is exciting new desires in them to leave old France that they may come to the New."[28]

Neither chapter bears any hint that its appearance in the *Relation* was prompted by specific questions from readers, but it is clear in both cases that the general interest in the mission expressed by devout readers who might wish to join the effort shaped how the Jesuits described their own experiences. Le Jeune and Brébeuf both warned would-be missionaries to expect to be faced with difficult challenges, and also reassured them that these were worth the trouble. Of the periods without enough food that he had to endure while working among the Innu, for example, Le Jeune hastened to add that he found a comforting spiritual abundance in the notion of his own possible death, "in order that those who read this Chapter may not have a dread of coming over to our assistance."[29] And he concluded the chapter by again trying to allay any fears his graphic descriptions might have inspired in potential colleagues, and by appealing to the religious fervour that had attracted their attention to New France in the first place: "This must not frighten any one; good soldiers are animated with courage at the sight of their blood and their wounds, and God is greater than our hearts. One does not always encounter a famine; one does not always meet Sorcerers or [*jongleurs*] with so bad a temper as that one had."[30] Brébeuf adopted a different rhetorical strategy, imagining a conversation with a would-be missionary and putting brave words in the fictional man's mouth, as if to acknowledge the fear that his fellow Jesuits may have felt at the prospect of joining a dangerous and difficult mission while also modelling for them a way to channel their anxiety into renewed determination: "Do you think by your arguments to throw water on the fire that consumes me, and lessen ever so little the zeal I have for the conversion of these Peoples? I declare that these things have served only to confirm me the more in my vocation."[31] The care Le Jeune and Brébeuf took to warn would-be colleagues of the mission's hardships while also calling for bravery and highlighting the spiritual rewards they could expect to reap shows that the Jesuit authors at least sometimes anticipated their readers' feelings and sought to address them in their texts.

This sensitivity to readers' potential reactions to the *Relations* raises the prospect that material that otherwise might have been included in the texts was omitted to avoid unduly frightening anyone or giving offence. And it is true that the missionary authors sometimes explicitly signalled that they had omitted something to avoid upsetting readers. In 1644, for example, Vimont reported that a concern for propriety had caused him to forego a detailed description of the particularly shocking treatment of his Jesuit colleague Francesco-Giuseppe Bressani at the hands of Haudenosaunee captors: "Seven days passed in this manner, and new tortures were added; for he was made to suffer in places and in ways concerning which propriety will not allow us to write."[32] Jérôme Lalemant's *Relation* for 1659–60 similarly reported that the Jesuits had learned new information about Indigenous behaviour toward captured enemies, but declined to describe it lest readers be too badly affected: "This has indeed been mentioned in the other relations; but what we have recently learned is so strange that all that has been said on the subject is nothing. I pass over these matters, not only because my pen has no ink black enough to describe them, but much more from a fear of inspiring horror by recounting certain cruelties never heard of in past ages."[33] Even simple discretion could, by the missionary authors' account, cause them to say less on certain subjects than they otherwise might have if addressing Jesuit authorities alone. In 1640, for example, Le Jeune lamented the death of the Jesuits' supporter François Fouquet, who was then serving as an interim but unofficial administrator of New France's trading company, writing, "I do not doubt that the loss of a man so useful to the State, and whose actions have merited so universal approbation, has been deeply felt by old France, but she will permit me to say that it has not been less felt by the new." He stopped himself from saying more, however, explaining cryptically that "my fear of offending the modesty of the living, and of violating the secret which continues binding even after death, will not permit me to say more."[34]

The Jesuits' explanations for the omission of material in these instances – propriety and discretion – align with the well-established policies of the Society of Jesus discussed in the first chapter of this book, and may reflect the missionaries' true motivations. But it is also true that on other occasions they signalled and then withheld their knowledge on particular topics, reminding readers and rivals in France that they possessed knowledge of Indigenous cultures and events in the French settlement that no one else was in a position to obtain. The New France Jesuits often touted their own growing knowledge of Indigenous languages, for example, but never shared it in detail, as if to highlight their privileged access to potential converts and rhetorically close the door on their former Recollet colleagues.[35] The authors of the *Relations* may have mentioned their knowledge in the above-cited cases and others like them without choosing to share it for the same reason, to enhance their own reputation as uniquely knowledgable and indispensable intermediaries between New France and the French reading public. Whether the missionary authors were motivated in any particular case to omit material by such concerns or by the Society of Jesus's longstanding norms for correspondence, the result was the same: their awareness of readers could lead them to leave things out of the *Relations* that otherwise might have merited inclusion in an account of a year's events.

The clues assembled above about how seventeenth-century readers experienced and reacted to the New France Jesuits' annual reports as they appeared year by year suggest that this audience ought to be understood as among the factors that shaped the texts, and not only as enthusiastic consumers of words written by distant missionaries. By complaining or asking questions, whether sympathetic to the mission or less so, readers could influence the contents of subsequent volumes in the series, or even, as in the case of Gaston d'Orléans' complaint about the 1637 *Relation*, their form. And the Jesuits' very awareness of their pious, refined, and powerful readers could also lead them to omit or moderate their comments on certain aspects of their experiences in New France, apparently even absent a specific request that they do so. French readers' interest in the texts is well known and generally cited as a sign of their curiosity about New France, its Indigenous inhabitants, and the Jesuit mission, or of the texts' potential to shape France's understanding of its relationship to the rest of the world.[36] These are fine explanations of the appeal and influence of the *Relations*, but they do not account for the capacity of readers to talk back to the Jesuits. The willingness of at least some readers to correspond with New France missionaries and of these authors to respond in the pages of their annual reports show that the texts ought to be thought of not only as rich accounts of the missionaries' experiences and perspectives, but also as the result of an ongoing conversation between interlocutors at home on both sides of the Atlantic Ocean. This was, of course, a conversation that was only possible while the annual reports were still rolling off the press each year, and after the series ended in 1673, the texts steadily faded from prominence.[37] This would not, however, be the last time readers took an intense interest in the Jesuits' *Relations* from New France.

* * *

In mid nineteenth-century North America, a surge of interest in old books, especially those related to colonial history, brought renewed attention to the *Relations* among antiquarians, bibliophiles, and historians. The resurrection of books that were by this time nearly forgotten and perceived to be at risk of disappearing was part of a growing historical consciousness in the United States in particular, a still-young nation that was perceived, both then and now, to not yet have its own robust literary traditions or even, in Meredith L. McGill's words, "the romantic associations – the picturesque ruins and storied places – that would make such a literature possible."[38] In this context, books written in seventeenth-century colonial settlements, which were rarer and therefore thought to be more at risk of being lost than works from the comparatively recent eighteenth century, could be useful in establishing such associations, as well as grafting the nation to a deeper set of roots and thereby implying its permanence.[39]

The Jesuit *Relations* from New France were particularly hard to come by in North America at this time. They had not been printed in luxury editions that were intended to withstand the passage of time, and many copies had been lost by the time interested parties began looking for them in the nineteenth century.[40] Surviving copies had not been grouped together in complete sets in the two centuries after their initial appearance, but were instead scattered in the hands of various individuals and institutional collections, mostly in Europe.[41]

In this atmosphere of scarcity, reading the *Relations* was necessarily a more complicated affair than it had been in Paris at the time of their initial publication. Whereas the texts' earliest readers could purchase them as they became available or expect to find them in Jesuit colleges, nineteenth-century readers and collectors were operating in a climate of more uncertainty. Indeed, it was not even immediately clear to such parties what they were looking for. The texts themselves contain no detailed description of the entire corpus, and could not have done so, because the series' end date was unknown to the Jesuit missionaries until after it had already passed. A *Relation* describing events in 1672–73 had been prepared, but was not printed at the time because political tensions between the French king Louis XIV and Pope Clement X had made it impossible to do so without incurring the wrath of one or the other, a situation that permanently ended the published series.[42] In the following century, the Jesuit Pierre-François-Xavier de Charlevoix provided a very brief description of the series in a list of authors whose works he consulted to prepare his 1744 *History and General Description of New France*. His list included Le Jeune's 1632 report and described it as "the first of the relations on New France which the Jesuits continued to publish from this year to 1672," but he did not provide any details – authors, titles, or other basic facts – about the rest of the texts in the series.[43] In the absence of any more detailed surveys, nineteenth-century readers and collectors initially knew only that an annual report was believed to have been published for forty years without interruption. Under these circumstances, any effort to study or acquire the texts was necessarily also an exercise in locating copies and filling in the missing information about the series. The rest of this portion of this chapter traces the interest in the *Relations* at this time among scholars and lovers of old books. Because such figures were numerous, many of them will be mentioned only in passing, including well-known names in American history like Francis Parkman and John Gilmary Shea. The following pages focus on three men in particular because their stories add up to a useful overview of how the Jesuits' annual reports came to be understood as a set – both a physical one and a bibliographical one – which in turn set the stage for the large-scale modern editions that now constitute scholars' primary ways of consulting the texts. These are Edmund Bailey O'Callaghan, Félix Martin, and James Lenox.

Credit for bringing the *Relations* out of obscurity is often given to O'Callaghan, who described them in an address to the New York Historical Society printed in that organization's proceedings in 1847.[44] It is unclear how O'Callaghan became interested in the Jesuits' annual reports, but it is easy to imagine that his particular life experiences could have drawn him to the texts. Born to a Catholic family in Ireland in 1800, he faced discrimination at the hands of the British during his early life and witnessed a movement in favour of emancipation.[45] He departed in 1820 or 1821 for the friendlier religious territory of Paris to study medicine, and then moved to Quebec in 1823 to continue his studies, beginning to work in a Montreal hospital several years later. In Canada, he became involved in resistance to the British, joining Louis-Joseph Papineau's Patriote Party, taking up the editorship of a resistance newspaper, and serving as an elected member of the Parliament of Lower Canada. O'Callaghan participated in the unsuccessful armed rebellion of 1837, avoiding the death or imprisonment that befell many others and fleeing to New York.[46] Perhaps, as a Catholic himself, he was drawn to the missionaries' accounts of their efforts to introduce Christianity to Indigenous Peoples. Or maybe curiosity about his new home in upstate New York, the territory of the Haudenosaunee Indigenous Peoples who feature prominently in the *Relations* as adversaries of the French and their Indigenous allies, was what spurred his interest. After moving to New York, O'Callaghan refashioned himself as a scholar, publishing scores of works on the history of New Netherland and New York and eventually serving as New York City's official editor of historical records.[47] Whatever the initial source of his interest in the *Relations*, it is clear that O'Callaghan viewed their account of the past as key to understanding both Canada and the United States in his own time. The full title of O'Callaghan's printed address – "Jesuit Relations of Discoveries and Other Occurrences in Canada and the Northern and Western States of the Union, 1632–1672" – staked a claim to the texts for the history of both his own country of residence and his former home in Canada, neither of which, of course, had existed at the time the *Relations* were written.[48]

By his own account, O'Callaghan's intent in writing about the *Relations* was to make students of North American history more aware of them, and his essay was the first to describe the entire series text by text – in effect assembling the widely dispersed volumes into a corpus, at least on paper. In a "Catalogue Raisonnée" appended to his essay, O'Callaghan listed each of the texts in chronological order, starting with Le Jeune's 1632 *Briève Relation* and ending with Claude d'Ablon's annual report for 1671–72. He provided not only basic bibliographic information about each of them – its author, title, length, etc. – but also a concise summary of its contents, compiled on the basis of copies he had managed to read in various private and institutional collections. There were two of the annual reports, however, that O'Callaghan was not able to describe because he could not find them. In the entry for the 1654–55 *Relation* in his "Catalogue Raisonnée," O'Callaghan had to admit that "I have not been able to discover a copy of the Relation for this year, in any collection, either in Canada or this country, as far as my enquiries have extended." He noted that the same was true of the Jesuits' annual report for 1658–59, but expressed no doubt that either text had once existed and still might, dismissing a rumour that they had been suppressed due to militarily sensitive content.[49] Both his chronological list of the volumes and a table showing all the copies he had been able to identify in various collections included these two elusive texts, confirming that for O'Callaghan, as for Charlevoix before him, the Jesuit *Relations* was an annual series published between 1632 and 1673.

The French Jesuit Félix Martin had different reasons for his interest in the *Relations*, and offered a correspondingly different understanding of the series in his translation and adaptation of O'Callaghan's essay.[50] Martin arrived in Montreal in 1842 as part of a group that had been sent to re-establish a Jesuit presence in what is now Canada after the death in 1800 of the last member there, Jean-Joseph Casot. He sought not only to resume the work of his Jesuit forebears, but also to revive their memory in a population that had seemingly forgotten even the most consequential and sensational events in the Jesuits' early years in New France.[51] Martin retrieved materials that Casot had deposited with Augustinian nuns for safekeeping, searched collections in Paris and Rome for other relevant records, and established archives at the Jesuits' new Collège Sainte-Marie. This work coincided with a particularly fraught moment in the history of relations between the French- and English-speaking populations of Canada, a continuation and consequence of the tensions in which O'Callaghan had been embroiled in the previous decade. In the wake of the rebellions of 1837 and 1838, Upper and Lower Canada were merged into a single Province of Canada, under terms that reduced the power and influence of the French-speaking population of Lower Canada, which the English viewed as troublesome and disloyal. The French language was banned from official uses, French civil institutions were suspended, and the debt of the two former provinces was consolidated, to the advantage of the less populous but more indebted Upper Canada.[52] These provisions were perceived by many French speakers as a threat to their influence and to the very survival of a distinct francophone population. It is perhaps little wonder that this merger sparked a nationalistic backlash among French-Canadians, or that Martin, living in this context and working to restore the place of the Jesuits in collective memory, used his translation of O'Callaghan's essay as a way of claiming the Jesuit *Relations* for

French Canada. Wrote Martin, "It was right that such a work should be published in French. The work and the people it deals with belong to Canada. They personify a whole era, which is rightly regarded as one of the most glorious of its history, and which will never be too well known."[53]

In light of Martin's own interest in bringing attention to the role of the Society of Jesus in Canada's past, it is not surprising that his corrections and additions to O'Callaghan's essay appear to have been motivated more by a desire to portray the work of his Jesuit predecessors in maximalist terms than by a concern to offer a coherent definition of the corpus of *Relations*. Whereas O'Callaghan had identified the beginning of the New France mission as the 1625 arrival in Quebec of Charles Lalemant and his two companions, Martin asserted that "it would be more accurate to go back to 1611, the time when the first two Jesuit missionaries arrived in Acadia, of all these regions of North America."[54] He therefore added to O'Callaghan's "Catalogue Raisonnée" Pierre Biard's 1616 *Relation* from a short-lived Acadian mission and Charles Lalemant's 1626 letter to his brother Jérôme, both of which are discussed in the first chapter of this book.[55] A short essay Martin appended to his translation and adaptation of O'Callaghan's work also mentions several other texts, including unpublished reports or fragments of reports for several years in the 1670s, a report and a journal describing the Jesuit Jacques Marquette's explorations of the Mississippi River in the same decade, and the Italian *Relatione* of New France missionary Francesco-Giuseppe Bressani that had been published in 1653.[56] Martin does not seem to have considered these texts to be part of the *Relations*, which, he wrote, "begin in 1611 and go until 1672, but with several gaps," but he nonetheless highlighted them "to complete the author of this essay's research on the *Relations* of the Jesuits in Canada."[57] Extending the corpus to an earlier moment in the history of French settlement and also pointing out the existence of related writings served Martin's particular purpose of highlighting Jesuit contributions to Canadian history as well as the politics of the moment, by extending French-Canadian history back in time by the same interval.

At the same time O'Callaghan and Martin were describing and defining the *Relations* as a corpus, collectors in both Canada and the United States were scrambling to acquire them. Such men (and they do seem to have all been men) had their own particular reasons for seeking copies of the Jesuits' annual reports, but they are too numerous to discuss individually here. The story of one of them in particular, however – the New York bibliophile James Lenox – can give some sense of their approach to the texts. Lenox inherited a fortune in 1840 from his father, a Scottish immigrant and merchant, and soon began to put it to work in amassing an enormous collection of books.[58] His reasons for doing so are not entirely clear, at least partly because he seems to have been an intensely private man who left no record of his own motivations. But it is known that he long nurtured a deep appreciation for art, literature, and music even while working in the family business, and his wealth provided the means to pursue his interests with vigour. A devout Presbyterian, he began by collecting bibles, moved on to works related to religious history more broadly, and eventually turned his attention to books on the exploration and colonization of the Americas. Henry Stevens, an American who scoured Europe to procure books for Lenox and other clients, remembered him as a voracious collector who acquired books too quickly to even organize them properly. Wrote Stevens, "The truth was that from about 1845 to 1869 Mr Lenox was actively collecting his library so rapidly, and doing all the work himself, that he had no time to catalogue or arrange his accessions ... The great bulk of his book collections was piled away in the numerous spare rooms of his large house, till they were filled to the ceiling from the further end back to the door, which was then locked and the room for the present done with."[59] Lenox continued to seek elusive volumes of the *Relations* even after the first modern edition of the texts appeared in 1858. A letter he wrote to Stevens in 1866 lists the Jesuits' annual reports among the small number of works he was still hoping to acquire at that time: "Unless it be some volume like the Vespucius, or De Bry, or Hulsius, or Jesuit Relation, I have *almost* made up my mind to stop purchasing."[60] The other items on this list give some sense of the difficulty of finding some of the Jesuits' annual reports in Lenox's time as well as the strength of his desire to do so. Stevens wrote that Lenox's collection of editions and variants of the travel narratives published by Levinus Hulsius, for example, had been "picked up separately from many sources, cost[ing] him much research over a long time, besides many hundreds of pounds," a project that added up to "more than thirty years' struggle."[61] O'Callaghan and Martin had provided collectors with distinct but overlapping roadmaps to complete sets of the *Relations* around this time, but assembling all of the physical books was a much more difficult feat.

Many collectors other than Lenox tried to do so, relying on personal visits to European bookstores during trips abroad, the work of agents like Stevens, and catalogues of Americana that some European booksellers began to produce in recognition of the demand.[62] Competition among such collectors could be fierce. O'Callaghan's revelation in the 1847 essay discussed above that the retired diplomat Albert Gallatin had managed to collect twenty-two of the *Relations*, for example, was rumoured to have provoked an angry confrontation between the two men when it caused treasure hunters to come knocking at Gallatin's door, looking either to acquire or admire his collection.[63] The texts were scarce enough in the mid-nineteenth century that O'Callaghan was not able to identify any complete sets when he surveyed known collections. John Carter Brown, whose private collection of Americana would later form the basis of the library that now bears his name on the campus of Brown University in Providence, Rhode Island, had thirty-eight volumes of the *Relations* by 1847. Harvard College had forty, including some duplicates. Many others were scattered, in numbers that are not always known, in private and institutional hands on both sides of the border between the United States and Canada.[64] But even the Bibliothèque Nationale de France in Paris did not possess every one of the texts that was believed to exist.[65] The first known complete collection, at least as O'Callaghan had defined it, was finally assembled in 1853 when Quebec Parliament librarian George-Barthélemy Faribault located and acquired the elusive annual reports for 1654–55 and 1658–59, which took the form of brief collections of letters instead of annual reports divided into thematic chapters and had probably been overlooked by other collectors because their titles did not include the word *Relation*.[66]

Lenox himself would also succeed in collecting all of the *Relations* by the end of his life, including not only the forty consecutive texts that Charlevoix and O'Callaghan had identified as making up the series, but also Martin's more expansive vision of the corpus that included the works of Biard and Charles Lalemant.[67] It is easy, in the present time of readily accessible large-scale editions of the texts, to take for granted their status as a corpus, a series of reports that belong together. But without the work of O'Callaghan, Martin, Lenox, and their contemporaries, scholars' access to them now might be no better than it was for readers in the early nineteenth century. O'Callaghan, for example, had to consult copies of the *Relations* in at least two different cities, and, as mentioned above, could not find all of them.[68]

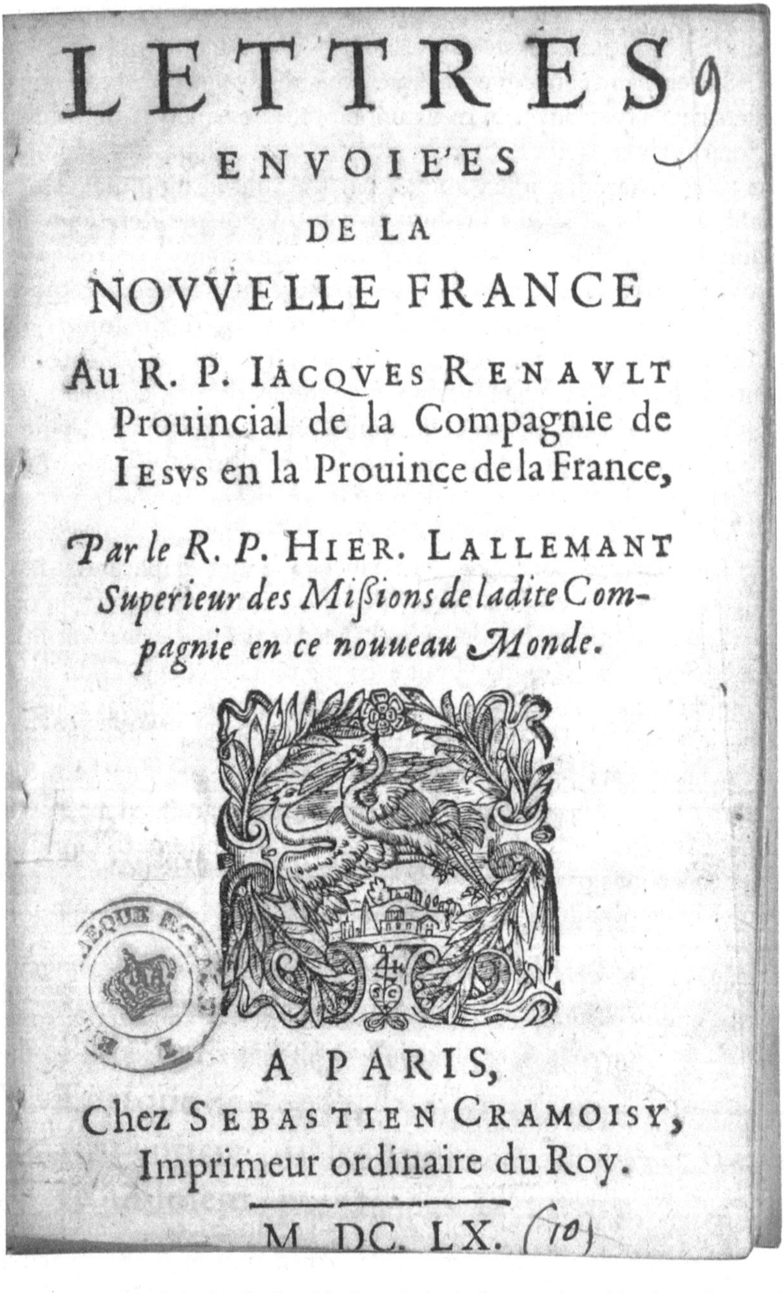

LETTRES
ENVOIE'ES
DE LA
NOVVELLE FRANCE
Au R. P. IACQVES RENAVLT
Prouincial de la Compagnie de
IESVS en la Prouince de la France,
Par le R. P. HIER. LALLEMANT
Superieur des Missions de ladite Compagnie en ce nouueau Monde.

A PARIS,
Chez SEBASTIEN CRAMOISY,
Imprimeur ordinaire du Roy.

M. DC. LX.

Figure 7.1 The New France Jesuits' annual report for 1658–59, like that of 1654–55, did not include the word *Relation* in its title, which likely contributed to researchers' and collectors' initial difficulty finding any copies of it.

The revival of interest in the *Relations* during the nineteenth century also has another legacy: it has left scholars in the present with enduring confusion about the extent of the series. Did the *Relations* begin with Biard's report that was published in 1616 but that describes events that took place several years earlier, as Martin contended, or were O'Callaghan and Charlevoix before him right to recognize Le Jeune's 1632 text as the first of the series? Scholars now routinely cite both texts as the starting point of the series.[69] It is debatable whether Biard's report from Acadia or Charles Lalemant's letter from Quebec can truly be said to fit with the rest of the texts that are commonly known as the Jesuit *Relations*. Both differ in important ways from the forty-year series of annual reports that began in 1632. As discussed in the first chapter of this book, Lalemant's letter was not intended for publication. Biard's text was from a different site in North America and was published almost two years after the author's return from France instead of several months after the events it describes, as was the norm for all of the texts starting with Le Jeune's 1632 report. This is not to say there are not good reasons to pay attention to Biard's and Lalemant's texts in studies of the Jesuit *Relations*. As the first chapter of this book showed, both texts appear to have influenced Le Jeune's understanding of Indigenous cultures and his own work when he started preparing accounts of his own experiences. But their inclusion in the series of texts known as the *Relations* requires overlooking fundamental aspects of the rest of these annual reports – the intention from the beginning that they be printed, their geographic focus, and their timely delivery of each year's news – in favour of a less specific vision of the series, one seemingly more motivated by Martin's goal of ensuring the place of the Jesuits in the collective memory of Canadians than by a concern to define the series in the most coherent terms possible. There was nothing inevitable about the inclusion of Biard's and Charles Lalemant's texts in many present understandings of the *Relations*. It is the result of Martin's particular perspective, and of the decision of the creators of the first modern edition of the texts to follow his lead.

* * *

Scholars around the world now use the New France Jesuits' annual reports to study the history of French colonization, Indigenous cultures as they existed at the time of contact with the French, and the dynamics of intercultural contact in the seventeenth century, usually by consulting one of the three major editions that have appeared since the mid-nineteenth century.[70] The first is the three-volume *Relations des Jésuites contenant ce qui s'est passé de plus remarquable dans les missions des pères de la Compagnie de Jésus dans la Nouvelle-France*, published in 1858 and reprinted in 1972 in six compact volumes. It was followed by the collection mentioned at the beginning of this chapter, Reuben Gold Thwaites' *Jesuit Relations and Allied Documents* in seventy-three volumes published in Cleveland, Ohio, between 1896 and 1901. A third major edition, the work of Canadian Jesuit Lucien Campeau, began appearing under the title *Monumenta Novae Franciae* in 1967. It remains incomplete, due to Campeau's death in 2003, but so far comprises nine volumes containing the annual reports and other documents related to the mission up to 1661.

This third and final part of this chapter examines these editions not to assess their relative merits or argue that one ought to be preferred over the others, but rather to show how each of them presents the *Relations* differently from the others, and how these differences have shaped the ways scholars have understood and characterized the texts. Such perceptions are not only the result of particular scholarly perspectives, the decisions made by writers and editors during the seventeenth century, or the ways the texts came to be grouped together in the nineteenth century, but also of the unmistakable messages modern editions – and especially Thwaites's *Jesuit Relations and Allied Documents* – send about the texts.

The 1858 *Relations des Jésuites* does not bear the name of any single editor or team who was responsible for its creation. It was only decades after the fact that scholars clarified that it was the result of a collaborative effort, initiated and led by a Catholic priest and life-long student of Canadian history named Louis-Édouard Bois, with key contributions from others and financial support from the government of Canada.[71] This edition was created during the time described above, when copies of the *Relations* were difficult to come by in North America, and just after a fire in the library of the Quebec Parliament in 1854 destroyed most of the above-mentioned complete collection of the original texts spanning 1632 to 1673, which had finally been assembled only the previous year.[72] A preface written by the edition's publisher, Augustin Côté, gives some sense of the difficulties encountered by Bois and his collaborators in this context. It reports that the editors made use of a large private collection owned by a priest named Hermann Plante, who served as chaplain at the Hôpital Général de

Quebec, to establish the text.[73] But they also relied on purchases made in France by the Canadian priest and historian Jean-Baptiste-Antoine Ferland, as well as his handwritten copies of instalments that could not be bought.[74] In short, the loss of a full set of the *Relations* and the above-discussed general scarcity of physical copies at this time made the assembly of this edition extremely difficult, but also extremely valuable. No longer would it be necessary for interested parties to track down copies on their own, or beg access to incomplete private or institutional collections. Bois described his own motive in creating the *Relations des Jésuites*, in personal correspondence, as a desire to be of service to scholars – "to put in the hands of those who will want to work on history some reliable and suitable documents."[75]

The publisher Augustin Côté's preface to this edition suggests that it is also understandable as a patrimonial project. Wrote Côté, "Since the fire that in 1854 devoured the palace of parliament, in Quebec, with the rich library of the legislative chambers it contained, some friends of our history were despairing of ever again finding gathered together all the volumes of the Jesuit *Relations* relating to New France. Others, more confident, believed that a feeling of patriotism would end up compelling some editor to rebuild this historical monument of our ancestors."[76] Côté's use of the second person plural – our history, our ancestors – attests to the publisher's vision of the Jesuits' reports as the work of some of the earliest French Canadians, and of the 1858 edition as the preservation of French-Canadian heritage, as does his characterization of the lost collection in the Quebec Parliament library as a monument to be rebuilt. This must have seemed like an urgent challenge not only because the fire had shown how easy it was to suddenly lose access to the New France Jesuits' annual reports, but also because American scholars were beginning to publish work that their northern counterparts perceived as encroaching on their own territory. The American historian John Gilmary Shea, for example, had published in 1882 an edition and translation of the exploration narratives of the Jesuits Jacques Marquette and Claude Allouez along with those of three Franciscan Recollet priests, prompting a strong reaction among French-Canadian historians – including some who were involved in preparing the *Relations des Jésuites* – who would have preferred to be able to rely on their countrymen for such work.[77] The above-mentioned priest and professor Jean-Baptiste-Antoine Ferland, for example, lauded Shea's short biographical chapter on Marquette's fellow explorer of the Mississippi River, Louis

Joliet, and translated some of it for inclusion in his own book, but also grumbled about having to rely on a foreigner for this information. Wrote Ferland, "Here, then, is yet another one of Canada's most remarkable men, rescued from oblivion by a foreigner: how many educated Canadians know the Sieur Joliet? We do have some vague notions that a man of this name discovered the Mississippi in the company of a Jesuit, and that some honour for this goes to Canada. That is all. We have, however, very few Canadian names to trace on the tablets of history. Is it not surprising that, for lack of children of the soil, writers not belonging to our country have to remind us of these names?"[78] Resurrecting the lost monument that had once existed in the library of the Quebec Parliament was not only a matter of honouring and bringing attention to missionaries whom some perceived as cultural ancestors, but also, it seems, of staking a claim to their writings for French Canada.

The *Relations des Jésuites* did not, of course, rebuild this monument exactly as it had existed in the library of the Quebec Parliament. It bound together several dozen books that had circulated independently and grouped them for the first time under a single title. The parliament's lost collection had included only the series of reports published from 1632 to 1673, but the *Relations des Jésuites* followed Félix Martin's example by including the two earlier texts by Pierre Biard and Charles Lalemant. This edition concretized Martin's notion that these particular texts constituted a set, but it also emphasizes the individuality of the texts published in the seventeenth century in a way that the more-popular Thwaites edition does not, as discussed below. Each of the texts is paginated separately, a decision that ensures that anyone who draws facts or quotations from this edition must identify the particular Jesuit report to which they refer in notes or parenthetical references, even if they choose not to specify the author's name or the year of the report in the body of a book or article. A citation of volume one, page ten of the 1972 reprint in six volumes, for example, could refer to any of the seven texts included in that tome. And so, scholars who use the *Relations des Jésuites* have always identified the particular annual report in question by the year it describes, by its author, or both.[79] One consequence of the way the texts are presented in this edition, then, is that scholarly references to it inevitably foreground particular authors or reports, and therefore do not look much different from references to the free-standing seventeenth-century editions.[80]

Approximately forty years after the appearance of the *Relations des Jésuites*, the head of the State Historical Society of Wisconsin, Reuben Gold Thwaites, began publishing the *Jesuit Relations and Allied Documents*, prepared with the help of a team of assistants and translators. Thwaites has sometimes been characterized as more of an entrepreneur than a scholar due to his own relative lack of formal education, his earlier career in journalism, and his team-based approach to quickly assembling and publishing the seventy-three volumes of this edition.[81] In his own time, however, he was regarded as remarkably accomplished in scholarly endeavours. Upon Thwaites's death, the well-known historian Frederick Jackson Turner observed that his work – fifteen monographs and approximately one hundred edited volumes in addition to the *Relations* – "compelled the recognition and respect of his associates throughout the United States."[82] Today, Thwaites is credited with modernizing the institution of the historical society, turning what had been a kind of club for antiquarians as it had long existed in the eastern United States into a publicly funded resource for all and cultivating close ties to the University of Wisconsin.[83] Perhaps naturally, in light of his service-oriented approach to his work leading the historical society, Thwaites presented his interest in the Jesuits' texts primarily as a desire to help scholars and students access the textual output of the New France mission. He wrote in the "General Preface" to the *Jesuit Relations and Allied Documents* that "no pains have been, or will be, spared to render all possible service to scholars, in the present work."[84]

Thwaites's motivations were similar to those of Bois before him, but his task in assembling his edition was much different from that of his predecessor, in at least two ways. First, he was not operating in a context in which a full set of the texts had just been lost and copies had to be scrounged across two continents in order to produce his edition. He instead benefitted from the above-described nineteenth-century efforts to assemble sets of the texts, and had access to the complete or nearly complete collections of James Lenox, John Carter Brown, and Harvard, among others.[85] Second, the decades leading to the publication of the *Jesuit Relations and Allied Documents* had seen the appearance of numerous editions of texts related to the New France mission in addition to the *Relations des Jésuites*, on both sides of the US-Canada border. These included Félix Martin's 1852 French translation of Bressani's Italian *Relatione*, a collection of previously unpublished mission reports from the 1670s, the journal kept by mission leaders in Quebec that is discussed in the second chapter of this book, twenty-five slender volumes of Jesuit texts pertaining to New France along with English translations that were published by Shea, and seven documents related to the earliest beginnings of the Jesuit presence in New France that O'Callaghan had printed between 1870 and 1871.[86] Many of these editions were already difficult to find by the time Thwaites began preparing his own work. He reported, for example, that copies of the *Relations des Jésuites* were only rarely offered for sale.[87] And Shea's volumes had appeared in just one hundred copies that quickly disappeared into the private collections of his friends and fellow scholars.[88] As Thwaites described his own project in his "General Preface," the *Jesuit Relations and Allied Documents* was intended partly as a consolidation of all that had already been published, augmented by facing-page translations into English: "We cannot promise for this series the entire body of existing Jesuit documents, either printed or in manuscript, which illustrate the history of New France in the seventeenth and eighteenth centuries ... We shall, however, reissue all of the documents usually designated as *Relations*, – the Cramoisys, the Quebec reissue, the Shea and O'Callaghan reprints; and to these will be added a very considerable collection of miscellaneous papers of importance, from printed sources and from manuscripts, in order to fill the chronological gaps and round out and complete the story."[89] This was an ambitious effort not only to republish and translate the *Relations*, then, but also to replace all the individual volumes and smaller series that had already made them and some related material available, at least to those who could read French.

In light of the sheer scale of this work relative to the more modest aim of the *Relations des Jésuites* to reproduce the published annual reports only, it is perhaps not surprising that the *Jesuit Relations and Allied Documents* presents the missionaries' texts very differently from the earlier edition. For one thing, individual texts are often split between two or more volumes. The annual report for 1639, to mention just one representative example, begins mid-way through volume 15 and continues nearly to the end of volume 17. And the journal prepared by the mission superiors in Quebec between 1645 and 1668 is spread across twenty non-consecutive volumes, so that entries for any given year precede the corresponding *Relation*, despite the fact that all this material originally appeared in single manuscript. Thwaites does not seem to have explained these choices, but it is easy enough to come to an understanding of them while contemplating the resulting uniform tomes neatly lined up on shelves stretching nearly floor to ceiling of almost any major research library. Each volume is approximately the same size, creating an impression of coherence and uniformity in the corpus, as does the consecutive pagination across all the texts contained in each volume. Whereas the creators of the *Relations des Jésuites* emphasized the integrity of the individual reports, Thwaites's decision to prioritize chronology and neat presentation sends an unmistakable message that he and his team regarded the coherence of the collection as a whole as more important.

This message is echoed in the way scholars now tend to cite the *Jesuit Relations and Allied Documents*. It is common to refer to it by using an abbreviated form of the title of the entire series – *Jesuit Relations*, *JR*, *JRAD* – or Thwaites's name instead of the names of particular Jesuit authors or the years in which individual reports first appeared.[90] This is understandable, because unlike in the case of the *Relations des Jésuites*, a reference to a particular volume and page number of the Thwaites edition is sufficient to allow interested parties to locate any given passage. And this is doubtless the most concise way to cite texts that appear in this edition. But it also sometimes results in a lack of clarity around what, exactly, is being cited when the author, date, or specific text being referenced is not explicitly mentioned in the body of a scholarly work.[91] It is not necessarily wrong that readers who focus on reconstructing historical situations instead of on the *Relations* themselves might find it sufficient to point to the source of particular facts without saying anything about the characteristics of the text in which they appear. But as this book has shown at various points, the Jesuits wrote differently when they knew their words would be published. Perhaps not surprisingly, given how this edition and common ways of citing it de-emphasize individual authors or particular texts and foreground the collection as a whole, scholars sometimes treat the *Jesuit Relations and Allied Documents* as a single massive but coherent work from which to draw facts, or in Luca Codignola's apt expression, "a sort of Jesuit encyclopedia, rather than a selective collection of edited sources."[92] It is not uncommon for scholars and other readers to call everything in Thwaites's edition a *Relation*, or to mistakenly attribute characteristics of the published texts to those that existed only in manuscript form until the nineteenth century and were never intended to reach the French reading public.[93] The full title of this edition makes clear that it includes material in addition to the published annual reports (the "allied documents"), but the result of the way it presents these texts has often been confusion about what is, and is not, a *Relation*.

The third major modern edition of the *Relations* is the late Canadian Jesuit Lucien Campeau's unfinished *Monumenta Novae Franciae*, which was a result of the same impulse that produced the two earlier editions, to make ever-more material related to the New France mission readily available to students and scholars. Campeau was not only a member of the Society of Jesus, but also a professional historian, with a long career as a professor at the Université de Montreal that yielded numerous studies of efforts to convert Wendat and Haudenosaunee people, the colony's civic affairs, and its general religious history, in addition to his edition of texts related to the New France mission.[94] *Monumenta Novae Franciae* is a subseries of the larger *Monumenta Historica Societatis Iesu*, which was established by Jesuits in 1893 in Madrid and initially devoted to editing and publishing documents related to the earliest years of the Society.[95] In 1944, it began to include secondary series devoted to publishing the textual records of the various Jesuit missions around the world, including, before the first volume of *Monumenta Novae Franciae* was published, tomes devoted to missions in Florida, Peru, Mexico, and Brazil. *Monumenta Novae Franciae* would, its editor promised, "contain the sources relating to the history of the French Jesuits' missions in North America during the seventeenth century."[96] It includes not only the *Relations* and all the other texts that had been presented in the *Jesuit Relations and Allied Documents*, but also hundreds of others related to the mission – letters, mission registers, memos, etc. – many of which had never been published before and would otherwise be accessible only in archival collections. These are all carefully described in *Monumenta Novae Franciae*, with annotations that are often illuminating, but critics have also complained about Campeau's sermonizing and faith-based interpretations in the volumes' critical material, as well as his apparent disregard for the work of his fellow historians.[97] This massive collection is also unforgiving of a reader's inability to read all the languages in which the missionaries wrote, presenting their texts in their original languages only: French, Latin, and occasionally Italian. These are likely among the reasons why *Monumenta Novae Franciae* has remained infrequently cited in studies of the New France Jesuits' annual reports, even among francophone scholars for whom its lack of translations poses no obstacle and despite occasional calls in recent decades for researchers to pay more attention to it.[98]

It may also be, however, that *Monumenta Novae Franciae* remains largely unknown as an edition of the *Relations*, despite its age and availability online in open access, because the edition itself does not place much emphasis on the published reports in its presentation of the mission's textual output.[99] The title page of each volume lists both of the two series to which it belongs – *Monumenta Historica Societatis Iesu* and *Monumenta Novae Franciae* – the volume number, and a subtitle that reflects Campeau's assessment of the most important event or theme in the period covered by that volume. The subtitle of the second volume, for example, is *Établissement à Québec (1616–1634)* (Establishment in Quebec), while the ninth is dubbed *Pour le salut des Hurons (1657–1661)* (For the Salvation of the Hurons). The word "*Relation*" does not appear in the title of any of the volumes or in the series titles, making it unlikely that anyone searching a library catalogue or the Internet for a modern edition of the New France Jesuits' annual reports would find and use Campeau's work instead of the two other options. And the *Relations* are not even particularly emphasized within the pages of the volumes, aside from the relatively large number of pages most of them take up. Each volume's table of contents arranges the documents it contains chronologically and numbers them consecutively. With the exception of the italic font used for texts on these lists that were published during the seventeenth century, the New France missionaries' annual reports appear as entries like any other, virtual needles that any casual observer might easily fail to notice in the haystacks of other documents related to the New France mission.[100] It is probably due at least in part to the way that *Monumenta Novae Franciae* presents the *Relations* that this edition is less frequently cited than the others, and that those who do use it usually do so only to refer to texts that are not included in Thwaites's *Jesuit Relations and Allied Documents*, or simultaneously offer references to one of the more familiar editions.[101]

Today, the vision of the texts implied by *The Jesuit Relations and Allied Documents* prevails: the missionaries' annual reports receive the most attention in scholarship, to the point of overshadowing the rest of the textual heritage of the mission, and very often the series as a whole, and not individual texts or authors, is placed in the foreground. This perspective on the Jesuits' annual reports is not necessarily incorrect. The missionary authors themselves sometimes made it clear they saw their textual project as cumulative, even if, as discussed at the beginning of this chapter, readers in the seventeenth century encountered them one at a time, as they appeared each year. In his 1637 report, for example, Paul Le Jeune repeatedly referenced past *Relations* in a chapter describing the Indigenous spiritual figures he called sorcerers, and suggested that there was no need to say more on this topic because additional information was already available elsewhere in the series: "As I have spoken of them in other Relations, I will say no more about them here."[102]

The two other modern editions discussed above nonetheless highlight other, less appreciated truths about the Jesuits' annual reports that are worth incorporating into scholarly understandings of the texts. The *Relations des Jésuites* presents them in such a way that it is practically impossible to completely lose sight of individual texts or authors, or confuse the published annual reports with texts that were never intended for non-Jesuit readers. As various chapters of this book have shown, the *Relations* are fundamentally different from other texts written by the New France missionaries and bear many traces of how the knowledge that they would be published influenced their form and contents. The way *Monumenta Novae Franciae* de-emphasizes the *Relations* and presents them as just one part of the Jesuits' textual output, on the other hand, can serve as an important corrective to decades of scholarship in which the published reports have overshadowed the missionaries' other writings.[103] Although this book has taken the *Relations* as its subject, the preceding chapters have also drawn on other texts written by the New France missionaries or others, showing that there is much to be gained by considering the published reports in the larger textual context in which Campeau placed them. It is understandable why Thwaites and his team presented the *Jesuit Relations and Allied Documents* as they did, and why scholarship now frequently reflects this vision of the texts. But aspects of the Jesuits' textual legacy that the most popular edition tends to obscure, and that are foregrounded in the other two major editions, also ought to be better reflected in contemporary scholarly understandings of the texts.

* * *

This chapter has shown that the way readers now tend to perceive and characterize the *Relations* – as a vast and coherent corpus – is at least partly a consequence of earlier moments in the long history of readers' engagement with the texts. The initial publication of these mission reports in small, inexpensive volumes undoubtedly served the immediate purpose of quickly getting them into the hands devout and powerful readers in the mid-seventeenth century. But the non-durable nature of these books also meant that the nineteenth-century scholars and bibliophiles who began looking for them in the context of broader nationalistic impulses to identify historical and literary roots for Canada and the United States struggled to locate copies, let alone complete sets. And this scarcity of the texts in the nineteenth century in turn led to efforts first to define and describe the corpus, and then to reproduce it in modern editions for the use of scholars and students of North American history. It is not difficult to imagine that modern editions of the *Relations* – and consequently scholars' perceptions of these texts – might look different if different choices about how to present them to readers had been made at various times in the past. If they had been published in a more robust format in the first place and then immediately assembled into whatever the missionaries or their Jesuit colleagues in France considered to be complete sets, they might not have been so hard to come by in the nineteenth century, eliminating the need for observers in that time to offer competing visions of the corpus rooted in the perceived needs of the moment.[104] If anyone in the seventeenth or eighteenth centuries had seen fit to reissue them in volumes including more than one annual report, perhaps devoted to particular authors, timespans, or key locations like Sainte-Marie or Quebec, the first modern edition and those that followed it might have maintained these configurations instead of taking their lead from Félix Martin. And modern understandings of the chronological boundaries of the series probably also would be different if O'Callaghan and Martin had chosen to define the corpus differently.

In sum, it is not only the intrinsic qualities of the *Relations* or the choices of those who wrote or contributed to them that have determined how the texts are now understood, but also the decisions of many others across several centuries. The way we read the Jesuits' annual reports now is in no small part a result of their near disappearance in the late seventeenth and early eighteenth centuries, their rediscovery in the nineteenth century, and the ways editors have presented them ever since.

Conclusion and Future Directions

In May 2017, Canadian prime minister Justin Trudeau met with Pope Francis in the Vatican to request an apology for the role of the Catholic Church in Canada's genocidal residential school system. This was an intentional step in efforts to reckon with the country's long history of mistreating Indigenous people, and one explicitly recommended by the 2016 Calls to Action of the National Truth and Reconciliation Commission. Wrote the report's authors, "We call upon the Pope to issue an apology to Survivors, their families, and communities for the Roman Catholic Church's role in the spiritual, cultural, emotional, physical, and sexual abuse of First Nations, Inuit, and Métis children in Catholic-run residential schools. We call for that apology to be similar to the 2010 apology issued to Irish victims of abuse and to occur within one year of the issuing of this Report and to be delivered by the Pope in Canada."[1] Trudeau's request was not unexpected, since he had already pledged to pursue implementation of the report's recommendations.

Perhaps more remarkable was a gift he gave the pope in a public session after their private meeting: the six-volume set of the Jesuit *Relations* published in 1972 by Editions du Jour, itself a reprint of the nineteenth-century edition of these mission reports from New France that is discussed in chapter 7 of this book. Trudeau's gift was understandable enough in diplomatic terms, as a reminder to a Jesuit pope of the Church's long association with Canada and the role of his own order therein. But his public comments about it brought into sharp relief the presumption of the centrality of European settlers in Canada's earliest history that continues to underlie common understandings of the texts. As reported by the Canadian Press, Trudeau called the

Relations "an essential tool for historians to understand the early years and stories of Jesuit missionaries documenting the origins of Canada," echoing the words of more than one scholar.[2]

This biography of the *Relations*, from conception to reception, has shown that it is possible to tell fuller, more complex stories about these texts than the familiar one repeated by the prime minister about Jesuits documenting their mission and providing to subsequent generations precious glimpses of the earliest beginning of settled Canada. It brings nuance to and sometimes directly challenges a number of aspects of how readers now tend to understand the Jesuits' annual reports from New France. The first chapter shows that it was understood from the very start of the series – not only after several years – that these reports would be published. Chapters 1, 2, and 3 show the degree to which their contents were shaped by the habits, preoccupations, and abilities of particular Jesuit writers who are often relegated to the background in scholarship that treats the series as a coherent whole. Chapters 3, 4, and 5 show that people who were not Jesuits could be involved in various ways in the creation of these annual reports, including figures who were sometimes identified in their pages like Marie de l'Incarnation and Joseph Chihoatenhwa and others about whom the Jesuit authors were careful to remain silent, like the *donné* Christophe Regnaut. Chapters 6 and 7 reveal France, and especially Paris, to have played a much more significant role in the history of the *Relations* than has sometimes been suggested, as editors and readers alike left clear marks on both the form and content of the texts. And finally, chapter 7 shows that the ways in which scholars now experience and understand the New France Jesuits' annual reports is a result not only of the work of seventeenth-century writers and editors, but also of how the texts have been characterized as a corpus and packaged together since the mid-nineteenth century. Along the way, this book has offered an account of the diversity in form and content to be found across the individual annual reports that is balanced with attention to the series as a whole. It has shown in more detail than ever before how the longstanding processes and standards of the Society of Jesus shaped the New France Jesuits' writing practices. And it has placed the *Relations* in the broader context of the many other texts that also contributed to the preservation and dissemination of news about events in New France, but that have received comparatively little attention. It is common and not necessarily wrong to think of the *Relations* primarily as reports composed by missionaries in New France that were lightly edited and then printed for enthusiastic readers. But this book has shown that it may be better to think of them as the result of many voices, not all of them belonging to Jesuits or others speaking from New France, and some of them clearly discernible only when the published reports are compared to other texts.

The story about the *Relations* that is told here brings to light much about them that was previously overlooked or poorly understood, but this should not be the last word on the subject. It is doubtful that any single study could ever fully plumb the depths of such a large and complex set of texts. For example, much more could be said about the individual Jesuits who were charged with writing or compiling the New France Jesuits' annual reports. The preceding chapters have focused on three of these authors: the oft-studied Paul Le Jeune, and two other prolific contributors whose writings have received comparatively less attention, Jérôme Lalemant and Paul Ragueneau, giving at least some sense of their personal preoccupations, abilities, and unique approaches to the task of reporting on a year's events in the mission. Only incidental attention has been paid to the other missionaries whose names appeared on the texts' title pages. Offering a comprehensive portrait of the writing life of any of the New France Jesuits – and perhaps especially the three particularly prolific writers mentioned above – would demand a full, dedicated volume. Le Jeune would obviously be an interesting figure to study from this perspective due to his unusual involvement in so many of the reports, including his inauguration of the entire annual series and his contributions to texts that he at least superficially would be expected to have nothing to do with, like the 1643 *Relation* to which he added at least one chapter during a visit to Paris several years after the end of his own term as superior. But others who receive scant attention in this book also merit sustained scholarly attention. François-Joseph Le Mercier, to mention just one example, wrote reports from both the Wendat mission and from Quebec during his thirty-seven-year career in New France. He later went on to serve as a visitor and then superior in the Jesuit missions in the Caribbean between 1674 and 1681.[3] He produced writings during his time leading the Society of Jesus's efforts there that are much less known than his New France *Relations*, and also less easily accessible to interested readers.[4] Sustained scholarly attention to this particular missionary would offer an opportunity to bridge a persistent gap in scholarship between New France and the early modern French Caribbean – and their respective Jesuit missions and textual records, for that matter – which have only rarely been examined together.[5]

Similarly, although this book has shown in various chapters that there is much to be gained by placing the Jesuits' annual reports in a broader textual context while being careful not to conflate published works with those that were meant to remain private, there are still many texts related to the New France mission that deserve fuller treatment. This book has engaged materials the New France missionaries wrote in Latin or Italian, for example, in only a limited way, drawing on their contents without considering their rhetorical qualities or particular form. Better accounting for the relationship between the Jesuits' published reports and the letters and other materials that the New France Jesuits and their counterparts in Europe wrote in Latin, especially, would be a major step forward in scholarly understandings of missionary writings from New France in general and the Jesuit *Relations* in particular. These works seem, in Zachary Yuzwa's recent estimation in a study of letters written in Latin by Paul Ragueneau, to be "generally regarded as a kind of abridged translation of the presumed French original ... and have therefore attracted little attention." But Yuzwa convincingly shows that Paul Ragueneau's Latin letters are carefully constructed and rich in literary allusion, and entirely worthy of close textual analysis.[6] It is to be hoped that classicists or other scholars competent in Latin might turn their attention in the coming years to texts produced in and about the New France mission in this language and produce translations that would facilitate their comparison to the rest of the New France textual record.

There is also, or may soon be, more to say about how scholarly perceptions and uses of the *Relations* are shaped by the form in which they are read, now that all three major modern editions of the texts are freely available online. Digitized versions of the texts are likely now a major tool scholars use to consult them due to the sheer convenience and searchability of such options. But it is impossible to know for certain without surveying such writers directly, because they generally do not specify in their books and articles whether they consult physical or digital versions of whichever edition has been selected. There is, of course, a difference between reading an individual text – or an entire series of them – from start to finish, and searching a digitized version for keywords to identify passages on particular subjects.

If the results of this difference are not yet plainly visible in scholarship, this may not always be the case. It is not difficult to imagine the emergence of a new transcription and encoding of the *Relations* that might allow a person to search across all of the texts simultaneously not only for particular words or phrases, but also for places, peoples, animals, environmental factors, or other thematic elements that might not always be associated with a single consistently spelled term.[7] In addition to improved searchability, a new digital edition might also enable computational approaches to the series as a whole. Such computer-assisted analyses have shown their value in recent years, producing insights about large corpuses of literary texts and historical documents that would otherwise be out of reach due to the difficulty of grappling with so much material, and this would surely prove true of the *Relations* as well should they ever be presented in a format that would allow for such an approach.[8] At the same time, however, presenting the texts in a high-quality digital edition could exacerbate the tendency discussed in chapter 7 to treat them as a homogeneous whole from which to draw facts, at the expense of attention to the unique qualities of individual texts or authors. Whether or not such an edition ever appears, it will be worth observing whether any signs eventually emerge of how digitized versions of the texts influence scholarly analyses.

Finally, the New France Jesuits' annual reports are shown in these pages, to a greater degree than ever before, to be the product of diverse hands and voices, but the relationship between Indigenous people and the texts undoubtedly deserves much more attention. Scholars both Indigenous and settler, many of whom have been cited in the pages of this book, have begun in recent years to pay more attention to Indigenous agency and knowledge as important factors in understanding the textual record of colonization. This work is unquestionably of great value in casting Indigenous people not merely as passive objects of description, potential converts, or conversation partners for European writers, but instead as people whose world views, beliefs, and actions were as operative in contact situations as those of missionaries and other French people. Continuing to examine texts written by settlers in this light can only enrich scholarly understandings of the past and its echoes in the present. This book has contributed to this body of work by highlighting one case in particular – the participation of Joseph Chihoatenhwa in the missionaries' writing practices, in various ways – but this is only the tip of the iceberg. There are many other Indigenous people whose interactions with the Jesuits could be fruitfully examined anew in light of what is known about their pre-existing beliefs and practices, and a systematic study of the *Relations* from this perspective would be welcome.[9] Further clarifying the prospects of texts like these to contribute to more inclusive understandings of historical situations and interactions is a particularly urgent challenge in the context of Canada's national commitment to reconciliation with Indigenous people. In the meantime, it is hoped that the account of the New France Jesuits' annual reports offered here may be more useful to efforts to answer the pressing questions of our own time about relations between Indigenous Peoples and modern Canada than the standard version of the story that Canada's prime minister repeated to Pope Francis.

As described in this book, the Jesuit *Relations* are complex pieces of writing that were produced and read in particular contexts, for particular purposes, and as the result of countless choices made not only by Jesuit missionaries but also by many others. There are lessons in the preceding pages for scholars who read the New France Jesuits' annual reports from a variety of disciplinary perspectives, whether focused on their textual dimension or their status as precious records of historical events and situations. It is to be hoped that some of the threads explored here might be picked up by others and further examined, not only for the benefit of scholars but also because the New France Jesuits' annual reports have undeniably played a major role in public understandings of the colonial history of North America, and even colonialism more generally. They have frequently served in recent decades as a direct or indirect source of inspiration and information for novels and films. These have included works of historical fiction – like Brian Moore's 1985 novel *Black Robe* and Bruce Beresford's 1991 film adaptation of it, William T. Vollmann's 1993 *Fathers and Crows*, and Joseph Boyden's 2013 *The Orenda* – that depict the New France mission directly, as well as works of science fiction that draw on the *Relations* to explore missionary work and colonization in more abstract fashion, like Mary Doria Russell's 1996 *The Sparrow* and 1998 *Children of God*. And, as mentioned above, they have even played a role in Canada's efforts to grapple with the ongoing legacies of the mistreatment of Indigenous people at the hands of settlers. Prime Minister Justin Trudeau's gift of the New France Jesuits' annual reports to Pope Francis and characterization of them in ways reflective of their general reputation among scholars provided the spark of inspiration for this book. But it can also serve as an illustration of the importance of developing more nuanced understandings of the *Relations* than the typical portrait of them as texts written by missionaries for the edification of European readers that now serve as a precious trove of information about the past.

Notes

INTRODUCTION

1 See, to mention only a few prominent examples, Wroth, "The *Jesuit Relations* from New France," 117–18; Melzer, *Colonizer or Colonized*, 83; and *JRAD* 1.38. A partial but indicative portrait of past and current scholarly approaches to the *Relations* can be found in True, "Jesuit Relations." See also Codignola, "The Historiography on the Jesuits of New France."

2 Examples include Berthiaume, "Les Relations des Jésuites (1632–1673)"; Desbarats, "1616–1673. Les Jésuites: Relations des Jésuites"; Donnelly, *Thwaites' Jesuit Relations*, 1–26; Dubois, "The Jesuit Relations"; Greer, "Introduction"; Rigault and Ouellet, "Relations des Jésuites"; and Wroth, "The *Jesuit Relations* from New France."

3 See also Meredith Beck Sayre's 2014 dissertation, "The Process of Conversion."

4 Such works are too numerous to list comprehensively here, but examples include Carile, *Le Regard entravé;* Deffain, *Un Voyageur français en Nouvelle-France*; Doiron, "Rhétorique jésuite de l'éloquence sauvage"; Ertler,"Les Relations des Jésuites et la construction de l'observateur européen face au monde indigène"; Ferland, *Les Relations des Jésuites;* Goddard, "Canada in Seventeenth–Century Jesuit Thought"; Laflèche, ed., *Le Missionaire, l'apostat, le sorcier*; Le Bras, *L'Amérindien dans les Relations du Père Paul Lejeune*; Melzer, *Colonizer or Colonized*; Pioffet, *La Tentation de l'épopée;* Sayre, *Les Sauvages américains*; and True, *Masters and Students*.

5 Audiat, *La Biographie de l'œuvre littéraire*. Kevin Birmingham has coined the term "narrative historicism" as an alternative name for this approach. Birmingham, "'The Great Shame of Our Profession.'"

6 Kaplan, *Looking for The Stranger*; Birmingham, *The Most Dangerous Book*; Gorra, *Portrait of a Novel*; and Hitchings, *Defining the World*. This book is not the first work of scholarship to use this concept as a way of approaching the *Relations*. Meredith Beck Sayre's 2014 PhD dissertation, "The Process of Conversion," presents itself as a biography of the Jesuit *Relations*. It touches on some of the themes examined here, especially in its first two chapters, but for the most part proceeds in a different manner, focusing largely on Thwaites's *Jesuit Relations and Allied Documents* and its relationship to ethnography and ethnohistory. Still, it must be recognized that Sayre appears to have been the first to attempt to tell a "life story" of the *Relations*.

7 https://press.princeton.edu/series/lives-of-great-religious-books.

8 Kaplan, *Looking for The Stranger*, 3.

9 These details are drawn from McCoy, *Jesuit Relations of Canada*, which helpfully catalogues seventeenth-century printings of the texts.

10 Melzer, *Colonizer or Colonized*, 76.

11 For just a few representative examples of work on Le Jeune, see Ibbett, "Saved from the Waters"; Le Bras, *L'Amérindien dans les Relations du Père Paul Lejeune* and "La Parole amérindienne dans les Relations de Paul Lejeune"; Ouellet and Beaulieu, eds, *Rhétorique et conquête missionnaire*; Deffain, *Un Voyageur français en Nouvelle-France au XVIIe siècle*; Doiron, "Rhétorique jésuite de l'eloquence sauvage au XVIIe siècle"; Côté, "Portrait de Paul Lejeune en ecrivain"; Principe, "Trois 'Relations de la Nouvelle France'"; Laflèche, *Paul Lejeune*; and Lopenzina, "Le Jeune Dreams of Moose." Research that takes Brébeuf as its subject includes Laflèche, "La Spiritualité des Jésuites de la Nouvelle-France" and Le Bras, "Les *Relations* du Père Jean de Brébeuf en Huronie." For work on Ragueneau, see Anderson, *The Death and Afterlife of the North American Martyrs*, 54–97 (chapter 2); Dunn, *Where Paralytics Walk and the Blind See*, 90–118 (chapter 3); and Yuzwa, "The Fall of Troy in Old Huronia."

12 For a very brief summary of how Lalemant's focus in the *Relations* differed from those of his predecessors, see Trigger, *The Huron*, 9.

13 The full title of the *Relation* for 1635, to cite just one representative example, is *Relation of what occurred in New France in the year 1635. Sent to the Reverend Father Provincial of the Society of Jesus in the Province of France. By Father Paul Le Jeune of the same society, Superior of the Residence of Quebec.* JRAD 7.251 *Relation de ce qui s'est passé en la Nouvelle-France en l'année 1635, envoyée au Révérend Père provincial de la Compagnie de Jésus en la province de France, par le Père Paul Le Jeune de la mesme compagnie, supérieur de la résidence de Kébec.*

MNF 3.44. Here and throughout this book, Thwaites's *Jesuit Relations and Allied Documents* is abbreviated JRAD. Campeau's *Monumenta Novae Franciae* is abbreviated MNF.

14 Codignola, "Jesuit Writings," 237.

15 Scholars have occasionally acknowledged the potential usefulness of this material and called for more attention to be paid to it. See, for example, Desbarats, "1616–1673. Les Jésuites," 58.

16 On the limitations of this edition, see True, "Is It Time for a New Edition of the Jesuit *Relations* from New France?" and Codignola, "Jesuit Writings."

17 Sayre, *Les Sauvages Américains*, xv. For a rich examination of how French characterizations of flora, fauna, and people in colonial North America as *sauvage* cast these aspects of life there as remediable defects, as part of a broad discourse of cultivation, see Parsons, *A Not-So-New World*.

CHAPTER ONE

1 JRAD 5.11 "l'aise et le contentement que j'en resenti en mon âme fut si grand que, de vingt ans, je ne pense pas en avoir eu un pareil, ny qu'aucune lettre m'ait esté tant agréable." MNF 2.298.

2 These and other details of Le Jeune's life recounted here are drawn from Pouliot, "Le Jeune, Paul."

3 JRAD 5.31. "Je ne pensois nullement venir en Canada, quand on m'y a envoyé. Je ne sentois aucune affection particulière pour les sauvages, si bien à faire l'obéissance, quand on m'eust deu envoyer encor plus loin mille fois." MNF 2.306.

4 JRAD 5.13, MNF 2.299 and JRAD 5.27–31, MNF 2.305. On violent European practices as compared to those of Indigenous Peoples, see Jaenen, *Friend and Foe*, 120–1.

5 On this brief period of British control, see Nicholls, *A Fleeting Empire*.

6 JRAD 5.21. "Aussi m'est-il advis que je viens icy comme les pionniers, qui marchent les premiers pour faire les tranchées; et par après, les braves soldats viennent assiéger et prendre la place." MNF 2.302.

7 See, to cite only a few examples, Blackburn, *Harvest of Souls*, 124; Le Bras, *L'Amérindien dans les Relations du Père Paul Lejeune*, 116–17; Pioffet, "L'Arc et l'épée," 41; and Schock, "Catholicism's Militant Pioneers to North America," 4.

8 By Luca Codignola's count, sixty-two Jesuits left France for what is now Canada between 1632 and 1658 alone. Codignola, "Few, Uncooperative, and Ill-Informed?," 176.

9 *The Constitutions of the Society of Jesus*, 335.

10 Nelles, "Jesuit Letters," 45. See Clossey, *Salvation and Globalization in the Early Jesuit Missions*, 193–215 (chapter 9) for a general account of how the Society of Jesus used letters to circulate information among its members around the world at this time.
11 For examples of scholarly mentions of this Jesuit tradition in studies of the *Relations*, see Pioffet, *La Tentation de l'épopée,* 7–8; Melzer, *Colonizer or Colonized,* 80; Pouliot, *Étude sur les Relations des Jésuites*, 3–7; and Le Bras, *L'Amérindien dans les Relations du Père Paul Lejeune*, 14–7.
12 Author's translation. *MNF* 2.135 (introduction). See also *MNF* 2.297 (preface).
13 Author's translation. Pouliot, *Étude sur les Relations des Jésuites*, 16.
14 Donnelly, *Thwaites' Jesuit Relations*, 2–3.
15 For an additional example, see Nelles, "Seeing and Writing," 329. This is also the conclusion reached in True, *Masters and Students*, 127–38. The present chapter reflects a change of thinking about Le Jeune's awareness of the publication of his earliest texts. Exceptionally, Bronwen McShea noted in passing that "it is unlikely Le Jeune had no thought that his first *relation* ... might be circulated publicly" on the basis of the publication in Paris in 1616 and 1626 of Jesuit reports from Acadia and Quebec, discussed later in this chapter. McShea, *Apostles of Empire*, 22–3.
16 On the purposes of Jesuit correspondence as first conceived by the Society's founders, see Friedrich, "On Reading Missionary Correspondence" and Balsamo, "Les premières relations des missions de la Chine et leur réception française."
17 Young, trans., *The Letters of St Ignatius Loyola*, 62–3.
18 Costelloe, trans., *The Letters and Instructions of Francis Xavier*, 265.
19 Ibid., 404.
20 Bobadilla's case is frequently mentioned in scholarship on the history of Jesuit letters. See Pouliot, *Étude sur les Relations des Jésuites*, 5; Nelles, "Jesuit Letters," 45; and Delfosse, "La Correspondance jésuite," 74.
21 All excerpts from Loyola's letters in this paragraph are from Young, trans., *Letters of St Ignatius of Loyola*, 75.
22 Nelles, "Jesuit Letters," 51.
23 The details in this paragraph are drawn from Delfosse, "La Correspondance jésuite," 93–7.
24 Friedrich, "Circulating and Compiling the *Litterae Annuae*," 7.
25 Ibid., 6.
26 Delfosse "La Correspondance jésuite," 78.
27 Friedrich, "Circulating and Compiling the *Litterae Annuae*," 6.

28 This tally is based on Carayon, *Bibliographie historique de la Compagnie de Jésus.*
29 Young, trans., *Letters of St Ignatius Loyola*, 63.
30 Nelles, "Jesuit Letters," 44, 49–51.
31 As noted in the introduction, many of these letters are reproduced in Lucien Campeau's edition of texts related to the mission, *Monumenta Novae Franciae.*
32 JRAD 5.11 and 73. "Mon révérend Père" and "De Vostre Révérence très humble et obéissant serviteur selon Dieu." MNF 2.298 and 323.
33 JRAD 5.71. "C'est assez, nous sommes si empressez que je n'ay gardé aucun ordre en ce narré." MNF 2.322.
34 Pouliot, "Le Jeune, Paul."
35 Nelles, "Jesuit Letters," 57. On the centrality of colleges and universities in the Jesuit production of knowledge, see Harris, "Mapping Jesuit Science," 224.
36 Carayon, *Bibliographie historique de la Compagnie de Jésus*, 59, 62, 178–9.
37 McShea, *Apostles of Empire*, 9. Le Jeune's letter making this request is not included in *Monumenta Novae Franciae* or in the open-access Digital Indipetae Database hosted by Boston College, but its contents can be gleaned from Vitelleschi's noncommittal reply. See MNF 2.78. Such letters from Jesuits asking to serve in missions outside of Europe – thousands of them between the 1560s to the 1960s – are known as *indipetae*. See Frei, *Early Modern "Litterae Indipetae" for the East Indies.* On such letters as they related to the New France mission, see Fabre, "L'Horizon de la Nouvelle-France."
38 JRAD 5.33. "Je puis dire des Hurons tout ce que nous en a escrit il y a quelque temps le père d'un jeune homme des Paraquais, sçavoir est qu'il y a grandement à souffrir parmy eux, mais qu'il s'y peut faire de grands fruicts et que, si les consolations de la terre y manquent, celles du paradis s'y goustent dèsjà." MNF 2.306.
39 JRAD 5.33–5. "On a fait de grands fruicts dans les Indes orientales et dans l'Amérique méridionale, quoy qu'on ait trouvé en ces païs-là non seulement des vices à combattre, mais encor des superstitions estranges, ausquelles ces peuples estoient plus attachez qu'à leur propre vie. En la Nouvelle-France, il n'y a que les péchez à destruire, et encor en petit nombre. Car ces pauvres gens, si éloignez de toutes délices, ne sont pas adonnez à beaucoup d'offenses." MNF 2.307.
40 Campeau sorted out how this private letter came to be published on the basis of records held in the archives of the Jesuits of the province of France. MNF 2.136 (preface).

41 On the missionaries' frustrations with traders in these early years of the mission and the misalignment of the priorities of the various actors on the New France stage, see Dewar, *Disputing New France*, chapter 4 (123–57).

42 *JRAD* 4.219. "Le secours qui nous est venu de France est un bon commencement pour cette mission. Mais les affaires ne sont pas encore en tel estat que Dieu puisse y être servy fidellement. L'hérétique y a autant encore d'empire que jamais. C'est pourquoy je renvoye le Père Noirot, selon la permission que les supérieurs m'en ont faite, afin qu'il parachève ce qu'il a commencé. Il est le mieux entendu en cette affaire." *MNF* 2.152–3.

43 Champlain, *The Works of Samuel de Champlain*, 5: 489.

44 *JRAD* 4.223, *MNF* 2.154 and *JRAD* 5.33, *MNF* 2.306.

45 *JRAD* 5.39. "la plus grande partie d'un corps de logis que le Père Charles Lallement avoit fait dresser." *MNF* 2.309. For Lalemant's report on the work of clearing land and constructing buildings, see *JRAD* 4.209 and 217; *MNF* 2.146 and 150–1.

46 *JRAD* 4.211, *MNF* 2.147–8 and *JRAD* 5.113, *MNF* 2.418. The political stakes of this claim, in relation to the efforts in the 1630s of Franciscan Recollet missionaries to rejoin the missionary field they had previously shared with the Jesuits, are discussed in True, *Masters and Students*, 35–6.

47 *JRAD* 5.35. "Il est vray que celuy qui sçauroit leur langue les manieroit comme il voudroit. C'est à quoy je me vais appliquer. Mais j'avanceray fort peu cette année, pour les raisons que j'écriray en particulier à Vostre Révérence." *MNF* 2.307. This separate letter is not included in Campeau's edition of materials related to the mission, and he speculates in a footnote that it has been lost. *MNF* 2.307n16.

48 *MNF* 2.281. The text of the manuscript can be found in *MNF* 2.281–95. Since its existence was unknown in Thwaites's time, there is no widely available translation. Quotations from the manuscript in this chapter are adapted from the *Jesuit Relations and Allied Documents*' English version of the published 1632 text. Scholars who have noticed and commented on this manuscript include McShea, *Apostles of Empire*, 22–3 and Sayre, "The Process of Conversion," 47–9.

49 Adapted from Thwaites's translation of the published *Relation*. *JRAD* 5.21. "Après la messe, nous entrasmes dans les bois dont ce païs est tout couvert. Nous trouvasmes encor quantité de neige si ferme qu'elle nous portoit." *MNF* 2.284.

50 *JRAD* 5.21. "Après la messe, nous entrâmes dans les bois. Il y avoit encor quantité de neige, si ferme qu'elle nous portoit." *MNF* 2.302.

51 *JRAD* 5.25. "(Mais) Ils ressemblent tous à ce philosophe de la Grèce qui ne portoit rien sur soy qu'il n'eût fait." *MNF* 2.286 and 303.

52 Adapted from the Thwaites translation of the published *Relation.* *JRAD* 5.27. "A nostre arrivée à Tadoussac, les Montagnards revenoient de la guerre contre les Hiroquois et en avoient pris neuf. Ceux de Québec en tenoient six et ceux de Tadoussac, trois." *MNF* 2.286 and 2.304.

53 See, for example, *MNF* 2.281.

54 *MNF* 2.281 ("description"). An assistant was a particular region's senior representative to the Jesuit leadership in Rome, serving as an advisor to the Society's superior general. For a brief discussion of this role, see Fabre et al., *Les Jésuites*, 472–3.

55 Adapted from the Thwaites translation of the published *Relation.* *JRAD* 5.31. "Ils sont si enragés contre ceux qui leurs font du mal qu'ils mangent mesme les poux de leur teste: en un mot, toutes leurs vermines; non pour aucun goust qu'ils y treuvent, mais simplement, disent-ils, pour manger ceux qui les mangent." *MNF* 2.288.

56 *JRAD* 5.31. "Ils sont si enragez contre tout ce qui leur fait du mal qu'ils mangent les poux et toute autre vermine qu'ils trouvent sur eux, non pour aucun goust qu'ils y ayent, mais seulement, disent-ils, pour se vanger et pour manger ceux qui les mangent." *MNF* 2.305–6.

57 Adapted from the Thwaites translation of the published *Relation.* *JRAD* 5.21. "Il me semble que je suis comme ces pionniers qui marchent les premiers pour faire les tranchées, puis les braves soldats viennent après, qui assiègent et prennent la place." *MNF* 2.284.

58 *JRAD* 5.21. "Aussi m'est-il advis que je viens icy comme les pionniers, qui marchent les premiers pour faire les tranchées; et par après, les braves soldats viennent assiéger et prendre la place." *MNF* 2.302.

59 Adapted from the Thwaites translation of the published *Relation.* *JRAD* 5.13. "Nous eusmes de grands tempestes. A tous coups, nous craignions que les vents ne brisassent nos mats ou que les coups de mer, qui se jettoient avec furie contre nostre vaisseau, ne l'ouvrissent. Et de fait, il s'y fit une voie d'eau, laquelle nous eût coulé à fond, si elle fut arrivée plus bas." *MNF* 2.282.

60 *JRAD* 5.13. "Vous eussiez dit que les vents estoient déchaînez contre nous." *MNF* 2.299.

61 There are numerous other places where the published text uses *vous* in this way where the manuscript does not, despite otherwise following its wording closely. See, for example, the two texts' descriptions the ship's entry into the Gulf of Saint Lawrence, *MNF* 2.283 and 301.

62 Adapted from the Thwaites translation of the published *Relation*. *JRAD* 5.23. “C’est icy où j’ay veu des sauvages pour la première fois. Si tost qu’ils apperceurent nostre vaisseau, ils firent des feux, puis deux d’entre eux nous vindrent aborder dans un petit canot fait d’escorce d’arbres fort proprement. Le lendemain, il y en vint douze avec leur capitaine. Il me sembloit, les voiant entrer dans la chambre de nostre capitaine, où j’estois pour lors, que je voiois ces masques qui courrent à caresme prenant.” *MNF* 2.285.

63 Adapted from the Thwaites translation of the published *Relation*. *JRAD* 5.59. “L’un deux, s’adressant à moy, me dit: ‘Ania, kir capitana?’; mon frère, es-tu capitaine? Ils demandoient le supérieur de la maison.” *MNF* 2.293–4.

64 *JRAD* 5.23. “Or c’est icy que j’ay veu des sauvages pour la première fois. Si tost qu’ils apperceurent nostre vaisseau, ils firent des feux, et deux d’entr’eux nous vindrent aborder dans un petit canot fait d’escorce fort proprement. Le lendemain, un sagamo, avec dix ou douze sauvages, nous vint voir. Il me sembloit, les voyant entrer dans la chambre de nostre capitaine, où j’estois pour lors, que je voyois ces masques qui courent en France à caresme prenant.” *MNF* 2.303. For the manuscript version of this passage, see *MNF* 2.285.

65 *JRAD* 3.87. “l’aisné de quelque puissante famille, qui, par conséquent, aussi en est le chef et conducteur.” *MNF* 1.487.

66 *JRAD* 5.59. “l’un deux m’aborde et me dit: ‘Ania, kir capitana?’ Mon frère, es-tu capitaine? Ils demandoient le supérieur de la maison. Ils appellent leur capitaine sagamo, mais par la fréquentation des Européens, il se servent du mot de capitana.” *MNF* 2.318.

67 See *MNF* 2.304 and 315.

68 *JRAD* 5.115. “Le mot de ‘sagamo’ ne s’usurpe icy que par quelques-uns, pour dire capitaine. Le vray mot, c’est ‘oukhimau.’ Je croy que ce mot de ‘sagamo’ vient de l’Acadie. Il y a quantité d’autres semblables. Au commencement quand on entre en un pays, on escrit plusieurs choses, les pensant vrayes sur le rapport d’autruy. Le temps découvre la vérité. On m’a discouru de plusieurs façons de faire de ces nations. Nous aurons assez de temps pour voir ce qui en est.” *MNF* 2.419. Campeau points out that alternate spellings of the word Le Jeune eventually realized was the correct one were recorded in early dictionaries, including *Oukimau* and *Outchimau*. *MNF* 2.419n40.

69 Adapted from the Thwaites translation of the published *Relation*. *JRAD* 5.27. “Or comme il y a quantité de nations dans les grandes

estendues de ces contrées et qu'elles sont fort portées à la vengeance, elles se font la guerre les unes aux autres." MNF 2.286.

70 Jaenen, *Friend and Foe*, 120–1. On Jesuit descriptions of Indigenous torture of captured enemies, see True, *Masters and Students*, 83–112 (chapter 4).

71 JRAD 5.27. "Or comme dans les grandes estendues de ce païs-cy il y a quantité de nations toutes barbares, aussi se font elles la guerre les unes aux autres." MNF 2.304.

72 Antoine Furetière's 1690 *Dictionnaire universel* emphasized the cultural difference of those deemed to be barbarians, defining the term to mean a "stranger who is from a very distant land, wild, impolite, and who has customs very different from ours." Author's translation. "Estranger qui est d'un pays fort éloigné, sauvage, mal poli, cruel, & qui a des moeurs forts differentes des nostres." Furetière, "Barbare," *Dictionnaire universel.*

73 For a brief summary of the history and meaning of the term *barbare*, see Melzer, *Colonizer or Colonized*, 67–70.

74 Adapted from Thwaites's translation of the published *Relation*. JRAD 5.27. "faite de perches entourées d'escorces, ouverte par en haut pour recevoir le jour et donner yssue à la fumée." MNF 2.286.

75 JRAD 5.27. "faites de perches et couvertes d'écorces assez grossièrement – le faiste n'est point couvert, pour recevoir le jour par là et donner yssue à la fumée." MNF 2.304.

76 This was a common feature of the missionaries' rhetoric in the *Relations*. See True, *Masters and Students*, especially chapters 3 and 4.

77 Campeau, for example, characterized Le Jeune this way: "The new superior of the Canadian mission liked to write. When he started doing so, his plume ran at length and easily and even had some difficulty stopping." Author's translation, MNF 2.297 (preface to the 1632 *Relation*).

78 On this last point, see Emma Anderson's exploration of Le Jeune's relationship with the Innu man named Carigouan, whom the Jesuit called a sorcerer. Le Jeune both demonized the man and described his desire to learn from his French interlocutor and accept his help healing a venereal disease. See Anderson, *The Betrayal of Faith*, 174–82.

79 The fate of the manuscripts that the New France missionaries sent to France each year is unknown, although Campeau has theorized that they were in poor condition after making their way across the ocean and being marked up by editors in preparation for printing, and were therefore simply discarded. MNF 2.532.

80 JRAD 23.267, MNF 5.641–2.

81 *JRAD* 26.167. "La première coppie de la Relation de nos Pères des Hurons de l'an passé ayant esté surpris par les Iroquois, la seconde me vint trop tard entre les mains pour l'envoyer à Vostre Révérence, les vaisseaux estant dèsjà partis. Je l'envoye cette année avec une nouvelle lettre venue de leur part, touchant ce qui s'est passé depuis de leurs affaires en général." *MNF* 6.169–70.

82 *JRAD* 6.27. "Ce n'estoit pas mon dessein de tant escrire. Les feuillets se sont multipliés insensiblement et m'ont mis en tel point qu'il fault que j'envoie ce brouillard, pour ne pouvoir tirer et mettre au net ce que je croirois debvoir estre présenté à Vostre Révérence. J'escriray une autre fois plus précisément et plus asseurément." *MNF* 2.484.

83 *JRAD* 32.249. "L'empressement que nous apportent les vaisseaux ne me permettent pas de revoir ce chapitre où j'ay parlé de la maladie d'un second Job pour sa patience. Il me faut coucher icy quelques sentimens dont Dieu l'a bény à sa mort." *MNF* 7.335. The grammatical error ("permettent") is present in the original seventeenth-century edition.

84 For additional examples, see Le Jeune's 1634 *Relation* and the 1661 *Relation* prepared by Le Jeune in Paris. *JRAD* 7.231, *MNF* 2.739 and *JRAD* 47.67–9, *MNF* 9.613.

CHAPTER TWO

1 *JRAD* 28.245. "[le] plus grand désastre qui fût encores arrivé en Canada" and "Fort bon garçon." *MNF* 6.736.

2 Just 964 settlers arrived in New France between 1640 and 1659, far short of the targets set when the Compagnie des Cent Associés was granted a monopoly on trade in return for supporting the settlement and the mission in 1627. Havard and Vidal, *Histoire de l'Amérique française*, 87 (see also 67 and 98); and Delâge, *Le Pays renversé*, 252. See also the 1627 "Acte pour l'établissement de la Compagnie des Cent-Associés," 23–30.

3 *JRAD* 28.245. "Les Trois-Rivières manquant surtout de cierges, on prit l'occasion d'un canot qui s'y en alloit, pour y envoyer deux douzaines de cierges jaunes pris à la paroisse de Québek et deux douzaines de chandèles de cire blanche pris dans mon armoire." *MNF* 6.736.

4 See, for example, the *Relation* for 1645–46. *JRAD* 28.257. "Relation de ce qui s'est passé de plus remarquable ès missions des Pères de la Compagnie de Jésus en la Nouvelle-France." *MNF* 6.543.

5 The departure of the ships is recorded in Lalemant's journal. *JRAD* 28.237–9, *MNF* 6.733.

6 *JRAD* 31.161–3, *MNF* 7.145 and *JRAD* 30.229–31, *MNF* 7.74.

7 For typical accounts of the work of the New France superior, which mention his work copying, editing, and collating the letters of missionaries throughout the North American wilderness after they arrived in Quebec each summer, see Melzer, *Colonizer and Colonized*, 83; and Wroth, "The *Jesuit Relations* from New France," 117–18.

8 The journal kept by Lalemant and his successors as mission superior is certainly not unknown, but it has usually served only as a complementary source of information about daily life and particular events in Quebec and its surrounding area. See, for example, Grégoire, "L'Interprétation du tremblement de terre de 1663"; Delâge, "La Tradition de commerce chez les Hurons de Lorette-Wendake"; and Plante, "Le Paysage sonore de la Nouvelle-France." For rare scholarly examinations of the journal, see Giguère, "Journal des Jésuites"; Pouliot, "Le 'Journal des Jésuites'"; and Sulte, "Le Journal des Jésuites."

9 Pouliot, "Lalemant, Jérôme (Achiendassé)."

10 Charles Lalemant's 1626 letter discussed in chapter 1 opens with a reference to another letter he had sent to Jérôme Lalemant from Quebec the previous year. *JRAD* 4.191, *MNF* 2.138. This earlier letter and any others the pair may have exchanged do not seem to have survived.

11 *MNF* 5.561. See also Lalemant's reply to Vitelleschi, which acknowledges these personal shortcomings. *MNF* 6.15–16.

12 Campeau believed he detected a somewhat irritable tone in some parts of Lalemant's 1645 report from the Wendat mission, but this seems to be no more than mild exasperation at the circumstances of the mission – rampant illness, famine, and risk of violent death – and not irritation directed at any other person. *MNF* 6.394n8.

13 *JRAD* 30.187–9. "On retira le reste du corps, que nous ne jugeasmes point à propos d'enterrer en terre saincte, estant un yvrogne manifeste et public, incorrigible et mort sans signe de pénitence dans son yvrognerie. En suite, on ne fit aucune prière publique pour luy." *MNF* 7.217.

14 *JRAD* 34.47. "Les Ursulines firent une faute remarquable en ce que pendant les ténèbres des trois jours, ils n'eurent de chandelier triangulaire ny cierge allumés sur l'autel, sinon, le premier ou deuxième jour, deux cierges blancs." *MNF* 7.629.

15 *JRAD* 45.145–7. "fort mal fait." *MNF* 9.516.

16 *MNF* 6.13; *JRAD* 25.83, *MNF* 6.27–8.

17 *JRAD* 16.225–37, *MNF* 4.353–9.

18 Lalemant described this new Jesuit settlement and the corresponding shift in strategy in his 1640 *Relation* from the Wendat mission: *JRAD* 19.133–7, *MNF* 4.670–2. For an account of the mission under Lalemant's

leadership, including his innovations and uniquely detail-oriented nature, see Campeau, *La mission des Jésuites chez les Hurons*, 157–247. A succinct summary can be found in Trigger, *The Children of Aataentsic*, 576–7.

19 *JRAD* 19.125–7, *MNF* 4.668.

20 Author's translation. "C'est lui ... qui a mis le bel ordre qui se voit dans l'Eglise de Québec avec autant de majesté qu'au milieu de la France." Marie de l'Incarnation, *Correspondance*, 403.

21 *JRAD* 27.85. "Journal commencé 1645." *MNF* 6.418. Similarly, the website of the Musée de la Civilisation, where the manuscript journal is housed, describes it as "the first regular journal of the Jesuits in Canada." Author's translation. See https://collections.mcq.org/objets/319511.

22 For a brief examination of this diary and sample entries from the small portion of it that has survived, see Nelles, "Seeing and Writing," 320–1.

23 Ibid., 318.

24 Delfosse, "La Correspondance jésuite," 97–8; Friedrich, "Circulating and Compiling the *Litterae Annuae*," 22. See also Nelles, "Jesuit Letters," 52–3 and Pouliot, "Le Journal des Jésuites de Québec de 1632 à 1645," 45.

25 Nelles, "Seeing and Writing," 318 and 327. The full text of Montserrate's letter can be found in Hosten, ed., *Jesuit Letters and Allied Papers*, 518–20. For other traces of this practice, see Arcilla, "The Fall of Manila"; Burrus, "A Diary of Exiled Philippine Jesuits"; and Finegan, "Pages from a Jesuit Missioner's Diary."

26 Pouliot asserts the existence of journals for 1632 to 1645 as a fact, and even attempted to reconstruct them on the basis of material in the *Relations*. Pouliot, "Le Journal des Jésuites de Québec de 1632 à 1645," 46–8 and "Premières pages du Journal des Jésuites de Québec, 1632–1645," 15–106. Campeau agrees that earlier journals kept by Le Jeune probably existed: *MNF* 6.413 (préface).

27 *JRAD* 7.119–21. "Je ne laissay pas, néantmoins, pour luy monstrer que je ne m'estonnois pas de ses diableries, de faire toutes mes actions à l'ordinaire: de lire, d'écrire, de faire mes petites prières. Et l'heure de mon sommeil estant venue, je me couchay et reposay dans un profond silence." *MNF* 2.688.

28 *JRAD* 6.115. "Cette lumière s'y fit voir à mesme temps et a mesme heure, comme nous l'avons remarqué depuis, le Père Bréboeuf et moy, confrontans nos mémoires." *MNF* 2.545. For another reference to Le Jeune's preliminary notes as a record of events recounted in the 1634 *Relation*, see *JRAD* 7.115–7, *MNF* 2.687. Portions of Brébeuf's own journal, largely focused on spiritual matters, have survived. See *MNF* 7.473–83. For an

English translation of the surviving entries, which Brébeuf wrote in Latin and French, see O'Donnell, "Brébeuf's Spiritual Journal." See also Clair, "Les *Notes spirituelles* de Jean de Brébeuf."

29 "Appendice: Inventaire des effets saisis," 228.

30 On this poem and for a translation into French, see Westra, "Références classiques implicites et explicites," 27–37. The Latin text of the poem is also available in *JRAD* 27.75 and *MNF* 6.414.

31 Author's translation. "Un livre in-folio de Parchemin, la première feuille commençant, 'Continuation des Régîtres précédens, dans lesquels tous les Recteurs de ce Collége ont écrit ce qui s'est passé de considérable dans ce pays, etc.'" "Appendice: Inventaire des effets saisis," 229.

32 Author's translation. "Continuation des Registres précédents dans lesquels tout les Recteurs de ce Collége ont écrit ce qui s'est passé de considérable dans ce pays durant le temps de leur Supériorité, excepté le R.P. Vincent Bigot, qui n'y a rien marqué de tous ses six ans, de sorte que le R.P. Bouvar auquel il avait immédiatement succédé est le dernier qui a écrit dans le livre précédent, couvert de Rouge, et nous allons commencer d'écrire dans celui-cy, couvert de Parchemin, le 10eme jour de Septembre 1710." L.B.P., "Extraits du Journal des Jésuites," 41–4. These excerpts were reprinted in *JRAD* 69.233–9. The eighteenth-century editor of these excerpts, identified only by initials, identifies William Smith as their transcriber, using footnotes to indicate points of correspondence between Smith's book on Canadian history and the surviving excerpts of the Jesuits' journal. Smith himself also cited Jesuit journals for the period after the surviving manuscript ends. Smith, *History of Canada*, 170 and 223. Smith's rumoured possession of excerpts is also mentioned in the preface to the first published edition of the journal of 1645–68. *Le Journal des Jésuites*, ix.

33 Giguère speculated that four or five volumes of the journal once existed, including the three discussed here. Giguère, "Journal des Jésuites," 422.

34 The tumultuous journey of the surviving manuscript to publication after Casot's death and being lost for fifteen years is not relevant here, but it is not without interest. See *Le Journal des Jésuites*, vii; Giguère, "Le 'complément indispensable' des 'Relations' réédite" and Giguère, "Journal des Jésuites."

35 For examples of Lalemant's many brief records of marriages, see *JRAD* 27.89, *MNF* 6.420; *JRAD* 27.93, *MNF* 6.422; *JRAD* 28.203, *MNF* 6.718; *JRAD* 45.149, *MNF* 9.517–8; and *JRAD* 47.288–9.

36 For just a few examples, see *JRAD* 27.93, *MNF* 6.422; *JRAD* 28.157, *MNF* 6.700; *JRAD* 32.71–3, *MNF* 7.434; *JRAD* 35.31, *MNF* 7.783 and *JRAD* 47.274–5.

37 See, for just a few examples, *JRAD* 32.79, *MNF* 7.436; *JRAD* 32.107–9, *MNF* 7.451; *JRAD* 34.41, *MNF* 7.627; *JRAD* 34.45, *MNF* 7.629; and *JRAD* 35.39, *MNF* 7.786.

38 Pouliot, for example, wrote that the journal's "main reason for being" was to aid in the preparation of the annual *Relation*. Author's translation. Pouliot, "Le Journal des Jésuites de Québec de 1632 à 1645," 47. Campeau described Le Jeune's process of writing the 1633 report as "the writing up of notes thrown into the journal." Author's translation. *MNF* 2.136 (introduction). Mairi Cowan similarly suggested that this was the purpose of the surviving journal, citing both Pouliot and Campeau. Cowan, *The Possession of Barbe Hallay*, 185n79. See also Giguère, "Le 'complément indispensable' des 'Relations' réédité," 15.

39 *JRAD* 29.29–43, *MNF* 6.564–8.

40 *JRAD* 32.131–41, *MNF* 7.297–8. The date of this incident is noted in the journal but not included in the *Relation*.

41 *JRAD* 36.29, *MNF* 7.772.

42 *JRAD* 28.187, *MNF* 7.711; *JRAD* 32.87, *MNF* 7.441; and *JRAD* 34.61, *MNF* 7.636.

43 *JRAD* 28.231, *MNF* 6.729–30.

44 The ships departed on 31 October 1646. *JRAD* 28.237–9, *MNF* 6.733.

45 *JRAD* 29.61. "Partit des Trois-Rivières le 24 de ce mois, en compagnie d'un jeune homme françois et de quelques Iroquois et autres sauvages." *MNF* 6.575. For similar discrepancies in the dates or time spans given for particular events in the journal and the *Relations*, see Lalemant's 1647 comments on the delivery by the French of a Haudenosaunee captive into the hands of his enemies and his 1648 accounts of the baptism and death of a Wendat man who had accidentally been shot in the leg. *JRAD* 30.193–5, *MNF* 7.220; *JRAD* 32.21–5, *MNF* 7.189–91; *JRAD* 32.71, *MNF* 7.433; *JRAD* 32.243, *MNF* 7.332–3.

46 *JRAD* 48.38–9.

47 For another example, see Lalemant's account of a 1661 drowning event that is similar to the one he wrote about in the journal in 1648. *JRAD* 47.23–33, *MNF* 9.600–3.

48 *JRAD* 28.241. "Le cinq mourut la Mère Marie de St Ignace, première supérieure de l'hospital de Québec, sur les cinq heures du matin. Elle ne fut enterrée que le lendemain. Je dis la grande messe en leur église, respondue par monsieur de Saint-Sauveur et autres chantres. Après l'évangile, je dis l'espace de deux ou trois Miserere quelques considérations sur la mort à l'occasion de celle de cette bonne Mère. Nous entrasmes dans leur choeur, cinq prestres et un chantre séculier, Saint-Martin, pour faire l'office de la sépulture." *MNF* 6.734–5.

49 *JRAD* 31.161. "qui est passée saintement de cette vie en l'autre, en avoit un soing si particulier qu'elle ne pouvoit dormir d'un bon sommeil, si les âmes de ces malades n'estoient en asseurance autant que la charité les y peut mettre." *MNF* 7.144.

50 *JRAD* 31.163. "Elle n'a vescu que six ans et demi en la Nouvelle-France, mais en ce peu de temps elle y a grandement souffert et travaillé pour le bien de la colonie françoise et des sauvages." *MNF* 7.144.

51 It is not clear to which Algonquin people this man belonged. Campeau identified as possibilities the Kichesipirini (Island Algonquin) or the Weskarini (Petite Nation). *MNF* 5.833–4.

52 On an earlier Algonquin man by this name, see Grassmann, "Oumasasikweie."

53 *JRAD* 31.261–3, *MNF* 7.178.

54 *JRAD* 31.265. "écumoit comme un possédé." *MNF* 7.179.

55 *JRAD* 28.249. "Ce mois, on receut nouvelle de la mort d'un malheureux apostat des Trois-Rivières, nommé Abdon où la Grenouille." *MNF* 6.738.

56 *JRAD* 31.257. "Trois hommes de considération parmi les sauvages mettoient quelques obstacles à l'amplification de la foy par leur polygamie, retenant publiquement deux femmes. Un carreau de foudre lancé du ciel, je veux dire un chastiment extraordinaire, a tué leurs corps et peut-estre malheureusement leurs âmes." *MNF* 7.176.

57 *JRAD* 31.261. "Quelques sauvages en furent touchez, mais commes les oreilles ne sont pas si proches de l'âme, pour ainsi dire, que les yeux, il falloit que quelques apostats et quelques payens endurcis vissent un autre coup pour estre ébranlez." *MNF* 7.178.

58 *JRAD* 31.267. "Ce careau de foudre, en tuant un homme, en résuscita plusieurs. Les bons chrestiens donnèrent mille bénédictions à Dieu. Les tièdes se rechauffèrent. Les apostats se réconcilièrent à l'Eglise et les payens, honorant Jésus-Christ, demandèrent son sainct baptesme. Personne n'osoit plus ouvrir la bouche contre la foy. On n'en parloit qu'avec une crainte et un respect tout aymable." *MNF* 7.180.

59 *JRAD* 32.95, *MNF* 7.444.

60 *JRAD* 32.159, *MNF* 7.305.

61 Both the journal and the *Relation* contain more information about the aftermath of this attack. See *JRAD* 32.105, *MNF* 7.449 and *JRAD* 32.159–71, *MNF* 7.305–8.

62 *JRAD* 32.95. "dans les lettres aux archives ou dans la Relation." *MNF* 7.444.

63 *JRAD* 27.85, *MNF* 6.418–19.

64 *JRAD* 27.119. "Deux de nos François, s'estant mis à boire attendant la messe de minuit, s'enyvrèrent avec beaucoup de scandale des François et des sauvages qui les virent." *MNF* 6.432.

65 For an example in addition to those mentioned here, see *JRAD* 34.39, *MNF* 7.625. The only other mention of alcohol in the journal was written by Jean de Quen, concerning a contradictory pronouncement of the Sulpician superior of the Séminaire de Saint-Sulpice in Montreal concerning whether it was a mortal sin to provide alcohol to Indigenous people. *JRAD* 44.93, *MNF* 9.306.

66 *JRAD* 30.189, *MNF* 7.217.

67 *JRAD* 32.83, *MNF* 7.438.

68 *JRAD* 27.119. "On prescha fortement contre, à raison de ce que les sauvages disoient: 'on nous fait prendre la discipline, quand nous nous enyvrons, et on ne dit rien aux François.' Il n'en falloit pas davantage que ce qui en fut dit en public. Monsieur le Gouverneur les fit mettre sur le chevalet exposés à un nord-est espouvantable." *MNF* 6.432.

69 This incident is also mentioned in Lalemant's journal. See *JRAD* 27.101, *MNF* 6.425.

70 *JRAD* 29.79. "payons à Dieu ce que nous luy avons dérobé par nostre offense. Je sçay bien que ceux qui ne croyent pas se mocqueront de nous, mais il ne faut pas que leurs gausseries nous empeschent de satisfaire pour nos offences." *MNF* 6.581.

71 *JRAD* 29.79. "ce qui consola les chrestiens, croyans que Dieu les préféroit aux infidèles, acceptant leur pénitence." *MNF* 6.581.

72 *JRAD* 29.77–81. "âme lasche" and "dérèglemens que les vaisseaux, à l'ordinaire, apportent par leurs boissons ... pendant qu'ils sont ancrez en nos ports." *MNF* 6.581–2.

73 The 1647 *Relation* reports on two Christian converts in nearby Sillery who found themselves on the receiving end of a Jesuit sermon against intoxication and then reportedly spoke out against their own behaviour and warned others not to follow suit. *JRAD* 31.171, *MNF* 7.147. For similar stories in the 1648 *Relation*, see *JRAD* 32. 219, *MNF* 7.324–5 and *JRAD* 33.33–5, *MNF* 7.359.

74 *JRAD* 28.251. "Le dernier jour de l'An, on représenta une action dans le magazin, du Sit. Nos Pères y assistèrent pour la considération de monsieur le Gouverneur, qui y avoit de l'affection et les sauvages aussi, sçavoir les Pères de Quen, Lalement, et Defretat. Le tout se passa bien, et n'y eut rien qui pût mal édifier. Je prié monsieur le Gouverneur de m'en exempter." *MNF* 6.739.

75 See, to cite just a few examples, Séguin, "Les Divertissements au Québec," 8; Laflèche, "Colonial Literature in New France," 62; and Dubé, *The Chevalier de Montmagny*, 215. On the performance of *Le Cid* in Quebec in 1652, see True, "Pierre Corneille's *Le Cid* in Colonial Quebec."

76 Laflamme and Tourangeau, *L'Église et le théâtre aux Québec*, 73 and Vance, *A History of Canadian Culture*, 47.

77 JRAD 51.145. "avec grand succez et satisfaction de tout le monde." JRAD 51.144. On the history of theatre in seventeenth-century Quebec, see True, "Beyond the 'Affaire *Tartuffe*.'"

78 JRAD 18.87. "Le Sieur Martial Piraube, qui conduisoit cette action et qui en représentoit le premier personnage, réussit avec excellence. Mais afin que nos sauvages en peussent retirer quelque utilité, monsieur le Gouverneur, doué d'un zèle et d'une prudence non commune, nous invita d'y mesler quelque chose qui leur pût donner dans la veue et frapper leurs oreilles. Nous fismes poursuivre l'âme d'un infidelle par deux démons, qui enfin la précipitèrent dans un enfer qui vomissoit des flames. Les résistances, les cris et les hurlemens de cette âme et de ces démons, qui parloient en langue algonquine, donnèrent sy avant dans le coeur de quelques-uns qu'un sauvage nous dit, à deux jours de là, qu'il avoit esté fort espouvanté la nuict par un songe très affreux: 'Je voyois, disoit-il un gouffre horrible, d'où sortoient des flames et des démons. Il me sembloit qu'ils me vouloient perdre, ce qui me donna bien de la terreur.'" MNF 4.566.

79 Farrell, *The Jesuit "Ratio Studiorum,"* 17.

80 On Jesuit pedagogical theatre, see Paschoud, "Puissance de l'image et efficacité de la représentation" and McCabe, *An Introduction to the Jesuit Theatre*, 11–18.

81 JRAD 18.87. "Bref, ce pauvre peuple se vient rendre à Jésus-Christ de jour en jour. Le secours qu'on leur donne pour défricher et pour cultiver la terre les encourage si fort que c'est une bénédiction de les voir prier et travailler [en] son temps." MNF 4.566–7.

82 This episode has attracted a fair amount of scholarly attention in recent years. See, for example, Dunn, "Sixteen and Possessed"; Grégoire, "Le Meunier, la domestique, et l'hospitalière"; and, especially, Cowan, *The Possession of Barbe Hallay*.

83 Author's translations. "Il faisoit venir des Démons ou esprits folets dans la maison de la fille avec des spectres qui lui donnoient bien de la peine et de l'effroi." And "L'on voioit des phantômes, l'on entendoit jouer du tambour et de la flûte, l'on voioit les pierres se détacher des murs, et voler çà et là, et toujours le Magicien s'y trouvoit avec ses compagnons pour inquiéter la fille." Marie de l'Incarnation, *Correspondance*, 668.

84 JRAD 45.167. "En ce moys fut amenée de Beauport Barbe Halé, infestée d'un démon folet depuis cinq ou six moys, mais à diverses reprises. Elle fut mise au commencement dans une chambre du vieux hospital, où elle

passoit la nuit avec compagnie d'une garde de son sexe, et quelque prestre et serviteurs. *Longa historia, de qua alibi fuse.*" MNF 9.526. The final sentence of this quotation appears untranslated, in Latin, in Thwaites's translation. It has been translated here for the sake of comprehensibility. Lalemant also recorded the execution of Daniel Vuil either by hanging or by musket on 7 October 1661. *JRAD* 46.187, MNF 9.638.

85 Marie de l'Incarnation, *Correspondance*, 814; Cowan, *The Possession of Barbe Hallay*, 110.

86 For an excellent summary of what various missionaries seem to have believed about the role of demons in Indigenous life, with references to their own words on the subject, see Cowan, *The Possession of Barbe Hallay*, 99–100. See also Goddard, "The Devil in New France."

87 *JRAD* 46.79. "qu'un missionnaire qui est destiné à ce grand employ doit se résoudre à mener un genre de vie bien estonnant et dans un dénuement de toutes choses plus grand qu'on ne peut s'imaginer, à souffrir toutes les injures de l'air sans soulagement, à endurer mille impertinences, mille brocards et souvent bien des coups de la part des sauvages infidelles, incités quelquesfois par les démons, et cela sans consolation humaine." MNF 9.497.

88 *JRAD* 47.61. "quoyque nos ennemis nous empeschent d'aller partout, pour recueillir des fruits si doux et si meurs, nous n'avons pas laissé cette année, malgré tous les Iroquois et tous les démons, d'étendre nos missions dans les quatre parties de ce nouveau monde et d'aller quasi partout chercher ces pauvres brebis errantes." MNF 9.610.

89 For additional examples, see *JRAD* 11.73, MNF 3.537 and *JRAD* 29.81, MNF 6.582.

90 See, for example, Goddard, "Canada in Seventeenth-Century Jesuit Thought"; Pioffet, "La Nouvelle-France dans l'imaginaire jésuite"; and True, "Une Hierusalem bénite de Dieu."

91 *JRAD* 28.269. "la piété et le bon exemple des habitans." MNF 6.547.

CHAPTER THREE

1 On this campaign against the Wendat, carried out by more than one thousand Haudenosaunee, see Labelle, *Dispersed but Not Destroyed*, 49–50.

2 On the Wendats' departure from their territory and the various decisions they made regarding where to settle, see Labelle, *Dispersed but Not Destroyed*, 47–140. For a long time, Western historiography tended to assert that the Wendat ceased to exist as a distinct group after 1650,

a thesis that Labelle and others have convincingly disputed, insisting on their agency in charting multiple paths forward after departing their territory in the wake of devastating Haudenosaunee attacks. In addition to Labelle's above-cited book, see Peace and Labelle, eds, *From Huronia to Wendakes*.

3 On the subject of martyrdom in New France, see Anderson, *The Death and Afterlife of the North American Martyrs* and Pearson, *Becoming Holy in Early Canada*, 35–61 (chapter 2).

4 The publication history of this particular *Relation*, and more specifically the unusually large number of distinct editions in which it immediately appeared, is documented in James Comly McCoy's bibliography of seventeenth-century editions and variant printings of the Jesuits' annual reports. See McCoy, *Jesuit Relations of Canada*, Synoptic Table (unpaginated).

5 See Donnelly, *Jean de Brébeuf*, 265–86 and Latourelle, *Jean de Brébeuf*, 211–14.

6 See Greer, "Colonial Saints"; Knox, "The Rhetoric of Martyrdom"; and Stevens, "The Historiography of New France and the Legacy of Iroquois Internationalism," 153.

7 Carson, "Brébeuf Was Never Martyred"; Anderson, "Blood, Fire, and 'Baptism'"; and Anderson, *The Death and Afterlife of the North American Martyrs*, chapter 1 (especially 38–52).

8 Wroth, "The *Jesuit Relations* from New France," 117–18.

9 The exceptions are years in which no *Relation* from the Wendat mission arrived in Quebec in time to be sent to Paris (1643, 1645, and 1647) and years in which the entire printed text was devoted to violent and disruptive events in the Wendat mission, including the *Relations* for 1649 and 1650.

10 For just two more examples, see Melzer, *Colonizer or Colonized*, 83 and Pouliot, *Étude sur les Relations des Jésuites*, 21.

11 For Ragueneau's *Relation*, see *JRAD* 34.139–57, *MNF* 7.591–7. His letter to Carafa does not appear in Thwaites's *Jesuit Relations and Allied Documents*. The original Latin version is in *MNF* 7.500–20.

12 Regnaut's account can be found in *JRAD* 34.25–37 and *MNF* 7.488–92. See Marie de l'Incarnation, *Correspondance*, 364–7.

13 Du Creux, *The History of Canada or New France*, 2: 521–2.

14 On Ragueneau's 1652 manuscript containing accounts of the deaths of Brébeuf, Gabriel Lalemant, and others who had been killed in the mission, see Muriel Clair, "Le Manuscrit de 1652 sur les martyrs jésuites canadiens" and Boss, "Writing a Relic." For Bressani's account, see *JRAD* 39.245–63, *MNF* 8.508–14.

15 Pearson, *Becoming Holy in Early Canada*, 56 and Sandoz, *The Beaver Men*, 56.
16 See, to mention only a few examples, Anderson, "Blood, Fire, and Baptism"; Carson, "Brébeuf Was Never Martyred"; Donnelly, *Jean de Brébeuf*, 265–86; Latourelle, *Jean de Brébeuf*, 211–14; Trigger, *The Children of Aataentsic*, 763–4; and Bourrie, *Crosses in the Sky*, 340–55.
17 These and other details of Regnaut's life are drawn from Campeau's biographical note. *MNF* 3.859.
18 This detail is drawn from a brief, unsigned history of the introduction of this practice to the Wendat mission that was apparently prepared there in 1641 in response to objections from the Jesuit leadership in Rome, discussed below. *MNF* 5.51.
19 Côté, "Domestique séculier d'habit," 183.
20 Côté, "L'Institution des donnés," 344.
21 Ibid., 345. On *donados* in the sixteenth- and seventeenth-century missions in South America, see Lavrin, "Lay Brothers."
22 Campeau, *La Mission des Jésuites chez les Hurons*, 336–7.
23 *MNF* 3.859 and 7.805–23.
24 For Gendron's published text, see *MNF* 7.252–63. On Gendron, see Nadeau, "Gendron, François"; Vallée, "François Gendron et Christophe Regnaut"; and *MNF* 5.824.
25 *JRAD* 34.33, *MNF* 7.491.
26 No complete roster of the *donnés* exists. For a list of those known to have been in Wendat territory between 1648 and 1650, see Laflèche, *Les saints martyrs canadiens*, 3: 285.
27 *JRAD* 21.305. "Pour servir et assister de tout mon pouvoir et industrie les Pères de la dicte Compagnie ... et particulièrement ceux qui sont employez à la conversion des pauvres sauvages et barbares de la Nouvelle-France aux Hurons ... sans plus rien prétendre au monde que de vivre et mourir avec les dicts Pères en quelque part au monde où il me faille trouver avec eux." *MNF* 4.259.
28 *JRAD* 21.303. "son désir de se consacrer au service de Dieu et de nostre Compagnie." "l'entretenir selon sa condition en son vivre et vestir, sans autres gages ou prétension de sa part, et de le soulager charitablement en cas de maladie jusques à la fin de sa vie, sans le pouvoir congédier en ce cas, sinon de son consentement, pourveu que de son costé il continue à vivre avec probité, diligence et fidélité à nostre service, ainsy que par ces présentes il promet et s'oblige." *MNF* 5.7.
29 On Boursier dit Desforges, see *MNF* 6.746. On Guérin, see *MNF* 5.825 and 7.842.

30 *MNF* 4.768.
31 *MNF* 6.575.
32 On Lambert, see *MNF* 6.762. On Ouré, see *MNF* 9.696.
33 Andréanne Vallée reported in her 2002 MA thesis that she had specifically searched for Regnaut's contract in various archives in France and Canada, without success. Vallée, "François Gendron et Christophe Regnaut," 73n8.
34 *JRAD* 35.57, *MNF* 7.797.
35 *MNF* 4.778.
36 On Gendron, see note 24 above. On Boursier dit Desforges, see *MNF* 6.746. On Lauzier, see *MNF* 6.763. On Goupil, see *MNF* 8.967–8 and Pouliot, "Goupil, René."
37 Both Côté and Vallée recount the history of negotiations on this subject between Lalemant, Jesuit authorities in Paris, and the Society's superior general Mutio Vitelleschi in more detail than is possible here. See Côté, "L'Institution des donnés," 353–78 and Vallée, "François Gendron et Christophe Regnaut," 70–93.
38 Côté, "L'Institution des donnés," 364–6. The Latin letter from Vitelleschi to Lalemant communicating this decision, dated 25 January 1643, can be found in *MNF* 5.561.
39 Côté, "L'Institution des donnés," 376. The original letter, in Latin, can be found in *MNF* 6.52.
40 Côté, "L'Institution des donnés," 344.
41 *MNF* 3.857. For more on Ragueneau's life and career, see Pouliot, "Ragueneau, Paul." Pouliot and Campeau disagree on the question of whether Ragueneau arrived in Quebec in 1636 or 1637.
42 *JRAD* 25.83, *MNF* 6.27–8. Ragueneau, for his part, does not appear to have aspired to this role, at least not openly. In his own letter to Vitelleschi in March 1644, he urged the superior general to allow Jérôme Lalemant to continue as superior or, failing that, to appoint either Brébeuf or their colleague François-Joseph Le Mercier. *MNF* 6.12–14. No English translation of this letter appears to be available.
43 *JRAD* 32.63. Brébeuf's original letter, in Latin, can be found in *MNF* 7.264–6.
44 Author's translation. Rochemonteix, *Les Jésuites et la Nouvelle-France*, 2:185n.
45 Yuzwa, "The Fall of Troy in Old Huronia," 403.
46 Author's translation. *MNF* 7.500.
47 For examples of sustained scholarly attention to Ragueneau in addition to Yuzwa's above-cited work, see Anderson, *The Death and Afterlife of the North American Martyrs*, 54–97 (chapter 2) and Dunn, *Where Paralytics Walk and the Blind See*, 90–118 (chapter 3).

48 This letter can be found in *MNF* 7.500–20. No translation of it seems to have appeared.

49 *JRAD* 34.139–57, *MNF* 7.591–7.

50 *JRAD* 34.143, *MNF* 7.593.

51 *JRAD* 34.29 and 193. "Double supplice." *MNF* 7.490 and 593.

52 *JRAD* 34.37 and 141. "accablé sous la pesanteur de ces coups" (with minor variation in spelling between the two texts). *MNF* 7.489 and 592.

53 *JRAD* 34.33 and 139. "Dès le lendemain matin, que nous eusmes assurance du départ de l'ennemy." *MNF* 7.491 and 591. This phrase appears word-for-word in both texts, but Thwaites translates it slightly differently in each case. Here I follow his translation of Ragueneau's *Relation.*

54 *JRAD* 34.141. "une gresle de coups de bastons sur leurs espaules, sur les reins, sur les jambes, sur l'estomac, sur le ventre et sur le visage, n'y ayant partie de leur corps qui n'eût dès lors enduré chacune son tourment." *MNF* 7.592.

55 *JRAD* 34.27. Thwaites's translation here has been corrected to match his translation of the corresponding passage in the *Relation*, which opens the same way. "Une gresle de coups de baston sur les épaulles, sur les reins, sur le ventre, sur les jambes et sur le visage, n'ayant aucune partie de leurs corps qui n'ayt enduré ce tourment." *MNF* 7.489.

56 Author's translation. *MNF* 7.489n2.

57 In Guy Laflèche's estimation, the factual discrepancies between Regnaut's manuscript and Ragueneau's *Relation* suggest of the manuscript that "the person who wrote it never had the 1649 *Relation* in front of him." Laflèche, *Les saints martyrs canadiens*, 3:173.

58 *JRAD* 34.237.

59 Laflèche, *Les saints martyrs canadiens*, 3:173–4. See also Vallée, "François Gendron et Christophe Regnaut," 145.

60 Author's translation. "coajuteur Frère au Jésuites de Caen, 1678, compagnon des Pères Brébeuf et Lallemand cy-dessus." *MNF* 7.492. Campeau does not indicate in any way that this information, and even Regnaut's full name, was added later, apparently by someone else. Thwaites's edition omits these details entirely, giving only Regnaut's first and last names at the end of the text, with no date. *JRAD* 34.37. The characteristics of the manuscript described here are plainly visible on page thirteen of the digitized version hosted by Library and Archives Canada. https://recherche-collection-search.bac-lac.gc.ca/eng/home/record?app=fonandcol&IdNumber=2395454&new=-8585533620934242954, accessed 31 March 2022.

61 Vallée, "François Gendron et Christophe Regnaut," 56.

62 *JRAD* 34.29. "Voicy la façon que j'ay veu faire ce collier pour d'autres captifs. Ils font rougir six haches, prennent une grosse hart de bois vert, passent les six haches par le gros bout de la hart, prennent les deux bouts ensemble et puis le mettent au col du patient." *MNF* 7.490.

63 *JRAD* 34.31. "le Père de Bréboeuf avoit esté bien courageux à souffrir tant de mal qu'ils luy avoient fait et qu'en beuvant son sang ils deviendroient courageux comme luy." *MNF* 490–1. On the significance to the Wendat and other Indigenous Peoples of the consumption of the heart of a particularly brave slain enemy, see Sioui, *Huron-Wendat*, 173–4.

64 *JRAD* 34.147, *MNF* 7.594.

65 *MNF* 7.503.

66 *JRAD* 34.27–9, *MNF* 7.489–90.

67 *JRAD* 34.145, *MNF* 7.593–4.

68 Regnaut: *JRAD* 34.29, *MNF* 7.490. Ragueneau: *JRAD* 34.145, *MNF* 7.593. In both accounts, the quoted expressions appear as "en dérision du sainct baptestme" and "railleries piquantes," but the Thwaites edition renders the second expression differently in each case. For consistency, Thwaites's translation of the *Relation* has been followed here.

69 *JRAD* 34.33. "j'ay veu faire le mesme traitement aux captifs iroquois que les sauvages hurons avoient pris en guerre, à la réserve de l'eau bouillante, que je n'ay point veu verser sur aucun." *MNF* 7.491.

70 *JRAD* 34.29–31. "Après cela, ils luy mirent une ceinture d'écorce toute pleine de poix et de raisine et y mirent le feu, qui grilla tout son corps. Pendant tous ces tourments, le Père Brébeuf souffroit comme un rocher insensible aux feux et aux flammes, qui estonnoient tous les bourreaux qui le tourmentaient." *MNF* 7.490.

71 *JRAD* 34.143. "Ils leur mirent des ceintures d'escorce toute pleine de poix et de rasine, où ils mirent le feu qui grilla tout leurs corps. Dans le plus fort de ces tourments le Père Gabriel Lallement levoit les yeux au ciel, joignant les mains de fois à autres et jettant des soupirs à Dieu qu'il invoquoit à son secours. Le Père Jean de Brébeuf souffroit comme un rocher, insensible aux feux et aux flammes, sans pousser aucun cry et demeurant dans un profond silence qui estonnoit ses bourreaux mesmes." *MNF* 7.593.

72 *JRAD* 34.25. "Ce fut le seizième jour de mars au matin que nous apperceûmes un grand feu au lieu où estoient allés ces deux bons Pères." *MNF* 7.488.

73 *JRAD* 34.33. "le mesme jour de sa prise, sur les quatres heures du soir." *MNF* 7.491.

74 *JRAD* 34.33–5, *MNF* 7.491.

75 *JRAD* 34.145, *MNF* 7.594.

76 *JRAD* 34.139. "ayant eu avant cela des nouvelles certaines par quelques captifs eschapez de la mort du Père Jean de Brébeuf et du Père Gabriel Lallement, nous envoyasmes un de nos Pères et sept autres François chercher leurs corps au lieu de leur supplice." *MNF* 7.591–2.

77 *JRAD* 34.143. "son coeur n'estant pas encore arraché." *MNF* 7.593.

78 *JRAD* 34.147. "Ils avoient tailladé leurs corps en diverses parties et, pour accroistre le sentiment de la douleur, ils avoient fourré dans ces playes des haches toutes en feu. Le Père Jean de Brébeuf avait eu la peau arrachée qui couvre le crâne de la teste. Ils lui avoient coupé les pieds et décharné les cuisses jusqu'aux os et luy avoient fendu d'un coup de hache une machoire en deux." *MNF* 7.594.

79 *JRAD* 34.147, *MNF* 7.594.

80 *JRAD* 34.27. "Voicy ce que nous dirent ces sauvages de la prise du bourg de Saint-Ignace et des Pères Jean de Bréboeuf et Gabriel L'Allemant." *MNF* 7.489.

81 *JRAD* 34.31–3. "Voilà ce que nous avons appris du martyre et de la bienheureuse mort du Père Jean de Bréboeuf par plusieurs chrétiens sauvages dignes de foy, qui ont toujours esté présents depuis que le bon Père fut pris jusqu'à la mort. Ces bons chrestiens estoient captifs des Iroquois et les menoient en leur pays pour les faire mourir, mais notre bon Dieu leur fist la grâce de se pouvoir sauver par les chemins et nous sont venus raconter tout ce que j'ay mis par escrit." *MNF* 7.491. The non-standard spelling of Brébeuf's name here is Regnaut's.

82 *JRAD* 34.27. "Ils nous dirent encore." *MNF* 7.489.

83 Sayre, "Communion in Captivity," 56–7.

84 *JRAD* 34.35. "J'ay veu et touché quantité de grosses ampoules qu'il avoit en plusieurs endroits de son corps, de l'eau bouillante que ces barbares lui avoient versé en dérision du saint baptesme. J'ay veu et touché la plaie d'une ceinture d'écorce toute plaine de poix et de raisine qui grilla tout son corps. J'ay veu et touché les brûleures du colier de haches qu'on luy mist sur les épaulles et sur l'estomach. J'ay veu et touché ses deux lèvres qu'on luy avoit couppées à cause qu'il parloit tousjours de Dieu pendant qu'on le faisoit souffrir." *MNF* 7.491–2.

85 Pearson, on the contrary, sees this passage as akin to "a litany recited at mass – a ritual performance of the Catholic liturgy" that serves as a kind of "official witnessing" since the Wendat witnesses themselves "could not be trusted in a matter so important to Jesuit views of themselves as worthy and innocent victims." Pearson, *Becoming Holy in Early Canada*, 55–6.

86 *JRAD* 34.149. "personnes dignes de foy, qui l'ont veu et me l'ont rapporté à moy mesme et qui alors estoient captifs avec eux, mais qui, ayant esté réservez pour estre mis à mort en un autre temps, ont trouvé les moyens de se sauver." *MNF* 7.595.

87 A number of scholars have pointed out the apparent reluctance of the Jesuits to assign to Indigenous people roles other than martyr maker in hagiographical texts and images. See Pearson, *Becoming Holy in Early Canada*, 76 and Greer, "Colonial Saints," 335–6, 343.

88 Detailed comparisons of the facts recounted in each text can be found in Vallée, "François Gendron et Christophe Regnaut," 168–84, and Laflèche, *Les saints martyrs canadiens*, 3:171–204.

89 As Carole Blackburn has observed, "Many Jesuits thought that martyrdom was necessary in order to plant the faith in New France … the 'Blood of the Martyrs' was 'the seed and germ of Christians' … not least because the Jesuits believed that their willingness to die would impress people with the truth of their teaching." Blackburn, *Harvest of Souls*, 65.

90 *JRAD* 34.25, 29–31. "indignez contre luy de ce qu'il leur parloit toujours de Dieu et de leur conversion" and "en dérision du saint baptesme." *MNF* 7.488 and 491.

91 *JRAD* 34.139. "Je les appellerois volontiers, s'il m'estoit permis, de ce nom glorieux" and "la haine de la foy et le mespris du nom de Dieu." *MNF* 7.592–3. What kinds of death counted as martyrdom was a subject of debate within the Catholic Church during the seventeenth century, in which Jesuits played a significant part. See Gay, "Finding Martyrs at Home?"

92 As Mary Baine Campbell has observed of a different textual account of torture among Indigenous people, Lafitau's *Moeurs des sauvages amériquains*, scenes of violent abuse inevitably cause readers to *feel*, not merely to understand: "They force upon us the impression of the victim's subjectivity. We may repudiate that victimization, but if we do, then we share the weaker sensations of the torturers and flesh-eaters, who are also Americans, and at their most 'sauvage.' Either way we are sharing a virtual experience with American persons, rather than coolly observing a systematic pattern of lineage." Campbell, *Wonder and Science*, 304.

93 Melzer, *Colonizer or Colonized*, 78–80.

94 Marie-Christine Pioffet, for example, observed in passing that a perspective of passionate engagement pervades how the *Relations* are narrated, but stopped short of elaborating. Pioffet, *La Tentation de l'épopée*, 62. Historians most often hail the texts as a rich repository of facts, albeit framed rhetorically to advance the Jesuits' own arguments. Examples include Greer, "Introduction," 1 and Beaulieu, *Convertir les fils de Caïn*, 19.

95 Author's translation. Pouliot, *Étude sur les Relations des Jésuites*, 20.

96 Regnaut: *JRAD* 34.31, *MNF* 7. 490. Ragueneau: *JRAD* 34.143, *MNF* 7.593. The language is identical in both original French texts – "souffroit comme un rocher, insensible aux feux et aux flammes" – but Thwaites translates it differently in each instance. The translation here follows Thwaites's rendering of the *Relation*.

97 *JRAD* 34.31. "Son zèle estoit si grand qu'il preschoit toujours à ces infidelles pour tascher à les convertir." *MNF* 7.490.

98 *JRAD* 34.143. "preschoit à ces infidèles et plus encore à quantité de bonne chrestiens captifs." *MNF* 7.593. *JRAD* 34.143–5. "sa langue ne laissa pas de luy rendre service jusqu'à son dernier soupir, pour bénir Dieu de ces tourmens et pour animer les chrestiens plus puissamment qu'il n'avoit jamais fait." *MNF* 7.593. Although not mentioned in the published *Relation* or in any of the specific texts examined here, it is worth noting that the Jesuits learned years after Brébeuf's death that an attempt by a Haudenosaunee man to ransom him with wampum – and thereby save his life from the violent end examined in this chapter – failed, apparently at least in part due to Brébeuf's own zealous preaching throughout his ordeal. See Anderson, *The Death and Afterlife of the North American Martyrs*, 42, 45, 392n94.

99 *JRAD* 34.141. "Mes enfants ... levons les yeux au ciel dans le plus fort de nos douleurs; souvenons-nous que Dieu est le tesmoin de nos souffrances et en sera bientost nostre trop grande récompense. Mourons dans cette foy et espérons de sa bonté l'accomplissement de ses promesses. J'ay pitié plus de vous que de moy, mais soustenez avec courage le peu qui reste de tourmens. Ils finiront avec nos vies. La gloire qui les suit n'aura jamais de fin." *MNF* 7.592.

100 *JRAD* 34.141, *MNF* 7.592.

101 *JRAD* 34.27. "Il ne laissoit pas de toujours parler de Dieu et d'encourager tous les nouveaux chrétiens qui estoient captifs comme luy de bien souffrir, afin de bien mourir, pour aller de compagnie avec lui dans le paradis." *MNF* 7.489.

CHAPTER FOUR

1 The spelling of Chihoatenhwa's name varies widely in scholarship and in the seventeenth-century sources: Chihwatenha, Chiwatenhwa, Chihouatenhoua, Chi8atenh8a, etc. This chapter follows the spelling used by ethnolinguist John Steckley, who reports that the name is "pronounced

shee-ho-a-ten-hwa and mean[s] roughly 'He Is Brought From Afar.'" Steckley, *Untold Tales*, 5.

2 Drawing on censuses conducted by the Jesuits, their accounts of the impact of disease on the Wendat and other nearby peoples, and archaeological data, Gary Warrick has concluded that the Wendat numbered approximately twenty-one thousand in 1633 and fewer than nine thousand at the end of the decade, after enduring deadly epidemics of measles, influenza, smallpox, and perhaps other diseases. Warrick, *A Population History of the Huron-Petun*, 222–7.

3 *JRAD* 15.95. "Devant et après les instructions qu'on luy fait, il y a du plaisir de le voir à genoux pour demander la grâce de l'Esprit divin, jusques-là qu'il s'est captivé luy-mesme à apprendre cet hyver à escrire, pour retenir et répéter ce qu'on luy dit, mais surtout pour remarquer, disoit-il, plus clairement le nombre de ses péchez." *MNF* 4.163.

4 *JRAD* 15.111. "L'opinion qu'il a de nous luy fit naistre un grand désir de sçavoir lire et escrire, comme il nous voyoit faire ... avec une telle pureté d'intention qu'il nous demandoit naguères s'il y auroit du péché de désirer sçavoir l'escriture, non seulement pour pouvoir coucher par escrit ce qui regarde l'avancement de son âme, mais aussi les affaires du pays." *MNF* 4.168–9.

5 *JRAD* 15.111–13. "Ce travail n'a pas esté inutile. Pour l'escriture, il y aura une grande facilité; la lecture luy coustera un peu plus. La difficulté que nous avons eu à luy en expliquer le secret l'a un peu retardé; néantmoins, nous espérons que dans peu de temps, il en viendra à bout." *MNF* 4.169.

6 *JRAD* 15.113. "Vous serez consolé de recevoir une de ses lettres. Je vous donne dèsjà parole qu'elle est toute de sa main." *MNF* 4.169.

7 See, to mention only two prominent examples, Parkman, *The Jesuits in North America in the Seventeenth Century*, vi; Tooker, *An Ethnography of the Huron Indians*, 5–6.

8 See, for example, Sayre, *Les Sauvages Américains*; Le Bras, *L'Amérindien dans les Relations du Père Paul Lejeune*; and True, *Masters and Students*.

9 See, for example, White, *The Middle Ground* and Blackburn, *Harvest of Souls*. Most recently, Emma Anderson has argued that Indigenous people ought to be understood as having profoundly contributed to Enlightenment thought. See Anderson, "The First Philosophes."

10 For accounts of Chihoatenhwa's life, some of which offer more detail than is possible here, see Poirier, *Religion, Gender, and Kinship in Colonial New France*, 73–126 (chapter 3); Trigger, "Chihwatenha

(Chihouatenhoua, Chiohoarehra) (baptized Joseph)"; Pouliot, *Le premier retraitant du Canada*; and Steckley, *Untold Tales*, 5–17. Other scholarly treatments of Chihoatenhwa include Greer, "Colonial Saints," 342–3 and Anderson, *The Death and Afterlife of the North American Martyrs*, 67–8, 269–70, and 331–2.

11 Author's translation. Sagard, *Le grand voyage du pays des Hurons*, 164.

12 *JRAD* 15.79–81, *MNF* 4.157.

13 Poirier, *Religion, Gender, and Kinship in Colonial New France*, 73–5, 120.

14 Ibid., 106.

15 *JRAD* 15.79. "Il a l'esprit excellent, non seulement en comparaison de ces compatriotes, mais mesmes à nostre jugement il passeroit pour tel en France. Pour sa mémoire, nous l'avons souvent admirée, car il n'oublie rien de ce que nous luy enseignons et c'est un contentement de l'entendre discourir sur nos saincts mystères." *MNF* 4.157.

16 For a summary of what is known about Wendat sexual and marriage practices, see Sioui, *Huron-Wendat*, 122–4. A good sense of how Jesuits and other settlers perceived these practices can be gleaned from Trigger, *The Children of Aataentsic*, 48–50.

17 It is not clear what kind of feasts Le Mercier had in mind. On Wendat feasts and festivals in general, see Sioui, *Huron-Wendat*, 160–1. On the periodic feast of the dead, see Seeman, *The Huron-Wendat Feast of the Dead*.

18 For accounts of Chihoatenhwa's life that focus primarily on his faith, see Henry, *Friends of God*; Pouliot, *Le premier retraitant au Canada*; Campeau, *La Mission des Jésuites chez les Hurons*, 54–215 (the story unfolds slowly over the course of Campeau's historical and religious analysis of the situation among the Wendat). For other perspectives, see Abé, *The Jesuit Mission to New France*, 110n54 and 118; Dunn, "Bedside Manners," 583; Labelle, "Oky Ontatechiata," 203; Porterfield, "Witchcraft and the Colonization of Algonquian and Iroquois Cultures," 111; and Poirier, *Religion, Gender, and Kinship in Colonial New France*, 73–126 (chapter 3).

19 See, for example, Henry, *Friends of God*, 102; Monet, "The Jesuits in New France," 188; Steckley, *Untold Tales*, 14; and Trigger, *The Children of Aataentsic*, 598–9.

20 Pearson, *Becoming Holy in Early Canada*, 62–3.

21 O'Donnell, "Brébeuf's Spiritual Journal," 48. "Le sentiment que j'eus pour lors est que Dieu vouloit donner à entendre l'estat de l'âme de ce bon chrestien." *MNF* 7.480–1.

22 Anderson notes that Indigenous Catholics often prefer another, more modern candidate: Rose Prince, a Dakelh woman from British Columbia whose body was reportedly found to have not decomposed two years

after her 1949 burial. Anderson, *The Death and Afterlife of the North American Martyrs*, 375–6. On Rose Prince, see also Anderson, "Residential School Saint."

23 See Henry, *Friends of God*, 26–7 and Pouliot, *Le premier retraitant du Canada*, 19. Poirier also comments briefly on Chihoatenhwa's effort to learn to write, seeing it as a possible contributing factor in his alienation from his fellow Wendat, who may have viewed writing with suspicion. Poirier, *Religion, Gender, and Kinship in Colonial New France*, 90–1.

24 For examples of the Wendat and their neighbours expressing unease about the Jesuits' ability to write and its potential relationship to disease, see *JRAD* 19.129, *MNF* 4.669 and *JRAD* 21.219–21, *MNF* 5.198. On this subject, see also Poirier, *Religion, Gender, and Kinship in Colonial New France*, 92–3 and Blackburn, *Harvest of Souls*, 110–11.

25 *JRAD* 8.113. "ils ne pouvoient concevoir comme ce qu'un de nous, estant au village, leur avoit dit et couché en mesme temps par escrit, un autre, qui cependant estoit dans la maison bien esloignée, le disoit incontinent en voyant l'escriture. Je crois qu'ils en ont fait cent expériences. Tout cela sert pour gaigner leurs affections et les rendre plus dociles, quand il est question des admirables et incompréhensibles mystères de nostre foy. Car la croyance qu'ils ont de nostre esprit et de nostre capacité fait que sans réplique ils croyent ce qu'on leur annonce." *MNF* 3.100.

26 *JRAD* 10.121–3, *MNF* 3.344–5. Birgit Rasmussen has cited this passage as a sign that the Wendat language had its own word for writing, and that writing was therefore "a common and familiar practice in Huron society." Rasmussen, *Queequeg's Coffin*, 19. The Wendat certainly had their own ways of preserving and transmitting information, as discussed later in this chapter, but it is entirely possible that this word was introduced by the Jesuits because the New France missionaries understood their linguistic work to be as much a process of invention as of documentation. See True, *Masters and Students*, 55–82 (chapter 3).

27 *JRAD* 15.121. "L'art de coucher sur le papier les choses esloignées." *MNF* 4.172.

28 See *JRAD* 10.27, *MNF* 3.314.

29 *JRAD* 13.51–3. "Un autre luy demanda d'où nous sçavions qu'il y avoit un enfer et d'où nous tenions tout ce que nous disions de l'estat des damnez. Le Père dit là-dessus que nous en avions des asseurances indubitables, que nous le tenions par révélation divine. Que le Sainct-Esprit avoit luy-mesme dicté ces véritez à des personnages et à nos ancestres, qui nous les ont laissées par escrit, que nous en conservions encor précieusement les livres." *MNF* 3.699.

30 JRAD 5.245, MNF 2.469. For more on Amantacha/Louis de Sainte-Foi, see Trigger, "Amantacha, Louis de Sainte-Foi." For a more literary exploration of his life, see Vollmann, "An Incomplete Biography of Amantacha the Huron."

31 JRAD 22.197. "Ma bonne Mère, je suis sur le poinct de partir. Je vous remercie de ce que vous avez eu tant de soin de moy et de ce que m'avez enseigné à bien servir Dieu. Seroit-ce pour peu de chose que je vous remercie? Jamais je ne m'en oublieray." MNF 5.436. This note was written in Wendat and translated into French for inclusion in the *Relation*. On Thérèse Oionhaton, see Anderson, "'Thine Own by Adoption'" and Poirier, *Religion, Gender, and Kinship in Colonial New France*, 127–74 (chapter 4).

32 It was not only Wendat people who sometimes learned to write. The well-known Innu convert Pierre-Antoine Pastedechouan did as well, to judge by the references to his writings in the work of Gabriel Sagard. See Sagard, *Histoire du Canada*, 206. On Pastedechouan, see Anderson, *The Betrayal of Faith*.

33 See, for example, Axtell, "The Power of Print" and Carpenter, *The Renewed, the Destroyed, and the Remade*, 53–6.

34 Susan M. Hill, *The Clay We Are Made Of*, 9. Georges Sioui, a Wendat philosopher and historian, has similarly written that sources like the *Relations* "were intended to give readers a low opinion of Amerindians and create general indifference to their existence and disappearance in order to justify colonial activity." Sioui, *Huron-Wendat*, xx. A number of non-Indigenous scholars have argued along similar lines that claims about Indigenous Peoples' surprise and enthusiasm about writing – not only in New France but throughout the world – may have had more to do with the importance missionaries and other settlers placed on the written word than with the actual reactions of Indigenous people. A useful if dated survey of such work can be found in Wogan, "Perceptions of European Literacy in Early Contact Situations."

35 Poirier, *Gender and Kinship in Colonial New France*, 106–7.

36 Pollack, "Chihoatenhwa's Prayer," 94–5. Trigger speculated that Chihoatenhwa was interested in learning to write primarily as a way of gaining prestige or at least notoriety among his own people. Trigger, *The Children of Aataentsic*, 550–1.

37 JRAD 10.293. "luy mit auprès de luy son atsatonewai, c'est-à-dire son pacquet de buchettes de conseil, qui sont tous les livres et papiers du päis." MNF 3.397. As Elisabeth Tooker noted in her classic ethnography of the Wendat, these were probably akin to the sticks and canes that are

known to have been used as mnemonic devices by other Iroquoian peoples, including the Haudenosaunee. Tooker, *An Ethnography of the Huron Indians*, 47n68. On this Wendat ceremony, see Seeman, *The Huron-Wendat Feast of the Dead*.

38 For a concise collection of what colonial observers – French, Dutch, and English – reported about the use of sticks for this purpose among the Wendat and other Indigenous Peoples, see William M. Beauchamp, "Aboriginal Use of Wood in New York," 169–71.

39 *JRAD* 29.103–5. "Ce pauvre homme tire un petit faisseau de bois comme une botte d'alumette et, les monstrant au Père, luy dist: 'voilà tous mes péchez. Je les ay escrits dessus ce bois à nostre mode, de peur d'en oublier.' Il se confesse avec de grands regrets, les yeux pleins de larmes, la bouche pleine de sanglots et le coeur tout remply de regrets et de douleur. Après sa confession, il raconta au Père comme il estoit tombé dans l'abysme de ses péchez." *MNF* 6.589.

40 *JRAD* 30.61. "Ils ont coustume en semblables rencontres de raconter les histoires qu'ils ont appris de leurs ancestres et les plus éloignées, afin que les jeunes gens qui sont présens et les entendent en puissent conserver la mémoire et les raconter à leur tour, lorsqu'ils seront devenus vieux, pour ainsi transmettre à leur postérité l'histoire et les annales du païs, tâchans par ce moyen de suppléer au défaut de l'escriture et des livres qui leur manquent. On présente à celuy duquel on désire entendre quelque chose un petit faisceau de pailles d'un pied de long, qui leur servent de jettons pour supputer les nombres et pour aider la mémoire des assistans, distribuant en divers lots ces mesmes pailles, selon la diversité des choses qu'ils racontent." *MNF* 6.665.

41 *JRAD* 39.149. "Non hanno eglino nè libri nè scrittura alcuna, come habbiam detto." *MNF* 8.476. See also *JRAD* 39.103; *MNF* 8.460.

42 Tooker, *An Ethnography of the Huron Indians*, 47n68.

43 A rich survey of the history of the production and use of wampum can be found in Lainey, *La 'monnaie des Sauvages'*, 11–26 (chapter 1).

44 Sioui, *For an Amerindian Autohistory*, 91; Lainey, *La 'Monnaie des Sauvages'*, 18.

45 To cite just three examples of Jesuit comments on the exchange value of wampum among the Wendat from the period under discussion here, Brébeuf in his 1636 *Relation* wrote that *porcelaine* "takes the place of gold and silver in this Country." *JRAD* 10.29; "tient lieu d'or et d'argent en ce pays." *MNF* 3.315. Two years later, Le Jeune indicated that this was the primary function of wampum more broadly, not just among the Wendat, writing that "these are the pearls and diamonds of the country"

and also that "these are the pistoles of the country." *JRAD* 14.163, 15.37. "ce sont les perles et les diamans du pays" and "ce sont les pistoles du païs." *MNF* 4.90, 142.

46 Sioui, *For an Amerindian Autohistory*, 91.

47 *JRAD* 40.165–7. "Ce capitaine fit étaler ses présens, qui servent parmy tous ces peuples barbares comme parmy nous les escrits et les contrats ... Ces présens consistoient en castors et en porcelaine et chacun d'eux avoit son nom et faisoit voir le désir de celuy qui parloit et de ceux qui l'avoient délégué." *MNF* 8.597–8.

48 Sioui has pointed out that wampum records continued to be useful to the Wendat long after the end of the Jesuit mission. In 1829, a wampum belt served as a record of the geography of Wendat territory in a dispute with the government of Lower Canada and other Indigenous Peoples. Sioui, *For an Amerindian Autohistory*, 90–1.

49 Sayre, *The Indian Chief as Tragic Hero*, 252. Sayre traces this motif in accounts of the Natchez Massacre and Pueblo Revolt and argues that such sticks served not as a means of counting down the days to a significant event, as suggested in written accounts that emphasize the innumeracy of Indigenous groups, but rather of communicating their commitments. Sayre, *The Indian Chief as Tragic Hero*, 236–7, 251–61.

50 Rasmussen, *Queequeg's Coffin*, 3; Mignolo, *The Darker Side of the Renaissance*, 83–7; and Wogan, "Perceptions of European Literacy in Early Contact Situations," 413.

51 Rasmussen, *Queequeg's Coffin*, 3. See also Mignolo, *Local Histories/Global Designs*, 259; Warkentin, "In Search of 'The Word of the Other'"; and Warkentin, "Dead Metaphor or Working Model?"

52 Kelsey, *Reading the Wampum*, xxv. See also Rasmussen, *Queequeg's Coffin*, 62.

53 Rasmussen, *Queequeg's Coffin*, 49–78 (chapter 2).

54 Haas, "Wampum as Hypertext."

55 *JRAD* 17.49. "Je vous demande, quand au commencement vous veistes de leurs haches et chaudières, après avoir recognu qu'elles estoient incomparablement meilleures et plus commodes que nos haches de pierre et que nos vaisseaux de boix et de terre, avez-vous pour cela rejetté leurs haches et chaudières, parce que c'estoit chose nouvelle à vostre païs et la coustume de France de s'en servir et non pas la vostre? Que s'ils nous pressent de croire ce qu'ils croyoient et de vivre conformément à ceste creance, nous leur en avons beaucoup d'obligation, car en effet si ce qu'ils disent est vray, comme il est, nous sommes les plus misérables gens du monde, si nous ne faisons ce qu'ils nous dissent." *MNF* 4.382.

56 *JRAD* 41.167, *MNF* 8.713.

57 Haas, "Wampum as Hypertext," 89. U. Vincent Wilcox, then curator of the Museum of the American Indian, similarly wrote that "in its very essence wampum signified sincerity and truth ... Wampum became the symbol of the power of the word. Words spoken over wampum became embodied in the beads." Wilcox, "The Manufacture and Use of Wampum in the Northeast," 12.

58 Rasmussen, *Queequeg's Coffin*, 62.

59 *JRAD* 15.113. "le profit a esté bien grand pour nous, car en luy servant de maistres pour la lecture, nous nous sommes façonnez un bon maistre en la langue. Quand nous luy demandons les initiales ou finales des mots, ce qui est quelquefois quasi imperceptible, il nous les dit fort distinctement; si qu'il nous servira fort, avec l'ayde de Dieu, pour les conjugaisons. Il nous a mesme dicté plusieurs beaux discours sur nos saincts mystères, dans une suite fort judicieuse, mais si distinctement que vous ne perdrez pas une syllabe." *MNF* 4.169. For additional examples, see *JRAD* 15.91–3, *MNF* 4.162 and *JRAD* 15.95, *MNF* 4.163.

60 For just a few examples, see *JRAD* 17.47–9, *MNF* 4.382; *JRAD* 19.137–63, *MNF* 4.672–81; and *JRAD* 20.63–5, *MNF* 4.734.

61 The full prayer can be found in *JRAD* 21.251–65 and *MNF* 4.209–14. John Steckley has offered an alternative translation, from the original Wendat directly to English, which is much smoother than the English version based on the Jesuits' French translation found in the Thwaites edition. See Steckley, *Untold Tales*, 14–16. It has been reprinted as an appendix in Poirier, *Religion, Gender, and Kinship in Colonial New France*, 209–11. For a scholarly examination of this text as it appeared in the *Relation*, see Pollack, "Chihoatenhwa's Prayer."

62 *JRAD* 21.251. "Quelques-uns ont souhaitté de voir un eschantillon de la langue huronne, pour en recognoistre l'oeconomie et leur façon de s'énoncer. Je n'ay pu choisir rien de meilleur qu'un des entretiens des plus ordinaires qu'eut avec Dieu sur la fin de ses jours Joseph Chih8atenh8a, ce brave chrestien dont nous avons fait mention. On y pourra par mesme moyen recognoistre l'Esprit de Dieu qui le poussoit." *MNF* 5.209–10.

63 See, for just a few additional examples of words that were reportedly dictated by Indigenous people, *JRAD* 55.260–3 (this text is not included in *MNF*); *JRAD* 25.131–3, *MNF* 6.67–8; *JRAD* 37.77–9, *MNF* 8.152–3; and *JRAD* 24.39–43, *MNF* 5.669–71.

64 On this aspect of pious speeches by Indigenous people, including Chihoatenhwa, that appear in the *Relations*, see Susini, "Dépaysement et détours d'une scénographie édifiante."

65 As prescribed in the *Constitutions* of the Society of Jesus, "They will exercise themselves in preaching and in delivering [sacred] lectures in a manner suited to the edification of the people, which is different from the scholastic manner; they should strive to learn the vernacular language well, to have prepared and have ready at hand the topics most useful for this ministry, and to avail themselves of all appropriate means to perform it better and with greater fruit for souls." *The Constitutions of the Society of Jesus*, 171.

66 On the gap between communicative intent and result that can sometimes be perceived in the Jesuits' efforts to explain their message in Indigenous languages, see True, "*Il faut parler pour estre entendu*" and *Masters and Students*, 55–82 (chapter 3). See also Leavelle, *The Catholic Calumet*, 97–125 (chapter 5). For some enlightening commentary suggesting that Jesuit missionaries' mastery of Indigenous languages may not have been quite what they sometimes appeared to claim, see Stevens, "The Language of Belief."

67 *JRAD* 19.161. "Ha! Que nous sommes bien esloignéz de cette amitié." *MNF* 4.680.

68 *JRAD* 19.251. "L'esté passé, allant et retournant de Kébec, dans les saults et portages, il faisoit trois et quatre voyages chargé quasi au-dessus de ses forces, et tout cela pour Dieu. Au commencement du portage, il offroit son travail à Nostre-Seigneur; dans le chemin, il s'entretenoit continuellement avec luy; et à la fin, il le remercioit de luy avoir donné la force de faire quelque chose pour luy." *MNF* 4.712.

69 *JRAD* 19.251–3. "Dans les pacquets qu'il rapporta pour nous, il y avoit entr'autres choses des reliques précieuses de quelque sainct. C'estoit là sa consolation, et jamais ne voulut permettre qu'autre que luy se chargeast d'un si sainct quoyque pesant fardeau, et ses devis plus ordinaires dans le plus fort de ses travaux estoient avec ceux qu'il ne cognoissoit mesme de nom, mais qu'il aimoit et honoroit, puisqu'ils estoient amis de Dieu." *MNF* 4.712.

70 *JRAD* 13.17. "Nous receusmes un pacquet de lettres de Vostre Révérence par le moyen d'un sauvage." *MNF* 3.688.

71 *JRAD* 15.61, *MNF* 4.151. Brébeuf's letter is also reproduced in the *Relation*. See *JRAD* 15.61–5, *MNF* 4.151–3.

72 *JRAD* 31.219, *MNF* 7.164.

73 *JRAD* 13.7. "Les secours, tant spirituels que temporels, ne nous viennent icy que par l'entremise et les mains des sauvages." *MNF* 3.685.

74 *JRAD* 20.77–9. "Je me disposois à escrire à Vostre Révérence pour la dernière fois de cette présente année, par la voye de Joseph Chihouatenhoua,

nostre bon chrestien, et voilà que le mesme papier dont il devoit estre le porteur est employé pour porter à Vostre Révérence la nouvelle de sa mort." *MNF* 4.739.

75 *JRAD* 22.271–3, *MNF* 5.467–8.

76 *JRAD* 33.135–7, *MNF* 7.392.

77 *JRAD* 15.35. "Nous ne pûmes faire sçavoir de la santé du Père à l'habitation de Sainct-Joseph qu'après la huictaine, faute de messager. Les lettres qu'ils nous escriverent monstrent évidemment que la chose passoit pour véritable parmy ceux de leur bourgade." *MNF* 4.141.

78 *JRAD* 21.231, *MNF* 5.201–2.

79 Jogues' ordeal is recounted in more detail than can be offered here in Giguère, "Jogues, Isaac."

80 These details are recounted across two of the *Relations*. See *JRAD* 24.295, *MNF* 5.766 and *JRAD* 31.89, *MNF* 7.120.

81 Melzer, *Colonizer or Colonized*, 83.

82 For other examples, see Wroth, "The *Jesuit Relations* from New France," 117–8 and *JRAD* 1.38.

83 Donnelly, *Thwaites' Jesuit Relations*, 3; Melzer, *Colonizer or Colonized*, 83.

84 Stevens, "The Language of Belief," 65–6.

CHAPTER FIVE

1 *JRAD* 38.69. "La Mère Marie de l'Incarnation, supérieure du séminaire des Ursulines de Kébec en la Nouvelle-France, voulant consoler ses soeurs sur la mort de la Mère Marie de Sainct-Joseph, leur a envoyé un abrégé de sa vie, de sa mort et de ses vertus. Ces mémoires estans tombez entre mes mains, j'ay creu que ce seroit faire tort au public de renfermer ce thrésor dans les seules maisons des Ursulines. J'en ay donc tiré la pluspart des choses que je vay déduire dans ce chapitre." *MNF* 8.344.

2 Oury concluded in a footnote to his edition of Marie de l'Incarnation's letters that Le Jeune "draws inspiration from her text more than he reproduces it." Author's translation. Marie de l'Incarnation, *Correspondance*, 468n1. See also Jamet's footnotes to his edition of this letter: Marie de l'Incarnation, *Écrits spirituels et historiques*, 4: 345–413.

3 On this aspect of the *Relations'* circulation, see True, *Masters and Students*, 151–3.

4 Marie de l'Incarnation, *From Mother to Son*, 129. "Il m'a beaucoup obligée de le faire, mais il m'eût fait un singulier plaisir de ne point faire paroître mon nom. Moy qui ne sçavois rien de tout cela, étant Lectrice au réfectoir, je me trouvé justement à commencer par cette histoire. J'en eus

de la confusion et la quitté pour la faire lire à une autre." Marie de l'Incarnation, *Correspondance*, 521.

5 On the norms and expectations surrounding women's participation in seventeenth-century French epistolary and autobiographical writing, see Farrell, *Performing Motherhood*, 27–56 (chapter 1); Zecher, "A New-World Model of Female Epistolarity," 95; and Dunn, *The Cruelest of All Mothers*, 26–9. See also the parallel case of Teresa of Avila as described in Weber, *Teresa of Avila and the Rhetoric of Femininity*, especially 17–41 (chapter 1).

6 Author's translation. "L'on m'écrit à son sujet de divers endroits de la France d'une manière qui fait voir l'amour et la dévotion que l'on a conçue pour elle. C'est un effet de nos lettres et du récit de sa vie, que le R. Père le Jeune a fait dans la Relation." Marie de l'Incarnation, *Correspondance*, 505.

7 Marie de l'Incarnation, *From Mother to Son*, 129. "J'avois donné charge qu'on vous envoiât une copie du récit que j'ay fait à nos Mères, de la vie et de la mort de notre chère défunte. On me mande qu'on ne l'a pas encore fait, parce que cet écrit est tombé entre les mains du R. Père Le Jeune. Ce bon Père en a pris ce qu'il a voulu pour mettre dans la Relation, sans que je l'en eusse prié." Marie de l'Incarnation, *Correspondance*, 521.

8 Marie de l'Incarnation, *Correspondance*, 853.

9 These and other details of Marie de l'Incarnation's life are drawn from Davis, *Women on the Margins*; Deroy-Pineau, *Marie Guyard de l'Incarnation*; Dunn, *The Cruelest of All Mothers*; Grégoire, *Marie Guyart de l'Incarnation*; Marie de l'Incarnation, *Marie de l'Incarnation, Ursuline de Tours*, 1: 17–100; and Oury, *Marie de l'Incarnation*. A short, informative overview can be found in Chabot, "Guyart, Marie named de l'Incarnation (Martin)."

10 Author's translation. "Dieu m'avoit donné du talent pour le negoce, et qu'il se trouvoit bien des personnes qui s'offroient de me faire des avances pour cela." Martin, *La Vie de la Vénérable Mère Marie de l'Incarnation*, 31.

11 Martin, *La Vie de la Vénérable Mère Marie de l'Incarnation*, 48–9. For a succinct summary of her writings during this period of her life, see Davis, *Women on the Margins*, 68–9.

12 On the history of the Ursulines in France, see Gueudré, *Histoire de l'ordre des Ursulines en France*. A rich but dated account of the Quebec Ursuline monastery can be found in *Les Ursulines de Québec depuis leur établissement jusqu'à nos jours*, authored anonymously, perhaps by an Ursuline, in the mid-nineteenth century.

13 On this act of abandonment in relation to the norms of seventeenth-century French family life, see Dunn, *The Cruelest of All Mothers*, 47–70 (chapter 2, especially 67).

14 Author's translation. "Rendez-moy ma mere; rendez-moy ma mere." Martin, *La Vie de la Vénérable Mère Marie de l'Incarnation*, 181, 186.

15 Ibid., 229.

16 Davis, *Women on the Margins*, 78.

17 Marie de l'Incarnation, *Correspondance*, 42–4; Martin, *La Vie de la Vénérable Mère Marie de l'Incarnation*, 305; Davis, *Women on the Margins*, 77–8.

18 Marie de l'Incarnation, *Correspondance*, 27, 34, and 56.

19 Le Jeune's *Relation* for this year includes an excerpt of a letter from an unnamed Ursuline that expresses a desire to work in New France, in a chapter recounting the favourable comments he had received from readers and supporters in France. *JRAD* 8.239, *MNF* 3.196. This letter cannot be attributed to Marie de l'Incarnation with certainty, but her interest in New France was blossoming at this time and the account of her life that her son prepared after her death on the basis of her own writings reports that she corresponded with Le Jeune before her arrival in Quebec. Martin, *La Vie de la Vénérable Mère Marie de l'Incarnation*, 347. Oury was sufficiently convinced to include the *Relation's* excerpt of the unnamed Ursuline's letter in his edition of her correspondence. See Marie de l'Incarnation, *Correspondance*, 60–1.

20 Davis, *Women on the Margins*, 81–2. On La Peltrie and her relationship with Marie de l'Incarnation, see Chabot, "Chauvigny, Mary-Madeleine de (Gruel de La Peltrie)" and Deroy-Pineau, *Madeleine de La Peltrie*.

21 A succinct summary of her writings can be found in Chabot, "Guyart, Marie, named de l'Incarnation (Martin)." Albert Jamet's 1929 edition of her writings remains the most complete collection of them with the exception of her correspondence, which has been surpassed by Oury's edition. Marie de l'Incarnation, *Ursuline de Tours: Fondatrice des Ursulines de la Nouvelle-France*, vols 3 and 4.

22 See Oury's summary of recipients in Marie de l'Incarnation, *Correspondence*, 61–2.

23 Mahoney, ed., *Marie of the Incarnation*, 225. "C'est icy la lettre du coeur; car mon autre qui vous parle de ce qui est arrivé en cette nouvelle Eglise du Fils de Dieu peut être commune et communiquée." Marie de l'Incarnation, *Correspondance*, 172. The second letter referenced here has been lost.

24 Dunn, "Introduction," 19n53; Davis, *Women on the Margins*, 100. For an overview of women's participation in epistolary culture in seventeenth-century France, see Farrell, *Performing Motherhood*, chapter 1 (27–56). For an examination of Marie de l'Incarnation's correspondence alongside that of well-known French women letter writers like Sévigné, see Zecher, "A New-World Model of Female Epistolarity."

25 For the 1644 and 1647 tallies reported here, see Marie de l'Incarnation, *Correspondance*, 240 and 320. For estimates of her total output, see Mahoney, ed., *Marie of the Incarnation: Selected Writings*, 6; Deslandres, "De Marie Guyart de l'Incarnation aux femmes 'ordinaires' de la Nouvelle-France," 266–7; and Marie de l'Incarnation, *Ursuline de Tours: Fondatrice des Ursulines de la Nouvelle-France*, 3: 13–14.

26 On Marie de l'Incarnation's mysticism, see Bruneau, *Women Mystics Confront the Modern World*; Mali, *Mystic in the New World*; and Deslandres, "Qu'est-ce qui faisait courir Marie Guyart?" On her missionary activities and participation in colonial life, see Grégoire, *Marie Guyart de l'Incarnation*; Peelman, "Marie Guyart de l'Incarnation et la spiritualité amérindienne"; Galvani, "Apprendre enfin des Indiens"; Deslandres, "L'Éducation des Amérindiennes"; and Zecher, "Life on the French-Canadian Hyphen." On her status as a mother, see Dunn, *The Cruelest of All Mothers*. Many other works along these lines can be found in the various edited collections of scholarship devoted to Marie de l'Incarnation. See especially Deroy-Pineau, ed., *Marie Guyart de l'Incarnation*; Brodeur, ed., *Femme, mystique, et missionnaire*; and Roy-Lysencourt et al., eds, *Marie Guyart de l'Incarnation.*

27 Davis, *Women on the Margins*, 80, 82–3.

28 Choquette, "Ces Amazones du Grand Dieu," 632, 636–7.

29 On this episode, see Grégoire, *Marie Guyart de l'Incarnation*, 138–41.

30 Choquette, "Ces Amazones du Grand Dieu," 637–8. See also Noel, *Along a River*, 66.

31 Noel, *Along a River*, 53. Although work certainly remains to be done, much scholarship has appeared in recent decades that places the experiences of women, both Indigenous and settler, at the centre of colonial life and intercultural contact. For just a few examples in addition to those cited above, see Anderson, *Chain Her by One Foot*; Devens, *Countering Colonization*; and Sleeper-Smith, *Indian Women and French Men.*

32 Davis, *Women on the Margins*, 100.

33 Bruneau, *Women Mystics Confront the Modern World*, 86.

34 *JRAD* 19.45. "Mais voyons ce que m'escrivit la Mère Marie de l'Incarnation touchant la première communion de ces jeunes enfans." *MNF* 4.640.

35 *JRAD* 19.39. "Escoutons-les parler de leur thrésor, c'est-à-dire de leurs enfans. Si je voulois coucher icy toutes les lettres de joye qu'elles m'ont escrites sur ce sujet, je ferois quasi un livre au lieu d'un chapitre." *MNF* 4.637.

36 *JRAD* 22.181, *MNF* 5.431.

37 *JRAD* 22.183. "Cette lettre a semblé digne de ce lieu. Venons au détail." *MNF* 5.431.

38 *JRAD* 22.183–5. "Il n'y a pas de doute que si on avoit de quoy en loger un nombre, qu'on les rendroit aussi adroittes et aussi gentilles que nos Européannes. Ce n'est pas ce qu'on cherche à présent, mais bien de graver dans leurs coeurs l'amour et la crainte de celuy dont elles ont maintenant cognoissance. C'est à quoy visent les travaux de ces bonnes Mère, ausquels Nostre-Seigneur semble donner sa bénédiction." *MNF* 5.432.

39 *JRAD* 22.187–9. "Deux de nos filles, âgées d'environ huict à neuf ans, dist la Mère, ont pressé quasi un an durant leur maistresse de les disposer à la communion. Se voyans rebutées, elles s'adressent à moy, me suppliant avec beaucoup de caresses de leur accorder cette faveur. Leur ayant dit qu'elles estoient trop jeunes, elles ne perdent point courage. Le révérend Père Vimon les estans venues voir pendant l'advent pour leur donner quelque instruction, elles se jettent à ses pieds et le conjurent de leur donner Nostre-Seigneur, du moins au temps de Pasques." *MNF* 5.433.

40 These three paragraphs can be found in *MNF* 5.432–4 (paragraphs 7, 10, and 13) and Marie de l'Incarnation, *Correspondance*, 146–8.

41 On this phenomenon, see Bilinkoff, *Related Lives*, 46–75 (chapter 3). See also Timmermans, *L'Accès des femmes à la culture*, 544–5.

42 Davis, *Women on the Margins*, 129; Dunn, *The Cruelest of All Mothers*, 8–9, 29; Oury, "Introduction," xiii; and Zecher, "A New World Model of Female Epistolarity," 96–7. As Oury summarized Martin's work, "Dom Claude rewrote, so to speak, the text he had before his eyes. The variants are extremely numerous and are not only justified by the archaism of certain turns of phrase." Author's translation. Oury, "Introduction," xx. See also Marie de l'Incarnation, *Ursuline de Tours: Fondatrice des Ursulines de la Nouvelle-France*, 3: 24–8.

43 On the preparation of this edition and its relationship to Martin's earlier work, *La Vie de la Vénérable Mère Marie de l'Incarnation*, see Oury's introduction to his 1971 re-edition of Marie de l'Incarnation's correspondence (ix–xvi).

44 These are the letters excerpted in the *Relations* and attributed to Marie de l'Incarnation in 1640 and 1642, and the 1636 excerpt from an unnamed Ursuline who, as noted above, is usually understood to be her. See Marie de l'Incarnation, *Correspondance*, 60, 91, 93, and 146.

45 *JRAD* 20.137, *MNF* 5.67.

46 *JRAD* 25.231. “J’advoue, disoit la Mère supérieure, que les interrogeant pour reconnoistre si elles estoient capables de recevoir ce pain céléste, qu’elles ont surpassé mon attente, les voyant instruites et touchées au-delà de mes espérances.” *MNF* 6.102.

47 *JRAD* 30.153, *MNF* 7.201 and Marie de l’Incarnation, *Correspondance*, 359.

48 *JRAD* 56.246–63.

49 For brief mentions of the Ursulines’ activities after the Jesuits stopped devoting a full chapter to the subject, see *JRAD* 31.175–81, *MNF* 7.149–50 and *JRAD* 32.213–17, *MNF* 7.322.

50 For additional examples, see Marie de l’Incarnation’s 1642 mention of an Indigenous convert named Charles who she said had been discussed in the *Relations*, and the corresponding passages of the Jesuit’s annual report for the previous year: Marie de l’Incarnation, *Correspondance*, 160–1; *JRAD* 20.145, *MNF* 5.69; *JRAD* 20.185–213, *MNF* 5.82–93; and *JRAD* 21.81–105, *MNF* 5.147–56. In 1643 she mentioned the marriage of a girl named Angelle, and noted the favourable comments about her that had appeared in the previous year’s *Relation*. See Marie de l’Incarnation, *From Mother to Son*, 59; Marie de l’Incarnation, *Correspondence*, 201; *JRAD* 22.115–25, *MNF* 5.407–11. And in 1645, she pointed to the 1644 *Relation* for information on the exploits of a Christian convert named Pieskaret. See Marie de l’Incarnation, *Correspondance*, 250; *JRAD* 26.53–73, *MNF* 6.133–40.

51 Marie de l’Incarnation, *From Mother to Son*, 46. “Mr nostre Gouverneur les a chassé dans un combat qui leur a livré pour sauver nos bons néophites. La relation vous le dira.” Marie de l’Incarnation, *Correspondance*, 132.

52 *JRAD* 21.61–3, *MNF* 5.139–40.

53 Author’s translation. “L’on voit des Sorciers devenus Apôtres et prêcher hardiment l’Evangile à leurs compatriotes: La Relation vous le dira, car les lettres sont arrivées si tard que je n’ay pas le loisir de m’étendre. Comme vous êtes jaloux de la gloire du Roy des Nations, votre coeur sera comblé de joye d’apprendre que douze cens personnes ont été baptisées: Ce sont des effets du bras tout-puissant, qui par les travaux de sa vie et de sa passion, s’est acquis tous ces peuples: on en a encore découvert de nouveaux, à la conversion desquels on va travailler.” Marie de l’Incarnation, *Correspondance*, 112–13.

54 *JRAD* 18.95, *MNF* 4.570; *JRAD* 18.189, *MNF* 4.604; and *JRAD* 18.205, *MNF* 4.609.

55 *JRAD* 18.119. “Nous avons baptisé cette année environ douze cens sauvages, tant aux Hurons qu’icy bas.” *MNF* 4.578.

56 *JRAD* 18.227–49, *MNF* 4.617–27.

57 Author's translation. "Encore que vos occupations vous empêchent de m'écrire, ou que les accidens de la mer m'eussent privée d'une si précieuse lettre, je n'eusse pas laissé de vous mander des nouvelles de ce cher païs, en attendant que la relation vous en donne de plus amples." Marie de l'Incarnation, *Correspondance*, 94. She mentioned the relation a second time in closing this letter, as a source of more information than she was able to provide herself. See Marie de l'Incarnation, *Correspondance*, 99.

58 Author's translation. "Il y a eu une grande persécution aux Hurons, où un des Pères a pensé être martyrisé d'un coup de hache. On a rompu un bâton sur lui en détestation de la foy qu'il prêchoit." Marie de l'Incarnation, *Correspondance*, 94.

59 *JRAD* 19.213–15. "Ce jeune homme que nous avions instruit m'arache avec effort le crucifix que je portois au col. Il prend une hache en main, dit que résolument j'en mourois ... Il lève la hache droit sur le milieu de ma teste alors descouverte et descharge son coup si roidement que le Père Chaumonot et moy croyons voir en ce moment ce que nous souhaittons il y a si longtemps. Je ne sçay ce qui arresta le coup, sinon la grandeur de mes péchez. Mais à moins de sentir la hache fendre une teste en deux, on ne peut pas se voir plus proche de la mort." *MNF* 4.699.

60 *JRAD* 19.263. "Il se saisit d'un gros baston au défaut d'une hache qu'il ne put pas trouver. Il descharge sa colère fortement sur le Père, ne donnant autre response à tout ce qu'il peut dire sinon de redoubler ses coups. Et quoyque son baston se fust rompu en deux après cinq ou six bonnes descharges, il continue de qui luy restoit en main." *MNF* 4.715.

61 Author's translation. "Souvent ... le Reverend Pere, qui étoit chargé de travailler aux Relations, lui communiquoit ses Memoires, pour en tirer ce qu'elle jugeroit à propos, afin d'en faire part en France à ses Amis et aux Bienfaiteurs de sa Maison." Marie de l'Incarnation, *Lettres de la Vénérable Mère Marie de l'Incarnation*, "avertissement" (unpaginated).

62 Oury, "Introduction," xvii–xviii.

63 Author's translation. "Les Hiroquois ont massacré un bon Dogique en detestation de la Foy. C'est un second Martyr dont la relation vous racontera l'histoire, et toutes les affaires de cette Eglise." Marie de l'Incarnation, *Correspondance*, 350.

64 *JRAD* 33.229–49, *MNF* 7.423–30. For the little that is known about Douart, see Campeau's biographical note: *MNF* 6.753–4. For a concise summary of this incident in its political context, see Trigger, *The Children of Aataentsic*, 746–50. Anderson sees Douart as an unacknowledged martyr. Anderson, *The Death and Afterlife of the North American*

Martyrs, 35–6, 53, 68. Oury concluded that Marie de l'Incarnation meant to reference this incident in her mention of the murder of a dogic. Marie de l'Incarnation, *Correspondance*, 351n4.

65 On the origin of the term dogic (*dogique*) and for an intriguing argument that its use in New France constitutes evidence that the mission was influenced by the example of Iberian missions in Japan, see Abé, *The Jesuit Mission to New France*, 156–63.

66 Author's translation. "j'ai bien voulu vous faire le récit en abrégé, en attendant que vous le voiez plus au long dans la relation, où vous verrez encore les grandes calamitez de cette Eglise, et les grandes risques, que courent les Ouvriers de l'Evangile." Marie de l'Incarnation, *Correspondance*, 366.

67 Marie de l'Incarnation, *From Mother to Son*, 142. "Dans celles que je vous ai écrites de ce qui s'est passé, je ne vous ai point parlé de cette nouvelle Église. Je ne veux pas laisser partir ce vaisseau sans vous en dire un mot en attendant la relation qui vous en parlera plus au long." Marie de l'Incarnation, *Correspondance*, 602. For additional examples, see Marie de l'Incarnation, *From Mother to Son*, 214 and Marie de l'Incarnation, *Correspondance*, 865–6 and 156.

68 See Davis, *Women on the Margins*, 107–8 and 116–17 and Dunn, "Introduction," 2 and 18. See also Noel, *Along a River*, 56.

69 Marie de l'Incarnation, *From Mother to Son*, 203. "fait seulement mention du progrès de l'Evangile, et de ce qui y a du rapport." Marie de l'Incarnation, *Correspondance*, 803.

70 Landy-Houillon, "Marie de l'Incarnation et les Jésuites," 74–6.

71 On this particular epistolary relationship, see Dunn, "Introduction"; Grégoire, "Une Correspondance transatlantique au 17ème siècle"; Landy-Houillon, "'Au bruit de tous les infinis'"; and Zecher, "A New-World Model of Female Epistolarity."

72 Author's translation. "Je ne vous puis dire combien j'ay d'interruptions. Cette lettre est courte, et cependant il m'a fallu faire tantôt une ligne tantôt une autre." Marie de l'Incarnation, *Correspondance*, 392–3. For another example, see her 1647 letter to Martin: "I am so constrained by the nuisance of exterior affairs that I write you only when I steal a brief moment ... See how one must pass this life in waiting for eternity." Marie de l'Incarnation, *From Mother to Son*, 97. "Je suis si enfoncée dans le tracas des affaires extérieures, que je ne vous écris qu'à petits momens que je dérobe ... Voilà comme il faut passer cette vie en attendant l'Eternité." Marie de l'Incarnation, *Correspondance*, 320.

73 Author's translation. "Je suis extrêmement fatiguée de la quantité de lettres que j'ay escrittes." Marie de l'Incarnation, *Correspondance*, 240.

74 Marie de l'Incarnation, *From Mother to Son*, 61. "Je vous écris la nuit pour la presse des lettres et des vaisseaux qui vont partir. J'ay la main si lasse qu'à peine la puis-je conduire, c'est ce qui me fait finir en vous priant d'excuser si je ne relis pas ma lettre." Marie de l'Incarnation, *Correspondance*, 202. For a convenient collection of Marie de l'Incarnation's descriptions of her writing life, see Oury, "Introduction," xiv–xv, and xx.

75 Marie de l'Incarnation, *Correspondance*, 430.

76 *JRAD* 7.231. "Il est temps de sonner la retraitte. Les vaisseaux sont prests à partir et cependant, je n'ay pas encore releu ny interponctué cette grande Relation, qui peut suffire pour trois années. Vostre Révérence jugera … que je n'ay pas tout le loisir que je pourrois désirer. Je ne sçay comme cela se fait que les nouvelles s'escrivent tousjours avec empressement." *MNF* 2.739. See also Jérôme Lalemant's comments blaming the shipping schedule for his inability to make his 1648 *Relation* as coherent as it could have been. *JRAD* 32.249, *MNF* 7.335.

77 *JRAD* 5.201, *MNF* 2.451. For additional examples, see *JRAD* 7.257, *MNF* 3.46 and *JRAD* 36.217, *MNF* 7.748.

78 One notable exception to the Jesuits' tendency to say less about the difficulties of writing than Marie de l'Incarnation is Paul Le Jeune's 1633 complaint that "the cold was at times so violent that we heard the trees split in the woods, and in breaking make a noise like that of firearms. It happened to me that while writing very near a big fire, my ink froze; and I had to place a little pan full of hot coals near my inkstand, otherwise I should have found black ice instead of ink." *JRAD* 5.125. "Le froid estoit par fois si violent que nous entendions les arbres se fendre dans le bois et en se fendans faire un bruit comme des armes à feu. Il m'est arrivé qu'en escrivant fort près d'un grand feu, mon encre se geloit et par nécessité il falloit mettre un réchaut plein de charbons ardens proche de mon escritoire; autrement j'eusse trouvé de la glace noire au lieu d'encre." *MNF* 2.422. Occasional comments about such individual discomforts are to be found in the *Relations*, but they generally do not speak to the physical toll of the summer rush to produce the annual report and other letters in time for the autumn ships.

79 *JRAD* 18.61, *MNF* 4.557–8 and *JRAD* 32.127, *MNF* 7.293.

80 *JRAD* 19.37–59, *MNF* 4.636–44. See, to mention just two additional examples of words written by women finding their way into the Jesuits'

texts, the long quotation in the 1641 *Relation* from a report written by Marie Guenet de Saint-Ignace, superior of the Augustinian nuns in Quebec, and the excerpt of a letter from a Carmelite nun in France that Le Jeune included in his 1637 *Relation.* *JRAD* 20.241–9, *MNF* 5.103–6 and *JRAD* 11.53, *MNF* 3.528–9.

81 On this relationship, see Anderson, *The Death and Afterlife of the North American Martyrs*, 54–97 (chapter 2) and Dunn, *Where Paralytics Walk and the Blind See*, 90–118 (chapter 3).

82 Anderson, *The Death and Afterlife of the North American Martyrs*, 58.

83 Author's translation. "c'est un nommé Nouel dont il est parlé aux *Relations.*" Marie de l'Incarnation, *Correspondance*, 957 (appendix). Oury sees this as a reference to the Innu leader Tekouerimat, also known as Noël Négabamat. For more on this figure, see Monet, "Negabamat, baptized Noël (Tekouerimat)."

84 Author's translation. "c'est une relation vivante qui vous poura donner toutes sorte de consolation." This letter is included in an appendix to Oury's edition of her letters. Marie de l'Incarnation, *Correspondance*, 973.

85 *JRAD* 50.155. "Vous apprendrez par la Relation comme le grand courage de Monsieur nostre Gouverneur luy fit faire une campagne contre les Iroquois durant les rigueurs de l'hyver passé." *JRAD* 50. 154–6.

CHAPTER SIX

1 The details of this incident recounted here are drawn from both the year's *Relation* and Ragueneau's journal. The latter source records several facts not mentioned in the published version of the story, including the names of Buteux's companions and the size of the group of Haudenosaunee that attacked them. For the *Relation*, see *JRAD* 135–45, *MNF* 8.279–83. For the relevant journal entry, see *JRAD* 37.99, *MNF* 8.380.

2 *JRAD* 37.143. "se ruèrent incontinent sur luy pour le percer de leurs espées and pour l'assommer à coups de haches, avec son compagnon." *MNF* 8.282.

3 *JRAD* 37.145. "Je n'ay rien pu dresser que cette lettre pour la *Relation.* Les Pères, qui ne font que de retourner de leurs missions, m'ont rendu trop tard leurs mémoires. Je les envoye au Père Paul Le Jeune, procureur de nos missions, qui les présentera à Vostre Révérence pour en estre fait selon sa volonté." *MNF* 8.283. Thwaites's translation has been corrected to use the common English term for the Jesuit office of *procureur*.

4 *JRAD* 37.143. "glorieuses à Dieu dans la mort de ceux qui consomment leur vie pour le salut des âmes." *MNF* 8.283.

5 Lawrence Wroth wrote that the Jesuit provincial in Paris who received the manuscript from New France "gave it a final editing" in light of current conditions in Europe before sending it off to be printed. Wroth, "The *Jesuit Relations* from New France," 117–18. Joseph P. Donnelly wrote that it was the provincial who "edited the material and sent it to Cramoisy for publication." Donnelly, *Thwaites' Jesuit Relations*, 3. And Reuben Gold Thwaites's introduction to his monumental edition of the texts said simply that each year's text "was forwarded to the provincial of the order in France." *JRAD* 1.38.

6 Desbarats, "1616–1673. Les Jésuites. Relations des Jésuites," 52; McShea, *Apostles of Empire*, 23.

7 Melzer, *Colonizer or Colonized*, 83 and Greer, "Introduction," 14.

8 Exceptions include Pouliot, "La Contribution de P. Paul Le Jeune aux Relations des Jésuites de 1650 à 1663," which focuses on the work of Le Jeune during his time as procurator; Pouliot, *Étude sur les Relations des Jésuites*, 285–6n6, which briefly mentions changes made in Paris; and True, "'On fait dire à un enfant ce qu'on veut, quand son père est absent,'" which examines additions, omissions, and substitutions made in Paris, but stops short of considering who was responsible for them.

9 Greer wrote that "there is no reason to suppose that the Jesuit superiors and provincials altered the sense of the texts that passed through their hands." Greer, "Introduction," 14. And although he elsewhere acknowledged the alterations made by various figures in Paris – and especially Paul Le Jeune – Pouliot wrote the that *Relations* were, aside from a few exceptions, "already ready to print" when they were sent to Paris each fall. Pouliot, *Étude sur les Relations des Jésuites*, 18 (author's translation).

10 *The Constitutions of the Society of Jesus*, 317.

11 Ibid., 122. The injunction against publishing books without examination and approval is also repeated in reference to compendiums of notes on various courses made by students in Jesuit colleges to aid their study. *The Constitutions of the Society of Jesus*, 164–5.

12 The foregoing draws on the summaries of this process in Hellyer, "Because the Authority of My Superiors Commands"; Gorman, "A Matter of Faith?"; and Manning, "Publication Protocol in the Seventeenth-Century Jesuit Province of Aragon."

13 O'Malley, "The Historiography of the Society of Jesus," 7.

14 For much more detail on this text and its path to publication, see Stolzenberg, "Utility, Edification, and Superstition."

15 Castelnau-L'Estoile, "Entre curiosité et édification," 131.

16 Stolzenberg, "Utility, Edification, and Superstition."
17 Manning, "Publication Protocol in the Seventeenth-Century Jesuit Province of Aragon," 134–5.
18 On this context and the French Jesuits' efforts to navigate it by cultivating a close relationship with the French Crown amid its claims of ecclesiastical independence from Rome, see Friedrich, *The Jesuits*, 31–2; Worcester, "Jesuit Dependence on the French Monarchy"; McShea, *Apostles of Empire*, 7; and Nelson, "The Historiography of the Pre-Suppression Jesuit Mission in France."
19 *MNF* 4.5–6.
20 For reasons that are unclear, this printed *permission* or *approbation* was absent from the *Relations* for 1632, 1633, and every instalment in the series after 1663. In a few cases, it was the vice provincial whose name appeared: 1648–49, 1650–51, 1653–54. These permissions are reproduced in the relevant volumes of both *JRAD* and *MNF*.
21 *JRAD* 22.23. *Relation de ce qui s'Est Passé en la Nouvelle-France en l'Année 1642, Envoyée au Révérend Père Jean Filleau, Provincial de la Compagnie de Jésus en la Province de France, par le Révérend Père Barthélemy Vimont, de la Mesme Compagnie, Supérieur de la Résidence de Kébec.* *MNF* 5.374.
22 This summary of the role of procurator is drawn primarily from Martínez-Serna, "Procurators and the Making of the Jesuits' Atlantic Network."
23 *The Constitutions of the Society of Jesus*, 138, 259, 408, and Friedrich, *The Jesuits*, 111–12.
24 Martínez-Serna, "Procurators and the Making of the Jesuits' Atlantic Network," 190.
25 For examples of the tendency to emphasize the procurators' role in managing finances, see Zubillaga, "El Procurador de la Compañía de Jésus"; Alden, *The Making of an Enterprise;* and Friedrich, *The Jesuits*, 283. On procurators' role in facilitating the movement of information, see Martínez-Serna, "Procurators and the Making of the Jesuits' Atlantic Network," 181. In the case of New France, see Pouliot, "La Contribution de P. Paul Le Jeune aux Relations des Jésuites de 1650 à 1663."
26 Noyrot is identified as procurator in a 1626 memo bearing his name and that of Charles Lalemant that attests to receipt of a piece of land along the Saint Lawrence and Saint Charles rivers. *MNF* 2.129–30.
27 *MNF* 2.152n33.
28 *JRAD* 4.181–3, *MNF* 2.134–5. Conflict between the New France Jesuits and their colleagues in Paris over resources for the mission would continue

during and after the period in which published series of *Relations* appeared. See McShea, *Apostles of Empire*, 194–5, 206.

29 *MNF* 2.160–1.

30 *MNF* 2.204.

31 Author's translation. "Pour nous, mon révérend Père, il nous faudroit deux choses: la première, liberté de recevoir ce qu'on nous offriroit: il suffit que Vostre Révérence obtienne sur cela le consentement de nostre révérend Père et qu'elle preine la peine de me la faire sçavoir; autrement nous sommes extrêmement gesnez; deuxièmement, que l'argent de monsieur et de madame de Gamaches soit emploié pour la mission et qu'il ne soit pas diverti ailleurs, et qu'on aye permission de s'en servir tout les ans. Et de ce deuxième poinct il faudroit que nostre révérend Père en escrivît au révérend Père Provincial et que j'en sceusse quelque chose. Et véritablement, je ne vois pas pourquoy on voudroit que ceste mission fût de pire condition que celle par example de Constantinople, celles des Indes, qui se servent du revenu qu'elles ont. S'il plaisoit à Vostre Révérence de travailler pour cela, elle obligeroit fort la mission." *MNF* 2.278.

32 Le Jeune reported Lalemant's return to France to serve in this capacity in a 1 August 1638 letter written in Latin to the Jesuit superior general in Rome, Mutio Vitelleschi. See *MNF* 4.56.

33 *JRAD* 14.277. "passe en France pour nos petites affaires [et] dira de bouche ce que je ne puis coucher sur le papier sans longueur." *MNF* 4.132.

34 *JRAD* 18.241. "Je n'ose icy spécifier ce que plusieurs y font, parce qu'ils m'ont fait entendre qu'ils ne veulent avoir que Dieu pour tesmoin. Ceux qui auront dévotion de les imiter ont par-delà le Père Charles Lalemant, procureur de toutes nos missions, qui sçaura bien leur dire ce qui sera le plus expédient, losqu'il sera adverty de leurs bonnes intentions." *MNF* 4.623.

35 *JRAD* 24.125. "Le Père Charles Lalemant m'escrit de France qu'entendant les larmes et les plaintes des sauvages de ces quartiers-là, sur ce qu'ils avoient si peu souvent des personnes pour les instruire, elle a fourny de quoy entretenir cette année les Pères nécessaires à cète mission." *MNF* 5.700.

36 For a succinct account of the "taxing life" of provincials in which they were "almost constantly on the move," see Friedrich, *The Jesuits*, 106.

37 For the complaint about typesetting mistakes, see *MNF* 2.705. For the descriptions of Innu practices, see *MNF* 2.617–18 and 639–41. The latter two passages are not included in Thwaites's *Jesuit Relations*, but the relevant location is *JRAD* 7.7–19. Guy Laflèche claimed that this

manuscript served as the basis of the published *Relation*, but Lucien Campeau built a much more convincing case that the *Relation* and the surviving manuscript copy were prepared independently of each other on the basis of another manuscript, probably the one sent from Quebec. See Laflèche, *Le Missionnaire, l'apostat, le sorcier*, 226 and MNF 2.532–4.

38 For a more detailed examination of these changes, their effect on the argument made in this part of the *Relation*, and what they might have communicated to Le Jeune when he received the printed version of his text in Quebec, see True, *Masters and Students*, 163–7.

39 JRAD 7.263. "nous n'avons aucune communication avec nos Pères qui sont ès résidences de Saincte-Anne et de Sainct-Charles, si ce n'est par la voye de France; et par conséquent il ne faut point nous adresser ny lettres, ny autres choses pour leur faire tenir, ains les donner aux vaisseaux qui vont en ces habitations de nos François. Il s'ensuit encor que ne je puis rien dire des choses qui se passent en ces résidences, pour la distance des lieux et le peu de commerce que nous avons avec elles." MNF 3.48.

40 Author's translation (The *Jesuit Relations and Allied Documents* follows a different variant and does not include a translation for this passage). "Il me vient quelquefois en pensée que ce grand homme, qui par son admirable sagesse, et non pareille conduite ez affaires s'est tant acquis de renommée sur la terre, se prépare une couronne de gloire très esclatante dans le ciel, pour le soing qu'il tesmoigne avoir en la conversion de tant d'âmes que l'infidélité perd en ces pays sauvages. J'en prie tous les jours affectueusement pour luy, et nostre compagnie, ayant par son moyen occasion de glorifier Dieu en cette si noble entreprise, luy en aura une obligation éternelle." MNF 2.452, footnote. For a more detailed discussion of this alteration to the 1633 *Relation*, see True, *Masters and Students*, 161–3.

41 JRAD 8.45. "Le quatriesme de juillet, une chalouppe envoyée de la part de monsieur du Plessis Bochart, général de la flotte, resjouit tous nos François et nous asseura de sa venue, et qu'il estoit suivi de huict forts navires: six pour Tadoussac et deux pour Miscou, sans ce que l'on envoyoit au cap Breton et coste de l'Acadie à monsieur le commandeur de Razilly." MNF 3.76; McCoy, *Jesuit Relations of Canada*, 40–4. On Razilly and his association with Richelieu, see MacBeath, "Razilly (Rasilly), Isaac de," and Havard and Vidal, *Histoire de l'Amérique française*, 86, 89–90.

42 The first, second, and third variants of the text read "It is called Muskrat because, in fact, its testicles smell of musk, if caught in the Spring, – at other times, it has no odour." Adapted from JRAD 8.45. Thwaites follows

the version of this passage in the fourth variant printing: "It is called Muskrat because, in fact, a part of its body smells of musk, if caught in the Spring, – at other times, it has no odour." *JRAD* 8.45. Campeau opts for the initial version in the body of his edition of the *Relations* and records the variant in a footnote: "On l'appelle Rat musqué, pource qu'en effect les testicules, pris au Printemps, sentent le musc; en autre temps, ils n'ont point d'odeur." *MNF* 3.75–6.

43 On this subject, see Candal et al, *Printing and Misprinting*. For examples of such corrections in the *Relations*, see McCoy, *Jesuit Relations of Canada*, synoptic table (unpaginated).

44 Lucien Campeau speculated, on grounds that he regrettably did not specify, that the metropolitan affairs of the mission were managed by the procurators of the Jesuit Collège de Clermont or of the Jesuit residence in Paris (the Maison Professe) in the years before a mission procurator in Paris was appointed. *MNF* 3.41n4.

45 *JRAD* 23.267. "Vostre Révérence n'aura pas ceste année tout le contentement accoustoumé de la Relation, car la meilleure partie, qui est celle des Hurons, a esté prise par les Hiroquois avec les lettres de nos Pères." *MNF* 5.641.

46 *JRAD* 25.19. "quelques François et quelques sauvages de nos alliez, marchants par après sur les brisées de ces barbares, nos ennemis, ont recueilly quelques papiers qu'ils avoients jettez dans les bois ou qui leur estoient eschappez des mains et, nous les ayans fait tenir en France, nous en avons recueilly ce qui suit pour consoler ceux qui s'intéressent avec tant d'amour en la conversion de ces pauvres peuples et pour leur donner une petite cognoissance de ce que Nostre-Seigneur va opérant dans cette extrémité du monde." *MNF* 5.772.

47 *JRAD* 25.43–75, *MNF* 5.780–94.

48 Vimont explained the reasons for Le Jeune's journey to France in the prefatory letter to his 1643 *Relation*. See *JRAD* 23.269, *MNF* 5.642.

49 *JRAD* 25.33. "Un autre jeune chirurgien bien versé dans son art et bien cognu dans l'hospital d'Orléans, où il a donné des preuves de sa vertu et de sa suffisance, a voulu prendre la place de son camarade. Il est passé en la Nouvelle-France, et moy qui escri ce dernier chapitre, le voyant sur le poinct de monter aux Hurons, je luy représentay tous les périls où il s'alloit jetter." *MNF* 5.777.

50 On Gendron, see *MNF* 5.824 and Nadeau, "Gendron, François."

51 Campeau concluded on grounds similar to those presented here that Le Jeune wrote chapter 13 of the 1643 *Relation* in Paris, but also positively identified him as the writer of chapter 14, for reasons that he did not

specify. This second case, as outlined here, is less certain. *MNF* 5.772n1, 777n10, 778n13, 789n17.

52 *JRAD* 34.223–35, *MNF* 7.619–24; *JRAD* 36.47–57, *MNF* 7.777–81; *JRAD* 37.79–87, *MNF* 8.153–56; *JRAD* 41.199–203, *MNF* 8.724–25; *JRAD* 42.215–17, *MNF* 8.890–1; *JRAD* 44.311–17, *MNF* 9.301–3; and *JRAD* 46.197–9, *MNF* 9.572–3.

53 *JRAD* 36.45. "Je croyois que ce chapitre concluerоit la Relation de cette année, mais le Père Hiérôme Lallemant, estant retourné de la Nouvelle-France par le dernier vaisseau et n'ayant pas rencontré à Paris nostre révérend Père Provincial, nous coucherons icy la lettre qu'il luy a envoyée pour luy rendre compte des missions qu'il a si longtemps gouvernées en ce bout du monde." *MNF* 7.777.

54 *JRAD* 34.229–35, *MNF* 7.622–4.

55 See *JRAD* 36.21–45, *MNF* 7.769–76.

56 *JRAD* 37.79–87, *MNF* 8.153–6.

57 *JRAD* 40.77. "Nous envoyons au Père Paul Le Jeune, procureur de nos missions, les mémoires de nos bonnes et de nos mauvaises avantures, pour les présenter à Vostre Révérence." *MNF* 8.563.

58 *JRAD* 40.79–83, *MNF* 8.564–6.

59 *JRAD* 41.219. "ce que nous avons apris de quelques lettres et de la bouche de ceux qui sont nouvellement retournés de la Nouvelle-France." *MNF* 8.767.

60 *JRAD* 43.85. "le navire auquel on l'avoit confiée, ayant esté pris par les Espagnols et toutes les lettres qui s'y sont trouvées ayant esté jettées dans la mer, j'ay esté obligé de ramasser dans le livret que je présente à vostre Révérence ce qu'on a pu recouvrer de ces lettres et de quelques autres mémoires qui nous furent rendus trop tard l'année précédente." *MNF* 9.54.

61 *JRAD* 40.119. Thwaites's *Jesuit Relations and Allied Documents* does not include the bracketed portion of this passage in its English version of the text, despite including it in the facing-page French. "On a commandé au Père, à son retour, de coucher sur le papier sa prise et toutes ses avantures. Il a obéy avec répugnance, souhaittant que ses croix ne fussent connues que du Roy des crucifiés. Mais une partie de ses mémoires à esté déchirée par les Anglois. Nous suivons dans ce chapitre ce qui est venue entre nos mains, après avoir rapporté deux ou trois petits mots d'une lettre escrite sur ce sujet." *MNF* 8.581.

62 *JRAD* 40.191. "les lettres et les mémoires qui parlent de son arrivée et des conseils tenus pour la conclusion de la paix ont esté perdus dans le vaisseau pris par les Anglois." *MNF* 8.606–7.

63 *JRAD* 40.235. “je n’ay pas assez d’instruction pour parler en détail de tous ces peuples et de toutes ces nations. Je rapporteray quelque petite chose de ce qui est venu entre mes mains.” *MNF* 8.623.

64 For two more examples of Le Jeune’s comments about the fragmentary nature of his information in 1653, see *JRAD* 40.123, *MNF* 8.582 and *JRAD* 40.203, *MNF* 8.611.

65 *JRAD* 40.87–9. “J’ay leu dans une lettre que les chemins par où ils passèrent en s’enfuyans furent trouvés tous couvers de leur sang et qu’assés longtemps après leur départ les chiens rapportoient des lambeaux de corps humains en l’habitation des François. Il ne s’est passé aucun mois de l’année, disent les mémoires qui sont venus jusques à nous, que ces chasseurs ne nous ayent visités à la sourdine, tâchans de nous surprendre.” *MNF* 8.568. For two more examples, see *JRAD* 40.97, *MNF* 8.571 and *JRAD* 40.109, *MNF* 8.576.

66 *JRAD* 40.71. “Envoyée au R.P. Provincial de la Province de France. Par le Superieur des Missions de la mesme Compagnie.” *MNF* 8.561.

67 *JRAD* 48.153. “Comme l’on imprimoit cette Relation, il nous est tombé entre les mains le narré d’un voyage fait exprés par une personne de merite, pour reconnoistre la pays de la Nouvelle France, depuis l’entrée du Golphe Saint Laurent jusques à Montreal. Quelques personnes ont cru qu’il estoit à propos d’en faire un extrait, et de le communiquer au public dans cette Relation.” *JRAD* 48.152. The grammatical error by which *pays* is treated as feminine is present in the original.

68 *JRAD* 49.149. “Extrait d’une Lettre Escrite de Québec, du 22 Septembre” and “Depuis la Relation envoyée par le Navire qui partit d’icy le 31. D’Aoust, les Onionenhronnõs sont venus en Ambassade, and sont arrivez à Quebec le 18 Septembre.” *JRAD* 49.148.

69 *JRAD* 52.56–81.

70 *JRAD* 52.81. “Cette Lettre Circulaire a esté envoyée pour les Convents qui sont en France de l’Institut des Religieuses Hospitalieres de Dieppe. Celuy qui a eu soin de la faire imprimer ayant receu quantité de Memoires tres autentiques, sur la vie et la mort de cette heureuse defunte, a jugé à propos d’ajoûter icy les choses qui suivent.” *JRAD* 52.80.

71 On Ragueneau’s long relationship with Catherine de Saint-Augustin, see Anderson, *The Death and Afterlife of the North American Martyrs*, 54–97 (chapter 2) and Dunn, *Where Paralytics Walk and the Blind See*, 90–118 (chapter 3).

72 Ragueneau, *La Vie de la Mère Marie de Saint Augustin*, 352–5.

73 Ibid., Epistle (unpaginated).

74 See Pouliot, “La Contribution de P. Paul Le Jeune aux Relations des Jésuites de 1650 à 1663” and *MNF* 9.503n101.

75 Marie de l'Incarnation, *From Mother to Son*, 203. This translation has been altered to remove an apparently errant second "de" from the name of the Ursuline nun's illustrious correspondent, which does not appear in the French version of this passage: "lorsqu'on en envoye les exemplaires d'ici, l'on en retranche en France beaucoup de choses. Madame la Duchesse de Sennessay qui me fait l'honneur de m'écrire tous les ans, m'en manda l'année dernière le déplaisir qu'elle avoit de quelque chose qu'on avoit retranché, et elle me dit quelque chose de semblable encore cette année." Marie de l'Incarnation, *Correspondance*, 803.
76 Martin, *Print, Power, and People in Seventeenth-Century France*, 223.
77 Martin, *Le Livre français sous l'Ancien Régime*, 43.
78 Martin, *Print, Power, and People in Seventeenth-Century France*, 223.
79 Martin, *Le Livre français sous l'Ancien Régime*, 43, and Martin, *Print, Power, and People in Seventeenth-Century France*, 223. The *Relations* of 1643 to 1657 list Sébastien Cramoisy's brother Gabriel Cramoisy as a co-publisher on their title pages. On the involvement of various Cramoisy family members in this business, see Martin, *Le Livre français sous l'Ancien Régime*, 61.
80 McShea, *Apostles of Empire*, 107.
81 Martin, *Le Livre français sous l'Ancien Régime*, 45 and McShea, *Apostles of Empire*, 22. On the role of the trading company in the settlement of New France, see Dewar, *Disputing New France*, chapter 5 (158–96). For brief overviews, see Havard and Vidal, *Histoire de l'Amérique française*, 86–92 and Galland, *Pour la gloire de Dieu et du Roi*, 100–6.
82 McShea, *Apostles of Empire*, 20.
83 Martin, *Print, Power, and People in Seventeenth-Century France*, 224.
84 McShea, *Apostles of Empire*, 21.
85 For lists of books known to have once belonged to the Jesuit college library, see Drolet, "La Bibliothèque du Collège des Jésuites"; Filion, "La première bibliothèque canadienne"; and Pariseau, *La Bibliothèque du Collège de Québec*. On the New France Jesuits' library more generally, see Biron, "Les Livres que les missionaires de la Compagnie de Jésus ont apportés avec eux en Nouvelle-France" and Beaulieu, *La première bibliothèque canadienne*.
86 McShea, *Apostles of Empire*, 106.
87 Martin, *Le Livre français sous l'Ancien Régime*, 46–7. Martin provided a slightly different tally and some details on how the presses were distributed among the various shops in Martin, *Print, Power, and People in Seventeenth-Century France*, 247.

88 This and the following details of the printing process are drawn from Martin, *Print, Power, and People in Seventeenth-Century France*, 247–51.

89 The best summary available of such minor blemishes is McCoy, *Jesuit Relations of Canada*, synoptic table (unpaginated).

90 *JRAD* 36.59–61, *MNF* 7.781.

91 *JRAD* 49.198–211.

92 McCoy, *Jesuit Relations of Canada*, 267.

93 Ibid., 273. *JRAD* 50.150–63.

94 McCoy, *Jesuit Relations of Canada*, 280, 284. *JRAD* 51.104–15 and *JRAD* 52.102–9.

95 Some of Cramoisy's letters to the mother superior Marie de Saint-Bonaventure have survived, and can be consulted in the digital collection of the Bibliothèque National de France. See Cramoisy, "Lettre de Cramoisy à la Mère de St-Bonnaventure."

96 *MNF* 7.781.

97 *JRAD* 50.158–61, 51.112–15, and 52.106–9. This list is not included in Thwaites's presentation of the 1664–65 *Relation* or any other edition, and also does not seem to be available online.

98 Marie de l'Incarnation, *From Mother to Son*, 203. "M.C. qui imprime la relation et qui aime fort les Hospitalières d'ici, y inséra de son propre mouvement une lettre que la Supérieure luy avoit écrite, et cela fit bien de bruit en France." Marie de l'Incarnation, *Correspondance*, 803.

99 See, for example, Castelnau-L'Estoile, "Entre curiosité et édification" and Fabre, "L'Usage catholique des Juifs," 34–45.

100 *JRAD* 14.277. Thwaites's translation here has been altered to more accurately follow the original French. "Au chapitre 8, page 145, où il s'agist de quelque prise que j'eus avec un sorcier, au lieu de me servir d'exorcismes contre le diable, l'imprimeur me fait servir d'une espée. Voicy ce que j'avois couché dans l'original: 'En effet, j'avois dessein de me servir d'une espèce d'exorcisme'; l'imprimeur a mis: 'En effet, j'avois dessein de me servir d'une espée désormais.' Je vous confesse que ce beau rencontre m'a fait rire. Quand on parle de si loing, on ne fait pas si bien entendre ses pensées; l'escriture est une parole muette, qui se change aussi facilement qu'il est aisé de prendre un caractère pour un autre. On fait dire à un enfant ce qu'on veut, quand son père est absent." *MNF* 4.132.

101 Similarly, in the above-referenced manuscript copy of his 1634 *Relation*, Le Jeune included a note that was ultimately omitted from the printed *Relation* that shows he understood that whatever he wrote would not

necessarily be printed: "If these two short prayers are printed, I beg the printer to take care with the sauvage words. Those included in last year's *Relation* were corrupted and filled with printing errors." Author's translation. "Si ces deux petites oraisons sont mises soubs la presse, je supplie l'imprimeur de prendre garde aux mots sauvages. Ceux qui estoient dans la Relation de l'an passé ont esté corrompus et remplis de fautes à l'impression." MNF 2.705. Le Jeune asked that care be taken if – not when – this portion of his text was printed.

CHAPTER SEVEN

1 Examples include scanned volumes in the Internet Archive digital library, Hathi Trust, and on the website of the Canadian Research Knowledge Network. A plain-text version of Thwaites's translations (without the original French) is available on the website of Creighton University. There is also a 1959 reprint of this edition by Pageant Book Company in half as many volumes.

2 Randall, "Appendix: Cathedrals of Ice," 187; Dubois, "The Jesuit Relations," 51; Paschoud, "Aborder les *Relations jésuites* de la Nouvelle France," 3 ("la masse documentaire," author's translation). Strikingly, but also exceptionally, Randall uses the word "*Relations*" as a singular noun. See, for example, Randall, "Appendix: Cathedrals of Ice," 185.

3 See, for example, Cavallo and Chartier, *A History of Reading in the West*, 2; Hammond, "Book History in the Reading Experience," 243–4; and Darnton, "First Steps toward a History of Reading," 175.

4 See Desbarats, "1616–1673. Les Jésuites, Relations des Jésuites," 51; Dubois, "The Jesuit Relations," 52; Greer, "Introduction," 14; Martin, *Print, Power, and People in Seventeenth-Century France*, 138; Rigault and Ouellet, "Relations des Jésuites," 639; Wroth, "The *Jesuit Relations* from New France," 114.

5 Press runs of literary texts in seventeenth-century France could range in size from 750 to as many as 3,000 copies, with between 1,200 and 1,800 being typical, not counting reprints or new editions. Martin, *The French Book*, 3.

6 For an accounting of the known editions and variant printings, see McCoy, *Jesuit Relations of Canada*, synoptic table (unpaginated).

7 JRAD 11.45–61, MNF 3.526–32. Passages in the *Relations* that reflect an awareness of readers are collected in Debacq, "Le Lecteur malveillant"; Dostie, *Le Lecteur suborné dans cinq textes missionnaires de la Nouvelle-France*; and Pouliot, *Étude sur les Relations des Jésuites*, 23–5.

8 *JRAD* 5.145–7. “Il y a des dames dans Paris qui emploient tous les ans plus de dix mille francs en leurs menus plaisirs. Si elles en appliquoient une partie pour recueillir les gouttes du sang du Fils de Dieu respandu pour tant d’âmes qui se vont perdant tous les jours faute de secours, elles ne rougiroient pas de honte au jour qu’elles paroistront devant Dieu, pour rendre compte des biens dont il les a fait oeconomes.” *MNF* 2.430. For more examples, see *JRAD* 8.215–17, *MNF* 3.186–7; *JRAD* 15.233, *MNF* 4.271; and *JRAD* 18.117, *MNF* 4.578.

9 *JRAD* 32.195. “J’ay leu et releu autrefois les *Relations* sur ce sujet et tousjours avec admiration et avec satisfaction.” *MNF* 7.316.

10 Chartier, *The Cultural Uses of Print in Early Modern France*, 145–53. Reliable literacy rates are not available for this period. It has been estimated, on the basis of the none-too-certain metric of ability to sign one’s name in a parish register prior to marriage, that 29 per cent of French men and 14 per cent of French women may have been literate by the final decade of the seventeenth century. On these figures, their limitations, and comparisons to other places in Europe, see Melton, *The Rise of the Public in Enlightenment Europe*, 81–3.

11 *JRAD* 9.187. “Mais à qui est-ce que je parle? A des personnes qui n’ont garde de sçavoir rien de ce que j’écris, si plus capables qu’eux ne leur en font le récit.” *MNF* 3.268.

12 A concise overview of the forces opposing the Jesuits in France around this time can be found in Nelson, “The Historiography of the Pre-Suppression Jesuit Mission in France.” See also Worcester, “Jesuit Dependence on the French Monarchy,” 112.

13 On this moment in the mission’s history and the complaints lodged in France by the Recollets, see True, *Masters and Students*, 27–54 (chapter 2) and Galland, *Pour la gloire de Dieu et du roi*, 95–137 (chapter 2).

14 Author’s translation. Pioffet, “Introduction,” 21.

15 Sagard, *Histoire du Canada*, 401n1, 376n2, 378n2. Sagard’s recent editor Marie-Christine Pioffet has pointed out his many other apparent borrowings from the *Relations*. See 177n10, 181n5, 227n5, 263n12, and 368n1. In another case, an anonymous 1636 memo arguing for the Recollets’ return to New France cites what the Jesuits had sent to France as the source of the news that one of their own missionaries, Nicolas Viel, had been drowned intentionally by the Wendat instead of dying accidentally as previously believed. This assertion, the truth of which is uncertain, had been included in Le Jeune’s 1634 *Relation*. *MNF* 3.158–72. On the Recollets’ initial beliefs about Viel’s fate, see Sagard, *Le grand*

voyage du pays des Hurons, 324. For the relevant passage in Le Jeune's 1634 *Relation*, see JRAD 7.231–3, MNF 2.739.

16 Debacq, "Le Lecteur malveillant," 3.

17 JRAD 9.86. "Entre quelques propositions qu'on m'a fait de l'ancienne France, quelqu'un me demande d'où vient qu'en tant d'années, on a baptisé si peu de personnes. Il me semble qu'il faudroit renverser la proposition et dire: d'où vient qu'en si peu d'années, on a baptisé tant de personnes?" MNF 3.236.

18 When exactly this complaint was made, and to whom, is unclear. Vitelleschi's 1638 letter was dated 8 December, too late to have affected the composition of the *Relation* in Quebec. See MNF 4.72–3. A letter from Vitelleschi to the rector of the Jesuit college in Blois dated 4 January 1639 indicated that he had previously raised the alarm on 24 October of the previous year, but this letter is not included in any of the published collections of texts related to the Jesuit mission. See MNF 4.182. It is unclear if Vitelleschi had earlier communicated this complaint to the New France Jesuits or if another Jesuit in France had done so. Another possibility, that the 1638 *Relation* was shortened in Paris to respond to this criticism because it arose too late to be communicated to the Jesuits in Quebec, cannot be ruled out, although it seems unlikely in light of the limited extent of the changes apparently made to other texts around this time (see chapter 6). For an indication of the Jesuits' financial reliance on Gaston d'Orléans and hopes to encourage him to contribute more, see Vitelleschi's February 1636 letter to Jérôme Lalemant: MNF 3.812–13.

19 JRAD 14.123. "On est dèsjà si remply des façons de faire de nos sauvages et de nos petits travaux en leur endroit que j'appréhende le dégoust. C'est pourquoy je diray peu de beaucoup, omettant des chapitres entiers, de peur d'estre accusé de longueur." MNF 4.76–7. For an additional example, see JRAD 14.277, MNF 4.132. The physical characteristics of the texts are given in Campeau's prefaces: MNF 3.520 and 4.73–4. See also True, *Masters and Students*, 150–1.

20 JRAD 27.139–41. "Nous ne parlerons point en particulier des diverses résidences ny des diverses missions de nostre Compagnie, de peur d'user de redites. Les choses qui se passent de nouveau ont tant de raport avec celles qui ont dèsjà esté escrites que le danger du dégoust nous rendra succints de plus en plus." MNF 6.328. For another example, see Paul Ragueneau's *Relation* from the Wendat mission for 1647–48: JRAD 33.223, MNF 7.421.

21 JRAD 9.151–83, MNF 3.256–66.

22 *JRAD* 16.225. "Mon dessein n'est pas de redire icy ce qui se peut trouver dans les précédentes *Relations* ou dans les autres livres qui ont dèsjà traicté de ce sujet, mais seulement de suppléer au défaut de certaines circonstances sur lesquelles j'ay reconnu qu'on désiroit quelque satisfaction." *MNF* 4.353–4.

23 *JRAD* 23.179, *MNF* 5.535.

24 *JRAD* 12.219–21. "Il y a subjet de grande édification en tout ce qui est inséré dans la Relation qu'on a envoié. On demanderoit néantmoins quelque esclaircissement en ce qu'on peut espérer d'establissement de la religion chrestienne et en suitte de communication avec les païs attenans aux sauvages, leurs frontières et aboutissemens." *MNF* 3.669.

25 *JRAD* 12.223. "Pour la communication avec les païs voisins, on a pleinement satisfait dans les autres *Relations*, les livres qui traittent de ces contrées." *MNF* 3.670. For another example, see *JRAD* 35.101, *MNF* 7.711.

26 *JRAD* 7.35. "armes nécessaires pour le combat." *MNF* 2.651.

27 For a brief portrait of Carigouan, whose name is spelled Carigonan in the *Relations*, see Jury, "Carigouan (Carigonan)."

28 *JRAD* 10.87. "Nous avons appris que le salut de tant d'âmes innocentes, lavées et blanchies dans le Sang du Fils de Dieu, touche bien sensiblement le coeur de plusieurs et y allume de nouveaux désirs de quitter l'ancienne France, pour se transporter en la Nouvelle." *MNF* 3.334.

29 *JRAD* 7.51. "afin que ceux qui liront ce chapitre n'appréhendent point de nous venir secourir." *MNF* 2.657.

30 *JRAD* 7.63. "Cecy ne doit épouventer personne. Les bons soldats s'animent à la veue de leur sang et de leurs playes. Dieu est plus grand que nostre coeur. On ne tombe pas tousjours dans la famine; on ne rencontre pas tousjours des sorciers ou des jongleurs de l'humeur de celuy-cy." *MNF* 2.663. Thwaites's team translated *jongleur* as juggler, but the term is much more capacious than this, designating fortune tellers, sleight-of-hand artists, tumblers, minstrels, etc. For lack a suitable term in English, it has been left untranslated here.

31 *JRAD* 10.97. "Pensez-vous par vos raisons avoir jetté de l'eau sur le feu qui me brûle et diminué tant soit peu le zèle que j'ay pour la conversion de ces peuples? Je vous déclare que cela n'a servy qu'à me confirmer davantage dans ma vocation." *MNF* 3.337.

32 *JRAD* 26.47. "Sept jours se passèrent de la sorte et y adjoustèrent de nouveaux tourmens, car ils le firent souffrir en des lieux et en des façons que la bienséance ne permet pas d'escrire." *MNF* 6.131.

33 *JRAD* 45.211–13. "On en a parlé de vrai dans les autres Relations, mais ce que nous en avons appris de nouveau est si estrange que tout ce qu'on

en a dit n'est rien. Je les passe, non seulement parce que ma plume n'a pas d'ancre assez noire pour les décrire, mais bien plus de peur de faire horreur par la lecture de certaines cruautez dont les siècles passez n'ont jamais entendu parler." MNF 9.463–4.

34 JRAD 18.241–3. "Je ne doute point que la perte d'un homme si utile à l'estat et dont les actions ont mérité une approbation si universelle n'ayt esté extraordinairement sensible à l'ancienne France, mais elle me permettra de dire qu'elle ne l'a pas moins esté à la nouvelle ... La crainte que j'ay de faire souffrir la modestie des vivans et de violer le secret dont l'obligation dure mesme après la mort ne me permettra pas d'en dire davantage." MNF 4.623.

35 See True, *Masters and Students*, 27–54 (chapter 2).

36 See, for example, Dubois, "The Jesuit Relations," 52; Greer, "Introduction," 14–15; and Wroth, "The *Jesuit Relations* from New France," 114.

37 Individual *Relations* continued to be referenced by various writers for several decades after they ceased to be published. For some examples, see Le Clercq, *First Establishment of the Faith in New France*,1: 399 (footnote); Lafitau, *Moeurs des sauvages ameriquains comparées aux moeurs des premiers temps*, 2: 51; 2: 77; 2: 143; 2: 295; 3: 230; Charlevoix, *History and General Description of New France*, 1: 77; and True, trans., *The Jesuit Pierre-François-Xavier de Charlevoix's (1682–1761) Journal of a Voyage in North America*, 220n19, 262n6, 263n7, 268n2, 301n3, 303n5, 355n12, 361n1, 372n11. Charlevoix's ambitious effort to organize decades' worth of information about North America seems to have overshadowed the *Relations* after its appearance in 1744. It was a trusted source of the authors of the *Encylopédie* and Voltaire, novelists Chateaubriand and the Abbé Prévost, and even modern historians as late as the mid-twentieth century. Thierry, "Pierre-François-Xavier de Charlevoix," 42; Healy, "The French Jesuits and the Idea of the Noble Savage," 162–3; Hayne, "Charlevoix, Pierre-François-Xavier de."

38 McGill, *American Literature and the Culture of Reprinting*, 20. See also Gigante, *Book Madness*, 174.

39 DiCuirci, *Colonial Revivals*, 4–5, 9, 10. Emma Anderson has traced the nineteenth-century resurgence of interest in the Jesuits who were martyred in seventeenth-century New France, particularly among Catholics, and shows how this played out differently on each side of the United States-Canada border. See Anderson, *The Death and Afterlife of the North American Martyrs*, 98–164 (chapter 3).

40 JRAD 1.42.

41 O'Callaghan, "Jesuit Relations," 21.

42 This unpublished *Relation* can be found in *JRAD* 57.33–305 and 58.19–89. On the circumstances leading to the end of the published series, see True, *Masters and Students*, 171–2 and McShea, *Apostles of Empire*, 196–8.

43 Charlevoix, *History and General Description of New France*, 1: 77.

44 For examples of O'Callaghan's essay being cited as the starting point of serious scholarly attention to the *Relations*, see De Celles, "M. O'Callaghan et les 'Relations' des Jésuites," 256; Donnelly, *Thwaites' Jesuit Relations*, 8; Pouliot, *Étude sur les Relations des Jésuites*, 28; Verney, *O'Callaghan*, 186; and Walsh, "Edmund Bailey O'Callaghan," 475–6.

45 The story of O'Callaghan's life is told in much more detail than can be offered here in Verney, *O'Callaghan*. The biographical details in this and the following paragraph are drawn from this source. On his political preoccupations, see also Brundage, *Irish Nationalists in America*, 68.

46 For just a few perspectives on this much-studied rebellion, see Greer, *The Patriots and the People*; Dagenais and Mauduit, eds., *Revolutions across Borders*; and Laporte, *Brève histoire des patriotes*.

47 Verney, *O'Callaghan*, 205.

48 See also O'Callaghan's anachronistic claim that the Jesuits "were the first Europeans who reached the Atlantic shores of the State of Maine." O'Callaghan, "Jesuit Relations," 4.

49 Ibid., 7, 18, 19.

50 Details on Martin's life and career in this paragraph are drawn from Giguère, "Martin, Félix." For additional details on the restoration of the Jesuit presence in Canada, the archival work performed by Martin, and the atmosphere of budding "Québécois clerico-nationalism" in which he was working, as described in this paragraph, see Anderson, *The Death and Afterlife of the North American Martyrs*, 106–20.

51 Codignola, "The Historiography on the Jesuits of New France," unpaginated, and Côté, "La réception des écrits jésuites de la Nouvelle-France," 147–50.

52 For a concise overview of this political context, see Read, "Act of Union" and "Province of Canada."

53 Author's translation. Martin, *Relations des Jésuites*, v.

54 Author's translation. Ibid., 7 (footnote).

55 Ibid., 35.

56 Ibid., 61–7.

57 Author's translation. Ibid., 14, 61.

58 The general information on Lenox's life and collection in this paragraph is drawn from Stevens, *Recollections of James Lenox*, 3–9.

59 Ibid., 7.

60 Ibid., 104. Italics in original.

61 Ibid., 81.

62 Winship, *The John Carter Brown Library*, 12; Cannon, *American Book Collectors*, 66–7; Stevens, *Recollections of James Lenox*, 12–17; Wroth, *The First Century of the John Carter Brown Library*, 10.

63 This anecdote was related in the Montreal magazine *L'Opinion publique* in 1883 and reprinted more than forty years later: De Celles, "M. O'Callaghan et les 'Relations' des Jésuites," 256. In 1883, De Celles was working as a librarian in Ottawa while still contributing to his Montreal-based weekly magazine. It is unclear how he would have learned of this incident. See Roy, "Duclos De Celles, Alfred."

64 O'Callaghan catalogued twenty collections in the United States and Canada. O'Callaghan, "Jesuit Relations," 22. In his essay, he did not mention owning any of the texts, but he had approximately thirty of them at the time of his death in 1880, in addition to several related seventeenth-century texts and some nineteenth-century reprints. Nash, *Catalogue of the Library of the Late E.B. O'Callaghan*, 106–14. John Gilmary Shea owned fourteen of the *Relations* by the end of his life. Guilday, *John Gilmary Shea*, 131–4 (here, 131). Somewhat later, General Mills founder James F. Bell collected all but four of the *Relations*, including two or three copies of many of them. Walter and Doneghy, *Jesuit Relations and Other Americana in the Library of James F. Bell*, 3–128.

65 O'Callaghan, "Jesuit Relations," 6.

66 For details on Faribault's work, see Giguère, "Sous les auspices du gouvernement canadien."

67 Lenox's collection of the annual series of *Relations* as it stood around the time of his death in 1880 is catalogued in *Contributions to a Catalogue of the Lenox Library No. 2: The Jesuit Relations, etc.*, 4–12. It does not appear that anyone has sought in recent decades to characterize the current state of collections of seventeenth-century editions of the *Relations*.

68 O'Callaghan did not disclose his sources, but his entry on the *Relation* for 1648–49 references unique characteristics of Harvard's copy. And he must have consulted John Carter Brown's copy of the 1665–66 report, as this was the only one he had been able to locate. O'Callaghan, "Jesuit Relations," 18, 20, 22.

69 Scholars who cite Biard's text as the beginning of the series include, to mention only a few examples, Desbarats, "1616–1673. Les Jésuites,

Relations des Jésuites"; Oury in his notes to Marie de l'Incarnation, *Correspondance*, 470n24; Pioffet, *La Tentation de l'épopée;* and Randall, "Appendix. Cathedrals of Ice," 186. Those opting for Le Jeune's 1632 text include McCoy, *Jesuit Relations of Canada*; Rigault and Ouellet, "Relations des Jésuites," 637; Pouliot, *Étude sur les Relations des Jésuites*; Wroth, "The *Jesuit Relations* from New France"; and others.

70 Left aside for the present purposes are pedagogical or critical editions of individual *Relations* and collections of excerpts, which are cited less frequently in scholarship. Editions of individual reports include Beaulieu, ed., *Un Français au pays des "bestes sauvages"*; Côté, ed., *Brève relation du voyage de la Nouvelle France*; Guardiani, ed., *Breve Relatione d'Alcune Missioni dei Padri della Compagnia di Giesù nella Nuova Francia*; and Laflèche, ed., *Le Missionnaire, l'apostat, le sorcier.* Collections of excerpts include Greer, ed., *The Jesuit Relations*; Kenton, ed., *The Jesuit Relations and Allied Documents*; Randall, trans., *Black Robes and Buckskin*; and Thérien, ed., *Écrits en Huronie.* There is also a little-known translation of the *Relations* contained in *Monumenta Novae Franciae* by the late Jesuit physicist William Lonc, part of a larger self-published series entitled *Early Jesuit Missions in Canada*: Lonc, ed., *Early Jesuit Missions in Canada.*

71 Others whose contributions are acknowledged in the preface to the edition or in a 6 October 1858 letter from Bois to Jean-Baptiste Meilleur, just before the appearance of this edition, are the priest Charles-Honoré Laverdière, who proofread the text and assembled its index, and several others whose roles are not specified: Faribault, Henri de Courcy, John Gilmary Shea, and Francis Parkman. *Relations des Jésuites*, vol. 1, "Avis de l'éditeur" (unpaginated). Bois' letter is reproduced in Charland, "A qui devons-nous la réédition des Relations des Jésuites?" 217–18.

72 On this fire, see Giguère, "Sous les auspices du gouvernement canadien" and Pouliot, *Étude sur les Relations des Jésuites*, 30–2.

73 *Relations des Jésuites,* vol. 1, "Avis de l'éditeur" (unpaginated). O'Callaghan was aware of Plante's collection a decade earlier, and recorded its size as twenty volumes. O'Callaghan, "Jesuit Relations," 22.

74 The source used to establish the text of each annual report is duly noted on its first page in the *Relations des Jésuites*, but is usually given only as an unspecified copy of the text printed by Cramoisy. Exceptions include three texts prepared on the basis of published copies or manuscripts in France's national library in Paris: Biard's 1616 report from Acadia and the Quebec *Relations* of 1662 and 1666. *Relations des Jésuites*, vol. 1, 1611, 1; vol. 5, 1662, 1; vol. 6, 1666, 1.

75 Author's translation. Bois' 6 October 1858 letter to the physician and educator Jean-Baptiste Meilleur is reproduced in Charland, "A qui devons-nous la réédition des Relations des Jésuites?" 217–8. The quoted passage appears on page 218.

76 Author's translation. *Relations des Jésuites*, vol. 1, "Avis de l'éditeur" (unpaginated).

77 Shea, *Discovery and Exploration of the Mississippi Valley*. Other examples include O'Callaghan's above-discussed essay and Kip, *Early Jesuit Missions in North America*.

78 Author's translation. Ferland, *Notes sur les regi[s]tres de Nostre-Dame de Québec*, 38. Some additional examples are reproduced in Guigère, "Sous les auspices du gouvernement canadien," 368–70.

79 See, to mention only a few of the most prominent scholarly works that have used this edition, Delâge, *Le Pays renversé*; Parkman, *The Jesuits in North America in the Seventeenth Century*; and Pioffet, *La Tentation de l'épopée*. Pouliot cited both the *Relations des Jésuites* and *The Jesuit Relations and Allied Documents* in his *Étude sur les Relations des Jésuites*.

80 Parkman sometimes cited the *Relations des Jésuites* and other times opted for the seventeenth-century editions in references that are distinguished only by a parenthetical reference to the original publisher, in the latter case. For example, he cites the nineteenth-century editions as "Brébeuf, *Relation des Hurons*, 1635, 81" and the original editions as "Lalemant, *Relation des Hurons*, 1640, 38 (Cramoisy)." Parkman, *The Jesuits in North America in the Seventeenth Century*, xxvn1, xxvin2. More recently, the Jesuit historian Michael Knox consulted scanned images or physical copies of the original seventeenth-century editions and cited the texts in a way that closely resembles Parkman's references to the 1858 edition, for example: "Ragueneau, *Hurons* (1649–1650), p. 57." Knox, "The Rhetoric of Martyrdom in the Jesuit Relations of New France, 1632–1650," 1n2. See also Ferland, *Les Relations des Jésuites*, 23n48.

81 Codignola, "The Historiography on the Jesuits of New France," unpaginated; Donnelly, *Thwaites' Jesuit Relations*, 19.

82 Turner, *Reuben Gold Thwaites*, 54. On Thwaites's scholarly output, see Blessing, "Reuben Gold Thwaites," 42–9 (especially 45). A full bibliography of Thwaites's work is appended to Turner, *Reuben Gold Thwaites*, 63–94.

83 On this aspect of Thwaites's legacy, see Gietschier, "Reuben Gold Thwaites."

84 *JRAD* 1.x.

85 The specific copy Thwaites and his team used to establish the text of each *Relations*, primarily but not exclusively copies in the Lenox Library, is recorded in the bibliographical data at the end of each volume.

86 Martin, trans. *Relation abrégée de quelques missions des pères de la Compagnie de Jésus dans la Nouvelle-France*; Martin and Demontézon, eds, *Mission du Canada. Relations inédites de la Nouvelle-France (1672–1679)*; and *Le Journal des Jésuites*. On the series published by Shea and O'Callaghan and for other examples of texts that appeared around this time, see Donnelly, *Thwaites' Jesuit Relations*, 8–15.

87 *JRAD* 1.42. Additional support for Thwaites's impression of the rarity of the *Relations des Jésuites* comes from an anecdote in which an undersecretary of state in Canada's federal government is said to have ordered in 1869 a search of various government offices and archives for copies of this edition, but none were located. See Giguère, "Sous les auspices du gouvernement canadien," 359.

88 Donnelly, *Thwaites' Jesuit Relations*, 12.

89 *JRAD* 1.viii–ix.

90 To mention only a few very recent or particularly influential books that cite the Thwaites edition in these ways, see Blackburn, *Harvest of Souls*; Cowan, *The Possession of Barbe Hallay*; Lozier, *Flesh Reborn*; McShea, *Apostles of Empire*; and Trigger, *The Children of Aataentsic*.

91 For just a few examples of references to *The Jesuit Relations and Allied Documents* that do not specifically identify particular texts, see Blackburn, *Harvest of Souls*, 67–8; Cowan, *The Possession of Barbe Hallay*, 22, 169n42; McShea, *Apostles of Empire*, xxvii, 265n30; and Trigger, *The Children of Aataentsic*, 82. Some scholars – especially those who write in French – do routinely indicate specific texts when citing this edition, often by year. See, for example, Le Bras, *L'Amérindien dans les Relations du Père Paul Lejeune*; Doiron, *L'Art de voyager*; and Ouellet, *La Relation de voyage en Amérique*.

92 Codignola, "Jesuit Writings," 223.

93 Ibid., 219. See, for example, the characterization of Regnaut's manuscript description of Brébeuf's torture and death (discussed in chapter 3 of this book) in Pearson, *Becoming Holy in Early Canada*, 56; Sarah Rivett's description of Jesuit Julien Binneteau's 1699 letter praising his colleague Gabriel Marest in Rivett, *Unscripted America*, 100; and the novelist William T. Volmann's acknowledgment that he "labeled anything which appears in the Thwaites version a Jesuit Relation." Vollmann, *Fathers and Crows*, 902.

94 Among these are Campeau, *Les Finances publiques de la Nouvelle-France*; *Les Cent-Associés et le Peuplement de la Nouvelle-France*; *Catastrophe démographique sur les Grand Lacs II: Les premiers habitants du Québec*; *La Mission des Jésuites chez les Hurons, 1634–1650*; *L'Evêché de Québec, 1674*; *La première mission des Jésuites en Nouvelle-France*; and *Gannentaha*.

95 For more on this series of Jesuit documents and the place of Campeau's New France volumes within it, see *MNF* 1.53–4.

96 Author's translation. *MNF* 1.53–4.

97 See Dickinson, "Review of *Monumenta Novae Franciae*, vol. 4," 577–8; Jaenen, "Review Essay," 147–52; Codignola, "Jesuit Writings," 238; Beaulieu, *Convertir les fils de Caïn*, 157n2.

98 See Codignola, "Jesuit Writings" and True, "Is It Time for a New Edition of the Jesuit *Relations* from New France?"

99 For partial but indicative lists of scholars who have used, acknowledged, and ignored Campeau's edition, see Codignola, "Jesuit Writings," 220–2.

100 For reasons that are not clear, the convention of italicizing the titles of the *Relations* is not observed in the table of contents for the third volume of *Monumenta Novae Franciae*.

101 Recent examples include McShea, *Apostles of Empire*; Lozier, *Flesh Reborn*; and True, *Masters and Students*.

102 *JRAD* 12.17. "Comme j'ay parlé d'eux aux autres Relations, je n'en dirai point davantage en ce lieu." *MNF* 3.603. For additional examples, see *JRAD* 6.117, *MNF* 2.546–7; *JRAD* 6.157–9, *MNF* 2.564–5; *JRAD* 7.277, *MNF* 3.53; *JRAD* 12.17, *MNF* 3.603; *JRAD* 12.21, *MNF* 3.605; *JRAD* 14.155, *MNF* 4.88; and *JRAD* 16.225, *MNF* 4.353–4.

103 Desbarats is one of a small number of scholars who have called for more attention to texts that are related to, but distinct from, the *Relations*. Desbarats, "1616–1673. Les Jésuites. Relations des Jésuites," 58.

104 The editorial history of the Jesuit Pierre-François-Xavier de Charlevoix's 1744 *Histoire et description générale de la Nouvelle-France* may be instructive on this point. Unlike the *Relations*, it was initially published in large, sturdy volumes intended to stand the test of time. The final portion of it – an epistolary journal of Charlevoix's voyage through North America – was finally republished in a modern critical edition in 1994, but the first two volumes still have never been republished in French despite their influence and frequent use as a source of information about eighteenth-century French America. See True, trans., *The Jesuit Pierre-François-Xavier de Charlevoix's (1682–1761) Journal of a Voyage in North America*, 1–2, 20–1.

CONCLUSION

1 https://ehprnh2mwo3.exactdn.com/wp-content/uploads/2021/01/Calls_to_Action_English2.pdf, accessed 7 November 2023 (page 7, item 58).

2 Smith, "Trudeau Asks Pope for an Apology." For examples of scholarly characterizations of the texts that resemble the one offered by Trudeau, see Greer, *The Jesuit Relations*, 1; Beaulieu, *Convertir les fils de Caïn*, 19; Paschoud, "Aborder les *Relations jésuites* de la Nouvelle France," 3; and *JRAD* 1.41. For more on Trudeau's gift to the pope, see True, "As an Indigenous Delegation Prepares to Visit the Vatican, It's Worth Revisiting Trudeau's 2017 Papal Gift of the Jesuit 'Relations.'"

3 A visitor was a Jesuit specially appointed by the superior general to travel to every house in a particular region or province to identify and help correct problems large and small, and to help make clear the will and expectations of the Society's leadership. On this role, see McCoog, ed., *With Eyes and Ears Open*. For a brief summary of Le Mercier's life and career, see Campeau, "Le Mercier, François-Joseph."

4 Le Mercier's writings from the Antilles do not seem to have appeared in any readily accessible modern editions, but their existence is confirmed by occasional scholarly references to letters held in the French Archives nationales d'outre-mer and the Vatican's Archivio Storico De Propaganda Fide. See, for example, Peyronnin, "Contours d'une pastorale ultramarine," 45n33 and 58n68.

5 For notable exceptions to the scholarly tendency to examine New France and the Caribbean in isolation from each other, see Le Bras "Du Canada aux 'Îles de l'Amérique' et à la 'Terre Ferme'" and Ouellet, *La Relation de voyage en Amérique*.

6 Yuzwa, "The Fall of Troy in Old Huronia," 400, 403. For rare other examples of scholarly attention to Latin in the New France textual record, see Galucci, "'I Began to Teach ... ': Emotion and Performances in Isaac Jogues's Letter for Father Jean Filleau" and Westra, "Références classiques implicites et explicites dans les écrts des Jésuites sur la Nouvelle-France." For a general overview of the use of Latin in New France, see Cottier, "Écrits latins en Nouvelle-France."

7 Two attempts in recent years to secure funding from the United States National Endowment for the Humanities to produce such a sophisticated new digital edition of the texts were regrettably unsuccessful. These were a joint effort on the part of the author, Dr Christopher Parsons of Northeastern University, and Dr Robert Morrissey of the University of Illinois, with support from the John Carter Brown Library, the Institute

for Advanced Jesuit Studies at Boston College, and Northeastern University.

8 Recent examples include Paige, *Technologies of the Novel* and So, *Redlining Culture.*

9 Scholars have foregrounded the experiences of several Indigenous people in recent decades. See, to mention only a few prominent examples, Anderson, *The Betrayal of Faith*; Greer, *Mohawk Saint*; Pearson, *Becoming Holy in Early Canada* (especially chapter 3, "Evangelism: Indigenous Holiness"); and Poirier, *Religion, Gender, and Kinship in Colonial New France* (especially chapters 2 and 3, on Joseph Chihoatenhwa and Thérèse Oionhaton).

Works Cited

Abé, Takao. *The Jesuit Mission to New France: A New Interpretation in the Light of the Earlier Jesuit Experience in Japan*. Leiden: Brill, 2011.

"Acte pour l'établissement de la Compagnie des Cent-Associés." In *La Nouvelle-France par les textes: Les cadres de vie*, edited by Marcel Trudel, 23–30. Montreal: Hurtubise HMH, 2003.

Alden, Dauril. *The Making of an Enterprise: The Society of Jesus in Portugal, Its Empire, and Beyond, 1540–1750*. Stanford, CA: Stanford University Press, 1996.

Anderson, Emma. *The Betrayal of Faith: The Tragic Journey of a Colonial Native Convert*. Cambridge, MA: Harvard University Press, 2007.

– "Blood, Fire, and 'Baptism': Three Perspectives on the Death of Jean De Brébeuf, Seventeenth-Century Jesuit 'Martyr.'" In *Native Americans, Christianity, and the Reshaping of the American Religious Landscape*, edited by Joel W. Martin and Mark A. Nicholas, 125–58. Chapel Hill: University of North Carolina Press, 2010.

– *The Death and Afterlife of the North American Martyrs*. Cambridge, MA: Harvard University Press, 2013.

– "The First Philosophes: The Impact of Indigenous Thought upon Christianity and Modernity." *U.S. Catholic Historian* 41, no. 3 (Summer 2023): 1–31.

– "Residential School Saint: The Life, Death, and Turbulent Afterlife of Rose Prince of the Carrier Nation." *Church History: Studies in Christianity and Culture* 89, no. 2 (September 2020): 592–632.

– "'Thine Own by Adoption': Conversion, Integration, and Fictive Kinship in the Life of Thérèse Oionhaton, Seventeenth-Century Wendat Convert." In *Religious Intimacies: Intersubjectivity in the Modern Christian West*, edited by Mary Dunn and Brenna Moore, 46–64. Bloomington: Indiana University Press, 2020.

Anderson, Karen L. *Chain Her by One Foot: The Subjugation of Native Women in Seventeenth-Century New France*. New York: Routledge, 1991.

"Appendice: Inventaire des effets saisis par le shérif du district de Québec, à et pour l'usage de sa majesté, appartenant au Feu Révérend Pierre Cazot, comme représentant le ci-devant ordre des Jésuites dans la province du Bas-Canada, en vertu du writ du roi à lui adressé, portant date du huitième jour de Mars, 1800." In *Rapport du Comité spécial de la Chambre d'assemblée du Bas-Canada nommé pour s'enquérir de l'état actuel de l'éducation dans la province du Bas-Canada, ordonné le 2e Février 1824 par la Chambre d'assemblée du Bas-Canada qu'il soit imprimé*, 226–37. Quebec: T. Cary Co., 1824.

Arcilla, Jose S. "The Fall of Manila: Excerpts from a Jesuit Diary." *Philippine Studies* 37, no. 2 (1989): 192–214.

Audiat, Pierre. *La Biographie de l'œuvre littéraire: Esquisse d'une méthode critique*. Paris: Honoré Champion, 1924.

Axtell, James. "The Power of Print in the Eastern Woodlands." *William and Mary Quarterly* 44, no. 2 (April 1987): 300–9.

Balsamo, Jean. "Les premières relations des missions de la Chine et leur réception française (1556–1608)." *Nouvelle revue du XVIe siècle* 16, no. 1 (1 January 1998): 155–84.

Beauchamp, William M. *Aboriginal Use of Wood in New York*. Albany: New York State Education Department, 1905.

Beaulieu, Alain, ed. *Convertir les fils de Caïn: Jésuites et Amérindiens nomades en Nouvelle-France, 1632–1642*. Quebec: Nuit blanche éditeur, 1990.

– *Un Français au pays des "bestes sauvages"*. Montreal: Comeau & Nadeau: 1999.

Beaulieu, André. *La première bibliothèque canadienne: La bibliothèque des Jésuites de la Nouvelle France, 1632–1800 / The First Canadian Library: The Library of the Jesuit College of New France*. Ottawa: Bibliothèque Nationale du Canada, 1972.

Beresford, Bruce, dir. *Black Robe*. Santa Monica, CA: Metro Goldwyn Mayer, 1991.

Berthiaume, Pierre. "Les Relations des Jésuites (1632–1673)". In *Dictionnaire des journaux, 1600–1789*, edited by Jean Sgard. Paris: Universitas, 1991.

Bilinkoff, Jodi. *Related Lives: Confessors and Their Female Penitents, 1450–1750*. Ithaca and New York: Cornell University Press, 2005.

Birmingham, Kevin. "'The Great Shame of Our Profession.'" *Chronicle of Higher Education*, 12 February 2017.

– *The Most Dangerous Book: The Battle for James Joyce's "Ulysses"*. New York: Penguin, 2014.

Biron, Johanne. "Les Livres que les missionaires de la Compagnie de Jésus ont apportés avec eux en Nouvelle-France: Écrire l'histoire d'une bibliothèque jésuite." In *De l'Orient à la Huronie: Du récit de pèlerinage au texte missionnaire*, edited by Guy Poirier, Marie-Christine Gomez-Géraud, and François Paré, 165–84. Quebec: Presses de l'Université Laval, 2011.

Blackburn, Carole. *Harvest of Souls: The Jesuit Missions and Colonialism in North America, 1632–1650*. Montreal & Kingston: McGill-Queen's University Press, [2000] 2004.

Blessing, Matt. "Reuben Gold Thwaites and the Historical Resurrection of Lewis and Clark." *Wisconsin Magazine of History* 88, no. 2 (Winter 2004/2005): 42–9.

Boss, Julia. "Writing a Relic: The Uses of Hagiography in New France." In *Colonial Saints: Discovering the Holy in the Americas*, edited by Allan Greer and Jodi Bilinkoff, 211–33. New York: Routledge, 2003.

Bourrie, Mark. *Crosses in the Sky: Jean de Brébeuf and the Destruction of Huronia*. Windsor, ON: Biblioasis, 2024.

Boyden, Joseph. *The Orenda*. Toronto: Hamish Hamilton, 2013.

Brodeur, Raymond, ed. *Femme, mystique et missionnaire: Marie Guyart de l'Incarnation: Tours, 1599-Québec, 1672*, in *Actes du colloque organisé par le Centre d'études Marie-de-l'Incarnation sous les auspices du Centre interuniversitaire d'études québécoises qui s'est tenu à Loretteville, Québec, du 22 Au 25 Septembre 1999*. Sainte-Foy, QC: Presses de l'Université Laval, 2001.

Brundage, David. *Irish Nationalists in America*. Oxford: Oxford University Press, 2016.

Bruneau, Marie-Florine. *Women Mystics Confront the Modern World: Marie de l'Incarnation (1599–1672) and Madame Guyon (1648–1717)*. Albany: SUNY Press, 1998.

Burrus, Ernest J. "A Diary of Exiled Philippine Jesuits (1769–1770)." *Archivum Historicum Societatis Iesu* 20 (1951): 269–99.

Campbell, Mary Baine. *Wonder and Science: Imagining Worlds in Early Modern Europe*. Ithaca, NY: Cornell University Press, 1999.

Campeau, Lucien. *Catastrophe démographique sur les Grands Lacs; Les premiers habitants du Quebec*. Montreal: Éditions Bellarmin, 1986.

– *Les Cent-Associés et le peuplement de la Nouvelle-France, 1633–1663.* Montreal: Éditions Bellarmin, 1974.
– *L'Évêché de Québec, 1674: Aux origines du premier diocèse érigé en Amérique française.* Quebec: Société Historique de Quebec, 1974.
– *Les Finances publiques de la Nouvelle-France sous les Cent-Associés, 1632–1665.* Montreal: Éditions Bellarmin, 1975.
– *Gannentaha: Première mission iroquoise, 1653–1665.* Montreal: Éditions Bellarmin, 1983.
– "Le Mercier, François-Joseph." In *Dictionary of Canadian Biography.* Accessed 30 October 2023. https://www.biographi.ca/en/bio/le_mercier_francois_joseph_1E.html.
– *La Mission des Jésuites chez les Hurons, 1634–1650.* Montreal: Éditions Bellarmin, 1987.
– ed. *Monumenta Novae Franciae.* 9 vols. Rome: Monumenta Hist. Soc. Jesu, 1967–2003.
– *La première mission des Jésuites en Nouvelle-France (1611–1613) et les commencements du Collège de Québec (1626–1670).* Montreal: Éditions Bellarmin, 1972.

Candal, Geri Della Rocca de, Anthony Grafton, and Paolo Sachet, eds. *Printing and Misprinting: A Companion to Mistakes and In-House Corrections in Renaissance Europe (1450–1650).* Oxford: Oxford University Press, 2023.

Cannon, Carl L. *American Book Collectors and Collecting from Colonial Times to the Present.* New York: The H.W. Wilson Company, 1941.

Carayon, Auguste. *Bibliographie historique de la Compagnie de Jésus: Ou, Catalogue des ouvrages relatifs à l'histoire des Jésuites depuis leur origine jusqu'à nos jours* (1846). Geneva: Slatkine Reprints, 1970.

Carile, Paolo. *Le Regard entravé: Littérature et anthropologie dans les premiers textes sur la Nouvelle France.* Sillery, QC: Septentrion, [1987] 2000.

Carpenter, Roger M. *The Renewed, the Destroyed, and the Remade: The Three Thought Worlds of the Iroquois and the Huron, 1609–1650.* East Lansing: Michigan State University Press, 2004.

Carson, James Taylor. "Brébeuf Was Never Martyred: Reimagining the Life and Death of Canada's First Saint." *Canadian Historical Review* 97, no. 2 (June 2016): 222–43.

Castelnau-L'Estoile, Charlotte de. "Entre curiosité et édification. Le savoir des missionnaires Jésuites du Brésil." In *Sciences et religions. De Copernic à Galilée (1540–1610). Actes du Colloque International – Rome 12–14 Décembre 1996.* 131–57. Rome: École française de Rome, 1999.

Cavallo, Guglielmo, and Roger Chartier, eds. *A History of Reading in the West: Studies in Print Culture and the History of the Book*. Amherst: University of Massachusetts Press, 2003.

Chabot, Marie-Emmanuel. "Chauvigny, Mary-Madeleine de (Gruel de La Peltrie)." In *Dictionary of Canadian Biography*. Accessed 3 November 2023. https://www.biographi.ca/en/bio/chauvigny_de_la_peltrie_marie_madeleine_de_1E.html.

– "Guyart, Marie named de l'Incarnation (Martin)." In *Dictionary of Canadian Biography*. Accessed 3 November 2023. http://www.biographi.ca/en/bio/guyart_marie_1E.html.

Champlain, Samuel de. *The Works of Samuel de Champlain*, vol. 5. Edited by Henry Percival Biggar. Toronto: Champlain Society, 1933.

Charland, Thomas. "À qui devons-nous la réédition des Relations des Jésuites?" *Revue d'histoire de l'Amérique française* 3, no. 2 (1949): 210–26.

Charlevoix, Pierre-François-Xavier de. *History and General Description of New France*, 6 volumes. Translated by John Gilmary Shea. New York: John Gilmary Shea, 1872.

Chartier, Roger. *The Cultural Uses of Print in Early Modern France*. Princeton, NJ: Princeton University Press, 2019.

Choquette, Leslie. "'Ces Amazones du Grand Dieu': Women and Mission in Seventeenth-Century Canada." *French Historical Studies* 17, no. 3 (1992): 627–55.

Clair, Muriel. "Le Manuscrit de 1652 sur les martyrs jésuites canadiens: En deçà d'une perspective hagiographique et ethnologique." In *Penser l'Amérique: De l'observation à l'inscription*, edited by Nathalie Vuillemin and Thomas Wien, 43–55. Oxford: Voltaire Foundation, 2017.

– "Les *Notes spirituelles* de Jean de Brébeuf (1630–1640)." In *Relire le patrimoine lettré de l'Amérique française*, edited by Sébastien Côté and Charles Doutrelepont, 189–218. Quebec: Presses de l'Université Laval, 2013.

Clossey, Luke. *Salvation and Globalization in the Early Jesuit Missions*. Cambridge: Cambridge University Press, 2008.

Codignola, Luca. "Few, Uncooperative, and Ill-Informed? The Roman Catholic Clergy in French and British North America, 1610–1658." In *Decentring the Renaissance: Canada and Europe in Multidisciplinary Perspective, 1500–1700*, edited by Germaine Warkentin and Carolyn Podruchny, 173–85. Toronto: University of Toronto Press, 2004.

– "The Historiography on the Jesuits of New France." In *Jesuit Historiography Online*. Accessed 3 November 2023. https://doi.org/10.1163/2468-7723_jho_COM_220170.

– "Jesuit Writings According to R.G. Thwaites and Lucien Campeau, SJ: How Do They Differ?" In *Little Do We Know: History and Historians of the North Atlantic, 1492–2010*, edited by Matteo Binasco. Cagliari: Istituto di Storia dell'Europa Mediterranea del Consiglio Nazionale delle Ricerche, 2011.

The Constitutions of the Society of Jesus and Their Complementary Norms: A Complete English Translation of the Official Latin Texts. Saint Louis: The Institute of Jesuit Sources, 1996.

Contributions to a Catalogue of the Lenox Library No. 2: The Jesuit Relations, etc. New York, NY: Printed for the Trustees, 1879.

Costelloe, M. Joseph, trans., *The Letters and Instructions of Francis Xavier*. St Louis, MO: The Institute of Jesuit Sources, 1992.

Côté, Jean. "Domestique séculier d'habit, mais religieux de cœur." *Revue d'histoire de l'Amérique française* 10, no. 2 (1956): 183–90.

– "L'Institution des donnés." *Revue d'histoire de l'Amérique française* 15, vol. 3 (1961) 344–78.

Côté, Sébastien, ed. *Brève relation du voyage de la Nouvelle-France.* Quebec: Presses de l'Université Laval, 2020.

– "Portrait de Paul Lejeune en ecrivain: Les *Relations* de 1632 à 1634." *Argument: politique, société, histoire* 16, no. 2 (2014): 96–106.

– "La Réception des écrits jésuites de la Nouvelle-France dans l'histoire littéraire au Québec (1874–2007): Archiver la mémoire." In *Rencontre, réécriture, mémoire*, vol. 1 of *Textes missionnaires dans l'espace francophone*, edited by Guy Poirier, 145–64. Quebec: Presses de l'Université Laval, 2016.

Cottier, Jean–François. "Écrits latins en Nouvelle-France (1608–1763): Premier état de la question." *Tangence* 92 (2010): 9–26.

Cowan, Mairi. *The Possession of Barbe Hallay: Diabolical Arts and Daily Life in Early Canada*. Montreal & Kingston: McGill-Queen's University Press, 2022.

Cramoisy, Sébastien. "Lettre de Cramoisy à la Mère de St-Bonnaventure." *BAC Archives Nouvelle-France. Fonds de l'Hôtel-Dieu de Québec. Correspondance, rapports et autres documents*, 18 April 1655. https://archivesetmanuscrits.bnf.fr/ark:/12148/cc124960h/cN69585.

Dagenais, Maxime, and Julien Mauduit, eds. *Revolutions Across Borders: Jacksonian America and the Canadian Rebellion*. Montreal & Kingston: McGill-Queen's University Press, 2019.

Darnton, Robert. "First Steps Toward a History of Reading." *Australian Journal of French Studies* 23, no. 1 (1986): 5–30.

Davis, Natalie Zemon. *Women on the Margins: Three Seventeenth-Century Lives*. Cambridge, MA: Harvard University Press, 1995.

Debacq, Éric. "Le Lecteur malveillant dans les Relations de Pierre Biard (1616) et de Paul Lejeune (1632–1641)." *Mémoires du livre / Studies in Book Culture* 12, no. 1 (2021): 1–24.

De Celles, Alfred Duclos. "M. O'Callaghan et les 'Relations' des Jésuites." *Bulletin des recherches historiques* 31, no. 7 (July 1925): 256.

Deffain, Dominique. *Un Voyageur français en Nouvelle-France au XVIIe siècle: Étude littéraire des Relations du Père Paul Lejeune (1632–1641)*. Tübingen: Max Niemeyer Verlag, 1995.

Delâge, Denys. *Le Pays renversé: Amérindiens et Européens en Amérique du Nord-Est, 1600–1664*. Montreal: Éditions du Boréal, 1991.

– "La Tradition de commerce chez les Hurons de Lorette-Wendake." *Recherches amérindiennes au Québec* 30, no. 3 (December 2000): 35–51.

Delfosse, Annick. "La Correspondance jésuite: Communication, union et mémoire. Les enjeux de la *Formula Scribendi*." *Revue d'histoire ecclésiastique* 104, no. 1 (March 2009): 71–114.

Deroy-Pineau, Françoise. *Madeleine de La Peltrie, amazone du nouveau monde: Alençon 1603–Québec 1671*. Montreal: Bellarmin, 1992.

– ed. *Marie Guyard de l'Incarnation: Un destin transocéanique (Tours, 1599–Québec, 1672)*. Paris: L'Harmattan, 2000.

– *Marie de l'Incarnation: Marie Guyart, femme d'affaires, mystique, mère de la Nouvelle France, 1599–1672*. Montreal: Fides, [1989] 1999.

Desbarats, Catherine. "1616–1673. Les Jésuites: Relations des Jésuites." In *Monuments intellectuels de la Nouvelle-France et du Québec ancien: Aux origines d'une tradition culturelle*, edited by Claude Corbo, 51–62. Montreal: Presses de l'Université de Montréal 2014.

Deslandres, Dominique. "De Marie Guyart de l'Incarnation aux femmes 'ordinaires' de la Nouvelle-France." In Roy-Lysencourt, Nadeau-Lacour, and Brodeur, *Marie Guyart de l'Incarnation*, 265–76.

– "L'Éducation des Amérindiennes d'après la correspondance de Marie Guyart de l'Incarnation." *Religious Studies* 16, no. 1 (1987): 91–110.

– "Qu'est-ce qui faisait courir Marie Guyart? Essai d'ethnohistoire d'une mystique d'après sa correspondance." *Laval théologiques et philosophiques* 53, no. 22 (June 1997): 285–300.

Devens, Carol. *Countering Colonization: Native American Women and Great Lakes Missions, 1630–1900*. Berkeley: University of California Press, 2021.

Dewar, Helen. *Disputing New France: Companies, Law, and Sovereignty in the French Atlantic, 1598–1663*. Montreal & Kingston: McGill-Queen's University Press, 2022.

Dickinson, John A. "Review of *Monumenta Novae Franciae*, vol. 4, *Les grandes épreuves*, by Lucien Campeau." *Canadian Historical Review* 73, no. 4 (December 1992): 577–8.

DiCuirci, Lindsay. *Colonial Revivals: The Nineteenth-Century Lives of Early American Books*. Philadelphia: University of Pennsylvania Press, 2018.

Doiron, Normand. *L'Art de voyager: Le déplacement à l'époque classique*. Sainte-Foy, QC: Presses de l'Université Laval, 1995.

– "Rhétorique jésuite de l'éloquence sauvage au XVIIe Siècle: Les Relations de Paul Lejeune (1632–1642)." *XVIIe siècle* 173 (1991): 375–402.

Donnelly, Joseph P. *Jean de Brébeuf, 1593–1649*. Chicago: Loyola University Press, 1975.

– *Thwaites' Jesuit Relations: Errata and Addenda*. Chicago: Loyola University Press, 1967.

Dostie, Pierre. *Le Lecteur suborné dans cinq textes missionnaires de la Nouvelle-France*. Quebec: Éditions Huit, 1994.

Drolet, Antonio. "La Bibliothèque du Collège des Jésuites." *Revue de l'histoire de l'Amérique française* 14, no. 4 (1961): 487–544.

Dubé, Jean-Claude. *The Chevalier de Montmagny (1601–1657): First Governor of New France*. Ottawa: University of Ottawa Press, 2005.

Dubois, Laurent M. "The Jesuit Relations." In *A New Literary History of America*, edited by Greil Marcus and Werner Sollers, 50–4. Cambridge, MA: The Belknap Press of Harvard University Press, 2009.

Du Creux, François. *The History of Canada or New France*, 2 vols. Translated by Percy J. Robinson, edited by James B. Conacher. Toronto: Champlain Society, 1952.

Dunn, Mary. "Bedside Manners: Sickness and the Jesuit Mission in Early Modern New France." *Journal of Jesuit Studies* 5, no. 4 (2018): 567–85.

– *The Cruelest of All Mothers: Marie de l'Incarnation, Motherhood, and Christian Tradition*. New York: Fordham University Press, 2016.

– "Introduction." In *From Mother to Son: The Selected Letters of Marie de l'Incarnation to Claude Martin*, translated by Mary Dunn, 1–40. New York: Oxford University Press, 2014.

– "Sixteen and Possessed." *Spiritus: A Journal of Christian Spirituality* 22, no. 2 (September 2022): 232–51.

– *Where Paralytics Walk and the Blind See: Stories of Sickness and Disability at the Juncture of Worlds*. Princeton: Princeton University Press, 2022.

Ertler, Klaus-Dieter. "Les Relations des jésuites et la construction de l'observateur européen face au monde indigène." In *Jesuit Accounts of the Colonial Americas: Intercultural Transfers, Intellectual Disputes, and Textualities*, edited by Marc André Bernier, Clorinda Donato, and Hans-Jürgen Lüsebrink, 276–90. Toronto: University of Toronto Press, 2014.

Fabre, Pierre Antoine. "L'Horizon de la Nouvelle-France dans les provinces françaises de la Compagnie de Jésus au XVIIe et XVIIIe siècles: Lettres de demandes d'envoi en mission." In *Regards sur l'âme en Nouvelle-France: Histoire des spiritualités individuelles et collectives en espace colonial*, edited by Joy Palacios and Anne Régent-Susini, 27–43. Montreal & Kingston: McGill-Queen's University Press, 2024.

– "L'Usage catholique des Juifs de K'ai-feng dans la 'Querelle des rites chinois': Notes historiques et historiographiques sur l'ouvrage de Joseph Dehergne et Donald Daniel Leslie, *Juifs de Chine à travers la correspondance inédite des Jésuites du xviii*[e] *siècle*, Paris-Rome, 1980." *Cahiers du Judaïsme* 10 (2001): 34–45.

Fabre, Pierre Antoine, Benoist Pierre, Justine Cousin, and Xavier Gilly. *Les Jésuites. Histoire et dictionnaire*. Paris: Bouquins, 2022.

Farrell, Alan P. *The Jesuit "Ratio Studiorum" of 1599*. Washington, DC: Conference of Major Superiors of Jesuits, 1970.

Farrell, Michèle Longino. *Performing Motherhood: The Sévigné Correspondence*. Lebanon, NH: University Press of New England, 1991.

Ferland, Jean-Baptiste-Antoine. *Notes sur les regi[s]tres de Notre-Dame de Québec, première livraison*. Quebec: Augustin Côté, 1854.

Ferland, Rémi. *Les Relations des Jésuites: Un art de la persuasion: Procédés de rhétorique et fonction conative dans les Relations du Père Paul Lejeune*. Quebec: Éditions de la Huit, 1992.

Filion, Pierre-Emile. "La première bibliothèque canadienne: Le Collège des Jésuites à Québec; Historique et contribution à l'inventaire du fonds." In *Livre, bibliothèque et culture québécoise: Mélanges offerts à Edmond Desroches, SJ*, edited by Georges A. Chartrand, 273–98. Montreal: ASTED, 1977.

Finegan, Francis. "Pages from a Jesuit Missioner's Diary." *Clogher Record* 8, no. 2 (1974): 135–46.

Frei, Elisa. *Early Modern "Litterae Indipetae" for the East Indies*. Leiden: Brill Publishing, 2023.

Friedrich, Markus. "Circulating and Compiling the *Litterae Annuae*: Towards a History of Jesuit Communication." *Archivum Historicum Societatis Iesu* 77, no. 153 (January 2008): 3–39.

– *The Jesuits: A History*. Princeton, NJ: Princeton University Press, 2022.

– "On Reading Missionary Correspondence: Jesuit Theologians on the Spiritual Benefits of a New Genre." In *Cultures of Communication: Theologies of Media in Early Modern Europe and Beyond*, edited by Helmut Puff, Ulrike Strasser, and Christopher Wild, 186–208. Toronto: University of Toronto Press, 2016.

Furetière, Antoine. *Dictionnaire universel, contenant généralement tous les mots françois tant vieux que modernes, et les termes de toutes les sciences et des arts*. The Hague and Rotterdam: A. et R. Leers, 1690.

Galland, Caroline. *Pour la gloire de Dieu et du roi: Les Récollets en Nouvelle-France au XVIIe et XVIIIe siècles*. Paris: Cerf, 2012.

Gallucci, John A. "'I began to teach … ': Emotion and Performance in Isaac Jogues's Letter to Father Jean Filleau." In *Changing Hearts: Performing Jesuit Emotions between Europe, Asia, and the Americas*, edited by Raphaële Garrod and Yasmin Haskell, 167–86. Leiden: Brill, 2018.

Galvani, Pascal. "Apprendre enfin des Indiens: Une ouverture sur l'expérience transculturelle." In Deroy-Pineau, *Marie Guyard de l'Incarnation*, 375–86.

Gay, Jean-Pascal. "Finding Martyrs at Home? Jesuit Attempts at Redefining Martyrdom in the Seventeenth Century and Their Censure." *Journal of Jesuit Studies* 9, no. 1 (2022): 15–35.

Gietschier, Steven P. "Reuben Gold Thwaites." In *Dictionary of Literary Biography*, vol. 47, *American Historians, 1866–1912*, edited by Clyde Norman Wilson, 302–13. Detroit, MI: Gale, 1986.

Gigante, Denise. *Book Madness: A Story of Book Collectors in America*. New Haven, CT: Yale University Press, 2022.

Giguère, Georges-Émile. "Le 'complément indispensable' des 'Relations' réédité." *Le Devoir* 64, no. 98 (28 April 1973): 15, 20.

– "Jogues, Isaac." In *Dictionary of Canadian Biography*. Accessed 2 November 2023. https://www.biographi.ca/en/bio/jogues_isaac_1E.html.

– "Journal des Jésuites." In *Dictionnaire des œuvres littéraires du Québec*, vol. 1, edited by Maurice Lemire, 422–3. Montreal: Fides, 1980.

– "Martin, Félix." In *Dictionary of Canadian Biography*. Accessed 10 November 2023. https://www.biographi.ca/en/bio/martin_felix_11E.html.

– "Sous les auspices du gouvernement canadien," *Revue d'histoire de l'Amérique française* 8, no. 3 (1954): 359–79.

Goddard, Peter. “Canada in Seventeenth-Century Jesuit Thought: Backwater or Opportunity?” In *Decentring the Renaissance: Canada and Europe in Multidisciplinary Perspective, 1500–1700*, edited by Germaine Warkentin and Carolyn Podruchny, 186–99. Toronto: University of Toronto Press, 2001.

– “The Devil in New France: Jesuit Demonology, 1611–50.” *Canadian Historical Review* 78, no. 1 (1997): 40–62.

Gorman, Michael John. “A Matter of Faith? Christoph Scheiner, Jesuit Censorship, and the Trial of Galileo.” *Perspectives on Science* 4, no. 3 (1996): 283–320.

Gorra, Michael. *Portrait of a Novel: Henry James and the Making of an American Masterpiece*. New York: W.W. Norton & Company, 2012.

Grassmann, Thomas. “Oumasasikweie.” In *Dictionary of Canadian Biography*. Accessed 27 October 2023. https://www.biographi.ca/en/bio/oumasasikweie_1E.html.

Greer, Allan. “Colonial Saints: Gender, Race, and Hagiography in New France.” *William and Mary Quarterly* 57, no. 2 (April 2000): 323–48.

– ed. “Introduction.” In *The Jesuit Relations: Natives and Missionaries in Seventeenth-Century North America*, 2nd ed., 1–20. Boston: Bedford/St Martin’s Books, 2019.

– *Mohawk Saint: Catherine Tekakwitha and the Jesuits*. New York: Oxford University Press, 2006.

– *The Patriots and the People: The Rebellion of 1837 in Rural Lower Canada*. Toronto: University of Toronto Press, 1993.

Grégoire, Vincent. “Une Correspondance transatlantique au dix–septième siècle: L’échange épistolaire entre Marie de l’Incarnation et son fils, 1640–1672.” *Seventeenth-Century French Studies* 26, no. 1 (June 2004): 71–83.

– “L’Interprétation du tremblement de terre de 1663 en Nouvelle–France d’après les écrits des missionnaires.” *Seventeenth-Century French Studies* 30, no. 1 (July 2008): 64–76.

– *Marie Guyart de l’Incarnation (1599–1672): Le singulier parcours d’une ursuline missionnaire de Tours à Québec*. Brussels: Peter Lang, 2022.

– “Le Meunier, la domestique et l’hospitalière: Entre magie, ‘possession’ et ‘obsession’ en Nouvelle-France au 17eme siècle.” *Cahiers du dix-septième* 13, no. 1 (2010): 68–91.

Guardiani, Francesco, ed. *Breve Relatione d’alcune missioni de’ PP. della Compagnia di Giesù nella Nuova Francia*. Ottawa: Legas, 2011.

Gueudré, Marie de Chantal. *Histoire de l’ordre des Ursulines en France*, 3 vols. Paris: Éditions Saint-Paul, 1958–63.

Guilday, Peter. *John Gilmary Shea: Father of American Catholic History, 1824–1892*. New York: United States Catholic Historical Society, 1926.

Haas, Angela M. "Wampum as Hypertext: An American Indian Intellectual Tradition of Multimedia Theory and Practice." *Studies in American Indian Literatures* 19, no. 4 (2008): 77–100.

Hammond, Mary. "Book History in the Reading Experience." In *Cambridge Companion to the History of the Book*, edited by Leslie Howsam, 237–52. Cambridge: Cambridge University Press, 2014.

Harris, Steven J. "Mapping Jesuit Science: The Role of Travel in the Geography of Knowledge." In O'Malley, Bailey, Harris, and Kennedy, *The Jesuits: Cultures, Sciences, and the Arts, 1540–1773*, 210–40.

Havard, Gilles, and Cécile Vidal. *Histoire de l'Amérique française*. Paris: Flammarion, [2003] 2006.

Hayne, David M. "Charlevoix, Pierre-François-Xavier de." In *Dictionary of Canadian Biography*. Accessed 2 November 2023. https://www.biographi.ca/en/bio/charlevoix_pierre_francois_xavier_de_3E.html.

Healy, George R. "The French Jesuits and the Idea of the Noble Savage." *William and Mary Quarterly* 15, no. 2 (April 1958): 143–67.

Hellyer, Marcus. "'Because the Authority of My Superiors Commands': Censorship, Physics and the German Jesuits." *Early Science and Medicine* 1, no. 3 (1996): 319–54.

Henry, Bruce. *Friends of God: Joseph Chiwatenhwa and Marie Aonetta*. North Bay, ON: Tomiko Publications, 1991.

Hill, Susan M. *The Clay We Are Made Of: Haudenosaunee Land Tenure on the Grand River*. Winnipeg: University of Manitoba Press, 2017.

Hitchings, Henry. *Defining the World: The Extraordinary Story of Dr. Johnson's Dictionary*. New York: Farrar, Straus and Giroux, 2006.

Hosten, Henri, ed. "Jesuit Letters and Allied Papers on Mogor, Tibet, Bengal and Burma, Part I: Mongolicae Legationis Commentarius or The First Jesuit Mission to Akbar by Fr. Anthony Monserrate, SJ." *Memoirs of the Asiatic Society of Bengal* 3, no. 90 (1914–16): 513–704.

Ibbett, Katherine. "Saved from the Waters: The Drowning World of Paul Lejeune." In *Before Canada*, edited by Allan Greer, 246–67. Montreal & Kingston: McGill-Queen's University Press, 2024.

Jaenen, Cornelius. *Friend and Foe: Aspects of French-Amerindian Cultural Contact in the Sixteenth and Seventeenth Centuries*. New York: Columbia University Press, 1976.

– "Review Essay: Lucien Campeau, S.I. – *Monumenta Novae Franciae*, Volume 2, Établissement à Québec (1616–1634)." *Social History* 18, no. 35 (1985): 147–52.

Jury, Elsie McLeod. "Carigouan (Carigonan)." In *Dictionary of Canadian Biography*. Accessed 24 July 2024. https://www.biographi.ca/en/bio/carigouan_1E.html.

Kaplan, Alice. *Looking for The Stranger: Albert Camus and the Life of a Literary Classic*. Chicago: University of Chicago Press, 2016.

Kelsey, Penelope Myrtle. *Reading the Wampum: Essays on Hodinöhsö:Ni' Visual Code and Epistemological Recovery*. Syracuse, NY: Syracuse University Press, 2014.

Kenton, Edna, ed. *The Jesuit Relations and Allied Documents: Travels and Explorations of the Jesuit Missionaries in North America, 1610–1791*. New York: Vanguard, 1954.

Kip, William Ingraham. *The Early Jesuit Missions in North America: Compiled and Translated from the Letters of the French Jesuits, with Notes*. New York: Wiley and Putnam, 1846.

Knox, Michael. "The Rhetoric of Martyrdom in the Jesuit Relations of New France,1632–1650." PhD thesis, University of Oxford, 2015.

Labelle, Kathryn Magee. *Dispersed but Not Destroyed: A History of the Seventeenth-Century Wendat People*. Vancouver: University of British Columbia Press, 2013.

– "Oky Ontatechiata: Wendat Witchcrafts and the Panic of 1635–1645." *Journal of Early American History* 4, no. 3 (2014): 187–211.

Lafitau, Joseph-François. *Moeurs des sauvages ameriquains comparées aux moeurs des premiers temps*. 2 vols. Paris: Chez Saugrain l'Aîné, 1724.

Laflamme, Jean, and Rémi Tourangeau. *L'Église et le théâtre au Québec*. Montreal: Éditions Fides, 1979.

Laflèche, Guy. "Colonial Literature in New France." In *History of Literature in Canada: English-Canadian and French-Canadian*, edited by Reingard M. Nischik, 58–66. Rochester, NY: Boydell & Brewer, 2008.

– ed. *Le Missionnaire, l'apostat, le sorcier: Relation de 1634 de Paul Le Jeune*. Montreal: Presses de l'Université de Montreal, 1973.

– *Paul Lejeune (1591–1664), missionnaire de Nouvelle-France, le premier linguiste et grammairien de l'Innu*. Laval, QC: Les Éditions du Singulier, 2017.

– ed. *Les saints martyrs canadiens*, vol. 3, *Le Martyre de Jean de Brébeuf selon Paul Ragueneau*. Laval, QC: Singulier, 1990.

– "La Spiritualité des Jésuites de la Nouvelle-France: L'Interprétation des visions de Jean de Brébeuf (1640)." *Voix et Images* 11, no. 3 (1986): 464–74.

Lainey, Jonathan Christopher. *La "Monnaie des Sauvages": Les colliers de wampum d'hier à aujourd'hui*. Quebec: Septentrion, 2004.

Landy-Houillon, Isabelle. "'Au bruit de tous les infinis': La correspondance de Marie Guyart de l'Incarnation et de son fils, Claude Martin." *Littératures classiques* 71, no. 1 (2010): 303–25.
– "Marie de l'Incarnation et les Jésuites: Une exception culturelle?" In Brodeur, *Femme, mystique et missionnaire*, 69–97.
Laporte, Gilles. *Brève histoire des patriotes*. Quebec: Septentrion, 2015.
Latourelle, René. *Jean de Brébeuf*. Montreal: Bellarmin, 1993.
Lavrin, Asunción. "Lay Brothers: The Other Men in the Mendicant Orders of New Spain." *The Americas* 72, no. 3 (July 2015): 411–38.
L.B.P. "Extraits du Journal des Jésuites de l'an 1710 à 1759." *L'Abéille* 11, no. 11 (19 January 1878): 41–4.
Leavelle, Tracy Neal. *The Catholic Calumet: Colonial Conversions in French and Indian North America*. Philadelphia: University of Pennsylvania Press, 2012.
Le Bras, Yvon. "Du Canada aux 'Îles de l'Amérique' et à la 'Terre Ferme': L'Amérindien dans les Relations des jésuites Paul Lejeune, Jacques Bouton et Pierre Pelleprat." In *Rencontre, réécriture, mémoire*, vol. 1 of *Textes missionnaires dans l'espace francophone*, edited by Guy Poirier, 7–21. Montreal: Presses de l'Université Laval, 2016.
– *L'Amérindien dans les Relations du Père Paul Lejeune (1632–1641)*. Sainte-Foy, QC: Les Éditions de la Huit, 1994.
– "La Parole amérindienne dans les *Relations* de Paul Lejeune, premier supérieur jésuite de Québec." In *Voix autochtones dans les écrits de la Nouvelle-France*, edited by Luc Vaillancourt, Sandrine Tailleur, and Émilie Urbain, 251–64. Paris: Hermann, 2019.
– "Les *Relations* du Père Jean de Brébeuf en Huronie: Écriture missionnaire et ethnographie." In *De l'Orient à la Huronie: Du récit de pèlerinage au texte missionnaire*, edited by Guy Poirier, Marie-Christine Gomez, and François Paré, 139–48. Quebec: Presses de l'Université Laval, 2011.
Le Clercq, Chrestien. *First Establishment of the Faith in New France*. Translated by John Gilmary Shea. New York: Shea, 1881.
Le Journal des Jésuites: Publié d'après le manuscrit original conservé aux archives du Séminaire du Québec par MM. les Abbés Laverdière et Casgrain. Montreal: Léger Brousseau, 1871.
Lonc, William, ed. *Early Jesuit Missions in Canada*, 35 vols. Toronto: Lonc, 2001–11.
Lopenzina, Drew. "Le Jeune Dreams of Moose: Altered States among the Montagnais in the Jesuit Relations of 1634." *Early American Studies: An Interdisciplinary Journal* 13, no. 1 (2015): 3–37.

Lozier, Jean-François. *Flesh Reborn: The Saint Lawrence Valley Mission Settlements through the Seventeenth Century*. Montreal & Kingston: McGill-Queen's University Press, 2018.

MacBeath, George. "Razilly (Rasilly), Isaac de." In *Dictionary of Canadian Biography*. Accessed 1 November 2023. https://www.biographi.ca/en/bio/razilly_isaac_de_1E.html.

Mahoney, Irene, ed. *Marie of the Incarnation: Selected Writings*. New York: Paulist Press, 1989.

Mali, Anya. *Mystic in the New World: Marie de l'Incarnation (1599–1672)*. Leiden: Brill, 2021.

Manning, Patricia W. "Publication Protocol in the Seventeenth-Century Jesuit Province of Aragon." *Explorations in Renaissance Culture* 33, no. 1 (2007): 133–60.

Marie de l'Incarnation. *Correspondance*, edited by Dom Guy Oury. Solesmes: Abbaye Saint-Pierre, 1971.

– *From Mother to Son: The Selected Letters of Marie de l'Incarnation to Claude Martin*, translated by Mary Dunn. New York: Oxford University Press, 2014.

– *Lettres de la Vénérable Mère Marie de l'Incarnation, première supérieure des Ursulines de la Nouvelle-France, divisées en deux parties*, edited by Claude Martin. Paris: Louis Billaine, 1681.

– *Marie de l'Incarnation, Ursuline de Tours: Fondatrice des Ursulines de la Nouvelle-France: Écrits spirituels et historiques*, edited by Albert Jamet, 4 vols. Paris: Desclée-De Brouwer, 1929–39.

Martin, Claude. *La Vie de la Vénérable Mère Marie de l'Incarnation: Première supérieure des Ursulines de la Nouvelle France. Tirée de ses lettres & de ses écrits*. Paris: Chez Louis Billaine, 1677.

Martin, Félix-François-Marie, trans. *Relation abrégée de quelques missions des pères de la Compagnie de Jésus dans la Nouvelle-France*. Montreal: J. Lovell, 1852.

– trans. *Relations des Jésuites sur les découvertes et les autres événements arrivés en Canada, et au nord et à l'ouest des États-Unis (1611–1672), par le Dr E.B. O'Callaghan, membre correspondant de la Société historique de New-York, et membre honoraire de la Société historique du Connecticut: Traduit de l'anglais avec quelques notes, corrections et additions*. Montreal: Bureau des Mélanges Religieux, 1850.

Martin, Félix-François-Marie, and Fortuné Demontézon, eds. *Mission du Canada. Relations inédites de la Nouvelle-France (1672–1679) pour faire suite aux anciennes Relations (1615–1672) avec deux cartes géographiques*. Paris: C. Douniol, 1861.

Martin, Henri-Jean. *The French Book: Religion, Absolutism and Readership, 1585–1715*. Translated by Paul Saenger and Nadine Saenger. Baltimore: Johns Hopkins University Press, 1996.

– *Le livre français sous l'Ancien Régime*. Paris: Promodis/Éditions du Cercle de la librairie, 1987.

– *Print, Power, and People in 17th-Century France*. Translated by David Gerard. Metuchen, NJ: Scarecrow Press, 1993.

Martínez-Serna, J. Gabriel. "Procurators and the Making of the Jesuits' Atlantic Network." In *Soundings in Atlantic History: Latent Structures and Intellectual Currents, 1500–1830*, edited by Bernard Bailyn and Patricia L. Denault, 181–209. Cambridge, MA, and London: Harvard University Press, 2011.

McCabe, William H. *An Introduction to the Jesuit Theatre*. Edited by Louis J. Oldani. St Louis, MO: The Institute of Jesuit Sources, 1983.

McCoog, Thomas M., ed. *With Eyes and Ears Open: The Role of Visitors in the Society of Jesus*. Leiden: Brill, 2019.

McCoy, James C. *The Jesuit Relations of Canada, 1632–1673*. Paris: Arthur Rau, 1937.

McGill, Meredith L. *American Literature and the Culture of Reprinting, 1834–1853*. Philadelphia: University of Pennsylvania Press, 2013.

McShea, Bronwen. *Apostles of Empire: The Jesuits and New France*. Lincoln: University of Nebraska Press, 2022.

Melton, James Van Horn. *The Rise of the Public in Enlightenment Europe*. Cambridge: Cambridge University Press, 2001.

Melzer, Sara E. *Colonizer or Colonized: The Hidden Stories of Early Modern French Culture*. Philadelphia: University of Pennsylvania Press, 2012.

Mignolo, Walter. *The Darker Side of the Renaissance: Literacy, Territoriality, and Colonization*. Ann Arbor: University of Michigan Press, [1995] 2003.

– *Local Histories/Global Designs: Coloniality, Subaltern Knowledges, and Border Thinking*. Princeton, NJ: Princeton University Press, 2000.

Monet, Jacques. "The Jesuits in New France." In *Cambridge Companion to the Jesuits*, edited by Thomas Worcester, 186–98. Cambridge: Cambridge University Press, 2008.

– "Nebabamat, baptized Noël (Tekouerimat)," In *Dictionary of Canadian Biography*. Accessed 1 November 2023. https://www.biographi.ca/en/bio/negabamat_1E.html.

Moore, Brian. *Black Robe*. New York: Plume, [1985] 1997.

Nadeau, Gabriel. "Gendron, François," in *Dictionary of Canadian Biography*. Accessed 1 November 2023. https://www.biographi.ca/en/bio/gendron_francois_1E.html.

Nash, Edward W. *Catalogue of the Library of the Late E.B. O'Callaghan, M.D., LL.D., Historian of New York*. New York: Douglas Taylor, 1882.

Nelles, Paul. "Jesuit Letters." In *Oxford Handbook of the Jesuits*, edited by Inès Zupanov, 44–72. New York: Oxford University Press, 2019.

– "Seeing and Writing: The Art of Observation in the Early Jesuit Missions." *Intellectual History Review* 20, no. 3 (September 2010): 317–33.

Nelson, Eric. "The Historiography of the Pre–Suppression Jesuit Mission in France." In *Jesuit Historiography Online*. Accessed 8 September 2023. https://doi.org/10.1163/2468-7723_jho_COM_193392.

Nicholls, Andrew D. *A Fleeting Empire: Early Stuart Britain and the Merchant Adventurers to Canada*. Montreal & Kingston: McGill-Queen's University Press, 2010.

Noel, Jan. *Along a River: The First French-Canadian Women*. Toronto: University of Toronto Press, 2011.

O'Callaghan, Edmund Bailey. "Jesuit Relations of Discoveries and Other Occurrences in Canada and the Northern and Western States of the Union, 1632–1672." *Proceedings of the New York Historical Society* 5 (1847): 140–58.

O'Donnell, Kathleen. "Brébeuf's Spiritual Journal." *Canadian Literature* 53 (1972): 42–50.

O'Malley, John W. "The Historiography of the Society of Jesus: Where Does It Stand Today?" In O'Malley, Bailey, Harris, and Kennedy, *The Jesuits: Cultures, Sciences, and the Arts, 1540–1773*, 3–37.

O'Malley, John W., Gauvin Alexander Bailey, Steven J. Harris, and T. Frank Kennedy, eds. *The Jesuits: Cultures, Sciences, and the Arts, 1540–1773*. Toronto: University of Toronto Press, 1999.

Ouellet, Réal. *La Relation de voyage en Amérique (XVI–XVIIIe siècles): Au carrefour des genres*. Quebec: Presses de l'Université Laval, 2010.

Ouellet, Réal, and Alain Beaulieu, eds. *Rhétorique et conquête missionnaire: Le Jésuite Paul Lejeune*. Quebec: Septentrion, 1993.

Oury, Guy. "Introduction." In Oury, Marie de l'Incarnation, *Correspondance*, edited by Dom Guy Oury, 10–30. Solesmes: Abbaye Saint-Pierre, 1971.

– *Marie de l'Incarnation (1599–1672)*. Quebec: Les Presses de l'Université Laval, 1973.

Paige, Nicholas D. *Technologies of the Novel: Quantitative Data and the Evolution of Literary Systems*. Cambridge: Cambridge University Press, 2022.

Pariseau, Claude. *La Bibliothèque du Collège de Québec*. Montreal: McGill Graduate School of Library Science, 1972.

Parkman, Francis. *The Jesuits in North America in the Seventeenth Century*. Toronto: Morang, [1867] 1901.

Parsons, Christopher M. *A Not-So-New World: Empire and Environment in French Colonial North America*. Philadelphia: University of Pennsylvania Press, 2018.

Paschoud, Adrien. "Aborder les *Relations jésuites* de la Nouvelle France (1632–1672): Enjeux et perspectives." *Arborescences: Revue d'études françaises* no. 2 (May 2012): unpaginated.

– "Puissance de l'image et efficacité de la représentation: Le théâtre d'édification dans les missions jésuites d'Amérique méridionale (XVIe–XVIIIe siècles)." *Irish Journal of French Studies* 4 (2004): 5–15.

Peace, Thomas, and Kathryn Labelle, eds. *From Huronia to Wendakes: Adversity, Migration, and Resilience, 1650–1900*. Norman: University of Oklahoma Press, 2016.

Pearson, Timothy G. *Becoming Holy in Early Canada*. Montreal & Kingston: McGill-Queen's University Press, 2014.

Peelman, Achiel. "Marie Guyart de l'Incarnation et la spiritualité amérindienne: Un dialogue impossible?" In Deroy-Pineau, *Marie Guyard de l'Incarnation*, 365–74.

Peyronnin, Philippe. "Contours d'une pastorale ultramarine: Les missionnaires jésuites dans les sociétés d'habitation des Antilles et Guyane françaises aux xviie et xviiie siècles." *Bulletin de la Société d'Histoire de la Guadeloupe* 126 (2000): 25–80.

Pioffet, Marie-Christine. "L'Arc et l'épée: Les images de la guerre chez le jésuite Paul Lejeune." In *Rhétorique et conquête missionnaire: Le jésuite Paul Lejeune*, edited by Réal Ouellet, 41–52. Quebec: Septentrion, 1993.

– "Introduction." In Sagard, *Histoire du Canada*, 13–44. Saint-Laurent, QC: Septentrion, 2022.

– "La Nouvelle-France dans l'imaginaire jésuite: *terra doloris* ou Jérusalem céleste?" In *Jesuit Accounts of the Colonial Americas: Intercultural Transfers, Intellectual Disputes, and Textualities*, edited by Marc André Bernier, Clorinda Donato, and Hans-Jürgen Lüsebrink, 326–43. Toronto: University of Toronto Press, 2014.

– *La Tentation de l'épopée dans les Relations des Jésuites*. Sillery, QC: Septentrion, 1997.

Plante, Jean-François. "Le Paysage sonore de la Nouvelle-France." *Ethnologies* 35, no. 1 (2014): 125–44.

Poirier, Lisa J.M. *Religion, Gender, and Kinship in Colonial New France*. Syracuse, NY: Syracuse University Press, 2016.

Pollack, John H. "Chihoatenhwa's Prayer: A Wendat-Jesuit Print Encounter from Seventeenth-Century New France." In *American Contact: Intercultural Encounters and the History of the Book*, edited by Rhae Lynn Barnes and Glenda Goodman, 90–9. Philadelphia: University of Pennsylvania Press, 2024.

Porterfield, Amanda. "Witchcraft and the Colonization of Algonquian and Iroquois Cultures." *Religion and American Culture: A Journal of Interpretation* 2, no. 1 (1992): 103–24.

Pouliot, Léon. "La Contribution de P. Paul Le Jeune aux Relations des Jésuites de 1650 à 1663." *Bulletin des recherches historiques* 68, no. 1 (1966): 49–53; 68, no. 2 (1966): 77–85; 68, no. 3 (1966): 131–5.

– *Étude sur les Relations des Jésuites de la Nouvelle-France (1632–1672)*. Paris: Desclée de Brouwer, 1940.

– "Goupil, René." In *Dictionary of Canadian Biography*. Accessed 9 November 2023. https://www.biographi.ca/en/bio/goupil_rene_1E.html.

– "Le Jeune, Paul." In *Dictionary of Canadian Biography*. Accessed 9 November 2023. https://www.biographi.ca/en/bio/le_jeune_paul_1E.html.

– "Le 'Journal des Jésuites.'" *Le Canada français* 15, no. 3 (1927): 173–91.

– "Le Journal des Jésuites de Québec de 1632 à 1645." *Rapport – Société canadienne d'histoire de l'Église catholique* 28 (1961): 45–52.

– "Lalemant, Jérôme (Achiendassé)." In *Dictionary of Canadian Biography*. Accessed 10 November 2023. https://www.biographi.ca/en/bio/lalemant_jerome_1E.html.

– "Premières pages du Journal des Jésuites de Québec, 1632–1645." *Rapport des Archives de Québec* 41 (1963): 3–119.

– *Le premier retraitant du Canada: Joseph Chihouatenhoua, Huron*. Montreal: Bellarmin, 1958.

– "Ragueneau, Paul." In *Dictionary of Canadian Biography*. Accessed 21 October 2024. https://www.biographi.ca/en/bio/ragueneau_paul_1E.html.

Principe, Charles. "Trois 'Relations de la Nouvelle France' écrites par le Père Paul Le Jeune (1632, 1633, 1634)." *Cahiers de l'association internationale des études françaises* 27, no. 1 (1975): 83–108.
Ragueneau, Paul. *La Vie de la Mère Catherine de Saint Augustin, religieuse hospitalière de la Miséricorde de Québec en la Nouvelle-France composée par le Révérend Père Paul Ragueneau de la Compagnie de Jésus*. Paris: Florentin Lambert, 1671.
Randall, Catharine. "Appendix. Cathedrals of Ice: Translating the Jesuit Vocabulary of Conversion." In Randall, trans., *Black Robes and Buckskin*, 185–208.
– trans. *Black Robes and Buckskin: A Selection from the Jesuit Relations*. New York: Fordham University Press, 2022.
Rasmussen, Birgit Brander. *Queequeg's Coffin: Indigenous Literacies and Early American Literature*. Durham, NC: Duke University Press, 2012.
Read, Colin. "Act of Union." In *Oxford Companion to Canadian History*, edited by Gerald Hallowell. Don Mills, ON: Oxford University Press, 2004.
– "Province of Canada." In *Oxford Companion to Canadian History*, edited by Gerald Hallowell. Don Mills, ON: Oxford University Press, 2004.
Relations des Jésuites contenant ce qui s'est passé de plus remarquable dans les missions des pères de la Compagnie de Jésus dans la Nouvelle-France. 3 vols. Quebec: A. Côté, 1858.
Rigault, Claude, and Réal Ouellet. "Relations des Jésuites." In *Dictionnaire des œuvres littéraires du Québec*, vol. 1, edited by Maurice Lemire, 637–48. Montreal: Fides, 1980.
Rivett, Sarah. *Unscripted America: Indigenous Languages and the Origins of a Literary Nation*. New York: Oxford University Press, 2017.
Rochemonteix, Camille de. *Les Jésuites et la Nouvelle-France au XVIIe siècle d'après beaucoup de documents inédits*. 3 vols. Paris: Letouzey et Ané, 1895.
Roy, Fernande. "Duclos De Celles, Alfred." In *Dictionary of Canadian Biography*. Accessed 10 November 2023. https://www.biographi.ca/en/bio/duclos_de_celles_alfred_15E.html.
Roy-Lysencourt, Philippe, Thérèse Nadeau-Lacour, and Raymond Brodeur, eds. *Marie Guyart de l'Incarnation: Singularité et universalité d'une femme de cœur et de raison*. Laval, QC: Les Presses de l'Université Laval, 2019.
Russell, Mary Doria. *Children of God*. New York: Villard, 1998.
– *The Sparrow*. New York: Fawcett Columbine, 1996.

Sagard, Gabriel. *Le grand voyage du pays des Hurons, suivi du Dictionnaire de la langue huronne*. Edited by Jack Warwick. Montreal: Presses de l'Université de Montreal, [1632] 1998.

– *Histoire du Canada et voyages que les Freres Mineurs Recollects y ont faicts pour la conversion des infidelles*. Edited by Marie-Christine Pioffet. Saint-Laurent, QC: Septentrion, 2022.

Sandoz, Mari. *The Beaver Men: Spearheads of Empire*. Lincoln: University of Nebraska Press, 1978.

Sayre, Gordon M. "Communion in Captivity: Torture, Martyrdom, and Gender in New France and New England." In *Finding Colonial Americas: Essays Honoring J.A. Leo Lemay*, edited by Carla Mulford and David S. Shields, 50–63. Newark: University of Delaware Press, 2001.

– *The Indian Chief as Tragic Hero: Native Resistance and the Literatures of America, from Moctezuma to Tecumseh*. Chapel Hill: University of North Carolina Press, 2005.

– *Les Sauvages Américains: Representations of Native Americans in French and English Colonial Literature*. Chapel Hill: University of North Carolina Press, 1997.

Sayre, Meredith Beck. "The Process of Conversion: A Biography of the Jesuit Relations." PhD diss., University of Wisconsin-Madison, 2014.

Schock, Mark. "Catholicism's Militant Pioneers to North America: The Seventeenth Century Jesuits of New France." *Fairmount Folio Journal of History* 9 (2007): 1–14.

Seeman, Erik R. *The Huron-Wendat Feast of the Dead: Indian-European Encounters in Early North America*. Baltimore: Johns Hopkins University Press, 2011.

Séguin, Robert-Lionel. "Les Divertissements au Québec au XVIIe et XVIIIe siècles." *Outre-Mers. Revue d'histoire* 61, no. 222 (1974): 5–17.

Shea, John Gilmary. *Discovery and Exploration of the Mississippi Valley: With the Original Narratives of Marquette, Allouez, Membré, Hennepin, and Anastase Douay*. New York: Redfield, 1852.

Sioui, Georges E. *For an Amerindian Autohistory: An Essay on the Foundations of a Social Ethic*. Translated by Sheila Fischman. Montreal & Kingston: McGill-Queen's University Press, 1992.

– *Huron-Wendat: The Heritage of the Circle*. Translated by Jane Brierly. Vancouver: University of British Columbia Press, 2011.

Sleeper-Smith, Susan. *Indian Women and French Men: Rethinking Cultural Encounter in the Western Great Lakes*. Amherst: University of Massachusetts Press, 2001.

Smith, Joanna. "Trudeau Asks Pope for an Apology over Church's Role in Residential Schools." 29 May 2017. https://www.cbc.ca/news/world/trudeau-pope-vatican-1.4135553.
Smith, William. *History of Canada: From Its First Discovery, to the Year 1791*. Quebec: Printed for the author by J. Neilson, 1815.
So, Richard Jean. *Redlining Culture: A Data History of Racial Inequality and Postwar Fiction*. New York: Columbia University Press, 2020.
Steckley, John L. *Untold Tales: Joseph Chihoatenhwa, Eustace Ahatsistari, Estienne Annaotaha, Kandiaronk*. 2nd ed. Toronto: Associated Heritage Publishing, 1992.
Stevens, Henry. *Recollections of James Lenox and the Formation of His Library*. Edited by Victor Hugo Paltsits. New York: New York Public Library, 1951.
Stevens, Scott Manning. "The Historiography of New France and the Legacy of Iroquois Internationalism." *Comparative American Studies: An International Journal* 11, no. 2 (June 2013): 148–65.
– "The Language of Belief: Religious Conversion in Eighteenth-Century Iroquoia." In *Feeling Godly: Religious Affections and Christian Contact in Early North America*, edited by Caroline Wigginton and Abram Van Engen, 56–79. Amherst: University of Massachusetts Press, 2021.
Stolzenberg, Daniel. "Utility, Edification, and Superstition: Jesuit Censorship and Athanasius Kircher's *Oedipus Aegyptiacus*." In O'Malley, Bailey, Harris, and Kennedy, *The Jesuits: Cultures, Sciences, and the Arts, 1540–1773*, 336–54.
Sulte, Benjamin "Le Journal des Jésuites." *La revue canadienne* 9, no. 2 (1872): 108–20.
Susini, Anne Régent. "Dépaysement et détours d'une scénographie édifiante: Le converti des *Relations* jésuites, un prédicateur sans ministère." In *Voix autochtones dans les écrits de la Nouvelle-France,* edited by Luc Vaillancourt, Sandrine Tailleur, and Émilie Urbain, 265–90. Paris: Hermann, 2019.
Thérien, Gilles, ed. *Écrits en Huronie*. Saint-Laurent, QC: BQ, 1996.
Thierry, Eric. "Pierre-François-Xavier de Charlevoix (1682–1761): Un enseignant de Louis-le-Grand, explorateur et historien de l'Amérique française." *Bulletin de la Montagne Sainte-Geneviève et ses abords: Comité d'études historiques, archéologiques et artistiques* 317 (2014): 22–42.
Thwaites, Reuben Gold, ed. *The Jesuit Relations and Allied Documents: Travels and Explorations of the Jesuit Missionaries in New France 1610–1791*. 73 vols. Cleveland: Burrows Bros, 1896–1901.

Timmermans, Linda. *L'Accès des femmes à la culture (1598–1715): Un débat d'idées de Saint François de Sales à la Marquise de Lambert.* Paris: Garnier, 1993.

Tooker, Elisabeth. *An Ethnography of the Huron Indians, 1615–1649.* Washington, DC: US Government Printing Office, 1964.

Trigger, Bruce G. "Amantacha, Louis de Sainte-Foi." In *Dictionary of Canadian Biography.* Accessed 3 November 2023. https://www.biographi.ca/en/bio/amantacha_1E.html.

– "Chihwatenha (Chihouatenhoua, Chiohoarehra) (baptized Joseph)." In *Dictionary of Canadian Biography.* Accessed 10 November 2023. https://www.biographi.ca/en/bio/chihwatenha_1E.html.

– *The Children of Aataentsic: A History of the Huron People to 1660.* Montreal & Kingston: McGill-Queen's University Press, [1976] 2000.

– *The Huron: Farmers of the North.* Fort Worth, TX: Harcourt Brace Jovanovich College Publishers, 1990.

True, Micah. "As an Indigenous Delegation Prepares to Visit the Vatican, It's Worth Revisiting Trudeau's 2017 Papal Gift of the Jesuit 'Relations.'" *The Conversation*, 22 March 2022. Accessed 8 August 2024. https://theconversation.com/as-an-indigenous-delegation-prepares-to-visit-the-vatican-its-worth-revisiting-trudeaus-2017-papal-gift-of-the-jesuit-relations-179258.

– "Beyond the 'Affaire *Tartuffe*': Seventeenth-Century French Theatre in Colonial New France." *Romance Notes* 55, no. 3 (2015): 451–61.

– "Il faut parler pour estre entendu: Talking about God in Seventeenth-Century New France." *Cahiers du dix-septième* 12, no. 1 (2008): 17–36.

– "Is It Time for a New Edition of the Jesuit Relations from New France? Campeau vs. Thwaites." *Papers of the Bibliographical Society of Canada/Cahiers de la Société bibliographique du Canada* 51, no. 2 (2013): 261–79.

– trans. *The Jesuit Pierre-François-Xavier de Charlevoix's (1682–1761) Journal of a Voyage in North America.* Leiden: Brill, 2019.

– "Jesuit Relations." In *Oxford Bibliographies in American Literature*, edited by Jackson Bryer and Paul Lauter. New York: Oxford University Press, 2013. Accessed 28 October 2023. https://doi.org/10.1093/obo/9780199827251-0097.

– *Masters and Students: Jesuit Mission Ethnography in Seventeenth-Century New France.* Montreal & Kingston: McGill-Queen's University Press, 2015.

– "'On fait dire à un enfant ce qu'on veut, quand son père est absent': Contributions parisiennes aux *Relations* des Jésuites en Nouvelle-France." *Dix-Septième siècle* 299, no. 2 (2023): 327–43.
– "Pierre Corneille's *Le Cid* in Colonial Quebec." *French Forum* 43, no. 3 (2018): 391–406.
– "'Une Hierusalem bénite de Dieu': Utopia and Travel in the *Jesuit Relations* from New France." *Papers on French Seventeenth-Century Literature* 39, no. 76 (2012): 175–89.
Turner, Frederick Jackson. *Reuben Gold Thwaites: A Memorial Address.* Madison: State Historical Society of Wisconsin, 1914.
Les Ursulines de Québec depuis leur établissement jusqu'à nos jours. Quebec: C. Darveau, 1863.
Vallée, Andréanne. "François Gendron et Christophe Regnaut: Deux voix données en Nouvelle France." Master's thesis, University of Ottawa, 2002.
Vance, Jonathan F. *A History of Canadian Culture.* Toronto: Oxford University Press, 2009.
Verney, Jack. *O'Callaghan: The Making and Unmaking of a Rebel.* Montreal & Kingston: McGill-Queen's University Press, 1994.
Vollmann, William T. *Fathers and Crows.* Vol. 2 of *Seven Dreams: A Book of North American Landscapes.* New York: Penguin Books, 1993.
– "An Incomplete Biography of Amantacha the Huron." *Conjunctions* 17 (1991): 277–306.
Walsh, James J. "Edmund Bailey O'Callaghan: Physician, Historian, Antiquarian." *Studies: An Irish Quarterly Review* 22, no. 87 (1933): 468–79.
Walter, Frank K., and Virginia Doneghy. *Jesuit Relations and Other Americana in the Library of James F. Bell.* Minneapolis: University of Minnesota Press, 1950.
Warkentin, Germaine. "Dead Metaphor or Working Model? 'The Book' in Native America." In *Colonial Mediascapes: Sensory Worlds of the Early Americas*, edited by Matt Cohen and Jeffrey Glover, 47–75. Lincoln: University of Nebraska Press, 2014.
– "In Search of 'The Word of the Other': Aboriginal Sign Systems and the History of the Book in Canada." *Book History* 2 (1 January 1999): 1–27.
Warrick, Gary. *A Population History of the Huron-Petun, A.D. 500–1650.* Cambridge: Cambridge University Press, 2008.
Weber, Alison. *Teresa of Avila and the Rhetoric of Femininity.* Princeton, NJ: Princeton University Press, 1990.

Westra, Haijo. "Références classiques implicites et explicites dans les écrits des Jésuites sur la Nouvelle-France." *Tangence* 92 (2010): 27–37.
White, Richard. *The Middle Ground: Indians, Empires, and Republics in the Great Lakes Region, 1650–1815*. Cambridge: Cambridge University Press, 1991.
Wilcox, U. Vincent. "The Manufacture and Use of Wampum in the Northeast: Description and Manufacture." *The Bead Journal (Archive: 1974–1978)* 3, no. 1 (1 July 1976): 10–19.
Winship, George Parker. *The John Carter Brown Library: A History*. Providence, RI: The Associates for the John Carter Brown Library, 1914.
Wogan, Peter. "Perceptions of European Literacy in Early Contact Situations." *Ethnohistory* 41, no. 3 (1994): 407.
Worcester, Thomas. "Jesuit Dependence on the French Monarchy." In *Cambridge Companion to the Jesuits*, edited by Thomas Worcester, 104–19. Cambridge: Cambridge University Press, 2008.
Wroth, Lawrence. *The First Century of the John Carter Brown Library: A History with a Guide to the Collections*. Providence, RI: The Associates for the John Carter Brown Library, 1946.
– "The *Jesuit Relations* from New France." *Papers of the Bibliographical Society of America* 30 (January 1936): 110–49.
Young, William J., ed. and trans. *The Letters of St Ignatius of Loyola*. Chicago: Loyola University Press, 1959.
Yuzwa, Zachary. "The Fall of Troy in Old Huronia: The Letters of Paul Ragueneau on the Destruction of Wendake, 1649–1651." In *Brill's Companion to Classics in the Early Americas*, edited by Maya Feile Tomes, Adam J. Goldwyn, and Matthew Duquès, 398–423. Leiden: Brill, 2021.
Zecher, Carla. "Life on the French-Canadian Hyphen: Nation and Narration in the Correspondence of Marie de l'Incarnation." *Quebec Studies* 26 (October 1998): 38–51.
– "A New-World Model of Female Epistolarity: The Correspondence of Marie de l'Incarnation." *Studies in Canadian Literature/Études en littérature canadienne* 21, no. 2 (1996): 89–103.
Zubillaga, Félix. "El Procurador de la Compañía de Jesús en la Corte de España." *Archivum Historicum Societatis Iesu* 16 (1947): 1–55.

Index